M000314081

THE AUTHOR AS HE APPEARED AFTER THE
COEUR D'ALENE RIOTS.

A COWBOY DETECTIVE

A True Story of Twenty-Two Years with a
World-Famous Detective Agency

Giving the Inside Facts of the Bloody Cœur
d'Alene Labor Riots, and the many Ups
and Downs of the Author throughout
the United States, Alaska, British
Columbia and Old Mexico

Also Exciting Scenes among the Moonshiners
of Kentucky and Virginia

By CHAS. A. SIRINGO

Author of "A Texas Cowboy"

CHICAGO
W. B. CONKEY COMPANY
1912

COPYRIGHT, 1912
BY
CHAS. A. SIRINGO

Old Colt's 45 and the Hand That Has
Kept Her Under Control.

TO MY FRIEND
ALOIS B. RENEHAN
OF SANTA FE, NEW MEXICO

An eminent lawyer, advocate and writer,
as a token of appreciation of many
kindnesses done, this book
is dedicated.

PREFACE

This story of twenty years of active service as a detective, an autobiography of many thrilling adventures, on mountain and plain, among moonshiners, cattle thieves, tramps, dynamiters and other strong-arm men, has been delayed for a long time in coming from the press. The delay was due to the protests of the author's former employers. These protests were undoubtedly rightful, but it was considered in the beginning that no harm could come therefrom, for the reason that the identity of persons involved was not disclosed except in reference to past facts, matters that were done and over with. Now this difficulty has been overcome and the objections removed by the use of fictitious names in many places. But the story in no wise loses its interest, and it is believed the reader will find in the volume much with which to entertain himself.

The author is not a literary man, but has written as he speaks, and it is thought that the simplicity thus resulting will not detract from the substantial merit of the tales, which are recitals of facts and not of fiction.

CHARLES A. SIRINGO.

Santa Fe, New Mexico, January 6, 1912.

CONTENTS

CHAPTER VIII

CHAPTER IX

CHAPTER X

CHAPTER XI

CHAPTER XII

CHAPTER XIII

CHAPTER XIV

CHAPTER XV

CHAPTER XVI

CHAPTER XVII

CHAPTER XVIII

CHAPTER XIX

CHAPTER XX

CHAPTER XXI

CHAPTER XXII

LIST OF ILLUSTRATIONS

10

THE KIDLET AUTHOR AFTER HE BE-
CAME A COWBOY.

A COWBOY DETECTIVE

CHAPTER I

THE ANARCHIST RIOT IN CHICAGO—MY FIRST WORK FOR THE DICKENSON AGENCY—IN JAIL FOR SLUGGING A SLUGGER.

The writer was born in Matagorda county, Texas, in the extreme southern part of the State, in 1855, and was reared on the upper deck of all kinds and conditions of cow-ponies scattered throughout the Lone Star State, Kansas, Indian Territory and New Mexico. I spent fifteen years continuously in the saddle, seldom ever sleeping in a house or a tent. In these early days of the cattle business when the southern half of Texas was overrun with wild, long-horned cattle, the cowboys used the ground for a bed and the sky for covering.

I first started out as a full-fledged cowboy in 1867 when only eleven years of age. Of course, I naturally became an expert at riding "bad" horses and roping wild cattle. Besides, this strenuous, open-air life gave me health and a longing to see the world and to learn the ins and outs of human nature.

The chance came when the spring of 1886 found me in Chicago with a pretty young wife and a sweet little girl baby on my hands. We were boarding and rooming with a private family on Harrison avenue on the night of the Haymarket riot, when an anarchist's bomb killed and maimed over sixty of the city's police officers. We went to bed expecting a riot before morning, so we were not surprised when we heard the explosion of the bomb, and, soon after, the shooting which followed. A young lawyer, Reynolds by name, ran to our room to tell me to get ready and go with him to the riot, but my frightened girl-wife held on to me and wouldn't let me go, though I sent a representative in the shape of my silver-plated, pearl-handled "Colt's 45" pistol, which had been my companion on the cattle range and which still keeps me company as I write. Reynolds had borrowed my pistol and as he ran around a corner at the Haymarket with the "gun" in his hands, policemen opened fire on him, thinking that he was an anarchist. He dodged into a door, went up a flight of stairs and out an alley gate and flew for home like a scared wolf. With face as white as snow he handed me the pistol while I still lay in bed, saying that he had enough of the riot business, as several bullets had whizzed close to his head.

After the riot the city was all excitement, and I commenced to wish that I were a detective so as to help ferret out the thrower of the bomb and his backers. I knew very little about the detective business, though I had spent part of 1881 and 1882 doing secret work for Texas cattlemen against cattle thieves in western Texas and New Mexico. This had given me a taste for the work, and I liked it. Besides, I had been told by a blind phrenologist that I was "cut out" for a detective. At that time I didn't believe in phrenology, but this man being as blind as a bat and telling so many truths about people I knew, convinced me that there was something besides wind and graft in phrenology. Had this man not been blind, I would have attributed his knowledge to his ability to read faces.

It was in the year 1884. I lived in Caldwell, Kansas, a cattle town on the border of Kansas and the Indian Territory. Circulars were scattered broadcast over the town announcing the coming of this noted phrenologist. After supper, on the evening of his arrival, many leading citizens turned out to hear him lecture at the Leland Hotel. He stood in the center of a large parlor, holding to the back of an empty chair. He was a fine looking old man, regardless of the fact that both eyes were out. After making a few preliminary remarks on phrenology, he called for some one to come forward and have his head examined. The audience began calling for our popular city marshal, Henry Brown, who had only been marshal a short time, but who had won glory and a new gold star by killing several men, including an Indian chief, "Spotted Horse," who had taken on more "fire-water" than he could carry. Brown hesitated quite awhile about having his head "felt." He knew better than any one else in the audience as to what was in his head and he didn't want to risk having his faults told. He finally went out and sat down in the chair. But it was soon made plain by the color of his face that he regretted going. He stuck it out though, and heard some very uncomplimentary remarks said against himself. I knew that the phrenologist was telling the truth, because I had known Henry Brown when he was a member of the

notorious "Billy the Kid's" outlaw gang in the Panhandle of Texas, and the Territory of New Mexico. I
first became acquainted with him through introduction
by "Billy the Kid" in the fall of 1878. I had just returned to the Panhandle from Chicago, where I had been
with a shipment of fat steers, and had found "Billy the
Kid" and his gang camped at the L X ranch where I
was employed as one of the cowboy foremen. I presented "Billy the Kid" with a fine meerschaum cigar
holder, which I had bought in Chicago, and he in turn
presented me with a book containing his autograph. He
also introduced me to several of his men, one of them
being Henry Brown. During that winter Brown and
a half-breed Indian quit "the Kid's" outlaw gang and
went to the Indian Teritory, and I lost track of him until
I met him wearing an officer's star in Caldwell, Kansas.
He begged me to not give him away as he intended to
reform and lead an honorable life. But I regretted afterwards that I didn't tell the citizens of Caldwell of his past
record. For, while acting as city marshal of Caldwell,
and while wearing his star, he rode into Medicine Lodge,
a nearby town, with his chief deputy, Ben Wheeler, and
two cowboys, and in broad daylight held up the Medicine
Lodge Bank and killed the bank president, Wiley Pain,
and his cashier. After a lively chase by the citizens of
Medicine Lodge the four robbers were caught and jailed.
That night when the mob opened the jail door to hang
them, Brown and Wheeler made a break for liberty,
knocking men down as they ran. Brown was killed with
a charge of buckshot and Wheeler and the two cowboys
were hung to a nearby tree.

Henry Brown.

Ben Wheeler.

After the blind phrenologist had finished Brown's head, he called for another subject. This time the crowd began calling for Mr. Theodore Baufman, the Oklahoma scout. "Bauf" needed very little coaxing. He strutted out, carrying his two hundred and fifty pounds of flesh with the air of a king. The phrenologist ran his hand over "Bauf's" head just once, and then said: "Ladies and gentlemen, here is a man who, if the Indians were on the warpath and he should run across one lone Indian on the plains, he would tell his friends that he had seen a thousand warriors." This caused such yelling and laughter that Baufman was angry for weeks; but I, for one, knew that the phrenologist had told the truth, as I had worked with "Bauf" on the range as early as 1878 and therefore knew that his worst failings were a fear of hard work and the stretching of the truth.

Next the audience began calling for "Mamie," my sixteen-year-old wife. She took the seat and the blind man ran his hand over her head once. He then said: "Here is a good-natured little somebody who cannot tell a lie or do a wrong." The balance he told was what we all knew to be true.

Next the crowd called for me. I went forward and sat down in the chair. The blind man laid his hand on the top of my head and then said: "Ladies and gentlemen, here is a mule's head." When the laughter had subsided he explained that I had a large stubborn bump, hence was as stubborn as a mule. He then said I had a fine head for a newspaper editor, a fine stock raiser, or detective; that in any of these callings I would make a success. So, during the excitement following the anarchist riot in Chicago, this old man's words began to bear fruit and I concluded to try my hand as a detective.

But the question arose as to the best way to start in the business, my main object being to see the world and learn human nature. I wisely concluded to start right by entering the greatest detective school on earth—the Dickenson National Detective Agency. My steps were light and my hopes buoyant when on the 29th day of June, 1886, I stepped into S. A. Kean & Co.'s Bank and asked the cashier, Mr. Yure, for a letter of introduction to Mr. Wm. L. Dickenson. I was slightly acquainted with this cashier, as I had done business with his bank. He replied that he would speak to Mr. Kean. He soon returned and wrote me the letter. It read as follows:

"CHICAGO, ILL., June 29th, 1886.

Dickenson Detective Agency,
City.

Gentlemen ·—The bearer, Mr. Chas. A. Siringo, we know to be a person of good character, and having been a cowboy and brought up on the plains, his services and ability are commendable to you.   S. A. KEAN & Co, Bankers."

Armed with this letter of introduction I bolted into the Dickenson Agency. I found the air in the main office impregnated with mystery and suspicion. A dozen pairs of eyes were focused on me as though I were an anarchist with a bomb up my sleeve. I asked to see Mr. "Billy" Dickenson. I had often heard him called "Billy," and my lack of business knowledge prevented me from using his proper name. The attendant informed me that he couldn't be seen, but that any word or letter which I might have could be conveyed to him. I then wrote a note addressed to Mr. "Billy" Dickenson, stating my business, and enclosed it with the banker's letter of introduction. The young man disappeared with these letters. In about twenty minutes he returned with the S. A. Kean letter, on the bottom of which was written in Mr. Dickenson's own handwriting:

"Capt. Farley:—The party referred to in this letter is undoubtedly a good man.—Wm. L. Dickenson."

I was told to go down stairs and present the Kean & Co. letter to Capt. Farley. I did so. He read it, then handed it back to me, and I still retain it as a relic of bygone days.

After being put through a test by Capt. Mike Farley, I was allowed to see the "big chief," Wm. L. Dickenson. He asked for references and I gave him the names of David T. Beals, president of the Union National Bank of Kansas City, Mo.; Jas. H. East, a popular Texas sheriff, and Pat Garrett, the slayer of "Billy the Kid." In 1880 I had assisted Garrett in running down that noted outlaw and his murderous gang; hence I felt safe in giving this noted "bad" man-killer as reference.

Mr. Dickenson said he would write to these men at once, and if their replies were favorable, he would give me a position in a new office which they were opening in Denver, Colo. He said they would need a cowboy detective there, as they figured on getting a lot of cattle work. I had told Mr. Dickenson that the east was too tame for me, hence I wanted a position in the west.

After the interview I went home to wait a week or two for replies from my references, and while waiting, I broke into jail for the first time in my life.

It was Saturday evening after dark. The mix-up took

2

place at Barnum's circus near the ticket wagon, when the great crowd was scrambling to buy tickets to the circus. A large man, who would have made two of me, tried to be fresh and I called him down. He made a pass to put me to sleep the first punch but before he could get in his work the weight of my old Colt's 45 pistol had landed on his head. This was followed up with one more lick which buried the sharp pistol-sight into his skull. This brought the blood in a stream. By this time his partner had picked up a piece of board and had it raised to strike me from the rear. I saw him just in time. He found a cocked pistol in his face, and dropping the board, begged for mercy. Both of these men had wives with them and they were crying and screaming. No doubt they thought their "hubbies" had innocently stirred up a hornet's nest. A policeman came running up, but he was so excited that he forgot to take my pistol, so I put it back into my pocket. This good-looking young policeman informed me that I was under arrest. I told him that I wouldn't be arrested unless he also arrested the other two men. He then told them to consider themselves under arrest. The wounded man, whose face and neck and white shirt front were red with blood, begged not to be put in a patrol wagon. Therefore, as it was only a few blocks to the Harrison street police station, the officer consented to let us walk. The other two prisoners and their nicely dressed wives took the lead, while the officer and I brought up the rear. We had only gone a block when the wounded man balked. He wouldn't budge until I surrendered my arsenal to the policeman. He had suddenly remembered that I still had the pistol.

On reaching the Harrison street station we stepped up to a desk behind which sat a very old, fat man. My pistol was laid on his desk and the policeman told him I had used it on the red man. The old fellow eyed me, then the pistol, then the man covered with blood and his nice broadcloth suit ruined. He asked me if I had use'd this pistol on the man. I replied "Yes." Then he said, "I'll fix you, young man. I'll make the charge assault with intent to murder." He then began writing it down in his book. The tiger blood in me began to boil. I finally turned myself loose and called the old bald-headed "judge" some hard names. The policeman tried to stop me but failed. Then he leaned over the desk and whispered something to the "judge" who changed the charge to "assault with a deadly weapon." This satisfied me and I sat down.

Then the "judge" told the officer to call the patrol wagon and have me taken to jail. While awaiting the patrol wagon, I secured the consent of the kind-hearted policeman to deliver a message for me. I told him to go to Umbdenstock's Lithographing and Printing office and tell them I was in jail. I was well known there and hoped that some one would be in the office, as it was Saturday night. Shortly after, I had a nice free buggy ride in the "hurry up" wagon and was put behind steel bars. For an hour I paced up and down before the heavy bars like a caged lion. It seemed as though I was doomed to remain in jail until Monday morning without my wife knowing of it. That worried me the worst.

About 9 o'clock Mr. Mike Shea, a wood engraver, came to the jail and heard my tale of woe. He ex-

plained that he was the only person left in the Umbdenstock office when the policeman arrived with my message.
Shea told me to rest easy and he would have me out
soon. He then left to see the judge who ruled over that
district. Soon after, Mr. Shea and a lithographer friend
of mine drove up in a buggy. They said they would
have to drive sixteen miles to the judge's residence out
on the edge of the city. The lithographer, whose name I
have forgot, was a leading Elk and a particular friend of
the judge of the Harrison street police station, so for this
reason Mr. Shea was taking him along to "work" the
judge, whose name I cannot recall. At 2 o'clock Sunday
morning my good friends returned with the bond signed
by the judge and I was liberated. It was 4 A. M. when I
reached home.

Monday morning I was in the court room which was
crowded with people. I had no lawyer or witnesses, but
was trusting to luck, though the attorney who had used
my pistol at the Haymarket riot was present, ready to
offer assistance. When my case was called the two men
and their wives were put on the stand and they all swore
lies against me. I was then called up and told my story.
When I had finished the judge asked me if I had any witnesses. I replied "No." Here a nicely dressed old
Scotchman rose up in the crowd and said: "Your
Honor, I am a witness for that young man." This was
a great surprise to me and showed that luck was on my
side. The old gentleman was put on the stand and corroborated my statement. He said he was taking a shipment of draft horses back to his home in Scotland; that
he was trying to get up to the circus wagon to buy a

ticket to the show, when the fracas began, and thinking that I might need help, he had come up to the court room this morning. I thanked the old fellow later at his hotel, but I regret that his name has slipped my memory.

As soon as the Scotchman left the stand the judge dismissed the case. With a smile he said to me: "Here, young man, take your pistol and go home." Thanking him, I started out with the pistol and cartridges in my hand. I looked at the prosecuting witnesses with a happy smile. They looked daggers at me in return. I afterwards learned that these people owned a restaurant on South Clark street, and that the sore-headed one had a reputation as a slugger and prize fighter.

If Mr. Dickenson ever learned of my breaking into jail while waiting to be put onto the secret force of his agency, he kept it to himself. The secret might have prevented my securing the position, and again, it might have helped me, as I have since found out that the agency officials admire a fighter when it is known that he is in the right, though, of course, they want their men to use their brains to control their trigger finger.

My first work was on the great anarchist Haymarket riot case, and I remained on it to the end of the trial, when the ringleaders were convicted.

Parsons, Engel, Fischer and Spies were hung. Ling blew his head off in jail with a bomb, and Schwab, Fielding and Neebe were sent to the penitentiary for a long term of years.

I heard most of the evidence, but I couldn't see the justice of sending Neebe to the pen. All that he did was

to set the type in the "revenge" circular which was cir-
culated, calling a mass meeting on Haymarket Square to
revenge the killing of strikers in a late riot in the Mc-
Cormick factory. The evidence was in Neebe's favor,
except that he was running with a bad crowd, and did
his loafing where the beer schooners were the largest.
They were all tried in a bunch for the killing of Degan,
one of the policemen killed outright by the bomb which
was thrown from an alley by an anarchist, supposed to be
Shnoebelt. A witness or two swore that they recognized
Shnoebelt when his companion lit the match to light the
fuse; that then Shnoebelt threw the bomb into the squad
of policemen, whose commander, Bonfield, had just
ordered the mob to disperse. Albert Parsons was standing in a wagon making a speech at the time. The next
day Shnoebelt was arrested for the throwing of the bomb,
though a couple of days later it was claimed that he was
liberated for want of evidence to hold him. Still later,
they claimed to have positive evidence of his guilt, but
too late, as he had skipped for Germany. My own opinion
is that Shnoebelt was murdered in jail by angry policemen, and his body put out of the way. At least, I received hints to that effect from men who were on the
inside.

A million dollars had been subscribed by the Citizens'
League to stamp out anarchy in Chicago, and no doubt
much of it was used to corrupt justice. Still, the hanging of these anarchists had a good effect and was worth
a million dollars to society. Now, if the law-abiding
people of the whole United States would contribute one
hundred times one million dollars to stamp out anarchy

and dynamiting, the coming generation would be saved much suffering and bloodshed, for we are surely playing with fire when we receive with open arms anarchists from foreign countries and pat them on the back for blowing up Russian and English Royalty. These chickens will come home to roost in our back yard some day.

I had talked with Policeman Degan, a fine officer, before his death, as his beat was near where we lived, and knowing the man, I couldn't much blame his brother officers for losing their heads and wanting to wreak vengeance on all who upheld anarchy.

After the anarchist case was finished, I did all kinds of small jobs, such as "shadowing" bank clerks and officials, down to looking up a lost jewel or child. During this time I had to study the rules and regulations of the Dickenson Agency, which were in book form.

The next important case that I was put on was against the Irish National League, for the English government. About half a dozen of us "sleuths" were put on the case under the direct supervision of assistant superintendent John O'Flyn. This being such an important operation, Supt. Jamieson, a kind-hearted old man, called us all into his office and explained the importance of doing our best and not getting together when working around the Irish League headquarters.

I was on this case over a month, and learned many new lessons. Operative Jakey Teufel and I went to Cincinnati, Ohio, with two Irish would-be destroyers of the English crown.

During the next couple of months I had many operations in the city of Chicago. They were of every class,

some lasting for weeks, and others only for a few minutes or hours. A good share of the time was spent in the
slums, or what should be called "Hell's Half Acre."
Here I learned some valuable lessons in human nature
and saw many eye-openers.

I had one operation which was a picnic. It was easy,
"all same" getting money from your wife's relatives.

I was put to work "shadowing" a long-legged, red-
headed banker. He had to be in the bank most of the
day, but at night he showed me a touch of high life. He
would go into tough places and drink wine with the in-
mates. I had to do likewise so as to find out how much
money his Royal Nibs was blowing in. This was my
first experience in having a "good time" at some one
else's expense.

We were glad when fall came and Mr. W. L. Dickenson called me into his private office to tell me to get ready
and move to Denver, Colo., there to join the force of
their new office which was opened for business a few
months previous.

Our friends in Chicago were bidden farewell, and
Mamie and little Viola were put into a Pullman sleeper
and we turned our faces back toward the setting sun.

My work was of all kinds during this first winter in
Denver. I had quite a lot of investigating to do, as well
as helping to run down city crooks and law breakers in
general. I helped break up a gang of crooked street car
conductors who had duplicate punches to ring in on the
company and thereby make from ten to twenty dollars
a day each for himself. Horses were the motive power
then.

CHAPTER II

Early in the spring of 1887 I was sent out on my first
cowboy operation.

In the southwestern part of Colorado on the border of
New Mexico, was situated the County of Archuleta, the
county seat being Pagosa Springs, and the nearest railroad being Amargo, New Mexico.

What the Denver newspapers called anarchy, and a
great uprising, had broken loose in this county which
contained only about seventy-five voters. The residents
of Archuleta county were mostly "Americans," but the
Archuleta brothers of Amargo, New Mexico, ruled polit-
ically by flooding the county on election day with their
New Mexican sheep herders who voted.

Finally the citizens rebelled and drove all the county
officials with the exception of the sheriff and county clerk,
who joined the insurgents, out of the country. They
even burnt up some of their property and threatened
death if they ever returned.

In order to retain their office by law, the five deported
county commissioners, "Press" and "Don" Archuleta,
Bendito Martinez, Mr. Scase and J. M. Archuleta, had to
hold a county commissioners' meeting within sixty days;

hence my being sent on ahead as a Texas outlaw, so as to be one of the revolutionists should a battle take place.

In Durango, Colorado, I bought a horse and saddle and rode sixty miles to Pagosa Springs. Enroute I stopped at the G. cattle ranch and made myself solid with Gordon G., who was one of the ringleaders of the uprising and known as a "bad" man from Texas.

While at the G. ranch I confided in Gordon by telling him of how I had killed three Mexicans in Texas and had to skip. He also told me of trouble he had in Texas.

On reaching Pagosa Springs, I headed straight for the residence of E. M. Taylor, the County clerk, who was the brains and the leader of the revolutionists.

I had made up my mind to establish myself at the Taylor residence if nerve and gall could accomplish the feat.

Riding up to the porch I tied my horse and knocked on the front door. Mrs. Taylor appeared and informed me that her husband had gone to his sheep ranch, and would not be back till dark. I asked if I couldn't wait there until his return. She asked why I wished to see him. Told her that I wanted to live with them awhile. Here the little lady climbed upon her dignity and informed me that they did not keep boarders; that there were two hotels in town. She then slammed the door in my face.

Recalling that old saying: "Faint heart ne'er won fair lady," I determined to try it. So unsaddling my pony and placing the saddle on the porch, I took the horse to the stable and gave him a good feed of grain and hay. Then returning to the porch, I lay down on the saddle.

It was a damp, cold day, and through the window I could see Mrs. Taylor and her only child, a ten-year-old daughter, sitting by the blazing fire in the hearth. Through the window they could also see me.

About dusk Mr. Taylor rode up on his horse and wanted to know what was up. I told him my tale of woe —that I had got into trouble in Texas and was hiding out—hence did not want to stop at a hotel. Also that I was a friend of Gordon G.'s. He replied that if I was a friend of Gordon's I could stop with them, providing he could get his wife's consent. He was absent in the house long enough to get the consent of ten men.

Mrs. Taylor was a splendid cook, and the warm supper hit the soft spot in my heart. And the nice clean bed in a cozy front room put me at peace with all the world.

Shortly after I had established myself in the home of Mr. Taylor, the county commissioners, with the county judge, J. Archuleta, and the county attorney, Jas. L. Russell, returned from New Mexico under an escort of sixty mounted and well armed Mexicans.

We revolutionists, about seventy-five strong, met them at the bridge spanning the San Juan river, and prevented them from entering the town. Communications were carried on through flags of truce.

Our side were mostly wild and woolly cowboys and ranchmen, and we had plenty of liquor to keep up our fighting spirit.

The county officials were camped in an old house on the opposite side of the swift flowing San Juan river, while their armed escort were housed in the vacated government barracks, a quarter of a mile distant from the river.

A plot was laid to assassinate the seven officials at 3 A. M. Two men were to cross the river above town and slip along under the bank to a haystack which adjoined the house in which the officials slept. The haystack was to be set on fire. This would burn the house. Men secreted behind rocks on our side of the river were to shoot down the gentlemen as they ran out of the burning building.

About 11 P. M. I waded the river half a mile above town and made a swift run to notify the armed guards doing duty at the old government barracks.

Jose Martinez, brother to Bendito Martinez, promised that he would give me ample time to get back to the saloon where our mob was congregated, before notifying the officials. But this he failed to do; the result being that our guards on the bridge saw the officials running with their valises over to the camp of their fighting men. Then the drunken mob began counting noses to see who of their party were absent to have warned the enemy. Of course, I was missed. Hence when I returned there was something "doing," and they were determined to hang me. But my friends, Taylor, Dyke and Gordon, believed my protests of innocence and my life was spared.

They decided to set a trap for me the next night. They concluded that if I were the guilty party I must have communicated the secret to Mrs. Scase, and she sent the news to her husband by one of her small boys. It puzzled them to know how I could have waded the swift river, which was waist deep, without wetting my clothes. They had felt to see if they were wet. They did not know that I disrobed while crossing the river.

County Commissioner Scase had a Mexican wife, and when the mob burnt up their residence and livery stable and escorted Mr. Scase over the line into New Mexico, they allowed Mrs. Scase and her children to occupy an old shack on the bank of the San Juan river. So at this shack the trap was set to catch me. They felt sure that if I were a detective I would communicate with Mrs. Scase. Therefore, they had two men detailed to watch this shack. They secreted themselves in a large wood pile near the front door. These men took turns about guarding.

We had a dance that night. All attended but the men on duty guarding the bridge and the Scase shack.

About 11 P. M. I walked in a round-about-way to the Scase residence to deposit some short hand notes in the back of an old oil painting which hung on the wall, and which had escaped the fire. I passed within a few yards of the wood pile where the armed guard was doing duty.

Securing the door key under a board—where Mrs. Scase had promised to leave it—I entered the front room and deposited the notes. Then I sat on the edge of the bed talking to Mrs. Scase a moment. The children were sound asleep.

In taking my departure I slipped a board out of place along the wall, facing the river, and made a jump of about twelve feet onto the rocky edge of the river. Mrs. Scase replaced the board.

As soon as I entered the door the young man in the wood pile ran to the dance hall to tell the half drunken mob that the suspect was caught in the trap. All grabbed their rifles or shotguns and raided the Scase shack. I was told that Mrs. Scase stood pat and insisted that I had not been there.

When I entered the dance hall the ladies and children turned their gaze onto me. There were no men in the place but the two fiddlers. A runner was sent to inform the mob that I was in the hall.

In a few moments the hall was a surging mass of armed men. Gordon G. touched me on the shoulder, saying: "Anderson, I want to speak to you." He led the way into a side room where there was a carpenter's work bench, and pointing to this bench, he asked me to sit down as he wished to ask me some questions. Around my waist were old Colt's 45 and a pearl-handled bowie knife. My first impulse was to draw the pistol and fight my way out, but on second thought I concluded that would be showing bad detective ability.

I sat down on the bench facing Gordon, who stood six feet in his stockings, and was otherwise every inch a man. Placing both hands on my knees and looking me square in the face, he said: "Now, Anderson, I want you to tell me the truth. If you do I can save you, otherwise you are going to be killed. Now, remember, don't lie to me. I want the truth. Are you a detective?" I answered, "no." He then continued: "Well, what were you doing in Mrs. Scase's house tonight?" I replied that I did not know Mrs. Scase, nor had I ever been in her house. Said he: "Well, one of our men swears he saw you go in there."

At this I jumped off the bench and with my hand on old Colt's 45, demanded that he show me the dirty whelp that would tell such a lie on me. And that if he said it to my face, one of us would have to die. I said this in a loud angry tone so that the mob in the hall could hear me.

Gordon said: "I believe, Anderson, you are telling the truth. But keep cool, and I'll put you face to face with the man."

We then walked into the hall and Gordon called the young man. As he stepped up I asked if he had lied about me. The result was the poor fellow weakened and said he could have been mistaken, but the man who entered Mrs. Scase's looked like me, but it being dark, he might have been mistaken.

That settled it for the night, but next day the mob became drunk and unruly and were determined to hang me as a spy. It would require too much space to give the details. The result was that through hard lying I saved my neck and was promoted. Sheriff Dyke made me one of his special deputies at $4.00 a day, as long as I could remain. This money came in handy and it was all "velvet," that is, belonged to me individually.

Two days later, after being appointed deputy sheriff, I saved the lives of the county commissioners, the county judge and Attorney Russell, who, by the way, has since served as district judge of that district, and at the present writing, so I am told, is still an honored citizen of that county.

A plot had been planned for both sides to stack all the fire arms and leave two men from each side to guard them. Then a meeting of the commissioners could sit in the court house. The scheme was to have some rifles cached and make a raid on the fire arms and their guards. Then the slaughter was to begin.

All the county officials with the exception of Bendito Martinez had agreed to the plan. All were trying to get Martinez's consent. He finally caught my eye and I shook my head—as much as to say don't do it. That settled it. He stood pat and the plot fell through.

I have heard it said that a Mexican can't take a hint, but Martinez caught a hint in a very light shake of my head. Poor fellow, he soon afterwards shot a man dead in the Durango court room, which broke him up financially, though I hear he is getting on his feet again.

After holding the county officials and their armed escort at bay for about four days, peace was declared by the leaders of the revolutionists being promised an even division of the political pie in future. Then the commissioners held their meeting and all departed for New Mexico.

The blood of the insurgents had cooled off as the liquors in Bowland's saloon diminished, hence peace was declared under a flag of truce—a woman's white apron.

For the next six weeks I had nothing to do but play outlaw and eat Mrs. Taylor's good cooking. Whenever suspicious strangers appeared in town Sheriff Dyke would have me keep hid out until he could learn their business, for fear they might be Texas officers on my trail.

Often I would be the sole occupant of the Taylor residence and at such times I would read Mr. Taylor's private political letters. His old love letters would be laid to one side. I had secured a key that fitted his private desk.

There were piles of political letters and receipts for

votes bought during past elections. The ruling price of votes was two dollars in cash or one sheep. Most of the interesting political letters were from Billy Adams, brother of the twice governor of Colorado, Alva Adams. From these letters I learned many new lessons in up-to-date western politics.

I appeared before the grand jury in the adjoining county of La Plata, at Durango, the judge of the court being Chas. D. Hayt, and the prosecuting attorney, G. T. Summer, with the result that sixteen of the leaders in the uprising were indicted.

I then disposed of my horse and saddle and "sneaked" to an eastbound train for Denver.

I had been on the operation about two months and during that time I dared not write reports or letters to my wife, nor receive mail from Denver, as the postoffice at Pagosa Springs was in the hands of the insurgents. I had used the name of Chas. Anderson on this operation.

Arriving in Denver, I was hurried away to the Republic of Mexico to run down an A., T. & S. F. Ry. brakeman who had stolen $10,000 from the Wells-Fargo Express Company at La Junta, Colorado, during the excitement of a train wreck.

A ride of 700 miles on the Atchison, Topeka & Santa Fe Railway brought me to El Paso, Texas, and another 1,200 miles on the Mexican Central Railway brought me to the City of Mexico.

On arriving there the first thing I did was to write a nice letter to my friend Taylor in Pagosa Springs, telling him that I had got a telegram from my brother in Texas warning me to skip, as the grand jury had found a true

3

bill against me for murder, and that I intended to remain in the City of Mexico a month or so until my brother could get money to me; then I was going to lose myself in the wilds of South America. My address in the City of Mexico under a new assumed name was given to Mr. Taylor, and in the course of three weeks I received a nice long letter from him. He told me that the grand jury in Colorado had indicted him, Sheriff Dyke and fourteen of the other leaders, for running the county officials out of Archuleta county and burning their property. He said that they were all then under heavy bond, and on account of the mysterious way in which I left, they had laid their downfall on to my giving them away before the grand jury; that they were mad enough to murder me if I could have been found; that I only had one friend in Pagosa Springs who stuck up for me to the last and refused to believe me guilty, and that was his wife. He said that this showed how a woman could be a true friend when once her mind is made up. He assured me that no matter to what part of the earth I might drift, I could count on having true friends in Pagosa Springs, and that any time I should need money or help, to write him. I have never seen any of the Archuleta county warriors since leaving there, hence I do not know whether I am regarded as an outlaw yet or not. I see by the papers that Taylor still lives in Pagosa Springs, which has grown to be an important railroad town, and that he is judge of the court there.

In dismissing the Archuleta county uprising, I wish to state that these men had good cause for revolting, as politics in that county were rotten. Most of them were honorable citizens, though a little rough and wild. Of course, I felt "sore" at them for wanting to hang me up by the neck.

I shall always hold my friend Gordon G. as one of the "true blue" sons of the Lone Star State, as he knows how to stick to a friend.

A few nights after my arrival in Mexico City, a big earthquake shook up the city. It shook the Guadaola Hotel where I had a room on the fourth floor, from stem to stern. Many people in the city, according to reports, had been killed. The next morning the streets were still lined with natives praying.

A few days later the big day of the Republic, the Fifth of May, was celebrated, and I then saw my first bull fight, and I never want to witness another. If ever Uncle Sam should want a good soldier to help wipe Mexico off the face of the earth or make her promise to quit her cold-blooded cruelties to dumb animals, he can count on me and I will gladly furnish my own ammunition. They pitted three bulls imported from Spain against four native bulls. The ones from Spain were artists when it came to butchering horses. If they had killed a few of the ignorant and cruel Mexicans who were riding the poor beasts up to be gored to death, they would have won my applause. One horse was sewed up six times and each time ridden back to be gored again, until finally killed by the bull. It was enough to disgust a Piute Indian, and still men, women and little children went wild and shouted for joy at the sight of blood and the suffering of the dumb brutes.

To show what a great head I've got for avoiding

danger, I will cite a little instance. A Mexican National Railway engineer, whose arm was in a sling, having been injured in a recent wreck, was out with me to see the sights. We visited the noted Church of Guadalupe, which is said to have been built by Montezuma in memory of the angel Guadalupe. After going through the church and seeing the "serape" (blanket), which this angel saint wore on her flying trip from heaven to Mexico City, we climbed the hill to the graveyard where all the noted warriors are buried. It covers a couple of acres and a guard with a rifle and sword is kept on duty night and day.

On coming to old General Santa Ana's grave, I thought of poor Davy Crockett and his brave followers who met their fate in the Alamo at San Antonio, Texas, through the inhuman blood-craving of this same old general. The earth mound where he sleeps was plastered over with all kinds of fancy, many-colored pieces of broken china-ware. One particularly pretty piece took my eye and I told the engineer that it would be in my cabinet of curios even if it should cost me a leg. The engineer said it would mean possible death or a long term in a Mexican dungeon·if I were caught stealing from this "heap big chief's" grave, but when he found that I was determined to risk a fight to a finish with this copper-colored son of old Montezuma, he agreed to assist me by steering the watchman away to another part of the graveyard and keeping his back towards me by asking him questions about the city which lay at our feet in plain view. The guard stood in sight with the seat of his white cotton pants towards me when I and old Colt's 45 climbed over the sharp-pointed, tall iron pickets and secured the prize. We wondered if Davy Crockett turned over in his grave to smile.

When a cowboy, and on a tear, we used to often in fun get up on the bar and yell: "I'm a wolf, and to-night is my night to howl. I've got two rows of teeth, one for ransacking graveyards and the other for devouring human beings." Little did I dream then that in years to come I would ransack old Santa Ana's grave just to satisfy a greedy desire for a pretty relic and to break the slow monotony of a peaceful life.

Much of my time was spent with Supt. Daniel Turner and his assistants in the Wells-Fargo office. They had just gone through a siege of fool Mexican law. They had all been held prisoners in their own offices over a peeled duck—that is, a duck with the feathers off.

A few hundred miles north, as a passenger train was fixing to pull out for the capital, a Mexican came running up to the Wells-Fargo agent with a duck in his hand. He demanded that it be expressed to his friend in Mexico City. This the agent said was impossible, as his duckship had to be billed out in regular form and now the train was ready to start. The result was the train pulled out leaving Mr. Mexican and his duck on the station platform. But he had his revenge as soon as he could reach the office of the Alcalde and make complaint. For a week or two the agent lay in a dungeon and Supt. Turner and his assistants dare not venture on the streets, as the place was surrounded by guards day and night. For a week Mr. Turner and his men had to eat and sleep in the office on account of the measly little duck, for the law prohibited the officers from going inside the house to arrest them.

I had located my man who had stolen the $10,000. He was living under an assumed name, but he was free from arrest while on Mexican soil, so for that reason I had to keep track of him until he left Mexico. This suited me, as it allowed me a month or two to see the sights and to have a good time.

The thief invested some of the stolen money in diamonds. I kept track of the purchases. Finally he got ready to sail from Vera Cruz on a steamship for Havana, Cuba, thence to New York City, and by rail to his home in Leavenworth, Kansas. I was all ready to go with him on the ship and thereby see Cuba and the City of New York, but word came that yellow fever had broken out in Havana, and our trip was abandoned. However, we started for the United States by way of El Paso, Texas. I remained with my man until he reached his home in Leavenworth, then had him arrested, and I departed for Denver, reaching there after an absence of about two months. Being so busy and constantly on the jump, I never went to the trouble to find out how many years in the penitentiary my friend received.

After only a few days spent with Mamie and Viola, I had to "hit" the road again, this time for Roseta, a mining camp in Custer county, Colorado, to capture the world renowned Bassick mine.

Four of us operatives, John Rucker, who had traveled with Barnum's circus as a Dickenson man for years, a fellow by the name of Goods, a Frenchman with a name as long as my arm, and myself, started armed to the teeth with Winchester rifles, pistols and playing cards.

At Canon City we left the railroad and drove over the Greenhorn range of mountains in a vehicle loaded with ammunition and grub to stand a long siege. A drive of twenty miles or more brought us to the top of a mountain overlooking the great Bassick mine and the little village of Quereda nestling at its feet. A mile further was the town of Roseta, noted for its tough men and the bloody local battles fought in the early history of Colorado mining. Eight miles to the west lay the prosperous mining camp of Silver Cliff, and the railroad town of West Cliff.

During the night we moved down the hill and entered the large Bassick hoisting works by breaking in a rear window. The custodian, a Kentucky colonel and ex-sheriff of Custer county whose name was Schofield, was at his home in Quereda, a few hundred yards down the mountain side, asleep.

In law, possession is nine points to the good, therefore, we had gained the points aimed at for our client, Mr. David Bryan, the Minnesota millionaire; but the question was could we hold it in the face of the great odds which Schofield could muster.

We sat up all night and next morning when Schofield unlocked the big front door of the hoisting works, as was his custom as paid custodian for Bassick and his associates, we threw our rifles down on him and made him go away and leave the door open. He had a pistol but made no effort to draw it, his surprise being so great. After he had climbed down off the high platform in front of the door, he was in the main street of Quereda. Across the street was the postoffice and a couple of stores, the remaining buildings being vacant. Finally Schofield recovered from his surprise and demanded to know what we meant. We laughed and told him that we had merely captured his job from him while he slept. He swore that he would dispossess us if it cost all the blood in Roseta. He then got on a horse and galloped over the hill to that town. Anticipating that the men of Roseta would open war on us, our superintendent had sent his trusted bookkeeper, Lawton, to Roseta a few days previous, so as to post us of impending danger. That night a little after midnight, our man Lawton slipped up to a rear window of the hoist and called for us. He was too badly frightened to come in. He gave a note to one of our men and then began "hitting" the high places over the mountains for Canon City. The note read about as follows: "Boys, run for your lives. Don't wait. 300 armed men, many of them drunk and desperate are now on the way from Roseta under the leadership of Schofield to kill you and take possession of the mine. I am off for Canon City. Follow me quick, before it is too late."

We held a hurried council of war and decided to stand "pat" and die fighting "all same" the noted heroes under Davy Crockett at the Alamo. "Frenchy" was the only man who looked pale and he wondered what would become of his wife if he were killed.

Stationing ourselves at upper story windows from whence the little valley towards Roseta and the side of the mountain towards Canon City could be scanned, we awaited results with rifles ready. Soon the moon came out, but she had no blood on her face. I told "Frenchy" that this was considered a good sign during war times.

About 3 o'clock we heard fierce yelling over the hill towards Roseta. Soon, by the bright light of the moon, we saw a dark mass of something creeping over the crest of the hill, a distance of half a mile or more. The yelling still continued. On drawing nearer we discovered the black mass to be men. When within about a quarter of a mile of us the one hundred to two hundred men stopped and collected into a solid round bunch—holding a consultation preparatory to making the final charge, thought we. The yelling had ceased. In a few moments the men began to string out again towards us. We could see that many carried rifles or shotguns, and many were staggering as though loaded with "booze." The yelling had begun again. Soon all stopped and we could hear loud cursing as though they were fighting among themselves. At last, to our great delight, all but two men started back towards Roseta. The two staggered on to Schofield's house and disappeared inside. One of them was Schofield. Next day we heard through the postmistress, a young lady from Chillicothe, Mo., that the mob broke up in a drunken row. Thus ended my second bloodless war within a space of four months.

The Rocky Mountain *Daily News* of Denver gave the following account of our arrival:

"LAWLESSNESS AT SILVER CLIFF.

SILVER CLIFF, COLO., June 21, 1887.

This community was convulsed with excitement last evening about 6 o'clock, on receipt of news that the Bassick mine had been captured by an armed force of men from abroad. Nothing definite could be gleaned until this morning, when it was learned that four men armed with Winchesters marched at once to the mine, broke in the doors of the old and new works and took possession. They are strangers and have ammunition and provision for a long siege. It has been ascertained that they are under orders from President Brown of the Bassick Mining Company."

In a few days Mr. Chas. Handsell, of the Denver law firm of Mathewson, Thornes & Handsell, came to the Bassick mine to see how we were getting along. As there was some wild talk by Schofield and his friends about ousting us, Mr. Handsell hired two fighting men in Silver Cliff to assist us.

In the course of a week or so matters quieted down and all were called off the job but Rucker and me. After this Schofield, who had been drowning his trouble in drink, made friends with Rucker and me, but we wouldn't allow him to loaf with us on our front porch—the platform in front of the hoist. He had to stand on the ground and hand the bottle up for us to drink out of. He thought this wasn't treating him right after he had buried the hatchet. Then, too, we always made him drink out of the bottle first, so if there was poison in it he would die too.

Soon after this, Schofield put up a slick Kentucky job on me, but it failed to work. It was Texas against Kentucky, and the Lone Star State won with hands down.

One evening about dark, Schofield came to our front porch with only one good drink in his bottle, but he said there was a demijohn full of the same kind of stuff in his cellar, and that if I would go with him he would give me a quart bottle full. I went, and on starting down the cellar steps at his residence, they being on the outside of the house, he stepped to one side to let me go down first but I balked. He then went ahead and on passing through the inner door he stepped to one side to let me pass. Here I suggested that he keep in the middle of the road and in front. He then went to the opposite side of the cellar and filled the bottle from a jug, then gave me a drink and I backed out of the door and up the steps. Next day a friend told us that Schofield had failed to trap me in his cellar. He said the inner door had been arranged with a spring lock so that he could stand outside and pull the door shut, leaving me a prisoner inside; that then it was arranged to capture Rucker and take possession of the mine.

In the course of a few weeks the court appointed a custodian to take charge of the mine. Then Rucker and I left for Denver, and shortly after Rucker returned to the New York Branch of the Dickenson agency, where he still hangs out.

CHAPTER III

To White River as an Outlaw—The Ute Indian
War—Riding and Roping Under Name of "Dull
Knife" at a Denver Cowboy Tournament—Off
for Wyoming as an Outlaw.

A rest of a few days in Denver, and Supt. A—— instructed me to get ready for a trip among the Ute Indians
who were then reported to be on the warpath.

It was the fall of 1887. The work was to be done for
a wealthy widow by the name of Mrs. Tice. She
and a Mr. C—— owned a small cattle ranch in western
Colorado. She suspicioned that she was being robbed by
their foreman and her partner. So, for there I started out
in my cowboy rigging.

In Rifle, on Grande River, I left the Denver & Rio
Grande train and on the upper deck of a civilized pony
I started north over the mountains for Meeker, on White
River. A moderate ride of a day and a half brought me
to the town made famous by the "Meeker Massacre."
On my arrival in Meeker the excitement of a late Indian
war had subsided. A week or ten days previous, a battle
had been fought on the head of White River, a day's ride
from Meeker, and on leaving Denver I was instructed to
investigate this battle for an official of the U. S. Government, after finishing the cattle operation.

From Meeker, a day's ride down the river brought me
to the cattle ranch owned by Mrs. Tice and C. With the

44

foreman and cowboys I played myself off as an outlaw Texan, and by being an expert with a lasso I soon won their friendship.

In the course of two weeks I had secured sufficient evidence to show that our friend, Mrs. Tice, was being robbed.

I then returned to Meeker and from there went to the head of White River to investigate the killing of some Ute Indians by the sheriff and a crowd of ranchmen.

Before leaving Meeker I wrote a letter to Mr. Geo. L. Golding, of Denver, asking that my name be put on the list of wild-horse riders and steer ropers, in the grand Cowboy Tournament soon to take place. I signed myself "Dull Knife," with Meeker as my home, so that no one would know me.

The name "Dull Knife" was selected on account of it once having been my nickname on the cattle ranges of Texas. It was given to me by cowboy companions who were in the habit of borrowing my pearl-handled bowie knife, and always finding it dull, from having killed so many rattle snakes. Through years of practice I had become an expert in throwing the knife from my horse's back. By holding the point between my thumb and forefinger I would throw it at the snake's neck and seldom failed to pin his snakeship to the earth by burying the blade through his neck or head into the ground. Often the blade would sever the snake's head from his body. Of course the knife was kept dull from being stuck into the earth so often.

On the head of White River I visited the few ranchmen and hunters and was shown the battle ground where the

Ute Indians were murdered by the blood-thirsty Whites. From what I could learn from eyewitnesses, it was cold-blooded murder. The fight was started by the long-legged, wild and woolly sheriff of Garfield County, who soon after absconded with the county's funds. The excitement of the "Great Indian Uprising" caused the militia to be called out, and made fat pocket-books for the ranchers who had horses, hay and grain for sale. Besides, the sheriff lined his pockets with free silver at the county's expense.

This was my first peep behind the curtain of a great Indian war, as illustrated by glaring headlines in the daily press. We wondered who are the real savages, the Whites or the Reds.

On leaving the head of White River for Denver, I concluded to take a short cut across the Flattop mountains, a distance of sixty miles between ranches.

The start was made from the cabin of a hunter at the head of White River. From him I had bought an extraordinary fine pair of elk horns. These I undertook to carry on my pony by holding them up in front of me with the skull resting on the saddle-horn. In traveling that lonely sixty mile stretch over the old Ute Indian trail, I had plenty of leisure to ponder over that wise saying: "What fools these mortals be."

Crossing the "Flattops" I saw more deer than I ever expect to see again. There were hundreds of them in sight at all times and they were very tame. Often they would stand by the side of the trail and allow me to pass within fifty paces of them. I saw one herd of elk, but they ran into the heavy timber near by before I could get out my Winchester rifle and shoot. I would have followed on their trail, as I had never killed an elk, if it hadn't been for the pair of elk horns. I pitched camp about sundown and killed a fat buck for supper. I had brought with me some salt and cold biscuits. The venison was broiled on a stick over the fire.

By daylight next morning the horns and I headed south. We got off on the wrong trail and were lost part of the day, but by hard swearing and a little patience we managed to get down over the rim-rock of the "Flattops" into the Grand Valley about half way between Newcastle and Glenwood Springs. On the road in the valley a boy leading a bronco overtook us. The boy was persuaded to allow me to make a pack-horse out of his bronco, so Mr. "bronc" was blindfolded and the horns put astride of his back. When securely fastened with a rope the blind was raised and Hades broke loose. The bronco began bucking and running and the rope which was fastened to the horn of my saddle broke. Then the horns had a swift ride for quite a distance, but as the run was made towards Glenwood Springs no time was lost. The boy and I caught the bronco after he had become exhausted. Then the horns were strapped onto my civilized pony and I rode the uncivilized brute. It was long after dark when we landed in Glenwood Springs. Next day the horns were crated and expressed to Denver, and after selling my pony and saddle I took passage on the same train with the antlers.

On my arrival in Denver I secured permission from my superintendent to enter the Cowboy Tournament at River Side Park. It was to take place in a couple of days and I had no time to lose.

After making a search of all the livery stables in the city I finally found a small white cow-pony which I thought would answer my purpose. He was quick and active, but too light in weight for such work. I also secured an old Texas saddle, as I couldn't get used to the high horn kind in use by northern cowboys. This old Texas saddle was the cause of my losing the steer roping prize, as the horn flew off when the weight of the steer and pony went against it. I feel confident that I would have won the prize, as the best time made was many seconds slower than the time made by me at a Caldwell, Kansas, fair several years previous, at which time I won a silver cup; and in the Kansas contest I lost valuable time by having to throw the steer twice.

In the wild-horse riding contest luck was also against me. After throwing the big bay bronco in quick time, I sprang off the white pony onto the bronco's head. Then to prevent him from choking to death, I cut the rope, knowing that he was in my power with both my knees on his neck and a good hand hold on his nose. But when I reached for the hackamore (a cowboy halter) and the leather blind which had been carried under my pistol belt, I found they were gone. They had slipped out from under the belt when I leaped out of the saddle. I saw them lying on the ground just out of my reach. According to the rules, no one could hand them to me, therefore I could do nothing but free the bronco and lose my chance at the prize. In reporting the matter the newspaper reporters had failed to comprehend my situation: They were green and didn't know why I held the struggling bronco by the nose for several minutes before turning him loose. Of course my cowboy opponents realized the cause of my predicament and cheered with joy, as it made their chances of winning more secure. I had been told that they feared the "dark horse," "Dull Knife," from Meeker, and had made much inquiry as to my identity.

This is what two of the leading daily papers of the city—The Rocky Mountain News and the Republican—had to say about "Dull Knife" the next morning. One paper stated:

"None knew who the next man was who rode out on a white pony. They called him Dull Knife, and he was from Meeker. That was all the information obtainable. But Dull Knife was a daisy. With new white sombrero, Mexican saddle, leather-fringed chaparejos, flaming red 'kerchief, belt and pearl handled revolver and knife, he was all that the eastern imagination of the typical cowboy could picture. As a bronco breaker, however, he wasn't a brilliant success. A bay was pointed out to him and away they flew. It didn't take that cunning bay bronco more than a minute to find out that he was wanted. With all the natural cussedness of his breed it didn't take him more than a second to determine that he would fool somebody. Dashing here and there, with flashing eyes and streaming main and tail, the animal was a pretty picture. The white pony was too cunning for him though, and soon put his rider in a position where the rope could be thrown and the arched neck caught in the running loop. The captive was thrown by twining the rope around his limbs and then Dull Knife made a skillful move. He cut the rope loose and held the struggling animal by the nose. But while he was subduing the horse, the man had gotten too far away from his saddle and couldn't get back to it. The judges at length called time and the pretty bay was free."

The other paper gave this account:

"When Dull Knife rode in armed with pearl-handled pistol and knife, a gold embroidered Mexican sombrero on his head

4

and mounted on a beautiful, quick-reined, white pony, he was such a perfect and graceful type of a Texas cowboy that the audience gave one spontaneous Ah-h-h! of admiration. The little white was a daisy and ran up on Dull Knife's bronco easy. Dull Knife was the only man this day to rope and throw his bronco on horseback. But the rope had fouled in the bronco's mane, and it was choking to death, so Dull Knife cut the rope, mercifully, freed the bronco and lost his time to ride. Dull Knife assayed roping and tying, but luck was against him. The horn of his light Texas saddle broke off close to the fork. Regaining his rope he tied it in the forks of his saddle and tried it again, but his beautiful little cut horse was too light and tried to hold the big burly steer which dragged it all over the corral, so Dull Knife, chafing with chagrin, had to give in to hard luck and call it a draw.

"Dull Knife and E. A. Shaeffer next stretched a steer in quick time."

Several days after the tournament George Golding and Mr. B. G. Webster, while riding in a buggy, happened to see me on the street. Hailing me as "Dull Knife" they called me to them. They said they had been trying to find me but no one knew who "Dull Knife" was or where a letter would reach him. I was then informed that the judges had voted me $15.00 for skillful cowboy performance and that a check for that amount awaited me at headquarters. Of course I went after the check and still retain it as a relic, as it states that it was presented to "Dull Knife" for skillful cowboy work.

For many years afterwards, and even up to the present time, I meet men who call me "Dull Knife," from having seen me at this Cowboy Tournament. It was several years after, before Geo. Golding—who is still proprietor of the City Sale Yards and Stables, and has since served as Denver's Chief of Police—learned of my identity.

In the course of a week or two Mrs. Tice brought suit in a Denver Court to annul her partnership with Mr. C—— or for damages, I have forgotten which. I was the star witness, and on the strength of my testimony as to the way cattle were being stolen, Mrs. Tice won. The foreman and one of his cowboys who were present in court, were surprised on finding that I was a detective instead of an outlaw.

A few days after ending Mrs. Tice's case I was off for Wyoming as a cowboy outlaw.

Kalter Skoll, the Cheyenne, Wyoming, attorney, who has lately won fame through the conviction and execution of Tim Corn, the stock detective, had written my superintendent to send him a cowboy detective who could make friends with a gang of tough characters on the Laramie River.

Before starting, my superintendent informed me that I was going up against a hard proposition, as Gen. Dave Cook, head of the Rocky Mountain Detective Agency, had sent three of his men up into Wyoming to get in with this gang, but had failed, they being on the lookout for detectives, hence wouldn't allow strangers to enter their camp.

On my arrival in Cheyenne I called on District Attorney Skoll. He explained the case on which I was to work. He told how Bill McCoy had shot and killed Deputy Sheriff Gunn in Lusk, Wyoming, and of McCoy being sentenced to hang for the crime, but that he broke jail in Cheyenne just before he was to be executed, and was trailed up to the Keeline ranch, which was run by Tom Hall, a Texas outlaw and his gang of cowboys, who were supposed to be ex-convicts from Texas. He felt sure that McCoy was in hiding at the Keeline ranch, but he said it would be a difficult matter to get in with them as they were on their guard against officers and detectives.

I boarded the Cheyenne northern train and went north to its then terminus. There I bought a horse and saddle and struck out, ostensibly for Fort Douglas, about 100 miles north.

The second day out I stopped for dinner at "Round Up No. 5 Saloon." This place was run by Howard, an ex-policeman and saloon keeper from Cheyenne. His wife was an ex-prize fighter and dance hall "girl" during the palmy days of the Black Hill excitement in Cheyenne. She was now getting old, but could still hide large quantities of liquor under her belt. After dinner I proceeded to get drunk so as to kill time. Mr. and Mrs. Howard drank with me. In telling of my past I told just enough to lead them to believe that I was a Texas outlaw headed for the north.

About 4 P. M. I saddled my horse and made a start for Fort Douglas, but on shaking hands with Mr. and Mrs. Howard, they being the only people beside myself present, and bidding them goodby, they persuaded me to have one more drink at their expense. Then, of course, I had to treat before making another start. This program was kept up for half an hour.

I had never mentioned the Keeline ranch, which I knew lay over a small range of mountains five miles east. As winter had set in, there was very little travel on this Fort Douglas road, and the cowboys had all gone into winter quarters. Howard depended on the summer cattle round-ups for his business. He said he and his wife merely existed during the winter seasons. His saloon was located at No. 5 round-up grounds.

Finally, I mounted and made another start, pretending to be drunker than I really was. As I rode off, Howard wished me well. Checking up my horse I remarked that I would be all right if I could run across some Texas boys up at Douglas. Then I asked if he knew of any Texas boys in that part of the country. He replied: "There are several Texas fellers not far from here, but they are in trouble and won't let strangers into their camp." At this I wheeled my horse around and rode back. I asked where they could be found. He replied: "No use going there, for they would run you off and perhaps kill you. The officers have been trying to get detectives in with them. They swear they will kill the next ———— that looks suspicious."

I answered: "If they are from Texas I'm not afraid of them. Just tell me where they are and I'll take chances on the killing part."

He pointed out a bridle path around a high peak and said I would find their camp on the other side of this on the edge of a clump of cottonwood timber. We then went into the saloon and had two more drinks and I bought a quart of his best whiskey, which was the same as his worst, though labeled differently.

I explained that the boys could drink with me and then run me off if they wanted to; but Howard plead with me not to go.

On mounting I buried the spurs into my horse's flanks and gave a cowboy yell and away we flew through the

heavy grove of cottonwood timber. There was no trail,
and my horse had to jump fallen logs and trees and I
dodged projecting limbs. I wanted to prove to Howard
that I was a reckless cowboy who had no fear of danger.
Looking back I saw Howard and his wife watching me.
The saloon was finally lost to view and then I rode
slowly and began to lay plans, though it was quite an
effort as the whiskey had gone to my head.

Howard had told me that there were fourteen men at
the Keeline ranch, but he wouldn't tell me what kind of
trouble they were in.

On reaching the foot of the high peak I struck the
bridle trail which had been pointed out. This I followed
over the range. When on the opposite side, my horse
was made to gallop in the most dangerous places, for I
figured that my horses' tracks would be examined. In a
rocky place where the trail went around a point and
where a horse on a gallop could hardly keep his feet,
I stopped. Here I knew the horse's tracks couldn't be
seen. At this point I got above the horse and gave him
a shove over the rocky bluff. He landed on his side in
the soft sand in the dry arroyo, twenty feet below. The
fall knocked the wind out of him, but he soon recovered
and jumped to his feet. I held one end of the rope so
that he couldn't get away. The impression of the horse
and saddle showed plainly in the sand. Climbing down
on the rocks I fell on my left side, leaving the impression
of my body in the sand where it would have been had I
fallen with the horse. I then jumped up, and dragging
my crippled left leg through the sand, led the horse to a
place where we could get back to the trail. Here I pulled

off my left boot and ripped the seam of my pants' leg nearly to the knee. Then I rolled the knit woolen drawer's leg up above the knee. This made a tight roll which checked the flow of blood, causing the knee to become red. It also had a tendency to shove the flesh downward and make the knee look swollen. I then rubbed the knee with dry grass and poured some of Howard's "rattle-snake juice" on. After tying the left boot to the saddle I mounted and headed for the large grove of cottonwood timber on the bank of the Laramie River.

Just after the sun had set I came in sight of a group of log houses on the edge of the grove. Not a breath of air was stirring and a column of smoke from a chimney pierced the lead-colored clouds above. I was riding slowly across an open flat. Soon I saw a man come out of the large log house. Then others followed until there were about a dozen lined up against the yard fence. I wondered what kind of a game I was running up against and where it would end. It was a case of forward march, with me, even though it led to death "all same," a fool soldier who marches up to the cannon mouth to have his head shot off so that posterity can weep and plant flowers on his grave.

As I drew near my body reeled as though drunk. My left leg was kept stiff and out of the stirrup. When within sixty paces of the yard gate where all the men stood, a fine looking six-footer, who proved to be the boss, Tom Hall, asked: "What in the h—— are you doing here?" I replied that my leg was broken and I needed some help. Hall sprang out of the gate and running up to me asked in a soft, sympathetic voice, how it happened. There was a wonderful change in his looks as well as voice, when he found I was crippled.

Soon the whole gang, all heavily armed, were around me and I was taken off the horse and carried into the house where I was seated before a blazing log fire in the large fire-place. Then Hall got down on his knees before me to examine the wound. I took pains to roll up the pants' leg which was only ripped part way to the knee, so as to hide the roll of knit drawers, this being the secret of my swollen knee. I had previously been shot with a large caliber bullet through this knee, and there was a large scar where the bullet entered, and another on the opposite side where it was cut out by the doctor. This helped to brand me as an outlaw in their minds.

After pressing the swollen flesh with his hand, Hall asked me to move my toes. I did so, as I didn't want the leg to appear broken for fear they might haul me off to a doctor. On moving my toes he said my leg was not broken. I asked how he could tell by the moving of the toes, and he explained. Then he asked me to bend my knee and also to twist it around, but this I couldn't do on account of the pain. He decided that my leg was badly sprained or out of joint. He ordered hot water and a towel brought and my knee was bathed and the hot towel bound around it. Then he demanded an explanation as to how I came to leave the Douglas road to visit them. I explained matters fully, and told the place where my horse fell over the bluff. He asked why I left Texas to come up to such a cold country so late in the season. With a smile I told him that the people of Texas tried to get me to stay, and even followed me to Red River on the Indian Territory border; in hopes of overtaking me so as to compel me to stay. This caused a laugh, as it meant that officers of the law had chased me to the State line.

Here I looked over towards a sullen, dark complexioned young man whom I had recognized as Jim McChesney, a boy raised in Southern Texas, and I asked him what he had done with his old sweetheart Matilda Labaugh. He was surprised and asked who ·in the h—— I was, that I should know he courted Matilda Labaugh over twenty years previous. I wouldn't tell him, but did say that he could call me Charlie Henderson. He then asked if I knew his name. I told him, yes, that it ought to be Jim McChesney. This was another surprise, and he wanted to know when I left the part of Texas where Matilda had lived. I told him that I pulled out one night in 1872 when a boy, but that I had slipped back to see my friends many times since then. His face brightened, and walking up to me he shook my hand, saying: "I know you." Then he whispered in my ear and asked if I wasn't one of the Pumphry boys. I told him that my name was Henderson now. I had chosen the year 1872, for at that time two of the Pumphry boys, mere children, had committed murder and left the country. McChesney felt sure that I was one of these boys, and that suited me.

Finally, all left the room to hold a consultation. Two men were dispatched with a lantern to examine the place where I said my horse had fallen over the bluff, and to ride to Howard's saloon to find out if I had told the truth. Another man was sent in haste to a small ranch three miles down the river, after some linament. Supper was then brought in and set before me. In the course of an hour and a half the man returned with the linament and Hall applied it to the supposed wound, and he bound up the knee so tight with bandages that it pained, but the tight bandages did good in preventing me from thoughtlessly bending my leg and thereby giving myself away.

About 10 o'clock the two "boys" returned from Howard's. Then all went outside and held a long consultation. Next day Jim McChesney told me confidentially that Howard had confirmed the truthfulness of my story and had told of the reckless manner in which I had run through the woods. He said he was not surprised at hearing of my being hurt, that he expected to see me killed before I got out of his sight.

Several days later McChesney told me of their long council of war, after the two "boys" had returned from Howard's. He said most of the "boys," especially the three escaped convicts from the penitentiary in Huntsville, Texas, were afraid that I might be a detective and insisted that I be taken out to a tree and hung up by the neck, just to frighten me into a confession in case I was a detective; but said he and Tom Hall argued against it as they felt confident that I was all right. Hall argued that it would be a shame to take advantage of a poor crippled man. He said if I was a detective that I couldn't help from showing it before many days and then I could be hung for "keeps."

All the men slept on camp beds spread on the floor, except Hall. He had a private room cut off from a corner of the kitchen, and in it he had a single bedstead. This he kindly turned over to me and he slept with one of the "boys" on the floor.

It was after 1 o'clock A M. when I went to bed, as I pretended that my leg was paining so that I could not sleep, any way. After being put to bed by Hall I took off the bandages from my leg so that I could rest my knee by bending it. I retired with my Colt's 45 pistol in the shoulder scabbard under my overshirt, and my bowie knife was swung to my waist by a small belt under my drawers. Therefore no one had seen my gun and knife. The cartridge belt containing my supply of ammunition was in my "war-bag," and this I put under my head. I slept very little during the night. Before daylight next morning, I fastened the bandages back on my leg so as to keep it stiff while hobbling about the house. After breakfast, Hall and McChesney made me a pair of crutches.

A few of the "boys" seemed suspicious of me, especially Johnny Franklin, a bowlegged Texan, who had escaped from the penitentiary in that State, so McChesney told me.

During the day Hall played "foxy" and tried to find out more about me. In speaking of Texas cowboys he asked if I ever knew Bill Gatlin. I told him yes, that I had worked with him in the Panhandle country until he got into trouble and had to skip and change his name again. I told him that Bill Gatlin was a name he had adopted after coming to northern Texas. These were facts, as I had known Gatlin well, but I never dreamed that he was the Bill McCoy I was now trying to locate.

A few days later, after I had convinced Hall that I was all right and was really acquainted with Gatlin and many of his Texas friends, he confided in me and told me how Bill Gatlin, under the name of Bill McCoy, had killed Deputy Sheriff Gunn, and was sentenced to hang, and that he (Hall) and others paid a slick jail breaker from the East $500 to commit a petty crime in Cheyenne so as to be put in jail. The result was that he sawed the bars and liberated McCoy and the other prisoners. A horse was kept in hiding for McCoy and he came direct to the Keeline ranch where they had kept him hid out in the hills until a few days before my arrival, when he was mounted on Hall's pet roan race-horse and skipped for New Orleans, there to take a sailing vessel for Buenos Ayres, South America. For a pack animal McCoy used a large-hoofed bay horse that he had stolen from the sheriff's posse who were searching for him. Later, Hall and McChesney told many incidents of how they had fooled the sheriff's posse of 100 men who were scouring the hills for McCoy.

A week later we all rode 40 miles to attend a dance at John Owens' ranch, a mile above the "Hog ranch" (a tough saloon and sporting house) at Fort Laramie. I was still walking on crutches, therefore couldn't dance. The crutches were tied to my saddle en route. Late at night when the "boys" were pretty well loaded with liquor I rode to Fort Laramie and secured a room at the hotel where my first reports were written. About daylight my reports were mailed to Denver, and then I rode back to the dance. The crowd had simmered down to just a few ladies and many drunken cowboys who kept the air outside full of smoke from their revolvers. My friends, McChesney and Franklin, were the worst. I finally succeeded in getting my drunken friends into a room to lay down, but McChesney raised such a racket breaking the windows and furniture with his pistol, that we had to abandon sleep and start back to the Keeline ranch. As I was sober, it fell to my lot to get them all on their horses and headed for home.

Hall and the cook had not come with us.

A supply of whiskey was taken along, and my life was made miserable keeping the men from fighting. To prevent McChesney from killing some one, I slipped the cartridges out of his pistol without letting him know it. Soon after this, McChesney and one of the "boys" got into a fuss while riding along, and McChesney pulled his pistol and began snapping it at the fellow, who pulled his loaded pistol and would have killed McChesney if I hadn't shoved my cocked revolver into his face just in time. I made him ride on ahead while I kept McChesney behind with me. We arrived at the Keeline ranch before night, and were a hungry, sleepy crowd.

Our next excitement came a few days later, when Howard came running over on horseback one evening to tell us that his wife was dying. He had left her alone while he came after help. All of us, Hall and the cook included, rode over to Howard's and spent the night. What happened would have made angels weep. Howard turned the saloon over to us and the liquor was free. Whiskey was poured down the poor woman's throat up to the last breath. She died before midnight and then the "Irish wake" began in dead earnest. Poor Howard, a large fine-looking, middle-age man, cried as though his heart would break. Between drinks he "harked back" to the time when he first met the corpse. Then he was on the police force of Cheyenne, and she was a beautiful young woman who made a living by boxing and singing on the saloon stages.

Until morning, whiskey and wine flowed like water, and my friend McChesney was in clover. Cowboy songs, both nice and vulgar, were sung over the corpse. Tom Hall was the champion singer of the crowd.

Next day the body was put in a rough box and lowered to its last resting place amid the drinking of toasts and the singing of "There's a land that beats this all to h——l, etc." One of the songs which was sung at the burial amused me. It ran thus:

> "Oh, see the train go 'round the bend,
>   Goodby, my lover, goodby;
> She's loaded down with Dickenson men,
>   Goodby, my lover, goodby."

When we took our departure the Howard saloon looked like a cyclone had struck it. The walls were shot full of holes and the liquors were gone. Howard left for Cheyenne when he sobered up. Of course, I didn't have as much fun as the rest, owing to the fact that I had to use one crutch.

With Mrs Howard under the sod "Calamity Jane" had the field to herself. These two women were noted characters in that part of Wyoming.

Finally my crutch was discarded and we made another forty-mile ride to a dance at Fort Laramie. This time I danced, and pretended to fall in love with a young lady who lived at the terminus of the Cheyenne Northern Railway. I wanted to make the excuse of riding over to the railroad station to see this girl when my work was finished at the Keeline ranch.

Reports were written, and much liquor destroyed, the same as on our previous trip.

Soon after, Hall received a letter from Bill McCoy in New Orleans. He was ready to sail for South America. Hall had given him a letter of introduction to a dentist in Buenos Ayres, South America. This answered the purpose of a passport into a tough gang of outlaws in the cattle country 1200 miles from this seaport, Buenos Ayres. Hall showed me letters from one of the gang there. His name was Moore and he was a Texas murderer. He wrote that they were over 100 strong, and that double their number of officers couldn't come in there and arrest them.

Hall had been reared at Austin, Texas, and had to skip out and change his name on account of a killing. He also told me of his ups and downs in New Mexico when he was a chum to the noted outlaw, Joe Fowler, who was hung by a mob at Socorro, New Mexico. He told how Fowler, after killing one of his own cowboys in Socorro, had placed the $50,000 received for his cattle and ranch to the credit of his sweetheart, Belle, and that on the day when the mob was collecting to hang Fowler that night, Belle drew $10,000 out of the bank and turned it over to him (Hall) so that he could bribe the jailer and liberate Fowler. Hall said he had the jailor "fixed" but when the time for liberating Fowler came, the mob was collecting and the jailer backed out for fear they would hang him, if Fowler was gone. Then Hall said he hit the "high places" and came North. I didn't ask if he brought the $10,000 with him, but took it for granted that he did.

It happened that I was already familiar with Joe Fowler's crimes. He murdered Jim Greathouse, who was a friend of mine, and at White Oaks, New Mexico, in 1880, I knew of his murdering a cowboy whom he had never seen before. Two cowboys had a pistol duel in Bill Hudgen's Pioneer Saloon. One of them was mortally wounded when Fowler, who had heard the shooting, came running in. He asked the cause of the shooting. Some one pointed to the wounded cowboy on the floor. Then Fowler pulled out his pistol and shot him through the head. The other cowboy was caught and hung to a tree by Fowler and his gang, and by the rope route Fowler's life was ended.

Finally, I struck out from the Keeline ranch to see my girl at the railroad station. There my horse and saddle were sold and I boarded the train for Cheyenne.

The Grand Jury were in session and I appeared before them as a witness. Hall and his gang were indicted. The sheriff and a large posse surrounded the Keeline ranch at daylight one morning, and the Hall gang were arrested. I was told that Hall remarked when arrested: "That —— Henderson is at the bottom of this." The fact that I did not come back had created a suspicion.

They were all landed in jail at Cheyenne and I felt sorry for them, especially for Hall and McChesney. My sympathy was overflowing for Hall because he is a prince, and has a heart in him like an ox. The sympathy for McChesney was on account of having known him when a boy, and having known his father in Caldwell, Kansas, years later.

I lay in Denver waiting to be called as a witness against Hall and his gang. But before the case was tried, District Attorney Skoll, who at that time was trying to get away with all the liquor in Cheyenne, had a row with the judge on the bench, McGinnis, and the cases were nolle prossed by Skoll. At least, this is the story told by my superintendent, who was in Cheyenne at the time. Thus my friends were liberated to my great joy, as I didn't want to see them sent to the pen. I heard afterwards that three of the escaped convicts from Texas were returned there, but as to its truthfulness I do not know.

CHAPTER IV

In Jail With Denver & Rio Grande Hold-Ups—
Aspen Ore-Stealing Case—Testing Railroad
Conductors—The Mudsill Mine-Salting Case—
In Longmont as a Bronco-Buster—In the Bull-
Pen With Hoboes.

My next operation out of the city was a train robbery
case upon the Denver & Rio Grande Railroad. Doc.
Shores, the popular sheriff of Gunnison County,
Colorado, had charge of the case. He and I went to a
town in northwestern Kansas, Cawker City. Doc. Shores
remained until I went twenty or thirty miles out in the
country to work for a farmer by the name of Smith.

The train had been held up by three men, two of
whom were supposed to be the Smith brothers, sons of
this old farmer. The hold-up occurred near Green River
Station in western Colorado, and the Smith boys were
seen in the neighborhood under suspicious circumstances,
just before the hold-up.

Farmer Smith had a pretty black-eyed daughter and I
made love to her, as well as figuring on buying his farm.
The girl showed me a letter from her brothers, written
and mailed in Price, Utah, after the hold-up, showing that
they were in hiding in that neighborhood. In the letter
they stated they were going to a certain town in Arizona
soon. I also saw photos of the Smith brothers and secured their descriptions. Then my heart grew cold for

this pretty maiden and I "hiked" back to join Mr. Shores. He at once wired his brother-in-law, Roe Allison, who was his under-sheriff, to search around Price, Utah, for the Smiths, as their letter had been mailed there.

We then started for Denver. There we boarded a 9 p. m. Denver & Rio Grande train for the line of Colorado and Utah to take up the trail. After retiring in the sleeper, Shores received a telegram from Roe Allison at Green River, saying that they had captured the Smith brothers and Rhodes, and would meet our train with the prisoners at Montrose. After dark next evening our train arrived in Montrose ahead of the east-bound train containing the prisoners. Shores and I held a consultation and decided that the best plan was for him to put his hand-cuffs and leg-irons on me and pretend that I was a desperate character whom he had captured up the Gunnison River that day.

When the train pulled into the depot I was taken aboard and placed in a seat near the other prisoners. I acted sullen all the way to Gunnison, where we arrived about 10 a. m. The whole town of Gunnison turned out to see the desperate prisoners. We were marched with our leg-irons on through the streets to the Court House and jail, a distance of half a mile. The snow was over a foot deep and the sidewalks were lined with people, so that we had to walk in the street single file. I brought up the rear and gave the people some hard contemptuous glances. Mr. Shores told me afterwards that several people said I was the toughest looking criminal in the bunch.

All four of us were shoved into a steel cage just large

enough for us to lie down in. We were given a few greasy quilts and blankets and our meals were put into the cage. There were no other prisoners in the jail and it was my wish that we be kept in close confinement for a day or two, as confessions can be secured much easier in that way.

Shores had been sheriff of this county for three terms and had his residence over the jail in the second story. Owing to my being a prisoner Mrs. Shores saw that we were well fed. She often brought the meals herself.

Our cell was still spattered with human blood, where a short time previous a man had cut his throat from ear to ear, in the presence of an officer who was unlocking the cell to take the fellow into court. After cutting his throat he laid the knife carefully on a shelf and shaking his fist at the officer fell over dead. Shores told us this story when we asked about the blood. We also learned that this cell had been the home of the man-eater, Alfred Packard, who had killed and eaten the choice parts of five men. He had been taken to the penitentiary for life a few years previous.

My three bedfellows were a dirty lot and were alive with vermin, as they had been in hiding on an island in Green River for several weeks. And one of the Smiths had a bullet wound through the head, which gave out an odor that put on the finishing touch to the already foul air in the cell. Smith had received the wound in a fight among themselves; at least that was their story.

After a few days of solitary confinement I secured a full confession of how the train was held up, and they told how up to the time of their arrest, they had remained in hiding on an island in Green River.

After being in jail two weeks I was taken out by a supposed officer from Wyoming, who was taking me there to be executed for murder.

I had confided in my companions, telling them of breaking out of Wyoming jail after being sentenced to hang. The "boys" really shed tears when I shook hands with them previous to being hand-cuffed to the officer.

I didn't have to appear as a witness against these men, as they confessed to the train hold-up after they were convinced that Shores had a "cinch" case against them. They were each sentenced to a term of seven years in the Colorado penitentiary.

This was the beginning of a lasting and warm friendship between C. W. Shores, his lovely wife, two bright sons and me.

Soon after my return home, a "Frenzied Finance" cyclone of small calibre struck our Agency in Denver and knocked Superintendent A. sky high. Mr. W. L. Dickenson came out from Chicago and discharged him and all his pets. Mr. Dickenson had at last discovered that his Agency was being robbed. Superintendent A. had become so bold in his high finance that he started a patrol system to furnish merchants and others with private policemen. He did this on the sly and had the bookkeeper Lawton as a partner. They were coining money on the strength of the Agency's reputation. A new set of employes were sent from the East, I being the only one of the old "bunch" left. This swelled my head, of course.

Mr. James McCartney, who had gained a world-wide reputation through his good work in hanging twenty-three miscreants, was made superintendent in A.'s stead.

McCartney had been sent to Denver a short time previous to see how matters were working. His eagle eye soon caught on to the true state of affairs, with the above result. A patrol system to furnish uniformed policemen was organized and Captain John Holmes was imported from Chicago to take charge of it, under the supervision of Mr. McCartney, and a nice young lady, Miss Mollie Rucker, was sent from the east to act as chief clerk and cashier; but a few years later Captain Holmes nailed her to the matrimonial cross and we were minus a pretty cashier. This caused the Dickensons to put a veto on the fair sex as office employes in Denver. No doubt they didn't like the idea of making a matrimonial bureau out of the Agency. However, they gave the newly wedded couple a good send-off by presenting them with a fine set of bedroom furniture.

Shortly after McCartney took charge, I was sent to Aspen, Colorado, on my first mining operation. It was an ore-stealing case, and the parties were the Aspen Mining & Smelting Company, J. B. Wellman being the president and Fred Rucklan the general manager.

At that time Aspen was a booming silver mining camp. I went to work in the mine as a common miner, although I was green at the business. Of course, the foreman, Fred Comb, and the shift-boss, Tom Qualle, knew my business and overlooked my slow work while learning to strike a drill. I hadn't been at work long when my partner, who had taught me to mine, had both eyes blown out and both hands blown off, besides suffering other injuries. He had taken out his knife and was opening a new box of caps when they exploded, with the above results. He begged to be shot, and told me that he had no desire to live in that condition; but he did live and was sent to his mother somewhere in the East.

I came very near being killed myself while at work in this mine. Qualle and I had started down a ladder 100 feet long. Qualle was ahead, while I followed. I held the lighted candle and sharp pointed steel candlestick in my right hand and in some way the sharp point of the candlestick got stuck into the flesh under one eye. The pain was so sudden that I turned loose the hold with the left hand, but like a flash realized where I was and grabbed a round of the ladder with my right hand and thereby saved my life by a mere hair's breadth. Had I fallen my body would have knocked Qualle off the ladder and we would both have had a free ride of 70 to 80 feet straight down.

After working a month I quit mining and joined "Paddy Mack" and his gang of ore thieves.

Paddy McNamarra was the slickest ore thief that ever did business in the West, and he bragged of how he could tell a detective by his actions. He told me that he had handled over one hundred thousand dollars' worth of stolen ore in this camp alone, and that he had made a fortune in Central City and Blackhawk in the same business. His main graft was handling ore stolen by the miners and bosses of packtrains. He initiated me into the mysteries of the ore stealing business and I soon became an expert.

In order to have a "cinch" case against "Paddy Mack" and his gang, I would have Fred Rucklan and D. R. C.

White, the banker and wealthy mine owner, hide in empty freight cars or upper-story rooms where they could see the ore delivered to the samplers late in the night. In that way the owners and foreman of the samplers would be caught "dead to rights."

I shall never forget the cursing that "Paddy Mack" gave me one night when I lighted a match and held it close to his face so that Mr. Rucklan and his friends in an upstairs window could see his countenance. He knocked the match from my hand and gave me a strong lecture and cursing about the danger of being seen if any one were looking out of the windows upstairs. On this occasion we were receiving stolen ore worth $10.00 a pound, and while we were taking it out of the tent and loading it onto burros Mr. Rucklan and his witnesses, who were watching us from an upstairs window, hurried to the R. ore sampler and hid in empty freight cars so as to see us deliver it to the sampler foreman.

Besides being a partner of "Paddy Mack" I was doing business on the side with many other noted ore thieves. One of these fellows had a false cellar under his house and kept the stolen ore there until he got a wagonload. He would then hire a wagon and team and deliver the ore in broad daylight to the B. sampler. I once laid a trap so that Mr. Rucklan and his friends were in hiding and happened into the sampler in time to see the owner, Mr. B., receive the ore.

When the collapse came I was thrown into jail by Sheriff White and his deputy, West Calvin, along with others of the gang. Bonds were soon furnished by "Paddy Mack" and others.

While in jail I found out that Mike M——, one of my chums, intended to jump his bond and quit the country, so I arranged with him to do likewise. He was due to be out of jail a few days ahead of me, so it was agreed that should he skip out before I was liberated, he would write to me, General Delivery, Kansas City, Mo., telling where he could be found. He said he would first go to Omaha, Nebraska, where he had friends in the stone yards, he being a stonecutter by trade.

By the time my bonds arrived through the bank, Mike M. had shaken the dust of Aspen from his feet, so I then went on his trail. In the search for him I was assisted by one of our operatives, John S. Kaiser, later the superintendent of the Denver office. We searched the stone quarries and yards of Omaha and Lincoln, Nebraska, and Kansas City, Missouri without success. Finally I received a letter in Kansas City telling me to meet him in a small town in Oklahoma. This was the finish of poor Mike M. He was landed back in the Aspen jail.

When the case came up for trial, a start was made on a fellow by the name of E. In his case I was not required to show my hand by going on the stand, as he had been caught with the stolen ore, en route to Denver, on the train. We had a "cinch" case against him, but the jury hung and his case was put off to the next term of court. We found the gang had too many friends and too much influence to ever convict any of them. Therefore the cases against the small thieves were continued to the next term of court, which ended the matter. The big fellows, —the owners of the two sampling works where the stolen ore was sold, were let go free with the understanding that they sell out and quit the country.

Poor "Paddy Mack" died from a broken heart soon after being arrested.

Thus one of the worst gangs of ore thieves in the West was put out of business in Aspen, though I met some of them in Cripple Creek and other places in later years, following the same line of business, and prospering.

My next operation out of Denver was "testing" railroad conductors on a great western railway system through the States of Colorado, Nebraska, Kansas, Iowa and Missouri. This kind of work was not to my liking, though I had an opportunity of seeing the country and learning new points in human nature.

There were about a dozen of us operatives on this work.

In Beatrice, Nebraska, on this operation, I made the acquaintance of Gen. Colby and saw his noted stallion, Lindentree, presented to Gen. U. S. Grant by the Sultan of Turkey. Seeing this horse was a treat, as I had never before seen so much horse wrapped in such a small hide.

My next big operation started soon after returning to Denver from the railroad "test case," our client being the Lord Mayor of London, England, through his Agent Mr. McDermott of New York City. His royal 'Ighness, the Lord Mayor, had bought a gold brick by paying $190,000.00 in cash for the Mudsill Silver Mine at Fairplay, Park County, Colorado, and in addition to the cash payment, he had contracted to build a $40,000.00 ore-treating plant on the ground and to give the sellers Dan V. and Matches, $75,000 worth of stock in a new company to be organized under the title of the Mudsill Mining & Milling Co. Before making the deal, his 'Ighness had employed McDermott, a noted mining expert of New York City to examine the property. McDermott reported 30,000 tons of ore in sight, worth $30 per ton. To make sure, before loosening his grip on the dollars of his forefathers, the Lord Mayor sent another mining expert from London to examine the property. In the meantime Mr. Dan V. remained in London with the palms of his hands itching for the cash that would be his if his trusted lieutenant in Fairplay, whom we will call Jacky, did his duty.

The London expert made a more favorable report than McDermott. Then the contracts were signed and the cash turned over to Dan V. who "hiked" back to America.

Soon a contract was let to Parson & Ayllmers, the leading mill men of the United States, for a $40,000 mill to be put up on the Mudsill property. After the mill foundation had been completed, but before the machinery had been shipped from the factory, Mr. McDermott of New York had discovered a certain kind of silver in the Mudsill ore samples, which was foreign to that class of ore. This looked suspicious, and to protect his reputation, McDermott cabled his discovery to the Lord Mayor. His 'Ighness then cabled to McDermott to employ the Dickenson Agency to investigate the matter.

Superintendent James McCartney received a letter from our head office in New York to put one of his best men on this case, as it was an operation of great importance. I was called into Mr. McCartney's private office and shown the correspondence on the subject. I was told of the importance of not making a mistake on the opera-

tion, as it might mean the cancelling of the Parson &
Ayllmers' mill contract on the Mudsill. He explained
that Mr. Ayllmers of that firm was one of the Dickenson
family, he having married a daughter of Anson Dickenson.

After being detailed on the case I kissed Mamie and
Viola good-by and started for Fairplay, high up in the
mountains, on the eastern slope of the main continental
divide.

In Fairplay two tough dance-halls were running, and
night was turned into day by the tough element. Of
course, I joined them, as I was to play the part of a Texas
outlaw.

Soon after my arrival I ran on to an old cowboy chum
whom I had not seen since I was a boy in southern
Texas, about the year 1875. His name was Pete
Stewart and he was proprietor of a saloon in Fairplay
and one in Alma. Up to within a short time of the
closing of the operation, Stewart supposed that I had
really become a tough character, therefore he kept my
true name a secret. I had adopted the name of Charles
Leon.

In a natural way I learned that Jacky had been Dan
V's right-hand man at the Mudsill mine before the sale
of that property; therefore my plans were laid to win
the friendship of Jacky.

One day I saw Jacky wrestling with a wild bronco, but
he was afraid to mount him. Here was my chance; so
stepping up, I inquired if my services were needed.
Taking hold of the rope I volunteered to take the wire
edge off the bronco for him. He was a wiry Texas
four-year-old, and he gave me a ride, as he bucked

pretty hard at times. Even after I had taken off the wire edge, Jacky was afraid to mount him, as he still had a lame leg caused by the fall from the horse. The result was, that I promised to break the bronco gentle for Jacky, and that night he and I got on a glorious drunk together. We wore pistols strapped to our waists and ran the dance halls to suit ourselves. Jacky told his friends that I was a bad man from Texas, as I had given him a hint that I had to leave the Lone Star State for a killing.

After midnight a drunken gang tried to run things. One big fellow pulled a knife on a friend of Jacky's. Just then I struck the fellow over the head with old Colt's 45 and knocked him down. Then one of the fellow's friends knocked me to my knees with his fist, at the same time drawing his pistol; but in a jiffy my cocked pistol was in the man's face and I ordered him to put up his gun and leave the hall. This he did, and his gang soon followed. Then Jacky and I were heroes of the ball and the "girls" patted us on the back. But about half an hour later one of the "girls" from the other dance hall came running over to warn Jacky and me that the gang had blood in their eyes and had gone after reinforcements and more ammunition and were coming back to teach us a lesson. By main force the eight or nine "girls" pushed Jacky and me into a wine room and locked us in. Jacky was pretty drunk. I was playing drunker than I really was, and in truth I was glad the "girls" kept us prisoners in the wine room, though I pretended to be dying to get out to fight a battle.

The gang returned well armed and were told by the "girls" that we had gone to bed. They soon left, and when daylight came Jacky and I went to bed together. He and I were now bosom friends, and ever afterwards in Fairplay, I was regarded as a dangerous man to "monkey" with.

Every night Jacky and I spent our time at the dance halls drinking and dancing. Both of us spent money freely and were favorites with the "girls."

Jacky told me some of his experiences with the noted salter of mines, "Chicken Bill," in the early days of Leadville, and he told me enough to convince me that he had help "salt" the Mudsill mine for Dan V.

In my report I advised that work stop on the new mill, as the Mudsill mine was a fake. Soon the contract with Parson & Ayllmers for the building of the mill was cancelled and work ceased.

Finally I slipped into Denver and met Mr. McDermott of New York City. He gave instructions, after hearing my story, that we get at the bottom of the salting of the Mudsill, regardless of expense, so that the Lord Mayor could get his money back, through the courts.

I then returned to Fairplay and spent money freely. I had explained to Jacky confidentially, that my father in Texas was well-to-do and furnished me all the money that I needed; so Jacky and I made "Rome howl" every night at the dance halls. Jacky had considerable money of his own, and he spent it freely.

Shortly, I secured a partial confession from Jacky as to how he and his partner Andy, had spent three years salting the Mudsill mine; that they had kept the tunnel locked during this time, and not even their best friends were allowed to enter.

To help me out in my work the Mudsill Company advertised for bids to drive a 70-foot upraise from the lower workings in the mine. It was thought by Mr. McDermott that good ore might possibly be struck in this upraise. Jacky and I put in separate bids on this contract. Neither knew what the other's bid was, although Jacky had advised me of the lowest limit that it was safe to bid. He knew how difficult the blue limestone rock was to break down. Through manipulation in our Denver office my bid of $9 per foot proved the lowest, so I was awarded the contract. I made Jacky my foreman and John C. was appointed my shift-boss. Supplies were hauled to the Mudsill, eight miles up Horseshoe Gulch, and a force of men put to work. Jacky and I had rooms in town and rode to the mine on horseback. We couldn't do justice to the dance halls and liquor by living at the mine. In order to recuperate we would often remain several nights at the mine.

In the course of a few months, by the time my contract was finished, I had got a full confession from Jacky. He and I had also become partners in a mining claim which we located up in Mosquito Gulch. We went up there and camped out alone, and sunk the 10-foot assessment shaft ourselves. This gave me a good opportunity to work on Jacky.

A couple of years later, after I had forgotten that I owned a half interest in this claim, I sold it for $100 through the mail. Of course this money was pure velvet for the lining of my own pocket.

From Jacky I received all the particulars connected with the salting of the Mudsill mine, and the fixing up of the 9-foot vein out of the short-line, a decomposed lime rock which lay below and on top of the 30-inch ore-vein.

Jacky also told of how the Mudsill had been salted once before, and sold by Dan V. to a Cincinnati, Ohio, Jew for $90,000 and that later Dan V. bought the mine back for $8,000.

After being in Fairplay quite awhile, I sent for Mamie and Viola, so they could enjoy the cool mountain summer weather. My friend "Doc" Lockridge, who owned a pay-mine near Alma, lived in the leading hotel of that town, hence it was arranged that Mamie should go there as his "niece" from Kansas. I had been to Alma to arrange matters. It was agreed that Mamie was to call him uncle, and she was to be introduced as a widow whose husband had died a couple of years previous.

I had only met "Doc" a few times in Denver, but his dead brother, Bill Lockridge, had been a warm cowboy friend of mine in the Indian Territory and Kansas. Before Bill's death "Doc" and I first met at his home in Denver.

I will here digress so as to record a small section of cattle history and at the same time give Ex-President Grover Cleveland and his well developed stubborn bump their just dues.

It was about the year 1884. A crowd of cattlemen of the Indian Territory, through fraud in bribing a few Indian Chiefs, secured a ten year lease on the western part of the Cheyenne Indian Reservation.

During that spring, Bill Lockridge and the other lessees turned large numbers of steers onto the Cheyenne

MAMIE AND VIOLA.

Reservation to fatten for the fall market. President Cleveland got upon his high horse, and sent Lieutenant Sheridan of the United States Army out to investigate. Gen. Phil Sheridan also came out in connection with the case—he being a brother to Lieutenant Sheridan; and in the then wild and wooly cattle town of Caldwell, Kansas, I met the old General. He had his picture taken in a group with some of his old soldier friends, and I still retain one of the original copies as a relic.

When Lieutenant Sheridan sent in his report, President Cleveland issued a proclamation giving the cattlemen just forty days to vacate the Cheyenne Reservation.

The cattlemen had a special meeting in Caldwell and raised $100,000 in cash to bribe the President to extend the time to eighty days, which would give the steers time to fatten before having to move them. A committee of five was sent to Washington to work on the President, Bill Lockridge being one of them. On reaching the White House and being seated in the reception hall, the President gave orders through his lackey-boy, that the committee appoint one of their number to come into the Blue room to meet him. As Bill Lockridge was a good Southern Democrat, and as he was a chip from the noted Lockridge family of Revolutionary days, he was selected to do the bribe act.

On returning to Caldwell, Bill Lockridge had to tell me how he got turned down in the White House by a man who pretended to be a good Democrat. Here is Bill's own story in substance:

"The old devil shook my hand and said he was glad to see me. He then asked if I were related to the Lock-

6

ridges of Virginia, and it turned out that he knew my grandfather. After we had a pleasant chat, he asked what he could do for me. I explained the situation, telling him how it would ruin us to get our steers out of the Reservation in forty days. I told him that we had one hundred thousand dollars in cash to give him if he would extend the time to eighty days. He smiled, and getting up on his feet said: 'Well, Mr. Lockridge, how long did it take you to come here?' I told him we were five days coming. He then said: 'Well, it will take you that long to get back, so you are losing valuable time. Good-by Mr. Lockridge.' He had the gall to reach out his hand to bid me good-by, but d—— him, I just gave him a contemptible look and walked out, and you can bet it will be a cold day when I vote the Democratic ticket again."

Now, this just shows one phase of human nature. As a man Bill Lockridge was a prince, and honorable in all his dealings.

It was Sunday morning when I rode the seven miles on horseback to Alma from Fairplay. My excuse for going to Alma was to visit my old cowboy friend Pete Stewart, who conducted a saloon there.

I met "Doc" Lockridge in Stewart's saloon and he invited me up to the hotel to take dinner with him. In the ladies' parlor in the presence of other guests, "Doc" introduced me to his pretty young "niece" from Kansas. Little Viola had been left in the room for fear that she might call me papa. At the dinner table Viola did call me papa once, but it was after most of the guests had left the table. We finally got her trained to call me Mr. Leon.

That night I retired with "Doc" to his room, but I couldn't sleep, so got up to get some fresh air, and to do a little skirmishing like a thief in the night. It is certainly a funny business which makes it necessary for a man to tip-toe through a dark hall to his own wife's bed-. room. But, gee whiz! what a scandal would have been raised had I been caught going into this "young widow's" room.

My trips to Alma became frequent, and it was soon noised about that I was in love with "Doc's" niece. Then the landlady of the hotel and other lady guests, who had become attached to Mamie, aired my reputation as one of the worst toughs and dance-hall loafers of Fairplay and advised her not to associate with me. Some of the men who were "stuck" on the "young widow" had told of my doings in Fairplay. They tried to "knock" me with their little "hammers," but it didn't work.

For the next few weeks I led a double life,—about four nights of each week I was carousing with Jacky and the dance-hall "girls," and the balance of the time I was doing the tip-toe act and playing myself off as a respectable gentleman.

No doubt, dear reader, you think this was a rank injustice to poor, pure-hearted Mamie; and so it was, but she had confidence in me and sanctioned it, so long as it was part of my business.

After about eight months I wound up the Mudsill operation. Towards the last I was suspected by Dan V. of being a detective for the Mudsill Company, and one night when he, Pete Stewart and I were on a tear in Fairplay, he tried to raise a row with me, but I held my temper and laughed at his threats and insinuations.

Soon after my return to Denver, Supt. James McCartney took up the work and I dropped out of the game.

The first thing that "yours, etc." did was to decoy Jacky to Denver and have him brought into the private office. There poor Jacky was confronted with his own photo, taken in stripes at the Nebraska Penitentiary under the name of Jack Allen, years before. Jacky was stunned; so I was told. He had confided in me and showed me the ugly gunshot wound in his hip, received while leading a wild, reckless life in Dakota and Nebraska under the name of Jack Allen. He also told of serving a term in the "pen" at Lincoln, Nebraska, giving me the number of his cell, etc., so it was an easy matter for McCartney to secure a copy of his photo and his prison record. Those were used as a lever to make him confess, as he didn't want his identify known among his friends in Fairplay; hence he made a full confession to Mr. McCartney.

All of Dan V.'s property was attached and so was the property of Mr. Matches, an officer of Bay City, Mich., he being Dan V.'s partner and financial backer.

The case was tried in the United States Court and was passed on by the Circuit Court of the United States in our favor.

The Lord Mayor of London, so I was told by Mr. McCartney, recovered $150,000 of his loss.

Years later, my friend, Attorney W. T. Skoll of Spokane, Washington, showed me the new volume of the Federal Reporter, Vol. 61, p. 163, containing the decisions rendered on the Mudsill mine-salting case, and Mr. Skoll informed me that this was the only mine-salting case ever passed on by the Circuit Judges of the United States.

Thus did the Mudsill mine-salting operation end, and become part of our law history to be used as a precedent in future mine-salting cases.

After a month spent in Denver doing all kinds of work, from robbery cases to hiding in ash-pits in order to catch people stealing, I was sent to Longmont, Colorado, on an important operation.

In Helena, Montana, a young man by the name of Wraxhall had got into a "scrape" with a wealthy man of that section.

In the fight which followed, the wealthy man was badly wounded and now lay at the point of death. In case he recovered, nothing was to be done with Wraxhall, so as to prevent a scandal. But in case of death, then he was to be prosecuted.

The officers of Montana had lost trail of young Wraxhall and had turned the case over to us to locate him, so that he would not become suspicious. He was not to be arrested until his victim died.

It was thought that he might be in hiding at his brother Frank's ranch, a couple of miles out of Longmont. I was detailed on the case and left Denver dressed as a tramp cowboy. I carried a description and photo of young Wraxhall in my pocket.

I walked out from Longmont to the Frank Wraxhall ranch, arriving there just at noon. Hoping to get a peep into the home, I rang the bell at the front door of the nice white residence. A lady came to the door and I told her I wished to see Mr. Frank Wraxhall. She said he was eating his dinner, but that she would call him. Instead of seating me in the nice parlor, Frank Wraxhall conducted me out to the yard to hear my tale of woe. I told him that my name was Charlie Le Roy and that I was stranded in Longmont with not a cent to buy my dinner; that I heard he had some wild horses to break and I had come out to get a job to break a few for my board until money could reach me from my home in Texas. He said I could have a free dinner, so he conducted me to a dining-room built off from the kitchen, where the hired men ate their meals. He agreed to talk to me about the horse breaking after dinner.

About the time my dinner was finished, three men came out of the house. I asked one of the cowboys who these men were. He replied that they were all brothers. One he said, was the Rev. Wraxhall, a minister of a swell church on Capitol Hill in Denver, and another was Oliver, just home from college, and the third was Frank, the proprietor of this ranch. I asked if there were any more brothers in the family. He replied yes, that there was a brother in Montana, who was a little older than Oliver.

Finally Frank called me to him in the yard and asked if I could ride a wild bronco and stay with him if he bucked. I told him that I was brought up in southern Texas in the early days of the cattle business, and that ought to be recommendation enough. He replied that it wasn't, for he said he had been fooled in hiring riders from Texas, just on their word. So, for that reason, he kept an outlaw horse with which to test new riders. He said if I could stick on that horse until he quit bucking, and whip him every jump, that I could have a job with him as long as he raised horses on the ranch. I told him to trot out his outlaw horse, and he then sent a cowboy out in the big pasture to drive up the wild bunch. When corralled, the outlaw was caught. He was a vicious, iron-gray four-year old, and very strong. We put the saddle on him. Then Frank told me I had to ride him in the calf-pasture, a small tract of an acre in front of the residence. This tract was enclosed with a high barbed wire fence, and I protested that it was dangerous to ride a wild horse in such a small lot enclosed with barbed wire. He said the horse had never failed to throw every man who ever mounted him, and he was sure he would throw me too, and for that reason he didn't want to take chances on the horse getting away with the saddle on.

No doubt, his main object was to give his brother in hiding a chance to see a free exhibition without exposing himself to view.

In front of the picket fence, surrounding the residence, I held the blindfolded bronco. On the porch were three ladies, also Oliver and the Rev. Mr. Wraxhall from Denver. Frank stood near me at the front gate. Several cowboys and the man cook were witnesses from another place.

After mounting, and just as I reached forward to raise the blind from the horse's eyes, I glanced toward the front door and saw the head of a black-haired man peeping around the door casing. So here was my man, thought I, and I determined to get a better look at him while the horse was bucking.

As soon as the blind was raised, I struck the **bronco**

with my quirt and he went straight up in the air and changed ends before he hit the ground.

For the next twenty minutes I had to ride, and on one occasion I had to throw one leg above the saddle to keep from being cut by the wire fence.

Several times, as the horse bucked by the front gate, I got a good look at my man and he looked just exactly like the photo, and answered the description. In the excitement he stood among the ladies on the porch. All were clapping their hands and cheering.

After the outlaw had worn himself out bucking, my man had disappeared again, but my work was done. The instructions had been to discontinue and return to Denver as soon as I was positive that our man had been located.

When the horse was subdued, Frank Wraxhall asked me to ride out in the big pasture and help drive up a bunch of cattle, as he wanted all the meanness taken out of the bronco while he was under control.

The cowboy and I returned with the cattle about night. After eating supper I told Wraxhall that I was going to town to see if my money had arrived from Texas, as it should have been there several days previous. He complimented me on my good riding and assured me work at top wages, so long as I wished to say. He offered me a horse to ride to town, but I insisted on walking.

That night my bones ached from the strenuous day's work as a bronco "buster."

Next morning I boarded a train for Denver. On the same train was the Rev. Mr. Wraxhall and his wife returning home, but I kept them from seeing me.

Other men were then put on the case to shadow the

depot in Longmont and also the Rev. Wraxhall's residence, so that we would know if our man came to Denver
to visit his preacher brother, or left the country.

In the course of time the wounded man in Helena,
Montana, was out of danger, and then the operation was
discontinued.

Not long after this, Frank Wraxhall shot and killed
the noted prize-fighter Clow, in a Denver saloon, and
shortly after this, his father, General Wraxhall, a noted
pioneer of Colorado, died.

Since then I have lost track of the Wraxhalls.

Soon after finishing the Wraxhall case, I took my first
sleep in the "bull-pen" at the Denver city jail; and it is
rightly named the "bull-pen." That night it contained
about twenty of the worst specimens of humanity, both
black and white, that it was ever my misfortune to be
housed with in one small room. I envied my partner
operative, Blummer, who had been put alone in a steel
cage across the hall, as he was taken for a desperado,
owing to the fact that he had on two big pistols and a
bowie knife. I had slipped my pearl-handled pistol and
bowie knife to Blummer, thinking that he had a better
chance than I to get away from the city policemen who
had surrounded us. But he ran into the arms of a big
city "fly-cop," who took him to jail, and put him in the
steel cage, while poor me, not being armed, had to go
in with the drunken hobo bunch.

Blummer and I had been hiding in an ash-pit in a dark
alley to catch people stealing silk from the Daniels-
Fisher dry goods store. We were discovered and
arrested as suspicious characters. We were certainly a

tough looking pair, as we had put on the worst clothes we could find. We had orders not to disclose our identity, for fear that the policeman on that beat might be standing in with the negro watchman who was suspected of throwing the silk out of an upper story window to the thieves in the alley below. They were caught a few nights later.

Next morning Superintendent McCartney came down to the jail and fixed matters with Chief of Police Henry Grady and Lieutenant of Police James Hummer, and we were liberated.

CHAPTER V

Two Wealthy Mine-Owners of Tuscarora, Nevada, Blown up with Dynamite—A Confession Secured After Nine Months of Strenuous Life in Nevada and Indian Territory.

During the month of August, 1889, Superintendent McCartney called me into his private office where I was introduced to Mr. Geo. Pelling of the firm of Prinz & Pelling, of Tuscarora, Nevada. I was given the outline of a case on which I was detailed to work.

It was explained that Mr. C. W. Prinz and Mr. Geo. Pelling were wealthy mine and mill owners, and that on a certain night during the previous spring, dynamite had been put under their residences and "touched off;" that Mr. Pelling and his mattress went up through the roof and landed right side up with care in the middle of the street. He was still wrapped in the quilts and blankets, and the shock put him out of business for awhile, but otherwise he was not hurt.

Not so lucky was Mr. Prinz. He was badly used up, but soon recovered. He, too, was blown out into the street but not on a feather bed.

Knowing that they had an organized gang of desperate enemies to deal with, they sent to San Francisco for two of the best detectives who could be procured to ferret out the criminals. Two detectives from a local detective agency were sent to Tuscarora to work secretly. In addition, a large reward was offered through the news-papers, for evidence that would convict. Several months' work by the detectives had failed to show up even a clue as to who were the guilty parties, and the sleuths being suspected, they were called home, their chances of success being doubtful.

Then it was decided that Mr. Pelling go to Denver and consult with Mr. James McCartney, and if possible, get a man who could do the work.

At that time the Dickenson Agency had no branch office west of Denver.

Mr. Pelling explained to me that I was undertaking a ticklish job, as their enemies were on their guard and watching for detectives.

I was instructed to take the Union Pacific Railway for San Francisco, while Mr. Pelling would go by a southern route and stop off for a visit in southern California. I was told to put up at the Palace Hotel in Frisco and re-main there until Mr. Pelling arrived.

For the next few days my time was spent in selling our furniture, and starting Mamie and little Viola off for Springfield, Missouri, where my wife's father, H. Clay Lloyd, and her step-mother lived. Poor Mamie's health had begun to fail, and the doctors decided an operation for pleurisy was necessary to save her life. Her father, when he heard of it, begged that she be sent there to be operated on by his family physician, one of the best in the land.

After seeing my wife and baby off on an eastbound train, I boarded a flyer for the extreme edge of the Golden West. My trip would have been a treat, as I had never been to California, if it had not been for the worry of Mamie's illness and the fact that she had to undergo an operation without my presence to comfort her.

In Frisco I put up at the Palace, the swell hotel of the city. I was there a week before Mr. Pelling arrived, therefore had an opportunity to see all the sights, which were new to me.

I was furnished with $250 expense money by Mr. Pelling, and he then departed for Tuscarora, Nevada. I soon followed dressed in rough cowboy clothes.

At Elko, Nevada, I left the train and boarded a stage for a fifty mile ride into the mountains. Phil. Snyder, an old-timer of Tuscarora, and whose name had been given to me by Mr. Pelling as a possible friend to the dynamiters who blew up Prinz's and Pelling's homes, was a fellow passenger on the stage, and I won his applause and friendship by making a crack shot with my old Colt's 45 pistol.

We were sitting on the seat with the driver, when a coyote jumped up about 100 yards distant. I made one shot while the stage was on the move, and Mr. Coyote quit business by tumbling over dead. It was an accidental shot of course, but no one but myself knew it.

In Tuscarora, a lively mining camp, Snyder pointed me out to his friends as a cowboy just from Texas, who was a crack shot with a pistol. This gave me a standing in the lower crust of society. Soon after my arrival, I was out in the hills with Tim W., one of Prinz and Pelling's most bitter enemies. He told me that Snyder and the stage driver had given me a big send-off as a crack shot. He asked me to show him what I could do.

He pointed out a pine knot in a board on a fence about 50 yards distant, and asked me to hit that. Here was a chance to make myself solid with one of Prinz and Pelling's enemies, providing I could make another accidental shot. It was worth trying, so I cut loose off-hand, and out went the pine knot, which was the size of a silver dollar. He begged me to try again at another mark, but I had sense enough to let well enough alone. My reputation was made and I decided to take no more chances.

In order to be away from town for awhile, I got permission from a butcher named Morrison, to live on his ranch a few miles out. I bought a horse and saddle and used to ride into town once in awhile.

Here was a new experience for me, living with a Chinaman who could only talk a few words of English. He and I were the sole occupants of the ranch except when Mr. Morrison came out to butcher stock. Mr. Pigtail and I sat at the same table, but ate different kinds of food. He used a couple of chop-sticks to throw the rice, etc., into his mouth. It would have been fun for a man up a tree to look down and see us joking and trying to talk to each other.

Finally, after I had become well established in the mining camp, I moved into town, and soon after, I received a letter from Mr. C. W. Prinz requesting that I meet him in an old abandoned mine about half a mile from town on a certain night. A diagram of the incline-shaft which I was to go down was enclosed in the letter. He explained that he would go around through the main workings of the mine so as not to be seen.

It was a dark night, but I found the mouth of the old

shaft from the description given in the letter. But to descend into the bowels of the earth through a dark hole 5 by 7 feet, that I knew nothing about, required a lot of fool courage, and therefore I was quite awhile getting started. It was a great relief when I reached the bottom of the rotten ladder which had not been used for several years. The distance to the bottom was about 200 feet. On the way down, pieces of rock became loosened and rolled to the bottom, making a lonesome noise which sent cold shivers down my back. The ladder was damp and slippery and some of the rounds were missing. A walk of a few hundred feet through a drift brought me to Mr. Price, who had arrived on time. About midnight we separated, each going the way we had come. On reaching daylight, I vowed never to meet another client in a hole that I knew nothing about.

During the fall, Phil. Snyder and I went out into the mountains to hunt deer and grouse, and we bagged some of both. We were gone a week. On returning, I rode out to "Wild Bill's" camp on Lone Mountain, a distance of about twenty-five miles. I had previously made friends with "Wild Bill" who was an enemy of Price and Pelling and stood in with the gang who had blown them up.

"Wild Bill" was a genius when it came to working with steel. He was a counterfeiter and made his own plates to print counterfeit paper money. He made me a steel candle-stick with half a dozen instruments combined, which I still keep as a souvenir.

After this, I made many trips to "Wild Bill's" camp. We lived on nice fat calf-meat which we would steal from bands of range cattle.

From "Wild Bill" I learned some valuable pointers as to who blew up Prinz and Pelling. I finally selected Tim W. as a good subject for me to work on to get a confession from. I made a confident of him and told him that my father in Texas was rich and that I had got into a killing scrape and had to skip out. I explained that my father sent money to me through two friends, Smith and Long, of Reno City, Oklahoma; that these friends had money now of mine in their possession, but I didn't want to take chances on having it sent direct to me at Tuscarora, even though I was under an assumed name. I was using the name of Chas. T. Leon.

Poor Tim W. bit at my bait and agreed that the money could be sent to him and then he would hand it to me on the sly. He promised to keep the matter secret, and he did so. He felt honored at being trusted with my liberty and money.

I then wrote to Superintendent McCartney and had him send $150 to my friends Smith and Long in Reno City, with instructions that they send it to Tim W. I also wrote Mr. Smith a letter on the subject. In due time a money order for $150 came to Tim W. through the Post Office. He cashed the money order and handed me the money. That night he and I got on a big "hurrah" and I spent money freely with his friends who were all enemies to our clients. After this, all the money which I spent came through Tim W.

Tim was working as a miner for the Smith Bros. on their rich gold mine. He would fill his pockets with some of the rich ore worth about $10 a pound, on coming off shift. Of course he made a confident of me as I had trusted him.

Tim had a sweetheart, a Mrs. B., who was a widow and owned a small lodging house. He and I roomed in her building, but we were not in the same class when it came to burning midnight oil and basking in the sunshine of her sweet smiles.

Late in the fall I put a hungry man on his feet by helping him "salt" a mine.

One day I saw a man standing for hours in one place without moving. His features showed worry. I stepped up to him and invited him into a saloon to have a drink with me, my object being to cheer him up. Turning round and facing me he said:

"Partner, I would die before I would beg, but if you will give me the price of my drink I will get something to eat with it. That will do me more good than a drink." He then informed me that his name was Harnihan, or a name similar to that; that he had come from Angels Camp, California, where he worked for the millionaire mine-owner Lane; that he had paid his last dollar for a stage-ride from the railroad and that he hadn't tasted food since leaving Elko the morning before, and that he had hoped to get work but had failed. I slipped a dollar into his hand and told him to call for more when that was gone. He thanked me kindly.

When a boy, I had read the Bible a little, and recalled a passage therein about there being no harm to shear a lamb for the benefit of mankind. I either read this in the Bible or dreamed it. At any rate, I concluded to do a little shearing act, so as to give Mr. Harnihan a lift in the world, as he seemed to be a nice fellow with a proud spirit.

7

Morrison, the butcher, and his partner in the saloon business, were selected as the lambs to be shorn.

I had never salted a mine, but had received valuable lessons from Jacky in the Mudsill mine-salting case.

These two men owned a mining claim with a 30-foot hole in the ground, which they called a mine. I induced them to give Harnihan a working bond on this mine. Harnihan, who was a fine looking, healthy man, agreed to follow any instructions that I might give. After working in the shaft a short time, he asked Morrison to have some of the ore assayed so as to see if it was improving. Morrison agreed to go up and sample the vein next morning and have an assay made of the ore. I gave Harnihan some of the rich ore which Tim W. had been stealing from the Smith mine, and told him to sprinkle it moderately over the bottom of the shaft that night. I had previously pulverized this ore into fine powder.

The next morning Morrison went to the mine in the edge of town, with Harnihan. He took a sample from the small vein in the bottom of the shaft and then returned to town. I made it my duty to watch Morrison take the sample to the assay office, and I saw him go there in the evening after the assay certificate. He came out in an excited manner. I stepped into his saloon ahead of him to watch proceedings. He called his partner into one corner and showed him the assayer's certificate. It would require too much space to record these men's monkeyshines up to the time Harnihan came from work at 5 P. M.

I met Harnihan and informed him that the lambs were tied on the block, ready for the shearing, but advised him not to accept their first offer.

Morrison told Harnihan that the ore had improved just a few dollars per ton. He offered to pay for what work had been done on the mine at regular wages, and release Harnihan from his interest, but Harnihan, as per my instructions, told him that he would work another week and then send a sample of the ore to Burlingame of Denver, for a good test. This did the work. At 9 P. M. Harnihan had $600 in gold in his pocket. He insisted on my taking half of it, but I refused to accept "tainted" money.

That night Harnihan got on a glorious drunk, and next day I sold him my horse and saddle at a fancy price and he "hit" the road for a lower altitude. I advised him to cut across country for fear the cat might get out of the bag; but it didn't for several days. Then the air was blue with curse words for a whole month.

On riding away, Harnihan threw me a $20 gold piece and told me to take a drink on him. I have never seen or heard of him to this day. Thus the world moves and we all act our little part on the big stage.

I found out from Morrison, between curse-words, that the salted sample showed a value of $1,500 per ton of ore, and that he supposed he was a millionaire; that the sudden fall to poverty was what hurt the worst. He never suspected me, and if he sees this the air will be impregnated with oaths again.

On Christmas day I took my first sleigh ride, and for a few minutes I was "going some."

The liveryman had just received a brand-new sleigh. I hired it and a spirited team of horses and took Miss Aggie Dougherty for a ride. We drove ten miles out

on the stage road and then turned back. The stage and
freight road was a mass of packed snow. On each side
the soft snow was from 5 to 10 feet deep. On one side
of the road about every hundred feet the stage company
had a willow stuck into the snow so that on a stormy
night the driver could keep on the road. One of these
slender poles was bending over and the team ran into
it. The end flew up and caught one of the horses in the
flank. Then there was "something doing," and we began
to "go some." If I had had the use of both hands the
team might have been stopped before they got under full
headway. My left arm was around the girl's waist, to
keep her from falling out, as the sleigh had no side-
boards. Before my left arm could be disentangled and put
back in its proper place, the team of flying broncos made
a sharp turn off the road and went out of sight into the
deep snow. The sleigh naturally went over them, high
up in the air, upside down.

While standing on my head in the air, I could see my
old Colt's 45 pistol, which had been carried loose in my
hip pocket, flying through space. At this place the snow
was about 10 feet deep. I found poor little Aggie standing on her head in a hole that she had made in the snow.
I had made a hole of my own, so it took me quite a while
to reach Aggie. By the time I got her on her feet into
the hard road the team was a couple of miles away, going like lightning. They had floundered back into the
road.

In order to find my pistol I had to swim out to the small
hole where it had disappeared in the snow, and then do
some fancy diving.

A three-mile walk brought us to where the team lay tangled up in the harness. Both were on their sides. We had passed pieces of the sleigh scattered all along the road. Therefore, there wasn't much of it attached to the team. After the pretty sorrels were on their feet, we started for town afoot, leading them. They had never been ridden, so we had to walk the five or six miles.

On reaching town a large crowd greeted us and made me treat.

The liveryman let me off lightly, by only charging me $50 for the half day's sleigh ride. He said the experience was worth something to a beginner. I thought so too, for in future, I vowed that side-boards would have to be put on the sleigh to hold the girl in place before it could be hired to Yours Truly.

The fact that I was out riding with an 18-year old girl while my sick wife was just recovering from a successful operation, may seem naughty to you, gentle reader, but you must bear in mind that there are tricks in all professions but ours, and they are all tricks. The truth is, I was working on old man Dougherty, and Aggie was only a side-issue to win points in the game.

In the spring, Tim W. and I made preparation to leave for the Wichita Mountains in the western part of the Indian Territory, on a prospecting trip for gold. I had told Tim wonderful stories of gold being found in these mountains by soldiers and hunters.

I had concluded that the best way to get a confession out of Tim would be to get him in a strange country where he could talk with no one but myself.

When his gang found out that he was going to the

Indian Territory with me, they became frightened for fear I might be a detective. They had heard that Mr. Prinz said he would spend $150,000 to find out who the dynamiters of Tuscarora were. For several days and nights previous to our start, the gang held secret meetings in Mason's drug store, trying to persuade Tim to give me the "shake." They said it was positively known that I was a detective, but Tim insisted on their producing the evidence.

Among the gang was a hard character by the name of "Black Jack," and he made it hot for poor Tim. He swore that he should not go. Mrs. B. also worked on Tim to dissuade him. Finally, everything was ready for an early start on the next morning's stage. That night they held another secret meeting in Mason's drug store, and Tim got very little sleep. As a last resort they told Tim that they had positive evidence that all the money which I had spent in Tuscarora came from Prinz and Pelling's agents in San Francisco, and that if he would wait over another week they would produce my signature to the receipts for the money received at different times. Here's where the gang fell down. Tim told them that they were d——d liars, but he wouldn't tell them how he knew. He told me all about their meetings later, when we were on the road.

Next morning we boarded the stage for Elko, and most of the gang were at the Post Office to see us off, and to make one last effort to change Tim's mind. The faces of some of the gang appeared pale and care-worn, and "Black Jack" looked daggers at me.

The whip was cracked and away we went.

In Elko, Tim and I boarded a train for Denver, Colorado. We kept the sleeping car porter busy furnishing us with drinks while en route.

Tim's wealth consisted of $600 in cash and several hundred dollars worth of rich ore that he had stolen from the Smith Brothers' mine, which he had taken along to sell in Denver.

A few days were spent in Denver, where I was under a strain for fear of meeting some one who might call me by my own name in the presence of Tim. I was indeed glad when we boarded the Denver & Fort Worth train for Wichita Falls, Texas.

In Wichita Falls I went to see my old friends Charlie Word, Liash Stephens and Tom Jones, cattle men, to tell them of my new name, and to caution them so they wouldn't address me by my own name where Tim W. might hear it.

About ten years previous I had "bossed" a large herd of long-horned cattle "up the Chisholm trail," from southwestern Texas, for Charlie Word.

On my arrival at Wichita Falls I left Tim at the hotel while I went to spend the evening until bed time with Mr. Word and his family. I had last seen Mrs. Word in San Antonio, Texas, in 1879, when she was a beautiful black-haired young woman with a first-born in her arms. Now this first-born was almost a young lady.

Word and I sat up late "harking back" to the days of big herds on the "Chisholm trail" between southern Texas and Kansas.

In the Word herd which I had charge of there were about 3000 head of cattle with about ten cowboys, and five horses to the man, and last, but not least, a cook to dish up the "grub" and drive the "grub-wagon."

In "harking back" I thought of my first pistol duel, which died before it was fought, but its dying was no fault of mine or my opponent's, a hot-headed Southerner by the name of Best, who was one of the cowboys.

He had loaned Mr. Word some money to buy cattle, and had agreed to make a "hand," that is, do full duty at regular wages on the trail. When passing Fort Worth, Word, who had come around by rail on his way to Kansas, stopped off to see how we were getting along. He drove out in a buggy to where we were to stop over night. On his arrival Best and I had a fuss over the way I made him do the full work of a cowboy all the way "up the trail." In the threats which followed I told Best to get his pistol and we would shoot it out. He brooded over the matter for an hour or so and finally told Word that he or I had to die before the sun went down. Word tried to reason with him, but it was no use. He was mad and meant it. He insisted that Word notify me that if I didn't agree to fight a regular duel that he intended to kill me any way before the sun set. Word notified me and it was agreed that I wait until the sun was setting and then stand back to back and walk forward ten paces, and wheel and fire, until one or both were dead. We both began cleaning our pistols, as the sun was only an hour high. Word put in his time trying to persuade us to shake hands and call the duel off, but the stubborn bump, which the phrenologist in Caldwell, Kansas, said was like a mule's, prevented me from backing out. I hoped though, that Best would "crawfish," that is, back out, for I didn't want to die, even a "little bit."

When the sun looked to be only a few inches above the horizon, I imagined that I could feel myself growing pale behind the ears, but "praise the Lord," here came Word from behind the wagon where Best was sitting on a pile of bedding, with the good news that Best had agreed to shake hands with me and do his duty the balance of the way up the trail. Thus Mr. Word had won a bloodless battle.

Two days later Tim and I had bought a horse each, and started northeast for the Wichita Mountains, a distance of two days' ride. We crossed Red River at the Burnett ranch and were then in the Indian Territory. At night we camped on the plains, and the next evening we struck the mountains and had an old Indian woman cook a turkey gobbler which I had killed. She fried the breast of the turkey and made a batch of bread for us. The old dame's hands were black with dirt and she struck them into the dough without washing them. We were too hungry though, to make a kick.

From here we went to Quanah Parker's camp on the head of West Cache Creek. Quanah Parker was a big chief of the 7,000 Comanche Indians scattered around the borders of the Wichita Mountains. They don't like to live in the mountains, therefore pitch their camps on the edge next to the plains. Quanah Parker is half white, he being the child of Cynthia Ann Parker, the white girl stolen in Texas by the Comanches before the war. He is over six feet tall and sports a mustache which can be seen with the naked eye. At this mustache he keeps tugging, when talking in broken English with his white brothers.

Tim and I rode through the Wichita Mountains to Anadarko, the Indian Agent's headquarters. I made a confident of Indian Agent C. E. Adams, and he gave me a pass so that Tim and I could stay on the Reservation outside the mountains. He could not give me a permit to go into the mountains, as there was supposed to be gold in there and white men were kept out by the Indian Police.

From Anadarko, Tim and I rode to Fort Sill, the army post on the east side of Wichita Mountains, where we went to lay in such supplies as could be carried behind our saddles as we had no pack-horse.

For the next month Tim and I led a strenuous life in the mountains, dodging the Indian Police who were trying to capture us, but our horses were too swift. We would camp on the highest peaks from whence we could watch them hunting us. We had a fine time killing game. Turkeys were as plentiful as fowl around a Kansas barnyard. We could lie in bed any morning and kill a gobbler for breakfast. They were not killed by the Indians, as they regard them as evil spirits.

Tim and I named some of the highest peaks. One in the western part of the range was named after me. We called it Mt. Leon, and up on its highest point we planted an elk horn, around which was wrapped a copy of the Tuscarora, Nevada, daily paper, also a slip with our names and the new name of the peak on it. I often wonder if these elk horns have been found since the opening of these mountains to white settlers.

On two occasions I left Tim in the mountains while I rode the 25 miles to Fort Sill after "grub," and our mail. Poor Tim never received any of the many letters sent to him by his friends and sweetheart, for I started a little post office of my own and placed them in a pigeon-hole under a rock.

The letters sent by Tim to be mailed by me were treated likewise. Most of the letters warned Tim to "shake" me and come home, as they had positive information that I was a Dickenson detective.

On my second trip into Fort Sill I found Tim's sweetheart Mrs. B., there, but she didn't get to see me. She had dropped about half a dozen letters in the post office telling Tim of her arrival to save him from the clutches of that Dickenson detective, Leon. I felt sorry for the poor woman, but all I could do was to shed a silent tear over her pathetic letters.

After this when we needed "grub," I took Tim with me and we rode to the little town of Navajo, Texas, across the north fork of Red River in Greer County.

At one time old Quanah Parker had deputy United States marshals searching for us.

We failed to find a gold mine, and as I had got a full confession from Tim about the blowing up of Price and Pelling, we shook the dust of the mountains from our feet and landed in Union City, Oklahoma, a boom town on the South Canadian.

Finally, Tim and I arrived in the booming town of El Reno. We put up at the Stanley livery stable. Here young Todd, whom I knew in Caldwell, Kansas, a few years before, asked if my name was not Charlie Siringo.

When I told him no, he replied: "Well you look like Charlie, all right enough." Tim was present when the question was asked.

We picked up our "warbags" and started up town, walking in the center of the main street. Before reaching the hotel a large man standing with a group of men in front of a saloon yelled out at the top of his voice: "Well I'll be d——d, if there ain't Charlie Siringo!" He then started across from an opposite corner to meet us. As he approached he held out his hand, saying: "Well, Charlie Siringo, what in the h——l are you doing here?" By this time he was facing me, but I didn't put out my hand. I said: "I reckon you are mistaken, partner." He replied: "Not by a d——d sight, Charlie. I would know your hide in a tan yard in h——l." Still I didn't put out my hand, and pretending to be mad I said: "Well, I must say you've got your gall whoever you are. I tell you that's not my name." He replied in a contemptuous manner: "May be it ain't by ———." Then he wheeled around and went back to the crowd.

I knew him well, though I hadn't seen him for many years. He and I used to be cowboys together in Texas. I remembered his name then, but it has slipped my memory now. I was sorry for the poor fellow, as no doubt his companions gave him the laugh at the way he got "turned down" by me. Tim remarked that he believed the fellow really thought he knew me.

That night after Tim and I had gone to bed, I got up under the pretense of going to a saloon to get a drink, and went in search of my cowboy friend so as to explain matters to him. He was found at a dance, and when I explained the situation we shook hands and talked of old times. He was then in the butcher business.

Next day El Reno was lively, as the Rock Island Railway had just arrived there and it was the first anniversary of the opening of the Oklahoma Territory to white settlement. Oklahoma being just one year old that day, the whole Territory turned itself loose to celebrate. Tim and I did our share.

In El Reno I traded a lot there, which I owned, for a two-year-old race filly named Lulu Edson. She had lately won a big race; but she proved to be a costly piece of horse-flesh, as I heard the lot sold for $5000 a few years later. I had the consolation though of owning a two-year-old that could run a quarter of a mile in 22½ seconds, almost world-record time.

In order to get Tim back to Denver before making the arrest, so as to keep it out of the newspapers, we started on horse-back, using Lulu for a pack animal, a distance of about 600 miles.

Just before entering the Cherokee strip, we camped one day for dinner. While eating, an Oklahoma settler came galloping up on a black mare bareback. He recognized me and jumping off the horse, he said: "Hello, Charlie Siringo, what are you doing here?" I got up and shook hands with him, as we needed some pointers about the road, but I said: "You are the third crazy Oklahoma boomer who has called me that name, so I am beginning to think that I look like him. He replied: "Why Charlie, you can't fool me. I would know your hide in a tan-yard." He insisted so persistently, that I had to make him mad. He finally mounted his old nag and galloped off cursing. He and I had run cattle together in Texas, years before, and I knew him well, but I forget his name now.

That night we put up at a big cattle ranch in the Cherokee strip or outlet. There were about twenty cowboys present. The next morning it was raining hard and we concluded to lay over a day. As Lulu was tenderfooted I rode her back into Oklahoma, five miles, to get her shod.

After I had left, a man with two pistols buckled around his waist called Tim to one side and said: "Partner did you ever commit a crime?" Tim asked why, and he replied: "Well if you did, you had better shake that Dickenson detective you are traveling with. That's Charlie Siringo and he's after some one down here." Tim told the fellow that he must be mistaken. He replied: "All right, go ahead if you think so; but my advice to you if you have done anything, is to hit the road and hit her hard, before he gets back." The fellow then got on his own horse and pulled out. He had just dropped in to eat breakfast before I had left, and he recognized me.

On my return the cowboys told of the noted outlaw "Six Shooter Bill" being there for breakfast. They said there were big rewards for him, dead or alive. He had evidently not told any one but Tim, who I was.

Tim was sour and apparently worried for the next few days, but I never surmised the cause until he told of it after his arrest. He said he felt like killing me and skipping out, as he had already made a confession to me, but he didn't believe I was a detective.

On our arrival in Denver, after a hard ride, and before

we had time to wash and eat, Tim was arrested by Supt. James McCartney. He was taken to our office and there confronted by Mr. W. C. Prinz who had come all the way from Nevada to be at the wind-up. Poor Tim broke down, and before a Notary Public he made a full confession, implicating all who had a hand in the blowing up of Prinz and Pelling.

After getting his sworn confession down in writing and his signature to it, he was turned over to me to keep under guard until Mr. Prinz could get back to Nevada and have the leaders arrested. But we heard they had flown before the arrest could be made. It was reported that "Black Jack" had skipped for South Africa. I lost track of the case and never heard how the matter terminated.

Tim W. had promised to testify in court when the time came, under agreement that he be not put in jail. We had faith in him keeping his promise. I guarded Tim a week or so in order to give Mr. Prinz time to reach Tuscarora and swear out warrants. Then Tim was turned loose and he went back to his grass widow, Mrs. B., to repent in sackcloth and ashes for the letters "which never came," after he had promised so faithfully to write often. I never learned how long poor Mrs. B. remained in Fort Sill nursing her grieving heart. Hers was a case of sitting on the anxious seat with a vengeance, but such is often the penalty of blind love.

Just two days after our return to Denver, I took Lulu Edson out to the Overland Park where the big races were going on. I hobbled her two front feet with a piece of new rope so that she could hobble around and eat green grass. I hired a negro to watch her, but when the first race started she saw them and joined in the run, she being on the outside of the fence. In crossing a muddy slough, she went up to her ears in black mud, so that she was a black horse with a sorrel head. When half way around the mile track she jumped the five-foot fence and led the bunch of trotting horses past the wire. Her hobble had broken before she jumped the fence. She trotted up to the grand stand where sat many thousands of Denver's elite, and whinnied. The people cheered, for most of them saw her jump the high fence. I was in the grand stand, but at first, didn't know her, as she was black.

This was Lulu's last race, as I wouldn't trust her to others, and I was leading too strenuous a life to race her myself. I still own three of her colts. She died at my expense fifteen years after falling into my hands.

Thus ended the Prinz and Pelling operation so far as I was concerned. It was May, 1890, when Tim and I arrived in Denver. I had been on the operation nine months.

In his confession Tim told how the fuses were cut the same length and touched off at the same time so that the two wealthy mine-owners would go up in the air and sprout angel-wings at the same time, their homes being a block or two apart. Many men were connected with the plot and for this reason Tim was set free after the sworn affidavits were made.

Mr. C. W. Prinz, the last account I had of him, was a prosperous mining man of San Francisco with offices on Pine street. He and Pelling sold out their interests in Tuscarora, Nevada. Mr. Pelling I heard, had married millionaire Cox's daughter of Sacramento, California, and was now soaring high in society; quite a change from the time he soared high in the air through the roof of a house, with dynamite instead of $'s as the lifting power.

CHAPTER VI

SHOOTING OF ANCHETA—I JOIN THE "WHITE CAPS" OF
NEW MEXICO—TAKEN DOWN WITH SMALL-
POX AND GIVEN UP TO DIE.

After getting rid of Tim W., we furnished a new
home and started to housekeeping again. Mamie and
little Viola had returned from Springfield, Missouri, but
the doctors had little hope of saving my wife's life, as
both lungs had become affected.

Owing to the sickness in my family, I was not sent
out of the city on long operations.

During the fall my stubborn bump and quick temper
came very near landing me in the penitentiary. It shows
how a man's whole life can be changed by a mere hair's
breadth. Gamblers call it luck, but I would call it chance.

Mamie was at death's door and I had been sitting up
with her night and day. It was Saturday, and I went
down to the office to draw my week's salary and to ask
Mr. McParland if I couldn't remain at Mamie's bedside
until she got better.

With the salary in my pocket, I started home by way
of Laramie street, so as to get old Colt's 45 out of "soak."
Being short of cash I had pawned the pistol for $20.00
to H. Solomon of the Rocky Mountain pawn shop, and in
its place I was carrying a small pistol belonging to
operative Frank McC.

Next door to the Rocky Mountain pawn shop a chem-

114

ical factory had blown up and it was reported that a dead man was being brought out by the police and firemen. The police had ropes stretched to keep the crowds back, and a special policeman named Rease, was guarding the front door of Solomon's pawn shop and wouldn't let any one inside for fear a raid would be made on the valuable diamonds in the window and show cases. Being refused admittance, I stepped up on an iron railing to get a better view of the dead man who was being brought out. Just then young Solomon told me to get down and move away from the front of their shop. I told him to go to Hades or some other seaport. Then the big double-jointed special policeman pulled me down and tore my coat almost off. My gold-headed silk umbrella was broken all to pieces over his head and when he reached for his gun mine was pulled out of my hip pocket and pointed at his heart and the trigger was pulled. While using the umbrella on the fellow's head, other policemen rushed at me. Just as the trigger was pulled, a policeman by the name of Ball, threw both arms around me from the rear. His right hand grabbed the pistol and the hammer came down on his thumb instead of the cartridge, thus saving me the expense of a trip to the penitentiary, for had he been killed, it would have meant a trip "over the road." The sharp hammer had buried itself in his thumb, so I was told. I saw him many times afterwards, but never made myself known to him.

By main strength and awkwardness, six policemen put me in the "hurry-up wagon," and I was taken to jail, coatless, hatless and an umbrella less. That evening I was liberated by Chief of Police John Farley, after Mr.

McCartney had come to see me. This ended the matter after old Colts 45 was taken out of "soak," and I had tried to round up my hat and the gold head of my umbrella, but they had vanished.

Poor Mamie died in my arms early in the winter as I was holding her at the window to get fresh air. Her suffering had been something awful and our physician, Dr. Herman H. Martin, shed tears when the end came. This was a surprise to me for I didn't think a doctor could shed tears, as they become so accustomed to great suffering.

Mamie's aunt, Mrs. Will F. Read, formerly Miss Emma Lloyd, of Shelbyville, Illinois, one of nature's purest and noblest women, came out from her home in Anna, Illinois, to comfort my wife in her last days on earth. When Mrs. Read returned to Illinois, I let her take Viola along, as she had no children of her own and begged so hard for the child to raise, as I had no way of caring for her.

Shortly after the breaking up of my home, I was sent to Santa Fe, New Mexico, to work for the Territory. I was the only operative in the Denver office who was familiar with the Mexican language, hence this operation fell to my lot.

It was in the early part of February, 1891. The Territorial legislature was in session at Santa Fe, the capital, and one night armed assassins fired into the law office of Mr. Thos. B. Catron, where the executive committee of the senate was holding a meeting.

The men who did the shooting were on horseback and rode up to the glass front office building on the ground floor and fired. It was late at night. One charge of buckshot struck Ancheta in the neck and another lodged in some law books on a table lying in front of Mr. Catron. The books saved his life. One rifle bullet barely missed Ex-Governor Stover, then a Territorial senator.

A fierce fight had been raging in the legislature over a free public school bill which had been introduced by Ancheta, an educated Mexican, and was being fought by the Catholic church. The legislature had appropriated $20,000.00 as a fund to run down the guilty parties. Rewards were offered and a committee of three was appointed to handle this fund. On this committee were the governor, L. Bradford Prince, the attorney-general, Edward L. Bartlett and territorial senator, Thos. B. Catron, all being leading Republicans.

On my arrival in the oldest city in the Union, and the cradle of "Ben Hur," I had a consultation with Gov. Prince, and later with the other two members of the committee. I was made familiar with all the facts in the case, even to a peculiar track made by one of the horses ridden by one of the shooters in running over the frozen snow and slush. One hind hoof of this horse dug up the dirt in a peculiar fashion, showing that the hoof was crooked.

John Gray, the city marshal, and a crowd had followed the tracks of these horsemen to the junction of two roads, one leading to Las Vegas and the other to the Cow Springs country. Here all trace was lost.

I was told to work on the "White Caps," and if possible, join their order, as there was no doubt about members of that lawless gang being the guilty ones, and that possibly the whole organization was in the plot.

During the last election the "White Caps" had carried the county of San Miguel, Las Vegas being the county seat, and elected to the legislature one of its leaders, Pablo H., who had just finished serving a sentence in the territorial penitentiary at Santa Fe. My mind was soon made up to win the friendship of this ex-convict member of the legislature, and through him join the "White Caps."

The sheriff of Santa Fe county, Francisco Chaves, was a member of the "White Caps" organization and by spending money freely with him, we became fast friends.

One night on our rounds in the "hurrah" part of the city, we ran into Pablo H. and his gang of friends. Of course, I was introduced to the gang, and we proceeded to "whoop 'em up."

A few days later the legislature adjourned and by invitation from Pablo, I was a passenger with him on the train for Las Vegas. In Las Vegas, both the old and new towns, I was introduced to all the "White Cap" friends of Pablo H., among them being his two brothers, Judge Jose and Nicanor, the latter being a fine looking specimen of the Mexican race, with jet black wavy hair, reaching to the shoulders; but the fierce determined expression on his face portended evil for his enemies.

Days passed into weeks and Pablo and I became inseparable. We consumed much bad liquor and ate many fine meals in swell society at the Montezuma hotel, six miles from Las Vegas, at the Hot Springs. The only thing to worry me was a fear that H. H. Pierce, of the Stock Growers' Journal might give me away. I had been introduced to him by my old friend Lute Wilcox, of the

Pablo H. Standing.—His Two Brothers Sitting.

Field & Farm in Denver, Colorado, a couple of years previous, and now he recognized me and I had to trust him to keep my identity a secret. The county clerk, Rox. Hardy, who had been elected by the "White Cap" vote, was his running mate, and I feared that Pierce might tell the secret to him and the chances are he did. I afterwards found out that Rox. Hardy was a friend to the "White Caps" for revenue only, so then I had no fear.

I had an old time friend in the new town of Las Vegas by the name of "Nick" Chaffin. He owned a livery stable in partnership with a Mr. Duncan. He didn't recognize me as we had not met before for twelve years. The fact that I went by an assumed name, C. Leon Allison, threw him off his guard when Pablo introduced us one night.

Seeing "Nick" brought back memories of early days in the Panhandle of Texas. I was dying to make myself known to "Nick," so that I could "hark back" to a time in 1877 when he got me to ride a wild horse for him. This horse gave me a new kind of a ride and thereby impressed "Nick" Chaffin's photo on memory's tablet.

I had faith in Mr. Chaffin not giving me away intentionally, but the rules of my agency forbid making ourselves known where there is nothing to be gained by so doing.

I finally bought a horse and saddle and one night when Pablo H. had to attend an important meeting of "White Caps" near the Mexican town of Tecolote, about ten miles from Las Vegas, I went along. Pablo and I had been drinking considerably that day, as I wanted him to feel gay when the time came for him to start, so that he would invite me to accompany him, which he did. Each of us carried a bottle of whiskey as we galloped over the hills to Tecolote. We rode up to a large adobe hall standing on a hill, solitary and alone, about 9 P. M. The light of the candles inside could scarcely be seen owing to the heavy curtains over the windows.

I felt a little shaky for fear that Pierce might have given me away and that this might be a trap set to murder me. I suggested to Pablo that as I was not a member of the order, I remain outside. This was done for effect, but Pablo insisted that I was his friend and wherever he went I should go. Pablo gave the secret knock at the door and it was opened. Seeing a "Gringo" stranger entering at Pablo's heels, the guard tried to stop me, but Pablo, being a powerful man, brushed the fellow to one side and cursed him in Mexican.

In the rear of the hall several new members were being initiated into the "White Cap" order, which had a charter from the Knights of Labor and pretended to be a branch of that organization merely for effect. My presence in the hall came near starting a riot. The masterworkman ordered me put out. Pablo put his hand on his pistol and told the crowd to stand back. Then he made a fiery speech, such as he had lately made in the legislative halls at Santa Fe. He soared to the sky in his Spanish eloquence and told how he had bled and starved for their noble order and how he would suffer his eyes to be plucked out rather than bring a man into the lodge who couldn't be trusted. The large crowd of rough looking Mexicans and half-breed Indians were carried off their feet by this speech and they cheered loudly. The master-workman put a motion before the house that the rules be suspended and I be initiated into the order. It was carried.

The half dozen candidates still stood in the middle of the hall forming a circle and holding each other's hands. They seemed frightened. Pablo led me over and breaking the circle, he placed my hands into those of two Mexicans, and thereby patched up the broken circle. In the center of this circle strange chalk marks were made on the floor. They all represented something. The ceremony was started anew for my benefit. It consisted of weird chanting and gestures and sworn pledges to give up life if necessary for the good of the order or a brother in need. This last clause proved hard on my territorial pocket book as later I found hundreds in need of a drink.

I was the only "Gringo" (American) member of this lodge and I felt highly honored. Most of its members were "Penitentes," the religious fanatics who whip themselves with cactus and inflict all manner of cruelties upon themselves. In this county they were 2,200 strong, and most of them had joined the "White Caps" and ruled in politics.

The "White Cap" order had been formed for the purpose of cutting fences and even killing stockmen who fenced large tracts of land. They traveled in large bands, wearing white caps on their heads and on their horses' heads. The horses were also covered with white sheets at times. The leaders finally turned it into a political order to frighten voters into voting the Populist ticket. Some men who opposed them were murdered. I was let into their secrets of the past. One pitiful case was where they murdered a poor Turk because they thought he was a detective.

For quite a while I lived with Nicanor H. on his ranch near Tecolote.

In attending other lodges and visiting brother members in Moro county, I saw many cruel scenes performed by the "Penitentes."

I spent some time visiting with Col. Blake and his family at Rociada, in Mora county. I knew Col. Blake in White Oaks, New Mexico, in 1880, but he failed to recognize me. He was a strong Populist and hence sympathized with the "White Caps."

I satisfied myself that the "White Caps" had nothing to do with the shooting of Ancheta at Santa Fe. I then bade my "White Cap" friends goodbye, and left overland for Santa Fe, a distance of about 80 miles.

Soon after this Pablo H. became an outlaw and killed men for the fun of it, so it was said. He was finally arrested and broke jail. While court was in session at Las Vegas, he got drunk and defied the court and its officers. This angered District Judge Smith and he ordered Billy Green, a fearless officer, to bring Pablo H. dead or alive, before his court. Green carried out the court's order by bringing Pablo's corpse before the judge. But this proved the doom of Billy Green. He and a companion were waylaid and killed later.

Nicanor H., soon after we parted, killed a man and was sent to the penitentiary. But after serving a short sentence he was pardoned and my old-time friend, former attorney-general of New Mexico, Col. Geo. W. Prichard,

informs me that he is now living an honorable, indus-
trious life in Las Vegas. His brother, Judge Jose H.,
died a natural death.

On my way over to Santa Fe, I traded horses. In the
distance I saw a cloud of dust and two black objects
cutting all kinds of monkey-shines. I hurried to the
place and found a negro man trying to plow with a brown
mare. The mare was wild and wouldn't be hitched to
the plow. The air was impregnated with cuss words and
rivulets of perspiration were flowing from the negro's
manly brow. He recognized me as a brother "White
Cap" whom he had met at one of the lodges. Then there
was rejoicing. He asked me to help him hitch up the
"d—— old mar'." I replied that I was in too much of a
hurry, but to accommodate him I would trade horses.
He asked if mine would work. I told him yes, that he
was hankering to get into that plow and tear up the dirt.
With a grin on his face he called it a trade. His mare
was much larger than my horse, and worth more. I
didn't lie to make this trade, for in Texas where I was
brought up, a lie told in a horse trade is the truth.

Mr. "Coon" helped me saddle the mare and when I
mounted her she bucked hard and wicked. Between
jumps I could hear the negro's loud laugh and now and
then I caught a glimpse of his white teeth shining in the
sun. We finally got straightened out and headed west
in a gallop. It was a level stretch of country and in looking back all I could see was a cloud of dust where the
negro and the bay bronco were having a tug of war.
This horse had never had harness on. I never knew who
won in this battle, the negro or the horse, but I could

smell the brimstone from the cuss words thrown at me as long as I was in sight. Of course, it may have been imagination.

I arrived in Santa Fe after a hard ride. I thought a hard ride would take the "buck" out of the mare, but it didn't, for next morning when I mounted her on one of the main streets of Santa Fe, she bucked hard. In this bucking match my pistol flew out of its scabbard and was picked up by Cooley Beaver, thus starting a friendship which has lasted to this day.

After a meeting with Gov. Prince, I left for Cow Springs, the end of the other road which the assassins might have taken. It was at the junction of this and the Las Vegas roads where the trail had been lost on the night of the shooting.

Cow Springs is a long day's ride from Santa Fe. It is an out-of-the-way place and consisted of about a dozen Mexican families who had small farms and ranches. There was only one brother "White Cap" in the settlement. His name was Eustaquio P. He was a good fellow and we became warm friends. The balance were all republicans.

I lived with Francisco G. and his family.

Before being here a week I found that I was on the right track. I located the horse with a peculiar hind hoof, and to satisfy myself I went after cattle one day with the owner of this horse, which was his pet, and I examined the tracks. The crooked hoof threw up the dirt exactly as described after the shooting. I also found out that the owner of this animal, with other relatives of his, were in Santa Fe up to the night of the shooting. In fact, I satisfied myself that here lived the guilty parties.

Two weeks after my arrival in Cow Springs, we had a "big time" which broke the monotony of living on chili and other Mexican dishes.

It was Sunday and the Catholic priest came from Santa Fe to christen the new bell in the small adobe church. We all turned out and met him several miles from the settlement. We returned riding ahead of the priest, singing and playing musical instruments. Sixto G. had a violin and he led the procession. After the new bell was put in place, five cents was charged to ring it once. I spent about $1.00 ringing the bell. Quite a purse was collected. Even little babies at their mother's breast forked over a nickel to ring the bell.

Soon after this we received word that a Mexican woman had died from smallpox out in the hills and that there was no one to bury her. A crowd of us took shovels, etc., and struck out to do the job. In the house lay the corpse and by the side of two little twin babies lying on the floor with nothing but a sheepskin under them, sat the father feeding the babies. He had nothing to feed them with but dried raw beef which he would chew up and stick in their mouths so they could suck the juice out of it. Their little bodies were parched and cracked open from the smallpox. The winking of the coal-black eyes and the movement of their lips were the only signs of life left in them. After burying the woman I got a box of salve from my saddle pockets and greased those little babes from head to foot. It was a pleasure to see them smile and their little eyes wink. It no doubt relieved their pain.

I had no fear of catching the smallpox, as I had it in

1882 in Texas. On that occasion I had to ride 200 miles to a doctor and had to sleep out at night in rain with no covering but my saddle blankets. Therefore, you may know that I could sympathize with these babes. I had always heard that a person couldn't take smallpox more than once, but I know better now. Gen. Smith's son-in-law, I am told, died in Santa Fe the third time he had it, and doctors tell me that a case is on record where a man had the disease eight times. I know positively now of one poor d——l who had it twice.

On our return to Cow Springs we sent a nurse and food to those sick babies, but they died a few days later.

Shortly after the burial of the woman, I got sick with a burning fever. Late in the evening I started for Lamy Junction, the nearest store, a distance of 12 miles, to get a bottle of Carter's little liver pills, my favorite remedy when feeling badly. I secured a room in the Harvey hotel and taking a dose of pills, went to bed for the night. Next morning I felt worse and was burning up with fever. Still I had faith in a few doses of the pills curing me, so I concluded to return to Cow Springs.

After saddling my mare I dreaded to mount her, as her vicious bucking which she always practised after a night's rest, would be painful to my already aching bones.

I was sitting on the steps in front of Charlie Haspelmath's store holding the mare by the rope with my face buried in both hands to ease the severe headache. Just then a big drunken Irish car repairer for the railroad company came along and asked me to please give him a ride on my horse, as he hadn't been on a pony since coming west. Forgetting all about my headache and looking up with a smile, I handed him the rope. The mare stood still until he was seated in the saddle, then business started with a rush. Seemed to me as if the Irishman stayed up in the air long enough for birds to have built a nest in his coat pocket. I heard afterwards that he lay in the hospital quite a while. The mare went flying over the hills towards the southeast, dragging the long rope. I hired two Mexicans on good horses to stay on her trail and bring her back. She was found fourteen days afterwards twenty-five miles from Lamy, just about starved to death. The rope had wound around a tree. The saddle was gone.

In the evening the train started for Santa Fe, and I was one of the passengers. On arriving in the city I had a hack take me to Mrs. Aaron Gold's rooming house, where I had formerly roomed. She had two nice daughters, Rebecca and Zepora, and I had found it a pleasant place to live.

I was a very sick man, but kept on my feet long enough to slip into the Governor's Palace after dark to report to Gov. Prince. He was absent from the city, so Mrs. Prince, his wife, informed me. She entertained me in her elegantly furnished parlor for a couple of hours, so that I forgot about being sick. It was a treat to have my high-heel cowboy boots buried in Brussels carpet after being so long on dirt floors. But I smile even to this day when I think of how good Mrs. Prince would have stampeded had she known that I was at that moment burning up with a smallpox fever.

That night I slept very little and by the next morning I was beginning to lose faith in Carter's little liver pills.

I had already taken half the bottle and still the fever was growing worse. Despite my suffering, most of the day was spent writing reports. Late in the evening I went to bed and sent for Dr. J. H. Sloan. While waiting for him Miss Zepora Gold came and sat at the head of my bed and with her beautiful girlish face and sweet voice, cheered my drooping spirits, but it wasn't for long, for when the doctor came and pronounced it smallpox she stampeded.

It was raining hard and Dr. Sloan told me not to listen to the pleadings of Mrs. Gold and her daughters should they try to have me moved in the rain, as it would cause my death. I sent for my old "White Cap" Mexican friend, Francisco Lechuga, to come and nurse me. As Dr. Sloan was slow about returning, I became impatient and sent my nurse after Dr. Harroun. He also pronounced it smallpox and advised me not to be moved in the rain.

After dark Mrs. Gold and Zepora pled with me from a distance through the partly opened door, to vacate my room before the other roomers learned of my presence, as they would all leave. I could resist the pitiful pleading of Mrs. Gold, but not of the pretty daughter. I thought of the countless numbers who in past ages had given up their lives at the command of youth and beauty, and why not I? So I consented to be moved if a place could be found for me.

In the course of an hour Mrs. Gold returned saying that she had found a place at the house of Diego Gonzales, but that I would have to pay $3 a day for a room and board; that they would wait on me during the day, but I had to furnish my own nurse at night. I agreed to this.

Soon a hack drove up to Mrs. Gold's and throwing a quilt over my head I walked through a pouring rain for about 100 feet to where the hack stood. An hour later, when Dr. Harroun found me in my new quarters he was angry at me for moving in the rain. By this time I had broken out with sores from head to foot, and I was "swelled up" like a Chicago alderman.

About four or five days later, Dr. Harroun came to see me at about 8 P. M. as usual. He felt my pulse and then began walking up and down the floor with a worried look on his face. I could still see through a corner of one eye which hadn't swollen shut yet. I knew there was something wrong, so I asked for an explanation. The doctor sat down by the head of my bed and taking hold of my hand, told me that I couldn't live till morning, as my temperature had been up to the highest pitch, either 105 or 107, I forget which, for four or five days, which was the limit; that my vital energy would be burnt out before morning. He advised that if I had any word or will to leave, that I attend to it then. I made him promise that he would keep the matter of what he was to write down a secret; and that not a soul but himself should know of it until after my death. I got him to write down a last farewell to my mother and relatives, but didn't tell who they were, nor where they lived.

Before leaving, the doctor left some medicine for me to take every ten minutes. He instructed my nurse, a strange young Mexican whom Francisco Lechuga had sent to work in his place that night, to stay awake and

9

give me the medicine regularly. Then the doctor shook hands with me and departed.

After the doctor had gone, the band began playing in the Plaza, and we could hear shouting and firing of cannon. The sleepy old city had woke up that day from her 300 years' slumber. An election had been held, and it was voted to incorporate and have a city government. This music and noise was to celebrate the event.

After giving me the first dose of medicine, the nurse asked if he could go to the door and hear the music. I consented, with his promise to be back in 10 minutes so as to give me the medicine again. I had overlooked the fact that he was of the common peon class, and that free liquor was flowing like water down town.

The Gonzales house covered nearly half an acre of ground, and the family lived across an open court in a different part of the residence from my room. They had gone down town to the rally after turning me over to the nurse before the arrival of the doctor, hence they knew nothing of my dangerous condition. On returning at midnight, they went to bed.

After enduring a burning thirst for an hour or two, I tried to get up to find a drink of water and call for help, but failed. I was swelled up like a barrel, and every inch of my body even to the soles of my feet and the inside of my throat was covered with sores. In lying so long on my back, these sores had become calloused, but on undertaking to turn over on to the fresh sores so as to try to get up, I would scream with pain and fall over on my back again. By this time I was good and angry at my nurse for his long absence, and I surmised the truth of his long stay. The only consolation that I had during the night was the satisfaction of knowing how to curse in the Mexican language, for fear that the god who ruled over this truant son of old Montezuma might not understand my English swearing.

After my anger had cooled down somewhat, I began to think of dying and wondered what kind of a reception I would receive on the other shore from whence no cowboy detective has ever returned.

Towards morning I could hardly get my breath, and I was suffering the torments of hell. This I thought meant the approach of death and I cried at the thoughts of being dragged off by a lot of cheap peons before my body was cold, and thrown into a small-pox grave. Then, for the first time, I realized the satisfaction of being buried by loving hands and having flowers strewn on our graves.

When the cry was over my teeth were set and I made up my mind not to die. I was determined to fight off death with all the energy left in me.

Next morning at 7 o'clock the doctor was the first one to come. He was as tickled as a little boy with his first pair of pants, when he saw I was alive. My temperature was down to 101, and he said I was safe.

For the next two weeks I suffered greatly. Most of the time I was compelled to lie flat on my back, as turning over on to the fresh sores which had not been hardened through contact with the hard corn-shuck mattress, was too painful. These sores seemed to have melted and all run together, forming one solid scab from head to foot.

Diego Gonzales and his good wife had two daughters,

Braulia and Delfina; also some little grandchildren by a son, Perfecto, and they all made it pleasant for me while recovering. The baby grandchild, Manuel, spent half of his time playing in my room. Catarina, an adopted daughter, also did her share towards making life worth living.

It was the first part of July when Francisco G. came in from Cow Springs in his wagon and took me out home to where my bucking mare was waiting for a tussel with me. She hadn't been ridden since that drunken son of Ireland struck the earth on his head, and she had recovered from that hungry spell while fast to a tree for a couple of weeks. After buying another saddle, I gave the mare an opportunity to practise her favorite game. I finally traded her off though, as I had tired of her "monkey business."

For the next month or two my time was divided between Cow Springs and Santa Fe.

I received a partial confession from the Mexican with the crooked hoof horse, also other evidence that convinced me of the guilty parties who fired into Catron's office; but I was never able to satisfy myself positively, as to the motive, though I think it was done to kill Ancheta and Governor Stover for their part in helping to pass a public free school law for the Territory. Of course it could have been done by these few religious fanatics without the sanction of the Church, even though the priests and Church officials did fight Ancheta and Stover, "tooth and nail," through their representatives in the legislative halls.

The chances are the Borreago gang of "bad" men—four

of whom were hung for murder in Santa Fe a few years later—had a hand in the Ancheta shooting. For, in visiting Santa Fe with any of these Cow Springs suspects we would always call on the Borreago boys. There seemed to be a deep friendship between the two families.

On laying the matter before Governor Prince and General Bartlett, I advised that the suspects be arrested, as I felt sure one or more would become frightened and make a full confession. But this was decided not advisable, owing to the chance of failure, which would injure the Republican party, the suspects being members thereof. I believe in taking chances in such matters, and "sink or swim." The chances were favorable for a confession, had they been jailed under the impression that we knew all of their secrets. Of course it may have resulted in opening old sores in New Mexico politics, which I knew nothing of; for, in Spanish-speaking countries, politics make strange bed-fellows. It was decided best to drop the matter and discontinue the operation.

It was early fall when I took my departure for Denver. I hated to leave, as I had found the climate of Santa Fe the finest that I had ever been in. The summers can't be beaten anywhere, and the winters are better than most places. In fact, I liked it so well that I made up my mind to build a permanent home there, and with that end in view I secured a tract of land a short distance from the outskirts of the city and christened it the Sunny Slope Ranch.

During my eight months in sunny New Mexico on this operation, I saw much of the Mexican people, especially of the lower classes. I like them as a whole,

and would like them still more if the blood of their
Spanish sires could be eradicated so as to do away with
their cruelty to dumb animals.   As a whole, they are a
hospitable, law-abiding people, although their gait is not
very swift, except when they fill up on the rotten, poison
liquors which are manufactured in local cellars cheaply,
for this class of trade, by Jews and so-called Americans
of the money-grabbing races.

CHAPTER VII

THE BLOODY COEUR D'ALENE STRIKE—I BECOME RE-
CORDING SECRETARY OF THE UNION—DURING THE
RIOT I SAWED A HOLE IN THE FLOOR TO ESCAPE
FROM BLOOD-THIRSTY DYNAMITERS.

After the smallpox siege I found myself in Denver
without a home or family ties; but I had quite a fat little
bank account. My salary had piled up during the eight
months that I was gone, as I had no occasion to touch
it, all my expenses, even to my laundry, medicine and
doctor bills, having been paid by our client, the Territory
of New Mexico.

This goes to show that the business of a detective is
more suitable for a single man. In fact the business is
unjust and cruel to the wife, even though she does get
to spend the biggest part of her hubby's money while he
is absent. She is deprived of his company and protection
when most needed, and has to shut her eyes to the fact
that he has to associate with all kinds of women, in order
to win a case.

After a few weeks' rest in Denver, Mr. McCartney
called me into his private office and told me to get ready
for a long trip into the Coeur D'Alene mining district of
northern Idaho.

He explained that the Miners' Union of that district
was raising Hades with the mine-owners who had formed
themselves into a Mine-Owners' Association for self-

135

protection, and that the Association wanted a good operative to join the Miners' Union, so as to be on the inside of the order when the fast approaching eruption occurred.

I told Mr. McCartney that I didn't want this operation as my sympathy was with labor organizations as against capital. He replied that if such was the case I couldn't do the Agency's clients justice, and for that reason he would have to select another operative.

A few days later I was detailed on a railroad operation through Utah and California, along with several other operatives.

A month or more had passed when one day in Salt Lake City, Utah, I received a telegraph message from McCartney instructing me to come to Denver on the first train. This I did, and on meeting McCartney he said: "Now Charlie, you have got to go to the Coeur D'Alenes. You're the only man I've got who can go there and get into the Miner's Union. They are on their guard against detectives and they became suspicious of the operative I sent up there, and ran him out of the country. We know the leaders to be a desperate lot of criminals of the Molly Maguire type, and you will find it so. I will let your own conscience be the judge, after you get into their Union. If you decide they are in the right and the Mine-owners are in the wrong, you can throw up the operation without further permission from me."

This seemed fair, so I accepted and began making preparations for at least a year's absence.

In Wallace, Idaho, the central town of the Coeur D'Alene district, I had a secret meeting with a Mr. Hankins who represented Mr. John Hayes Drummond, the President of the Mine-Owners' Association, and John A. French, Secretary of the Association. The importance of my work and the difficulties under which I would have to operate, were laid before me. I was told that the Miners' Union were on the lookout for detectives, and that the Union in Burk had become suspicious of a Thiel detective by the name of Mitch G., and ran him out of the country a short time previous.

It was agreed that no one in Gem knew me, outside of the mine superintendent, John Monihan, and that I would be described to him so that he would put me to work when I applied for a job.

A day or two later I applied to John Monihan in a natural way, and he turned me over to one of his shift-bosses, Peterson, on the Gem mine, who was told to make a place for me, Peterson of course not knowing who I was. I gave the name of C. Leon Allison. I worked as a regular miner two weeks, on day-shift, and the next two, on the night-shift.

Gem was a camp of two or three stores and half a dozen saloons. The three mines, the Gem, Helen Frisco, and Black Bear, which supported the camp, were near by, so that the men boarded in town. About 500 miners worked in these three mines, besides hundreds of other surface workmen; hence the little camp was a lively place after night when the saloons and gambling halls were running full blast. I put in much of my time at the saloons and made myself a "good fellow" among "the boys."

My worst trouble was writing reports and mailing them. These reports had to be sent to St. Paul,

Minnesota, where our Agency had an office, with my Chicago friend, John O'Flyn, as superintendent. There they were typewritten and mailed back to John A. Finch, Secretary of the Mine-Owners' Association, where all the mine-owners could read them.

The Gem Post Office was in the store of a man by the name of Samuels, a rabid anarchist and Union sympathizer; so for that reason I dare not mail reports there. "Big Frank" was the deputy post-master and handled most of the mail. He was a member of the Gem Miners' Union, consequently I had to walk down to Wallace, four miles, to mail reports; and for fear of being held up I had to slip down there in the dark.

Two weeks after my arrival in Gem, I joined the Gem Miners' Union, and a couple of months later I was elected recording secretary of the Union. Geo. A. Pettibone, a rabid anarchist, was its financial secretary.

Now that I had become an officer of the Gem Union, I concluded to quit work; but I didn't want to quit of my own accord. I wanted shift-boss Peterson to discharge me so that I couldn't get any more work in the camp. In order to be "fired," I shirked my duty and was discharged.

That night I got on a big "jamboree," and spent my wages freely.

In order not to desert the Miners' Union to hunt work elsewhere, as trouble with the Mine-Owners' Association was expected soon, I pretended to send to my rich father in Texas for money to carry me through the winter.

Now that I was not working, I had plenty of time to accompany Geo. A. Pettibone and others to the houses of supposed "scabs," or of men who wouldn't pay their dues to the Union, and order them to leave the country. Often they were stubborn and wouldn't go. Then we would get up a mob by holding a citizens' mass-meeting to run them out of the State.

We would first hold a special meeting of the Union, to resolve on running certain ones out. Then boys, ringing bells, would be sent through the town calling a citizens' meeting in the Union Hall; but no one except members were allowed to enter the hall. Then it would be declared the sense of the citizens' indignation meeting that certain "scabs" be run out of the State. Often as many as half a dozen "scabs" would be taken from their homes, sometimes with weeping wives and children begging for mercy, and with tin pans and the music of bells, they would be marched up and down the street to be spit upon and branded as "scabs," before the public eye. Then, half clothed and without food, the poor devils would be marched up the canyon, a few miles beyond the big mining camp of Burk, three miles distant, and told to "hit the road" and never return at the peril of their lives. Pistols would be fired over their heads to give them a good running start.

By this route, during the winters, the snow is waist deep over the Bitter Root range of mountains, and not a living inhabitant until reaching Thompson's Falls, Montana, a distance of about thirty miles.

This thing was kept up all winter, and I learned a few new lessons in human nature. My mind had taken a regular "flop" on the labor union question, since telling Superintendent McCartney that my sympathies were with the unions. I had found the leaders of the Coeur D'Alene unions to be, as a rule, a vicious, heartless gang of anarchists. Many of them had been rocked in the cradle of anarchy at Butte City, Montana, while others were escaped outlaws and toughs from other States.

Of course, after a batch of these "scabs" were run over the range to Montana, the daily papers of Spokane, Washington and Anaconda and Butte, Montana, would come out with glaring head-lines of how the citizens had held a mass-meeting and ordered these "scabs" deported; that the unions had nothing to do with it. I knew better though, but the general public didn't.

Thus did the winter of 1891-92 pass.

Gem was not the only transgressor of our glorious Constitution. The deporting of "scabs" was going on in the other camps, though Gem and Burk took the lead.

During the winter I often attended the Burk Union meetings. At one of these meetings, I had the pleasure of seeing with my own eyes a Miners' Union Irishman, not many years from the "ould sod," who was for law, order and justice, first, last, and all the time. He was a fine-looking specimen of manhood, with jet black hair, eyes and mustache. He made a fine speech, but after he had finished he was sat down on so hard by the rabid leaders, that he couldn't get his jaws in working order again during the whole winter. I saw him at many meetings after that, but he never said a word. There had been talk of branding him as a "scab." This was a warning to others to fall in line and be true union men.

In joining the Gem Union, I had to take an iron-clad "Molly Maguire" oath that I would never turn traitor to the union cause; that if I did, death would be my reward, etc.

Early in the Spring of 1892 war was declared between the Mine-Owners' Association and the Executive Committee of the Coeur D'Alene Central Organization of the Miners' Unions. This Central Union was made up of delegates from each local union. Geo. A. Pettibone represented the Gem Union and he told me that they had selected a secret crowd of the worst men in the unions to put the fear of Christ into the hearts of "scabs"; that if these secret men committed murder the union would stick by them, but that no one outside the Executive Committee, of which he was a member, was to know who these secret men were, and their pay came from a fund reserved "for the good of the order."

After war was declared, all the mines in the Coeur D'Alenes were closed down. Shortly after this, a big mass-meeting was called in Wallace to hear both sides of the trouble.

The Unions of Gem, Burk, Mullens and Wardner, had the meeting packed with the intention of choking off the Mine-Owners' side of the question, but the man whom the Mine-Owners selected to represent their side of the case, was not of the quitting kind. He wouldn't be choked off. He would wait until the cursing, hissing and abuse ceased and then start in anew.

Back in my part of the Hall, where sat Paddy Burk and a gang of dynamiters, there was talk of making a rush for the stage and in the excitement pitch this speech-making "scab" out of the upstairs window to the pavement below. It looked very much as though the meeting would end in a riot, but finally cooler heads got control, and Attorney W. T. Skoll, now one of the leading lawyers of Spokane, Washington, was allowed to speak his little piece.

Shortly after this, a train load of "scabs" with Joe Warren at their head, were imported into the district from other States. We heard they were on the way. Then the Central Union's headquarters in Wallace became a busy place. I was made one of the despatchers to carry messages on horse-back, when necessary.

Tom O'Brien was the President, and Joe Poynton was the Secretary of the Central Union. I was in their company a good deal, and caught on to many of their secrets. One of them was that the sheriff of the county, Mr. Cunningham, was in with the union even to murder.

On the day the "scabs" were to arrive in Wallace, there was great excitement. The drunken sheriff was on his fine horse with a gang of union deputies to preserve order, but in reality to help shoot down "scabs," if the Central Union desired it.

The funny part of it was that the mine-owners caught the union napping and stole a march on them. Of course I had been keeping them posted as to the unions' intentions.

Instead of the train stopping in Wallace, as expected, the engineer put on a full head of steam and went flying up the canyon towards Burk. The poor sheriff waved his order of arrest under the State laws for importing armed thugs, as he ran after the train on his swift horse. Before the armed gang of union men could get back to Burk afoot, it being seven miles, Joe Warren had unloaded his 100 or more armed "scabs" and marched them up the mountain side to the union mine, which had been prepared secretly for their reception.

Late that evening Burke was jammed full of angry miners begging President O'Brien for permission to blow those "scabs" off the face of the earth. Joe Poynton, Geo. A. Pettibone, and the rest of the rabid leaders, were eager for bloodshed, but O'Brien was the dam which held the angry waters of anarchy back.

A committee of level-headed unionists was finally appointed to go with the sheriff and arrest Joe Warren peaceably, if possible. Warren submitted to arrest so as to test the law, and he left a good man to act in his place. In submitting to arrest, Joe Warren did a foolish thing, and he would have thought so, could he have heard the plots to assassinate him that night, as I did. Warren no doubt realized his danger when he was surrounded by the hundreds of angry miners. They were clamoring for his blood; but O'Brien and the drunken sheriff argued that if he was harmed while under arrest it would ruin the unions. During all this excitement Warren, who was in the prime of manhood and stood about six feet four in his bare feet, was cool, though a little pale behind the ears. Late at night he was taken to Wallace under a heavy guard.

To record the fights and cruel acts of the union on "scabs" for the next few months, would require a book twice the size of this.

Other train loads of "scabs" were brought into Gem and placed in the Helen-Frisco and Gem mines under armed guards.

A bloody revolution was planned for July sometime. On the 4th day of July the American flags were shot full of holes and spat upon.

Previous to this the secrets of the unions were published in the Coeur D'Alene "Barbarian," a weekly journal run in the interest of the mine-owners, and published at Wardner, by a Mr. Brown.

Everything pointed to these union secrets having leaked out of the Gem union. Therefore, Dallas, a one-eyed, two-legged, Irish hyena from the Butte City, Montana union, was sent to Gem to discover the spy and traitor within their ranks.

After Dallas had been in Gem a few days doing secret work, a special meeting of our Gem union was called. On that day a rank union man by the name of Johnny Murphy confided in me and told me that I was suspected of being the traitor who supplied the mine owners with the secrets of the union, as I had access to the books and made too many trips to Wallace to mail letters; that I had been watched mailing letters in Wallace often. He said that he felt confident that I was not a detective, but for my personal safety he advised me to skip out and not attend this special union meeting, as the chances were I would be killed. He said that h——l was going to be turned loose within the next few days or weeks, and that I would not be safe in the district, even though innocent.

I assured him that I was innocent and that I would be a true soldier by sticking to my guns.

That night the large union hall was packed, as it was known that Dallas would attempt to show up the spy who had given out the union secrets.

When the meeting was called to order by the President of the Gem union, a Mr. Oliver Hughes, I sat by his side upon the raised platform, or stage. With us on the stage were Pettibone, Eaton, of the Central Union, and Dallas, the Secretary of the Butte City, Montana union.

After I had read the minutes of the last meeting from my book as recording secretary, Dallas got up to make his speech. A pin could have been heard drop, everything was so still.

He started out with a shot at me, as he glanced in my direction. He said: "Brothers, you have allowed a spy to enter your ranks, and he now sits within reach of my hand. He will never leave this hall alive. His fate is doomed. You know your duty when it comes to dealing with traitors to our noble cause for the upbuilding of true manhood." Here the applause broke loose and I joined in. I clapped until the palms of my hands were sore, despite the fact that I felt a little shaky as to what lay in store for me.

In a "Wess Harding" shoulder-scabbard under my left arm, rested old Colts 45, and around my waist underneath my pants was strapped my pearl-handle bowie knife. My mind was made up to start business at the first approach of real danger. Of course I didn't expect to last long among those hundreds of strong men, many of whom were armed, but I figured that they couldn't get but one of me, while I stood a chance to kill several of them. I would have been like a cat thrown into a fiery furnace—spit fire so long as life held out.

After Dallas wound up his long fiery speech, which I must confess was delivered in a masterful manner, a

10

recess of ten minutes was announced. The president then asked me to step down off the stage while they examined my book. I did so. As these officials turned each leaf of the large book over, my eyes were on them. Finally they came to something wrong, and Dallas looked down at me, with a look of, "Oh we've got you now." I stepped up near the platform and said: "What's the matter gentlemen, you seem to be puzzled?" Dallas replied in an angry voice: "Here's a leaf cut out of this book. We want an explanation." I answered that the president, Mr. Oliver Hughes had ordered me to cut that leaf out. The president jumped up with an oath and said it was a lie. I then referred him to the time when the members of the Burk union came down to hold a joint meeting with us, at which time it was voted on and decided to pull up the pumps of the Poorman and Tiger mines at Burk, and flood the lower workings of these deep properties; that I wrote down the full facts of our resolution and read it at the following meeting; my duty requiring me to read the minutes of the previous meeting; and that then he (the president) ordered me to cut out this leaf and burn it, as nothing of that kind should be put in the minutes to be on record, in case the book fell into the hands of the enemy.

The president then acknowledged the fact, and Dallas smothered the wrath which he had been accumulating for the explosion to follow.

Instead of burning the leaf, I had sent it to St. Paul along with my reports.

Finally I got back on the stage when the meeting was again called to order, after my book had been carefully gone through.

The president then made a conservative speech and advised that nothing be done to-night that might bring discredit on the union. He said the time would soon be here when we could act. Of course I helped cheer, and it came from my heart this time, as I could see daylight ahead. The meeting was then adjourned.

I have no doubt but that Dallas and his gang thought that I would show my guilt during and after his blood-curdling speech, and that during the ten minutes' recess I would make some kind of an excuse to the outer guard at the door so as to get out. But I was too "foxy" to make a break like that. Neither did I show guilt in my actions or looks. I had learned to control my looks while playing poker in cow-camps on the range, so my opponents couldn't guess the value of my hand by the looks of my face.

A couple of days after the above occurrence, Mrs. Shipley called my attention to a man sitting on a box in front of the postoffice, and informed me that she had noticed him following me. Looking through the store window, I recognized Tim W's chum, "Black Jack" from Tuscarora, Nevada. He had helped in the blowing up of Prinz and Pelling and we had heard that he skipped out to Africa. Later I caught him watching me, but didn't pretend to notice it. Whether he had really recognized me or was trying to place me, I never knew; but as I later found out that he was a member of the Miners' Union, I concluded that he had recognized and given me away to the union, for the chances are by this time he knew my business.

I had bought a two-story building in the center of

town, and in the store part, Mrs. Kate Shipley and I started a small store. Upstairs there were 12 furnished rooms and I gave Mrs. Shipley half the income from these to run the place. She roomed back of the store with her little five-year-old boy, while my room was upstairs.

Mrs. Shipley, whose husband was on their farm in Dakota, had no idea that I was a detective.

To keep prowlers out of our back yard, I built a high board-fence and made it tight so as to shut out the public gaze. As a precaution in case of trouble, I left the bottom of one wide board loose so that I could crawl out instead of going over the fence.

At our next regular meeting night of the union, early in the evening, Billy Flynn, a brother-in-law to John Day, with whom I had previously roomed, called me off to myself. He was pretty drunk. He began crying and said he hated to go back on union principles by warning a spy and traitor of danger, but said he always liked me and he couldn't believe that I was a Dickenson detective. Of course I assured him that I was not. Then he shook my hand and said I didn't look degraded enough for a detective who would take a false oath by entering a union in order to give away their secrets. I asked Flynn to tell me all the facts as to why I was suspected of being a detective. He replied that he couldn't do that as he was sworn to secrecy; but said that some one who knew that I was a detective, had recognized me. He further said that I was doomed to die the death of a traitor, and he advised that I skip out and not attend the union meeting that night.

Dallas was still in town, and I saw him with "Black Jack" who no doubt had given me away to the union.

The day had been one of excitement. Many "scabs" had been caught and nearly beat to death. "Scabs" were fed at the mines and seldom ventured away from their quarters, but when they did, they were caught and pounded nearly to death.

Early in the day John A. French had come to Gem, and was almost mobbed by Joe Poynton and a gang. He was glad to get back to Wallace with a whole hide.

The time for me, as recording secretary, to be in the union hall had passed, the hour being 8 P. M. About 8:30 P. M. a committee of three came to my room to see what was the matter that I didn't attend the meeting.

In my room I kept a Winchester rifle and 100 cartridges, secreted under the mattress of my bed, and I had made up my mind to stay close to these. I told the committee to go back and I would be at the hall in 10 minutes. When they had gone I wrote out my resignation as recording secretary and as a member of the Miners' Union. In it I told of them planning to knife me in the dark under the false impression that I was a Dickenson detective, one of the lowest and most degrading professions that mortal man could follow, and to be accused of such a black crime behind my back was more than I could stand, and for that reason I would never put foot in their union hall again. I gave this resignation to the door-keeper at the union hall about half a block from my place, and then returned to our store.

After the union meeting had adjourned, the hall was thrown open for a public dance. Men kept pouring in from outlying camps.

While I was standing in the dark in front of the union hall watching the dancers through the window, a leading member of the Mullen union who had just arrived in town, recognized me and we had a confidential talk on union matters. Of course he hadn't yet heard of my downfall in the union. He supposed that I knew all the secrets of coming events and therefore it was easy for me to lead him on. From him I found out that blood would flow here within the next few days; that it would amount to a regular uprising against "scabs" and the mine owners. He said the Homestead, Pa., riots of a few days previous would be child's play as compared to our approaching storm. He thought it was billed to come off the following night, but wasn't sure, as the executive committee of the Central Union had not given out the exact date. But he said the outside unions had already been ordered to concentrate their forces and arms in Gem, which would be the center of action.

About 11:30 P. M. a member of an outside union, who had not learned of my being branded as a traitor, told me that two "scabs" from the Gem mine were to be murdered and thrown into the river just as soon as the lights in the union hall were put out, after the dance, which would only last until midnight. He said that these two "scabs" had slipped over from the Gem mine to get a drink, and that a gang of union men had them at Dutch Henry's saloon getting them drunk so as to kill them.

A few minutes before midnight I entered Dutch Henry's saloon in hopes of getting a chance to warn these two "scabs" of their approaching danger. They were surrounded by a dozen union men who were patting them on the back and making them think they were fine fellows. One of them was a giant in size and said he could whip any union man in Gem.

While I was seated in the saloon watching for a chance to warn these "scabs," I saw a crowd collecting outside in front of the saloon. I could see through the front window that they were watching me. It only lacked ten minutes of midnight.

Just then the front door opened and old Shoemaker Roberson walked up to me and said: "Say Allison, you had better duck your nut out of here, and do it quick." I told him that I would leave when I got good and ready. He then went out and joined the crowd outside. I stepped up to the bar and drank a glass of beer, then went out at the front door.

On reaching the sidewalk the crowd, led by a hair-lip son of the scum of society, called "Johnny get your gun," started to enclose me in a circle. I sprang out into the street and with my hand on my cocked pistol, threatened to kill the first man who undertook to pull a gun. In this manner I backed across the street to the hallway leading up to my room. As I entered the hall-way still facing the 25 or 30 men, "Johnny get your gun" said: "Oh, you d——d traitor, we'll get you before morning." At this the crowd split and ran around my building to prevent me from escaping. A few moments later, through a rear upstairs window I saw men with rifles guarding the rear of my high board fence: I could also see three men with rifles on the bridge spanning the river towards the Gem mine.

There were no back stairs to my building, but the window to my room opened out in a narrow alleyway between my building and Jerry Nelson's Hotel, and here I had placed an old ladder just for such an emergency as this.

With my Winchester rifle and pockets full of ammunition, I crawled down this ladder and thence to the board previously left loose at the bottom. A light shove displaced the fence board, and on my hands and knees I crawled out by the side of a large fallen tree. The board being put back in place, I was now in a timbered swamp near the bank of Canyon Creek. The night was dark, and by crawling between logs and in brush, I reached the river, which was waded in a dark place under overhanging trees. Then to prevent being seen by the guards on the bridge, I had to crawl on my stomach, inch by inch, for quite a distance. On reaching a place where it was safe to stand up, I ran to the Gem mine, a few hundred yards distant. I found John Monihan, the superintendent, up and expecting trouble on account of the town filling up with union men, and guards being placed on the bridge. I informed him that two of his men were to be murdered in Dutch Henry's saloon.

While we and some of the Thiel guards were figuring on the best way to rescue those men, the town constable under the Justice of the Peace, Geo. A. Pettibone, came over to tell Mr. Monihan that two of his men had been "slugged" and one of them was about dead, and that the badly wounded one had been dragged to the deadline at the bridge near where the company's office was located. Monihan and some of the guards returned with the constable to get the wounded man. This was the big fellow who had been drinking in Dutch Henry's saloon, and he was barely alive. He was beaten almost into a jelly, his jaw and several ribs being broken. In fact, he had lost all resemblance to a human being, except in shape. His face was one mass of bruised and bloody flesh.

Monihan called for volunteers to walk down to Wallace four miles, after the doctor, but only one of the Thiel guards would consent to risk his life, as it was feared the road to Wallace was guarded by union men, and this guard refused to go alone.

Rather than see this fellow die without the care of a doctor, I accompanied the Thiel guard. We arrived in Wallace, walking on the railroad grade, without mishap. Dr. Simms was awakened and went back with the guard. By that time it was about 3:30 A. M.

I then went to report matters to the Secretary of the Mine-Owners' Association, John A. French. Mr. French was himself a millionaire, owning many mines and steamships on the Pacific coast. I found him in bed and told him to prepare for riots within the next couple of days. He begged me to leave the country and not return to Gem, when I told him the facts; but I told him that I had enlisted for the war and would stay and see the finish. I figured that a good sailor never gives up his ship until she is going down.

I went to a saloon and held the Winchester rifle in my hand until daylight, at which time the morning train went to Gem and Burk, the latter place being the end of that branch line.

On the train I found Geo. A. Pettibone who had gone
to Wardner in the night. He had with him a delegation
of union leaders from Wardner and a Catholic priest.
I never knew what the priest was doing in such company.

Pettibone asked what I was doing with a rifle. I told
him that his union scalawags had made a raid on me
during the night, and that I was going back to kill the
first one who interfered with me. He tried to bulldoze
me from carrying a rifle into Gem. He said it wouldn't
be allowed; but it was allowed, as I marched through the
large crowd who came to the train to greet the priest
and union delegation.

Shortly after my arrival, Bill Black, a desperado who
had just recovered from a bullet wound through the
stomach, was sent to me to find out my intentions. He
asked if I intended to remain in Gem that night. I said
yes, that I would stay there until carried out a corpse.
This seemed to satisfy him. When he left he went direct
to the union hall to report to the meeting then in session.

The chances are they thought a raid on me then would
spoil their plans, so concluded, as I didn't intend to leave,
to not disturb me until the general uprising started.

I remained in our store, or in Mrs. Shipley's bedroom
back of the store, most of the time.

Mrs. Shipley would visit neighbor women and report
the news to me. It was said the uprising would start
just before daylight.

The whole day had been spent drilling men under
captains in the union hall. By dark the town was jammed
full of union men from all over the district. There were
over 1,000 present.

Mrs. Shipley had found out that a strong guard was placed all around the town at dark to prevent any one from leaving Gem. I suppose this was partly for my benefit.

About 8 P. M. I concluded to "take a sneak"; so I went down the old ladder out of my bedroom window, thence over the same route taken the night before. I crawled within 30 feet of three union guards.

I reported to Mr. Monihan that the riot was to start before daylight. He then armed his 120 "scab" miners, and guards were put out. Until daylight, a tall fellow known as "Death on the Trail" and I did scout duty, both sticking close together. No one slept that night to speak of.

When daylight came I concluded to beard the lion in his den and find out the latest news from Mrs. Shipley. Putting the rifle under my raincoat and holding it by my left side so it couldn't be seen, I walked right by the three union guards on the bridge. We didn't speak. I entered the rear door of the Nelson Hotel. In the kitchen I found the two cooks and a waitress, Miss Olson, but I only bowed to them. I raised the kitchen window and jumped through it into the narrow alley where my old ladder stood. I found Mrs. Shipley in bed. She reported that all night the union men were drilling in the union hall. I then went into the store and through a side door into the hallway and thence upstairs. A window to a vacant front room was raised so that I could look up and down the main street. There were only a few armed men doing guard duty in front of my place. Two men with rifles stood directly under me. An awning prevented them from seeing me, though I could see them through the crack between the awning and the wall.

About this time the long-nose clerk, Jim Ervin, in White & Benders' store, a few doors below, stuck his head out of the window to see what was going on. One of these union men, a big blacksmith, raised his rifle and said to his companion, Tom Whalen: "Watch me knock that ——— nose off." He fired and as I learned later, the bullet just missed the clerk's nose by a scratch. It being 6 A. M. this no doubt was intended as the signal shot, as shooting became general up the canyon towards the Frisco mill, where armed guards and "scab" miners were housed.

I concluded it was time for me to emigrate, so I hurried down my ladder and through the window into the kitchen of the Nelson Hotel. Then I opened the back door to make a break for the bridge to fight my way past the three guards there. Just as I opened the door, the French cook grabbed me by the arm and jerked me back. I raised the rifle to strike him, but he threw up his hands and said: "For Christ's sake, don't go out there. They are laying for you. There are 50 men with Winchester rifles right around the corner of the house. I saw them just now when I went after wood."

I had thrown the door wide open, and it still remained so.

From the end of the bridge across a swamp to this kitchen door, there was a board walk, and on it, coming towards us, was a lone man in his shirt sleeves, and un-armed. I recognized him as one of the Thiel guards at the Gem mine. He was about 50 yards from the kitchen door then. I said to the two cooks: "I'll wait and see what they say to that guard." We all three had our eyes on him when a voice around the corner said: "Go back you ———!" He stopped suddenly and threw up his hands. Just then a shot was fired and the poor fellow fell over dead, with a bullet through his heart. His name was Ivory Bean, and he was an honored member of the K. P. lodge. He had volunteered to come over to the drug store after some medicine for the big fellow who was wounded two nights before. He was supposed to be dying, and to relieve his suffering, Bean risked his life. He argued that the union miners surely wouldn't harm him on an errand of mercy if he went in his shirt sleeves to show that he carried no fire-arms. The poor fellow hadn't reckoned on the class of curs that he was dealing with.

This convinced me that I was "up against the real thing," so shutting the door and thanking the cook for saving my life, I crawled back through the window. Just as I did so, Miss Olson came into the kitchen.

After Bean fell, the men at the Gem mine began to pepper the town of Gem with rifle-bullets. A big part of their shooting was at the rear of Daxon's saloon— that being a union hang-out; but the men in there soon found the cellar. Billy Daxon had his clothes shot full of holes. A union man was killed by this shooting. The firing was still going on at the Frisco Mill. They were burning powder up there in a reckless, extravagant manner. I concluded that "war is hell," sure enough, and that I was right in the midst of it without a way to get out.

I had Mrs. Shipley keep the store door locked, and told her to not let any one in. I then went out in the back yard to see if the coast was clear in the vicinity of my hole in the fence. I looked through a crack in the fence and discovered two armed men hiding behind a big log. I then went into a storeroom adjoining the fence on the east, and through a crack saw my friend Dallas walking a beat with a shotgun on his shoulder. He was evidently guarding a rat in a trap, and I happened to be that rat.

In this storeroom I discarded my hat and coat and in their place put on an old leather jacket and a black slouch hat. Then I got a saw and went into Mrs. Shipley's room, and next to the store wall, tore up a square of carpet and began sawing a hole through the floor. I sawed out a place just large enough to admit my body. This done, I replaced the carpet in nice shape, loosely, over the hole.

At first I had planned a scheme to barricade the head of the stairs with furniture and bedding and then slaughter all who undertook to come up the stairs. Had I carried out this plan, the newspapers would have had some real live news to record; but I hated to wait upstairs for business to come my way, hence made up my mind to go under the floor and do some skirmishing, which would at least keep my mind occupied.

The back part of my store building rested flat on the ground, and the front part was up on piles three feet high.

Finally I bade Mrs. Shipley and her little five-year-old goodbye, and dropped out of sight. Then Mrs. Shipley pulled her trunk over the hole as per my instructions.

In scouting around under the house, I could find no possible way to get out, except up under the board sidewalk on the main street. Through a crack the width of my hand, on the east side, I saw Dallas resting on his beat. He was leaning on his shot-gun. I up with my rifle and took aim at his heart, but before pulling the trigger, the thought of the danger from the smoke going up through the cracks and giving my hiding place away, flashed through my mind, and the rifle was taken from my shoulder.

Just then an explosion took place which shook the earth. It was up towards the Frisco Mill. The rifle shooting was still going on, but it soon ceased.

In about 20 minutes Mrs. Shipley pulled the trunk from the hole, and putting her head down in it, cried: "Oh, Mr. Allison, run for your life. They have just blown up the Frisco Mill and killed lots of men and now they're coming after you to burn you at the stake, so as to make an example of Dickenson detectives." Crawling nearer to the hole I asked Mrs. Shipley how she had found this out. She replied that Mrs. Weiss, a strong union woman, who was a friend of mine while I was in the union, had just told her when she went across the street to find out the cause of the explosion. I told Mrs. Shipley to keep cool and put the trunk back over the hole. It was explained to her that I could find no way to get out, hence must stay.

Soon I could hear the yelling of more than 1,000 throats as they came to get me. It wasn't long until the street was jammed with angry men. I was directly under the center of our store and could hear the leaders commanding Mrs. Shipley to open the door, but she refused to do it. Then they broke it down and the mob rushed in. I could hear Dallas' voice demanding that she tell where I was, but she denied having seen me since the night before. He told her that they knew better, as Miss Olsen had seen me crawl through the window, since which time a heavy guard had been kept around the house. I heard Mrs. Shipley ask why they wanted me. Then Dallas replied: "He's a dirty Dickenson detective and we intend to burn him at a stake as a warning to others of his kind." Mrs. Shipley asked why they didn't kill me yesterday when they had a good chance. To this Dallas replied: "The time wasn't ripe yesterday, but it is now and we will find him, so you might as well tell us or it will go hard with you." Mrs. Shipley then told them to do their worst, as she didn't know where I was. I felt like patting the lady on the back, as one out of 10,000 who wouldn't weaken and tell the secret with that vicious mob around her. I feared the child would tell, as he was bawling as though his little five-year-old heart would break.

Now I could hear "We'll find the ———. He's in this house," etc. Then a rush was made into Mrs. Shipley's bedroom and out into the back yard and also upstairs. I couldn't help but think of what a fine chance I was missing for making a world's record as a man-killer; for had I carried out my first plan, this was the moment as the rush was being made upstairs, when there would have been "something doing."

As I feared they might find the hole in the floor and then set fire to the building, I concluded to get out of there, even though I had to fight my way out.

The only opening was under the sidewalk, which was about a foot above the ground. I had no idea where it would lead me, but I thought of the old saying, "Nothing risked, nothing gained."

Finally I started east, towards the Miners' Union hall. The store buildings were built close together, except at my building where there was a narrow alleyway leading to the rear. It was in this narrow passage where Dallas had his policeman's beat that morning. I had to crawl on my stomach, "all same" snake in the grass; but I had to move very slowly as I was afraid of being seen by the angry men who lined the sidewalk as thick as they could stand. Some of the cracks in the sidewalk were an inch or more wide. After going the width of two store buildings, I stopped to rest, and while doing so, I lay on my back so as to look up through a wide crack. I could see the men's eyes and hear what they said. Most of their talk was about the "scabs" killed when they blew up the Frisco Mill with giant powder. Finally one big Irishman with a brogue as broad as the Atlantic Ocean, said: "Faith and why don't they bring that spalpeen out. I'm wanting to spit in his face, the dirty thraitor. We Emericans have got to shtand on our rights and show the worreld that we can fight." Of course I could have told this good "Emerican" citizen the reason for the delay in bringing me out to be burnt at a stake; and I could also have told him that he was then missing a good opportunity of spitting in my face, while alive, for my mind had been made up not to be taken until dead.

This was a hint for me to be moving, knowing that I was exploring new territory.

11

Another twenty-five feet brought me in front of a saloon, and here I found an opening to get under the building, which was built on piles and stood about four feet from the ground. In the rear I could see daylight. At this my heart leaped with joy. The ground was covered with slush and mud and there were all kinds of tree-tops, stumps and brush under this building.

In hurrying through this brush, my watch-chain caught and tore loose. On it was a charm, a $3 gold piece with my initials C. L. A. I hated to lose this, so stopped to consider as to whether I should go back to hunt it. While studying, I wondered if I was scared. I had to smile at the thought, so I concluded to test the matter by spitting; but bless you, my mouth was so dry I couldn't spit anything but cotton, or what looked like cotton. I decided that it was a case of scared with a big S. I had always heard that when a person is badly frightened he can't spit; but this was the first time I ever saw it tested.

A week or so later I bought the watch-chain and charm from a boy who had found it while the union had "kids" searching for me under these buildings on the day of the riot. When the chain was found, I suppose they figured that the bird had flown, all but this relic of his breast-feathers.

On reaching the rear of the saloon, I found plenty of room to get out in the open, but before making the break, I examined my rifle and pistol to see that they were in working order.

All ready, I sprung from under the house and stood once more in glorious sunshine. The Winchester was up, ready for action. Only three men were in sight and

their backs were towards me.   They stood at the corner of the saloon building, looking up a vacant space towards the main street.   They had evidently been placed
behind these buildings to watch for me, but in their
eagerness to be at the burning, they were watching the
crowd in the street, knowing that the movements of the
mob would indicate when the "fatted calf" was ready,
for the slaughter.   My first impulse was to start shooting
and kill these three men, but my finer feeling got the
best of me.   It would be too much like taking advantage
and committing cold-blooded murder.

I glanced straight south.   There, in front of me, about
fifty yards distant, was the high railroad grade which
shut off the view from the Gem mill where I knew my
friends awaited me.   But to undertake to scale this high
grade I would be placing myself between two fires, for the
chances were, my friends would take me for an enemy
and start shooting.

Quicker than a flash the thought struck me to fool
these three men and make them think I was going up
to the top of the grade to get a shot at the "scabs."

A little to the left there was a swift stream of water
flowing through a culvert under the railroad grade, and
to avoid being shot by my friends I concluded to go
through this and sink or swim.

I started in a slow run, half stooped like a hunter
slipping upon game, as though intending to crawl up on
the grade and get a shot at the enemy, my course being
a few feet to the right of the boxed culvert.   I didn't
look back, as I knew my footsteps would attract the
attention of the three men, and I didn't want them to see

my face or to note that my movements were suspicious.
When within a few feet of the rushing water, I made
a quick turn to the left and into the culvert. Just then
one bullet whizzed past my head. This was the only shot
fired. It was all I could do to stem the force of the
water, which reached to my arm-pits. The Winchester
was now in my left hand while my right extended forward holding on to the upright timber on the west wall
of the culvert. After I had worked my way far enough
into this culvert so that I was in the dark and out of sight
of my enemy, I braced myself against an upright timber
and turned around to look back. There in plain view,
were three drunken Swedes trying to see me so as to
get another shot. Now I held the winning hand, and
raised my rifle to take advantage of my opportunity;
but my heart failed me at the thought of murdering a
drunken Swede, for I had found them to be a hard-work-
ing lot of sheep who were always ready to follow heartless Irish leaders. I also thought of the danger of shooting, as the flash from my rifle would indicate my whereabouts and shots might be fired in that direction. Although from the way these Swedes or Finlanders were
staggering around, I didn't think they could shoot very
straight. I began to work my way to daylight on the
other side, a distance of about fifty feet. I would reach
ahead and get hold of an upright timber and then pull
myself forward against the raging torrent. I finally
emerged from the culvert and found myself under a
Swede's house, which was built over the opposite end of
this culvert, with the entrance to the house fronting on
the railroad track. On walking from under the house,

which was built on piles, a Swede woman at her back door recognized me. She called me by name and asked what I had been doing under her house. Her husband had been one of my best union friends. I told her that I was just prowling around a little for exercise. She laughed.

Now I had to march across a 200-yard open space to reach the Gem mill and I had to take chances of being shot at by both sides.

On reaching the "scab" forts—high ricks of cordwood with port holes—I was halted by a voice behind the woodpile which said: "Drop that gun you —— and walk up here with your hands up." I replied that I was a friend. He answered: "It don't make a d——d bit of difference; if you don't drop that gun your head goes off." I dropped it, and with both hands raised, I walked up to the port hole which was made by a stick of the wood being pulled out. The fellow then told me to pull off my hat so he could see my face. I did so, and he said: "Are you that detective who came to our camp last night?" I replied yes. Then he told me to hurry and get behind the fort before the union —— took a shot at me. It was a relief to get behind the fort and shake hands with the Thiel guards there.

From here I went to the concentrator, or mill, where I found Superintendent John Monihan and a crowd, among them being Fred Carter, a wild and woolly cowboy who had been in the Frisco Mill blow-up and had run the gauntlet through a shower of bullets to reach this haven of safety. One bullet had torn the heel off one boot and crippled his heel, and another knocked one knuckle off his right hand. I afterwards saw the bullet-marks in the railroad ties where this fellow ran along the railroad track. No doubt 50 to 100 shots had been fired at him. He was the only man who escaped. The others who were not killed or wounded were taken prisoners.

This fellow Carter, had brought in bunches of "scabs" and I saw his courage tested on several occasions. He was not afraid of man nor the devil, when he had half a chance.

Shortly after my arrival at the Gem mine, a union man under a flag of truce, in the shape of a white rag, came to tell Monihan that if he didn't surrender in a given time the Gem Mill would suffer the same fate as the Frisco Mill by being blown up. Monihan refused to surrender, and the fellow went back.

Soon we could see squads of men going around over the mountains back of the mill towards the main tunnel of the mine, up the side of the heavily timbered mountain, from whence a tramway was run to conduct the ore into the mill. Monihan and I decided that they intended to capture the mine-tunnel and then turn a tramway car loaded with dynamite and a burning fuse, down the side of the mountain into the mill. This had been done, so Fred Carter told us, at the Frisco Mill, but they failed to make the fuse long enough and the charge went off before reaching the mill, and as to how the Frisco Mill was finally blown up, was then a mystery to Carter.

In order to offset a scheme of this kind, I suggested to Monihan that I go with some men half way up the tramway and there tie some heavy poles across the rails in order to ditch a car if sent down. A couple of men were sent with me. On reaching the station over the mill I discovered that one of the men supposed to be guarding this part of the works was a union spy, and I so reported to Monihan later. Though I didn't know it for a fact, I felt confident of it. About twelve years later the fellow confessed it to me. His name was Oscar W.

After tying the poles across the track, we continued on to the tunnel, being exposed to union bullets, as we could be seen from town.

At the tunnel I found among our guards, a rank union man who had been a shift-boss. I knew this fellow's record in the union. He acted sheepish as though he knew that I would tell Monihan of his past record, which I did.

Shortly after my return to the mill, Monihan received orders through Ed. Kinney, French and Campbell's confidential secretary, to surrender to the union in order to save their valuable mill from being blown up. Ed. Kinney who had been passing back and forth under a flag of truce, had received this message over the wires. Monihan asked my advice. I told him it was a bad mistake, as it placed the lives of all his men and himself at the mercy of a lot of cut-throats. He agreed that I was right, but said in the face of his orders he would have to surrender. I told him that I would never surrender alive, and that I would fight it out alone.

A young man by the name of Frank Stark, who had come in as a guard with Joe Warren and the first batch of non-union men, asked me if he couldn't stay with

me. He said he didn't care to risk his life by surrender-
ing. As he had an honest face and seemed to be made
of good material, I consented.

We then bade Monihan farewell and slipped through
the heavy timber and brush up a side canyon towards
the top of the mountain to the southwest. We knew
that the union had armed guards all around us, as they
could be seen moving to and fro. On reaching a secluded
spot on the side of the mountain from whence could be
seen Gem and the union miners, we waited to see the
surrender. Monihan and his 120 to 130 men marched
to the depot platform and surrendered their arms to the
union officials. Then we could hear loud cheering by the
unionists. Finally all the prisoners were lined up in
rows and a committee seemed to be examining them. I
afterwards learned that it was Dallas and his gang
searching for me; that after they had looked at the face
of each man Dallas remarked: "The —— must have gone
over the hill." Then I heard men were sent to guard
the approaches into Wallace.

While sitting here resting, I realized for the first time
that I was hungry, for all I had eaten since supper the
night before, was a sandwich and cup of coffee which
Mrs. Shipley had put down into the hole for me, and it
was in the middle of the afternoon now.

On reaching the top of the mountain range, we discovered three armed men standing in our trail, a footpath over the mountain. They were on the summit of
the mountain and we dare not go below them to get past,
for we could be seen. Here I got my 2 by 4 brain to
working and soon studied up a scheme that might work

without having to kill them. I laid my plan before Stark and he agreed to follow my instructions, which were as follows: To crawl just as near as possible to the men and then both take aim at separate ones. Then I was to say in a voice loud enough to be heard by them: "Now you shoot the —— on the right and I'll kill the one on the left," and then if they raised their guns to fight, we were to shoot and fight it out to a finish.

It worked like a charm, and we could hear the brush cracking where they were falling and rolling down the steep gulch to the right. We laughed until our sides hurt.

That night, just after dark, we reached the wagon road half a mile above Wallace. It was a relief to get in a smooth road after traveling so long through brush and fallen timber. We had traveled about ten miles the way we had come, and were worn out.

Just before reaching a high rocky point on the bank of the river, a few hundred yards above the depot, on the edge of Wallace, we discovered four men with rifles guarding the road, two being on one side and two on the other, about fifty feet apart. No doubt these men were guards sent to watch for me. Now it was a case of going miles around through the hills or to risk a fight with these four men. Stark agreed to leave the matter to my judgment. I decided to fight rather than quit the road, but I told Stark not to shoot until I said fire. He was to take charge of the two on the left of the road while I took care of the other two. They didn't see us until we were within fifty feet of them. We kept the middle of the road, I watching my men, and Stark his. After passing them we kept watch over our shoulders. They hadn't spoken or moved until we got passed them. Then my two ran over to the other two. We were soon around the high rocky point in the glare of the electric lights at the depot. Here it was as light as day, and I saw we were in a bad place.

I jumped down the bank and into the swift stream, Stark following. The water struck us about the waist and the stream was about forty feet wide. Reaching a dark place in the timber on the opposite bank we sat down to await results. But we didn't have a minute to wait, as the four men came running around the bluff. When they reached the full electric lighted space to the depot a few hundred yards distant, and didn't see us, they were puzzled. It was comical to see their maneuvers. Their actions showed that they never suspected the truth. Their whole minds seemed to be centered on the high cliff to the right of the road, as though we had hid in some crevice. They knew we didn't have time to have reached the depot, the first building. In a few minutes three of them started back to their post while the other ran as hard as he could to town. We then hurried through the timber to the rear of the Carter Hotel, which had been the stopping place for mine owners. Stark was secreted in a dark place to shoot whoever undertook to harm me.

I knocked on the rear door and the porter came out. I asked who of the mine owners were there. He replied that all the mine owners but Mr. Goss had "flew the coop" on a special train, but that Mr. Monihan and Mr. Goss a millionaire mine owner, from Wisconsin, who owned a big share of the Morning mine at Mullen, were upstairs in their rooms. I told him to tell them that Allison wanted to see them at the head of the back stairs. Soon both appeared greatly excited. They begged me to skip out and get away from the hotel as they would be murdered if I were found there. They said the union men were scouring the country for me. Here I shook hands and bade them goodbye.

We then "sneaked" into French and, Campbell's private quarters where I knew Ed. Kinney and young Harry Allen, the bookkeeper, slept. Both were there and tickled to see us, but they feared the union had guards watching the place and might have seen us come in through the rear gate. So for that reason, we concluded not to waste any time telling funny stories; but we remained long enough to fill up on sardines and crackers and to put on dry underclothes. Then we struck out up a side canyon towards the southwest for "tall timber," there to await future results.

Thus the first act in the great Coeur D'Alene miners' strike of 1892 ends.

CHAPTER VIII

United States Troops Fill the "Bull-Pen" with
Miners' Union Dynamiters—My Evidence Convicts Eighteen of the Union Leaders.

On reaching a place of safety on the heavily timbered mountain side about three miles from Wallace, Stark and I lay down to sleep on the ground, using the sky to cover us.

Towards noon the next day we found the cabin of a sourkrout dutchman whom I knew as a friend to the mine owners. Though a member of the union, he was opposed to the way the Miners' unions were conducted; therefore I concluded to risk entering his cabin in order to get something to eat. We found the kind-hearted fellow at home alone, and he was fearful lest the union find out that he had fed us. He knew me as secretary of the Gem union, and had heard through his Irish partner that I had turned out to be a "traitor."

This Irishman partner was a rank union man and had gone to take part in the riot at Gem, and now he was expected back any moment, so for that reason, we were put in a stone cabin nearby and given a key so as to lock ourselves in, while waiting for "Dutchy" to cook us something to eat.

Soon after the steaming coffee and food were set before us in our hiding place, the dynamiter partner returned with glowing accounts of the murdering of

172

"scabs," etc. He was worn out from his long siege and after filling up, was soon asleep. Then our German friend came to tell us to keep quiet for awhile, as his partner was going back to Wallace when he finished his nap. Stark and I then took a nap ourselves, as we knew no one could get at us without waking us up. Still, mine were cat-naps, as I feared that "Dutchy" and "Micky" might conspire to blow us into kingdom-come with giant powder, or else warn the union of our presence there.

Late in the evening "Micky" went back to Wallace to help uphold the principles of his noble union, and then Stark and I with a supply of grub and an old coffee pot, struck out again for "tall timber."

This time we climbed the mountain side for a mile, east. Here in a secluded spot in the heavy timber and underbrush, we built an Indian "wickiup" to shelter us from the rain which was falling, and that night we slept the sleep of the just.

Next morning we tramped north nearly to the edge of Wallace, secreting ourselves on the top of a round mountain overlooking the town. Here we had a free show which couldn't be beat for money. It was grand, viewed from a distance; especially one of the last acts wherein a tall lanky pilgrim was the "fall guy," though he didn't take time to fall. He just hit the high places, twenty feet to the jump.

It was the unions' grand day of reckoning with all "scabs," and business men who had opposed union principles in the past. They were gathered up in small droves and taken to the railroad yards and there told to "hit the road" for Spokane, Wash., about seventy-five miles distant; and to give them a good start, the union men would fire over their heads. In running, some would fall and turn somersaults, but not so with the lanky individual with the stove-pipe hat and valise. At the first mile-post this tall man was leading the herd by at least 200 yards, and besides, he was handicapped with a big valise.

At the funny things which happened during the day, Stark and I split our sides laughing.

Late in the afternoon the union men captured a railroad train, and in a body, went to bury their dead.

Some union Knights of Pythias wanted to bury Ivory Bean, the man whom I saw shot through the heart, under the rules of the order, but the union wouldn't allow it. He had to be buried as a "scab," so far as the unions were concerned. This we heard later.

That night Stark and I slept in our "wickiup" again.

Next morning we returned to our lookout mountain, and late in the evening saw train-loads of United States soldiers and State militia arrive from the State of Washington. It was indeed a grand sight to me, and for the first time in my life did I realize the value of our troops.

When the large American flag was planted near the Carter hotel my heart broke loose from its mooring, where it had been hitched under the Confederate flag of my babyhood. Stark and I gave three cheers for the Star Spangled Banner of our united country, and deep down in my heart I made a vow to die and bleed, if necessary, to uphold the honor of this flag.

Throwing a kiss of farewell back at our "wickiup" and coffee pot, we started on a run down the mountain-side for the Carter hotel. Arriving within a quarter of a mile of the hotel and soldiers' camp, on the outskirts of the heavy timber, I concluded to do a little detective work at the home of French Pete, a rank union man who had built a fine home on the hill, south of the Carter hotel. Pete had married an Irish mother-in-law, and it was on this old Irish woman that I got in my fine work.

I had cached Stark, with his rifle across a log, ready to shoot, while I went to French Pete's home to learn the news and to get all the information possible about union matters. The Irish mother-in-law and her young son-in-law greeted me in the yard. I gave an assumed name, and wondered what we Miners' union men would do now that the dirty cut-throat soldiers had arrived. I won the old lady's heart, and she slobbered over me as a poor tired union miner who had fought a noble cause.

I asked if there was any danger of President O'Brien and the officers of the Central union being arrested by the soldiers. She replied no, that they would never find them as they were hiding in her (Mrs. Hollihan's) cellar down town. Here the old lady went into the house and got the late daily Spokane Review, and Spokesman, for me. I then went out to my supposed union friend behind the log and she and her son-in-law followed. There I read the big head-lines aloud. They told of the riot and the blowing up of the Frisco mill and the killing of · "scabs" and the capture of John Monihan and his 130 or more armed men, and how the next day they were marched in a body to the Wallace bank to draw their wages and savings, and then with all their cash, they were taken on a train to the head of the Coeur D'Alene lake at which point they had to board a steamer for the other side of the lake; and that while waiting for the steamer at the Mission about dusk, they were fired into by the union men and many shot and robbed of their money; John Monihan being among the missing; also that a trainload of United States troops had been sent on the first day of the riot from Missoula, Mont., but that the union men of Butte City and the Coeur D'Alene blew up the bridges so they couldn't get through; so that they had to go around through Oregon and Washington.

Of course we all cheered at this good news against "scabs." Then Stark and I bade our friends goodby, and started ostensibly for Placer Creek where the Dutchman and his Irish partner lived.

On getting out of sight in the heavy timber, we lay down and watched Mrs. Hollihan who had just come up to visit her daughter, French Pete's wife. In a few moments she came out of the house and with an old-country stride of four feet to the stretch, she hurried down to her own home, and on arriving there, as I learned afterwards, she told her guests, the union leaders, that she had just met two poor union men who looked tired and worn out. She was asked to describe these two men, which she did. On describing me as being pitted with smallpox, President O'Brien spoke up and said: "Why, that's that ———— detective Allison that we have been scouring the hills to find," or words to that effect.

Then a runner was sent down town to gather a crowd of union men to go on our trail and head us off and capture us. A large crowd was sent up the creek on the run, to scour the woods back to the point where the old lady had seen us. This crowd running up the creek armed, created an excitement, and some one friendly to the mine owners, learned that they were after me. Then General Carlin, commander of the United States troops, was notified and he sent a detail of twenty-five soldiers on the double-quick up the creek to rescue us. The soldiers were given a good description of Yours Truly.

It was just dusk when Stark and I presented ourselves to General Carlin in the Carter hotel. When he heard my name he said: "Why, you are the man we sent out twenty-five soldiers half an hour ago to rescue. Of course this was news to me, though next day I learned the whole truth of the affair, as outlined above. Then General Carlin sent runners out to bring in the soldiers, as the lost had been found. It was late when the last ones returned. They reported seeing many armed men whom they couldn't capture owing to the heavy brush.

I told of President O'Brien being hid at Mrs. Hollihan's house, and a squad of soldiers were sent to surround the place, with the result that President O'Brien, Joe Poynton and others of the union leaders were captured. But Dallas was not among the prisoners, who were fixing to change their hiding place when the soldiers got there. He had no doubt gone with the crowd to capture me, and thus saved his bacon, as he was never caught.

Stark and I slept soundly that night in the Carter hotel, with the glorious American flag waving over our heads, and a thousand bayonets to insure our safety.

Next day Dr. Simms was made marshal of the whole Coeur D'Alene district, under military rule, the district having been put under marshal law; and I was made one of his chief deputies.

12

As I knew all the agitators and union leaders, I was kept busy for the next week or so putting unruly cattle in the "bull pen," a large stockade with a frame building in the center, for them to sleep and eat in.

We scoured the country to the Montana line. General Carlin refused to follow them over the line, out of Idaho. In less than a week we had 300 "bulls" in the corral. A word from me would liberate any of them and many were let go, as I knew the bad ones. Instead of burning me at a stake, they were now begging me for mercy, that is, a great many of them.

My friend, Geo. A. Pettibone, was not captured for a few days. He was hid up in the mountains wounded by being struck with a boomerang. He had touched off the fuse that blew up the Frisco mill, causing the death and maiming of many men.

After they had sent a car of giant powder down the mountain and it blew up before reaching the mill, they tried a new scheme. High up on the mountain-side there was a large wooden flume and from this to the water-wheel in the mill, there was a large iron pipe called a pen-stock, to conduct water to run the mill machinery. As the mill was not then running, there was no water in the penstock. In order to reach the upper end of this pen-stock, the water was let out of the large wooden flume, and along its bottom, Geo. A. Pettibone and his gang of three or four men walked. Then bundles of giant powder were dropped into the penstock and found lodgment at the bottom, inside the mill. When they thought enough had been sent down, Pettibone touched a match to a fuse attached to the last bundle. He made the fuse long enough so that it wouldn't go off till it reached the bottom among the other bundles.

Now, Judge Geo. A. Pettibone, the learned justice of the peace, of Gem, had a fine head for dishing out union justice and for crawling up a hollow tree of small caliber, but not for scenting a boomerang. He remained in the flume with his ear at the mouth of the penstock so as to hear the joyful sound of the explosion when it should take place.

Pettibone went up in the treetops and his companion picked him up outside of the flume, where he came down with a shattered hand and other injuries. He hadn't studied concussion in his school books. If he had, he would have known that the shock of the explosion would come back up the penstock.

In this explosion at the Frisco mill, many lives were saved from the fact that most of the seventy-five or more guards and non-union miners were at the further side of the mill building, shooting at union men on the opposite side of the mountain, from where Pettibone and his small gang were doing their work.

In rounding up these unruly cattle with squads of soldiers, I had some narrow escapes. Once in Burk it looked scary for me, as I only had a few soldiers and the miners were very angry at me. All they lacked was a leader to make a break for my scalp.

To show how I was hated by the miners in the bull-pen, I will quote the headlines from the "Barbarian" newspaper:

"Allison went into the bull-pen and a rush was made for him. He had to draw his pistol. His presence in their midst had the same effect as a red flag on angry bulls."

I made one trip with a train load of soldiers with General Carlin in active command, to the line of Montana, where Jack Lucy, "Long Shorty" and a large gang of dynamiters had a fort built on top of a mountain. From the train to the foot of the mountain, Lieutenant Page had charge. After marching about a mile it was found impossible to reach the enemy's fort in a body, owing to brush and fallen timber. Therefore, we had to return empty-handed. But on the trip I learned a lesson in military training. Funny things happened, which would have made a stone idol grin, but not so with General Carlin. He would never crack a smile. On making inquiry, I found that at the military schools he had learned to set the brakes on his mouth, at will.

In Gem, Capt. J. W. Bubb had charge of a company of United States troops, and I did much of my work through him. He would furnish me a squad of soldiers whenever I asked for them.

In my dealings with soldiers I found out the difference between "raw recruits" and "seasoned veterans." In going through old tunnels and caves, searching for dynamiters, the boys in the state militia would squat and often jump at the least noise, while, if I said the word, half a dozen United States soldiers would march right into a dark place where dozens of the enemy were supposed to be hidden. I would be right behind them and could note their maneuvers. A dozen bats or "bloody howls" could fly past their heads and they would never change their course or alter their steps.

On my first visit to Gem, after the soldiers came in, it was comical to see the surprise of Mrs. Shipley's little boy. He almost had a "duck fit" on seeing me. He supposed I was still down in that hole under the floor, and his mother said that he couldn't eat a meal without saving some for Mr. Allison. This he would drop down into the hole. Bless his little baby heart, wherever he might be. I have lost track of him and his mother, but I want them to know that my last crust of bread or dollar is theirs for the asking, should they ever be in need.

Of course, after marshal-law was declared, the mine owners and deported business men came back.

Joe McDonald, a brave man and a fighter, took charge of the Frisco mine.

After the soldiers came, John Monihan also returned. He told of his narrow escape at the Mission while waiting for the steamer to take them to Coeur D'Alene City. He said they were all sitting around on the grass, about 250 of them, under the guard of a few union men, when just about dusk a squad of union dynamiters, under the leadership of Bill Black, who was later shot and sent to the penitentiary, came swooping down on the defenseless men shooting and robbing them right and left. The murderers were on horseback. John Monihan and Percy Summers jumped into the water and swam to an island, thus saving themselves.

At the point where the shooting took place, the river is very deep, and after dark a wounded man, Abbott, who was hidden in the tall grass said he saw the union men rob several dead bodies and then cut open their stomachs, so they would sink, and dump them into the river.

After the count, fourteen "scabs" were missing and some of them have never turned up to this day, and the supposition is that they were the ones sunk in the river.

Most of the "scabs," who gave up their money without protest, were liberated. Some had a year's savings in their pockets, as many had been working for a long time under union rules, but had turned to be "scabs" after the strike.

Many times I visited the States' hospital in Wallace and talked with the non-union men wounded in Gem, and in the Fourth-of-July canyon on the lake. To see some of these poor fellows shot through the body, and others with their heads split open, would melt the heart of a stone man, and make him resolve to fight this kind of unionism to the last ditch.

One poor fellow seventy-five years old, lay with his head cracked open and his face and body pounded to a jelly, and this was done after he had surrendered, when the Frisco mill was blown up. And other men served in the same manner lay by his side, almost at the point of death.

This dastardly work was done under the leadership of Paddy Burke and Dan Connor, two of my brothers of the Gem union. All honor to the Irishman who had the manhood to stop these cut-throats and give orders that no more prisoners be ill-used, at the risk of their own lives. This Irishman was Peter Breen, a leader of the Butte City (Mont.) union, who had come over to help in the riots. I afterwards saw him sulking in the Wallace jail, and I felt like giving him my hand for his noble act, even though he had himself trampled the Constitution of the United States under his big brogans.

The old man referred to above, told me how he had come from California to work in the Frisco mine to save his little home from being sold under mortgage, over his old wife's head, and tears streamed down his bruised face as he told it. Furthermore, he was an American-bred citizen, while the men who beat him up were every one foreigners of the lowest order.

Finally, I had to go on a stage coach to Murray, the county seat of Shoshone county, Idaho, this being the county in which the Coeur D'Alene mining district is situated, to appear before the grand jury against union rioters.

Murray is an old gold camp across a range of mountains, and is made up of a good class of American citizens, many of them being old Grand Army men. So, for that reason the grand jury brought in many indictments. Charlie O'Neal was the prosecuting attorney for the county, and he worked faithfully to get indictments, though he said he knew it would be utterly impossible to convict a union man in the local courts, and he was right, for the strongest case was tried first, as a test. It was against Webb Leasier, the man who was seen to fire the bullet through Ivory Bean's heart. O'Neal had witnesses who saw Leasier fire the shot, and still he failed to convict.

While in Murray, and before I had appeared before the grand jury, the deputy sheriff in charge at that point under Dr. Simms, told me after supper one night, that he and his guards could not be responsible for my safety, as there was a well-laid plan to kidnap me by force. He said he had just got a tip from a reliable party who had seen a large crowd of union outlaws up the creek several miles, and from this gang of union men, about 300, the informant found out their intention of capturing the town of Murray in order to get me. This deputy appeared to be very nervous over the matter, and he hired several extra men to do guard duty, but said he had no hope of standing off a large gang of desperate men. He advised me to look out for myself and not depend on him.

There were no soldiers in Murray, and the town was filled with union men to act as witnesses for their side; therefore I felt a little shaky. Still, I figured that possibly it was a bluff to frighten me so I wouldn't remain to testify before the grand jury.

That night and every night following, until all my evidence was in the hands of the grand jury, I stayed awake and sat up on the mountain side overlooking the town, with my Winchester rifle ready for action. I would pretend to retire to my room for the night, not telling a soul of my intentions; then I would slip down the back stairs and up the mountain side. Next morning I would return to the hotel at daylight and slip into my room.

After I had testified before the grand jury, I was told that Dallas and his gang were laying for me on the road to capture me when I returned on the stage to Wallace. No doubt there was truth in this report, for the stage drivers told of men stopping the stage as though to see who were aboard. Each side of the road was covered with a dense growth of timber and underbrush, so that it would have been an easy matter to capture the stage at a given signal that I was a passenger. But I fooled them by hiring a saddle-horse to take a little exercise one evening, and that night I "hit the road" for Wallace on horse-back, a distance of about twenty miles.

Finally I was called to Coeur D'Alene City, Idaho, to testify in Judge Jas. H. Beatty's United States court against leaders of the Miners' union.

Before leaving Gem, I had the pleasure of seeing my little daughter, Viola, though no one was to know that she was my child.

Mr. Will F. Read had sold his home in Anna, Ill., and come out to Gem for his wife's health, on the strength of my advice. He then bought out Mrs. Shipley's interest in our store and became my partner. I agreed to give him half the profits from the rent of the twelve furnished rooms, which were now all occupied with non-union men, and a barber shop adjoining the store, for his trouble in running the place. Therefore, on leaving, I turned over to Mr. and Mrs. Read all my rights in Gem, including the good-will interest in Miss Gertrude Hull, a pretty young lady whom I rounded up in Spokane to clerk in our store. I had gone to Spokane City on this special round-up, and of course I roped in the prettiest girl I could find.

For the next few months my name was in the papers a good deal, as I was the star-witness against the leaders of the miners' union. Many people came to Coeur d'Alene City especially to hear my evidence.

The United States' prosecuting attorney was Freemont Wood, and a Mr. F. B. Crossthwaite from the Department of Justice in Washington, D. C., assisted.

The Mine Owners' Association employed Attorney Hagen and W. B. Heyburn, now a United States senator from Idaho, to assist in the prosecutions.

We also tried a batch of the dynamite leaders in Boise City, the capital of Idaho, in Judge Beatty's court there.

During these trials I had to keep wide awake, as it was known that the miners' union had turned me over to the Irish "Clan-na-gaels" to be killed, so that my evidence would not be used against President O'Brien and the other leaders.

In Boise City I received a "tip" that Kelly and four "Clan-na-gael" members of the Butte City, Montana union, who it was said had charge of assassinating Editor Penrose for opposing their union, a short time previous, would come to get me out of the way. The "tip" came from a man on the inside. Kelly and his four companions came to Boise by the time court opened, but they were pointed out to me, and their usefulness to the dynamite society was spoiled.

The Butte City, Montana, and Coeur d'Alene unions had employed one-armed Pat Reddy from California and Nevada, to protect their side. He was a noted criminal lawyer, and he and I had some hot tilts while I was on the witness stand, both at Coeur d'Alene City and at Boise, The "Barbarian" newspaper and others, came out with big headlines of how Siringo-Allison paralyzed Reddy and had him fighting mad. In Boise, Reddy frothed at the mouth and shook his fist in my face, but I only smiled. Judge Beatty upheld me. Attorney James Hawley, of Boise, a nice fellow, was employed to assist Reddy. The unions also had two other lawyers of smaller caliber.

We succeeded in convicting eighteen union leaders, among them being my friend, Judge Geo. A. Pettibone, who had recovered from his fly up in the tree-tops at the

Frisco mill explosion. He received a sentence of two years in the United States prison at Detroit, Mich.

I was really sorry for the "honorable president" of the Coeur d'Alene Central Union, Mr. O'Brien. He was not a bad man at heart, but his head had gone wrong through taking the advice of such men as Joe Poynton and "Judge" Pettibone.

I shall never believe that nature intended Mr. O'Brien to wear prison stripes, but every one of the other seventeen, with the exception of Dan Harrington, deserved hanging, among them being an ex-prize fighter, Tom Whalen, who did a noble deed when he shot Bill Black through the body in a drunken brawl. Had he killed Black, who led the charge in the Fourth-of-July canyon on Monihan and his helpless victims, several lives would have been saved.

Thomas Eaton, old man Mike Divine, "Spud" Murphy, C. Sinclair, Joe Poynton, Tom Whalen and John Nicholson, were among those convicted as leaders of the miners' union.

The peculiar twist in the names of all these convicted men would indicate that they were not Swedes, Chinamen or Scandinavians.

It was late in the fall when in Wallace, Idaho, I closed the operation and started back to Denver. I had been on the operation a year and two months.

I hated to part with my companion, Frank Stark, as we had become warm friends; but soon after my departure he lost one of his legs above the knee from a rifle bullet. It was done in my building at Gem where he was rooming, and the rifle was fired accidentally by Johnny Kneebone, the "scab" blacksmith, afterwards murdered by the miners' union, several members of the union going to his blacksmith shop at the Gem mine in broad daylight and shooting him full of holes.

After losing his leg, Stark went to his old home in Pennsylvania and learned to be an engineer. Since then I have lost track of him, though I hope he is alive and doing well; for he is a prince and there is not a cowardly drop of blood in his veins.

I arrived in Denver and discontinued the Coeur d'Alene operation just before Christmas. Superintendent McCartney was glad to see me back alive, after the strenuous life I had been leading.

On several occasions in the Coeur d'Alene I had saved my life by being handy with the pistol and getting the drop. I always avoided taking life, though I had the law on my side. I had a chance once in Coeur d'Alene City during the trial there, to kill a bad dynamiter right before the eyes of Prosecuting Attorney Wood, and be upheld by the law. Also another time on a crowded train between Gem and Wallace, when Mr. "Mace" Campbell and other mine owners were present. Some of the tough union men had raised a "racket" with me. I made them sit down and kept them covered with my gun till we arrived in Wallace. Then I had Sheriff Simms throw the leader, a big Irishman, in jail for threatening to kill me.

On reaching Denver I started out to have a good time by spending my money freely. I figured that I could afford it, as outside of my weekly salary, I was drawing $135.00 per month from the rent of my Gem, Idaho, building and furnished rooms, besides a good profit from my half of the store.

But with me, good things don't last long, for one morning early in January, 1893, Miss Mollie Rucker, our cashier, handed me a telegram from Mrs. Will F. Read in Gem, which stated that my building and store had burnt to the ground and that her husband was in jail for shooting the union dynamiter merchant, Samuels. Thus my $3,000.00 had taken wings and flown up in smoke, and my extra income was cut off. I had had $1,500.00 worth of insurance on the building, but a few weeks before the fire, $1,000.00 of it was canceled owing to a fear that the union would set the town afire. The $500.00 of insurance money was used to pay some debts in Idaho and to assist the Reads who later joined me in Denver.

While the fire was raging on our side of the street, Will Read had carried his wife's trunk containing her keepsakes across the street and put it upon Samuels' store porch where it would be safe from the fire. Then Samuels gave the trunk a kick out into the street, as Read was not liked by the union men on account of his friendship for me. Read at once went back into the burning building and got his double-barrel shotgun loaded with buckshot, and "winged" dynamiter Samuels by shooting his right arm off at the shoulder; but before doing so, Samuels fired a couple of shots at Read with a pistol, after Read had knocked him through his own glass-front store, shattering the plate glass.

Barrels of whisky had been rolled out of the burning saloons, which lay between the Union Hall, where the fire started and my place, and the union mob were all drunk on free liquor.

After the shooting Read was knocked down and the

"scab" Deputy Sheriff Frank Rose secured Read's gun. The drunken dynamiters seeing their brother with his arm shattered to threads and Rose with the smoking gun in his hand, supposed he did the job. Poor Rose tried to explain matters, but he was a "scab" and they wouldn't listen to his pleadings. While they were fixing to hang him, the truth was explained that Allison's partner shot poor Samuels. Then Rose was liberated and the mob started after Read, who by that time, was half way to Wallace.

Arriving in Wallace about 5:30 a. m. Read surrendered to Sheriff Simms who took him down to the jail as a matter of duty, but forgot and left the jail door open; and he also forgot and left a Winchester rifle and 100 rounds of cartridges where Read could get them.

Soon the mob came in sight. Read lay on top of a stockade with his rifle ready to do business. When within a few hundred yards of the jail, Webb Leasier the man who is said to have killed Ivory Bean, succeeded in stopping the mob. He had been pleading with them to let the law takes its course, as Read was a brother Odd Fellow of his; but they wouldn't listen, until finally Webb Leasier got in front of the leaders with cocked gun, and threatened to kill the first one who made another step forward. They knew he meant business, and besides, they loved him as a good "scab-killer," so they turned back and spoiled Read's chance of making a glorious name as a slayer of dynamiters.

Webb Leasier's action goes to prove that there is some good in all men, even in murderers.

At the preliminary trial before my friend, Judge Angel, in Wallace, Read was liberated.

This ends the second and last act of the bloody Coeur d'Alene strike of 1892, which taught me many new lessons in my study of human nature.

My only regret is that I couldn't have bottled up that hole in the floor before it went up in smoke, so as to keep it as a relic to be handed down to my descendants, to remind them of the first time their worthy grandsire had crawled into a hole in time of danger.

The Coeur d'Alene trouble had been caused through the miners' union wanting to dictate as to how the mines should be run. When they made a demand for shorter hours, and that "muckers" and common roustabouts receive $3.50 per day, the same wages as skilled miners, the mine-owners closed down the mines and sent out for non-union men.

CHAPTER IX

IN JAIL WITH TWO MURDERERS—TESTING RAILWAY
CONDUCTORS—TRAMPING AS A HOBO THROUGH COLO-
RADO, NEW MEXICO, ARIZONA, CALIFORNIA AND
TEXAS—ROBBERY OF THE TREADWELL GOLD MILL
IN ALASKA—WE CAPTURE THE THIEVES AND RE-
COVER THE GOLD.

From now on I shall merely skim over the surface of
some of my experiences, as I find that one medium size
volume will not contain it all if given in full.

One of my important operations was for the A. & B. C.
Ry. Co. My friends, Doc Shores and Ed Farr, had charge
of the work. And Attorney Charlie Johnson prosecuted
the case.

Dick Manley and Young Anderson had started out on a
robbery crusade, and had killed one man and wounded
another. I spent three weeks in the Pueblo jail with these
two young outlaws and secured a full confession from
them.

In Walsenburg, Colo., I appeared on the witness stand,
with the result that Dick Manley was sentenced to seventeen years in the penitentiary; but after serving several
years, I used my influence in getting him a pardon from
Governor McIntire. His sister, Mrs. Birmingham, whose
husband had been a former cowboy companion of mine in
Texas, had pled for Dick's release, as he had promised to
lead an upright life in the future.

Young Manley kept his promise about two months, then killed a man at Red River City, N. M. A few months later he held up a bank in Breckenridge, Colo., killing two officers, and being killed himself.

During the years 1893 and '94 I led an exciting life.

About three months of this time I was posing as a wealthy mining man in Denver, under the name of Chas. Le Roy. Our client was A.B. Farnum and the victim was N. D. Lewis, the case being a $25,000 mining suit. Our side won through Lewis being so foolish as to let me hear the secret discussions with his lawyers.

While on this operation I hob-nobbed with my friend, Dan V., of Mudsill mine fame, without his knowing that I was the same Chas. Leon who had once put him "on the bum." He was Lewis' chum and adviser.

After finishing the Farnum case I put on bum clothes and became one of the unwashed Coxeyites, in Wyoming, for the Union Pacific Railroad Co.

The Debs' A. R. U. strike was then raging through the West over the Pullman Car Co. dispute. I saw much "scab" blood spilled by union sluggers jumping onto unarmed non-union railway employes.

I also put in several months "testing" freight and passenger conductors all over one of the greatest railroad systems in Colorado and Texas.

On leaving Denver in a freight caboose, a drunken Irishman and I had a swift ride down a mountain side from Hilltop. Three loaded freight cars and the caboose had broken loose from the train while the crew were at the station of Hilltop. "Micky's" prayers to the Virgin Mary, and a white cow asleep on the track, saved our

13

lives, after going around ten miles of crooked mountain curves at a gait of about ten miles a minute.

My work took me over ground in the Panhandle of Texas, where I had run cattle, and many of my old cowboy chums were met. But I had to tell them whopping big lies about how I was on the lookout for a "bad" man.

One of my operations was playing hobo and tramping over the S. T. & G. R. Ry. through Colorado, New Mexico, Arizona, California and Texas. The work was being done for a high official.

I had many new experiences on this trip. At one point on the Mohave desert, I had been put off a train three times and had to walk fifteen miles without water. On this fifteen mile tramp I overtook a crippled Irishman with red sideburns and the map of the "ould sod" smeared all over his face. He walked with a stick and carried a small bundle wrapped in a red handkerchief. I had been walking fast to overtake him so as to have company. We sat down on the end of the ties to rest, and I asked him what he was doing out on this desert. He replied that he was hunting work. I asked if he had lost any work. He smiled and said: "No, begorry, but I'm going back east to find a job that will fit me complexion. I was offered a job last winter in Californy, but I belongs to a union and I won't work in a state that has so many scab Chinamen. They can all go to the divel, I won't scab."

We were both panting for a drink of water. Further on were a house and wind mill half a mile from the railroad track. This was the first house seen for many miles. When opposite the ranch, I wanted Irish to go with me and get a drink of water, but he said he was "peetered out" and couldn't stand the tramp over the grass and sage brush. He asked me to bring him a drink in a tin can. I then started.

Arriving within a few hundred yards of the house, a tall man came out holding a bulldog by a chain. In a loud voice he ordered me off his land or he would turn the dog loose. I hallooed and told him that I just wanted a drink of water. He called back that he had no water for me and that if I didn't move on he would turn the dog loose. The white dog was making frantic efforts to free himself, and old Colt's 45 under my left arm where it couldn't be seen was ready for a struggle too. I had no fear of the dog, but thought maybe the rancher might have a long-range rifle in the house; so I turned back.

On the way to the house I had noticed a few milk cows in a deep arroyo off to my right and not far from the railroad track. I angled towards this arroyo, in hopes of finding a gentle cow among them. On reaching the cattle I was out of sight from the house. I used diplomacy by sitting down near the cows so they could get acquainted with me. They soon came "nosing" around to satisfy their curiosity. Only one cow would let me go up and rub her head, and she was a Jersey with a bag full of baby-food. While she chewed the cud of contentment, I got down on my knees and milked the fluid into my mouth. This was no new experience with me, as I had practiced it for whole days when a little bare-foot boy in Texas, at times when I was afraid to go home on account of a promised whipping.

After I was full to overflowing, I went up on high ground and called Irish. He came and I told him about the rancher and the dog, and of what a soft snap the old cow was. Irish didn't think that he could connect a stream of milk with his mouth, so I gave him my white felt hat to use for a cup by crushing in the crown and using the outside for a vessel. His old straw hat was put onto my head. When Irish reached the bottom of the arroyo, the cows raised their heads and tails and flew for the house. If that isn't luck, what is it? I told Irish that I thought the cows had smelled his red side-whiskers. He tried to smile, but was too downhearted.

A walk of five miles brought us to the first little town. Here I put a "jolt of the critter"—good old red "licker"—under Irish's belt and then took him to a Chinese restaurant and filled him up on "scab" grub.

On this operation, which lasted a few months, I had some narrow escapes and saw many funny sights. Once I was locked up in a box car loaded with scrap-iron, and for awhile I sweated blood in fear of a wreck. And once I had to stand off a crew of railroad men, with my pistol, who wanted to pound me to death because I was found among some heavy timbers on one of the freight cars after I had been put off the same train three times. On the trip I spent half my salary feeding poor bums whom I thought deserved pity.

At Isleta Station, twenty-two miles south of Albuquerque, N. M., I found an honest tramp. He was hungry and wet after having been put off a train during the night in a rain storm. When I saw him first, early in the morning, he was under the watertank wringing the water from his clothes. He was a tall, well-built man, and he claimed to be a son of Judge Caldwell, a once popular judge of the Lone Star state, and he said that his widowed mother then lived in California; that about a year previous he had sold a mine in Hillsboro, N. M., for $20,000 and had gone to Europe to blow in the money; that now, he was getting back, flat broke. How much of this story was "hot air," I had no way of knowing. After the honorable fool Caldwell had donned his wet clothes I took him up to the Indian village where I had stopped all night at an Indian house, and filled him up on tortillas, frijoles and hot coffee. Then we both boarded a south-bound freight train, secreting ourselves in a loaded box car of coal. When the "brakey" found us I gave him fifty cents for my fare to Los Lunas, as far as I wanted to go with that crew, and one dollar for Caldwell's fare to the end of that division.

On bidding Caldwell goodby, I gave him $1.50 more to pay his way to Hillsboro. He insisted on having my address, so that he could send me this borrowed money when he reached his friends in Hillsboro. I gave him the address of Chas. Le Roy, El Paso, Texas, and on reaching that town a week later, I found a postoffice money-order for the amount of the debt, $2.50, also a nice letter of thanks. This shows that there is honor even among tramps.

About February, 1895, Superintendent McCartney called me into his office and told me to get ready for a trip to Alaska. He went on to tell of the importance to the agency of this operation. He advised me to do my best to make the operation a success, as our Portland office, which had lately been established under the superintendency of Mr. Wooster, had lately made a failure of the work. He also went on to tell me how the Treadwell mine, on Douglas Island, had been robbed during the winter of $10,000 worth of gold; that the next day Mr. Durkin, superintendent of the big Treadwell mine, had sent a letter to Victoria, B. C., on an outgoing steamer, to the Western Union Telegraph office with instructions to wire the Dickenson National Detective agency in Portland to send three good operatives to Juneau, Alaska, on the first steamer; that Mr. Wooster complied with the request, not knowing the nature of the work; that these three operatives remained in Alaska for a month or two, but failed to get a clue as to what became of the gold; then Mr. Durkin called the operation off and sent the operatives back to Portland; that soon after the work was called off as a failure, Mr. Durkin went to San Diego, Cal., on a pleasure trip, and there, by chance, met Mr. Wm. L. Dickenson; that the subject of the failure to recover the stolen gold came up, and Mr. Dickenson laid the failure to the fact that he (Durkin) had not written the agency the full details of the robbery instead of wiring for three operatives, for then, operatives who were fitted for that kind of work could have been secured from other offices in case the Portland branch didn't have them; then Mr. Dickenson told Superintendent Durkin that although it was late now to make a success, he believed they could select men who would get a clue as to what became of the gold, and possibly get the gold itself; that then Superintendent Durkin told Mr. Dickenson to go ahead and put two men on the case, regardless of expense; that Mr. Dickenson then wrote Superintendent McCartney recommending me for the operation. This, of course, put me on my dignity, and I determined to do my best.

It was agreed that a few weeks later, Operative W. O. Sayles would be sent to Alaska to assist me.

In the early part of March I boarded the **Topeka**, at Tacoma, Wash., for Juneau, Alaska. The trip on smooth waters, among whales and "totem-poles" opened my eyes to a new world of which I had never dreamed.

On arriving in Juneau, a swift little city built on stilts mostly, I at once wrote to Superintendent Durkin on Douglas Island, across the bay, of my arrival. At night in a secluded place I met Mr. Durkin and his assistant, Mr. Bordus.

It was agreed that I apply for work in the big Treadwell gold mill, the largest in the world, in a regular way, and Mr. Bordus would make a place for me. No one but Mr. Durkin and Mr. Bordus were to know of my identity or my business. I secured a job as machine oiler. This work took me to all parts of the mill where I could make the acquaintance of all the employes. Part of the time I was on the day-shift, then I changed to the night-shift. In oiling the machinery, I had to climb around in ticklish places where a misstep or a false move would land me in the "kingdomcome."

Once I came within a hair's-breadth of going down into the midst of revolving wheels. I had barely room to walk between two large revolving belts. I had stooped to oil a piece of machinery and in raising up, swerved a little to the right and was struck on the head by the belt on that side. My hat, I suppose, is going yet, for I haven't seen it since.

By the time Operative W. O. Sayles arrived, three weeks after my arrival, I concluded that we had a clue and that Charlie Hubbard and Hiram Schell, two mill hands, who had quit work and bought a small schooner and sailed westward a month after the robbery, were the thieves. No one knew what had become of these men, as they didn't tell any one where they were going with their little schooner.

Operative Sayles and I discussed matters in Juneau, between drinks, at the big dance hall where fish-eating Indian maidens do the dance act to relieve the noble white man of his dollars.

We decided to buy a large canoe, one that would hold two cowboys (Sayles had been a cowboy in Montana) and twenty-five gallons of whisky and go on the trail of Hubbard and Schell. We had both trailed horses, cattle and men, but never a schooner on water.

It was agreed that Sayles keep his weather eye open for a good Indian canoe, while I returned to the mill to break my arm and recover from the wound. In order to keep down suspicion, it was necessary for me to have an excuse for quitting my job, therefore I concluded to break my arm that night.

It was on the night-shift, and after midnight lunch, I found a secluded place in the basement, and started the scheme. The point of my left shoulder was rubbed with chips and stuff until the skin was almost off, and it looked red. Then I went to work in the upper stories of the mill. At the foot of a slippery pair of stairs there was a floor covered with slush and mud. Here was just the place for me to land, so as to put on a muddy appearance. Near the foot of these stairs stood two men working at the "plates." I waited until their backs were towards me, then I went tumbling down the last flight of the stairs. I landed broadside in the mud, and my lantern was struck with such force against the floor that it flew all to pieces.

Of course the men heard the fall and ran to my assistance. I was picked up and the company doctor sent for. I complained the most about the pain in my left shoulder, which I said had struck against an upright timber in front of the stairs. My shirts were pulled off and the doctor made an examination of the seat of the pain. He looked wise and decided that the shoulder was not broken, but that the muscles of my arm were badly bruised from the contact with the post. What fooled him was the fact that I couldn't raise my arm beyond a level. He saturated cotton with liniment and put it on the shoulder. Then the arm was put in a sling and I was put to bed with much sympathy from the hired men who assisted me to my bunk. The next day at noon I was able to take my place at the table where a hundred or more men ate their meals. "Reddy" sat next to me and wasted much of his valuable time cutting my meat as I only had one hand, the other being in a sling. And poor "Reddy" kept up his sympathetic lick for several days until I drew my pay and left for Juneau.

Just before drawing my wages and quitting the mill job, Sayles had found Hubbard and Schell and their schooner lying on the water front among the other boats in Juneau. He had been watching for the little schooner which we had a description of. She had mysteriously slipped into port one evening and just as mysteriously slipped out next morning. But while she lay in port that evening, Sayles went aboard and searched the locker. Later, when the owners came from uptown, Sayles got into a conversation with them and found their names were Schell and Hubbard, and that they had just come from the west coast of Admiralty Island, but what particular place he couldn't find out.

The news of Schell and Hubbard having been in Juneau, cured my sore shoulder quickly. On my arrival in Juneau we bought one of the large Indian canoes which Sayles had "spotted." It was forty feet long and painted with all the colors of the rainbow. Her bow and stern were built high above the water to ward off the heavy seas.

After our new ship was rigged up with a sail which could be taken down, mast and all, we loaded up with the necessaries of life, including twenty-five gallons of good Canadian rye whisky. The main object in taking the whisky along was to pass ourselves off as whisky peddlers among the Indians, and as bait for Schell and Hubbard in case we found them. Before starting, we bought a fine chart of the Alaskan coast.

So as to prevent hard feelings, I suggested to Sayles that we take turns about being captain or boss of the ship; that when he was captain I was to be the slave, and vice versa. He agreed to this.

Sayles was captain the first day out and we had smooth sailing, but the next day we got caught in a mighty storm and were tangled up in a tide-riff. We had never heard of a tide-riff, where two tides meet, and in a storm make the sea "choppy" and very dangerous for small boats. But we were not long learning that the Indians dodge these tide-riffs, "all same" a Kansas Populist dodges prosperity and cyclones.

During this storm on an inlet several miles wide, Sayles turned pale and began bossing as to what was best to be done, but I laughed and told him to keep his "fly-trap" shut, as he was only a slave. He tried to smile but couldn't, as his heart was not in a smiling mood; besides, he was kept busy bailing out the water which washed over the canoe's side to the windward. I sat in the stern manipulating the Indian paddle used for a rudder, and the sail. The only thing that kept me from getting scared was the importance of my position as captain. It was amusing to me to have "Hold Hengland" at my feet begging to be saved. You see, Sayles was an Englishman, or at least, a misborn Irishman, he having been born in Ireland of quite wealthy English parents, therefore missed the chance of being born at home. Sayles had had very little experience on salt water, while most of my barefoot days were spent on the Gulf of Mexico in southern Texas, chasing coons, crabs, oysters and sea-fowls. Therefore when it came to handling a small sail-boat I was right at home.

It is said that "An honest confession is good for the soul," so I must confess that before being out a month Old England had America at her feet, begging for mercy. We were crossing the mouth of Hood's Bay in a severe storm which was drifting us out to the big water ten miles across, Hood's Bay itself only being three miles wide. I begged Sayles to turn back after we were out from shore only half a mile, but he just laughed and reminded me of the fact that he was captain that day. He had learned to be fearless on the water.

On reaching shore on this, our second day out, we had to both jump out in the white-capped breakers to keep our canoe from being pounded to pieces against the rocks; for in these Alaskan inlets and channels it is a hard matter to find a safe landing place. The heavily timbered mountains with their craggy edges come right down to the water's edge, the only sandy beaches being at the mouth of fresh-water streams, or at a projecting point.

On landing, a big Indian slipped out of the timber and, jumping into the water, helped us pull the canoe out high and dry on the shore. Then Mr. "Ingin" helped us get a fire started in the rain, by using wide bark for a shelter from the water which was falling. For this kind help we filled his hide full of Canadian-rye juice, and he was soon laid out on the dry side of a large spruce tree. Of course Sayles and I didn't forget to put a few "jolts" of the rye under our belts, as we were wet and cold. For the next few weeks we were sailing unknown waters, and most of the time among Indians who couldn't speak any English. Often the channels would be so narrow that we could throw a stone on either side and hit the land, while other times the water would be ten miles across.

From Indians, who could talk and understand a little English, we heard of our little schooner and the two strange white men sailing westward. Thus we knew we were on the right trail.

From now on, we had some narrow escapes from being swamped. Once in a storm we got our canoe tangled up in about a hundred acres of sea-weed, and couldn't get out for a long time. But at last, we made a landing on a small island and camped for the night.

We finally learned by experience that the storms all came in the daytime, so then we travelled at night when the water is generally as smooth as glass. But there being no wind at night for our sail, we had to take turns about rowing.

The sun went to roost between 9 and 10 o'clock, and from that time until 11:30 p. m. it was dusk, almost as light as day. Then at 1:30 a. m. day would begin to break.

One of our narrow escapes happened one night about 11 p. m. The water was like crystal, not a breath of air was stirring. Sayles was rowing and I was steering with the paddle. Seeing a black object like a small island ahead, I steered for that. When within a few hundred yards of the supposed island, Sayles' bump of caution began to work and he advised me to steer away from it as it might be a sleeping whale. He said they were very dangerous when suddenly awakened and that they were liable to scoot straight towards us, which would mean possible death to both. He confessed that his knowledge on the matter had been gained from books, so I told him that actual experience was the best teacher. It was my night to be captain, so that he had no right to "chip in." My phrenology bump of curiosity was at work, therefore I steered just a little to the left of the half an acre of black substance. When nearly opposite at a distance of about 100 yards, we discovered that it was a whale without a doubt. There could be no mistake, for there was his head and about one or two hundred feet further down the line was his tail. Sayles was pulling hard, and apparently sweating blood. He said we must get further away before the thing woke up. Just then a new thought struck me and I said, "Holy smoke, Sayles, here's the chance of my life to shoot big game!" As I raised the large caliber Winchester rifle which reclined by my side Sayles threw up both hands and said, "For God's sake, don't do it, Charlie!"

I had aimed just back of Mr. Whale's gills or throat. The bullet hadn't more than struck him when I wished I had taken my partner's advice. He went around and around with the rapidity of a cyclone, churning the water into a foam, the waves reaching our canoe. Then straight down he went, leaving a hole in the water. This hole filling up again, sucked us toward it, and I imagined I could see Hades at the bottom of the hole. But here, luck got in her work in my favor again, and the hole was closed up before we reached it. This was my last shot at that kind of big game. I hit him all right, for there was much blood on the water.

Sayles "sulked" the balance of the night, and when he tried to drown me in the mouth of Hood's Bay in that storm I believe he was trying to "play even" on me and the whale.

At a place called "Cootch-in-aboo Head," which was designated on our chart, we concluded to explore the mouth of what looked to be a river. The tide was running into it like a mill-race, so we went at a swift gait up the stream. By night we came to a large Indian village and the Indian bucks came down to the water-front with rifles to meet us. We let them smell and taste our "fire-water" to see if it was the right kind to use as a blind, in passing ourselves off for whisky peddlers. Finding these

Indians friendly and hospitable, we lay here all next day and I tried hard to fall in love with a young maiden whose sire and dame encouraged my suit, but she smelled "fishy" like all the Alaskan Indians do from living on fish, and I couldn't get my phrenology love-bump in working order.

After leaving this village and returning to "Cootch-in-aboo Head," we laid over a day to fish for halibut. They are plentiful here. We had brought along two halibut lines which were over 100 feet long.

There is no end to the different kinds of fish, crabs and clams which inhabit these waters. We tried them all and towards the last began to smell "fishy" ourselves.

On this trip we stopped at Funter's Bay and visited a noted character, old man Willoby, who was about eighty years old and had four Indian wives and a good undeveloped gold mine. He had come to that country twenty-five years previous as a missionary, and after seeing these fat, pig-eyed squaws he fell from grace.

Often we would travel for days and never see even an Indian. Then we would begin to feel lonesome. The Indians we met were mostly Chilcats, Sitkas and Chiekes. Many of them had their faces and hands painted black to guard against the swarms of mosquitoes and flies.

We had very little fresh meat on the trip, as the many deer, bear and goats were too poor at that season of the year to make good eating.

After following the mainland and searching many channels and inlets, we crossed over a wide water to the east coast of Bishcoff Island, thence south nearly to Sitka, the capital, thence east across the big water to the west coast of Admiralty Island. This island is over a hundred miles wide, and I think from one hundred and fifty to two hundred miles long. After traveling about 600 miles, counting the waste miles when we were lost and went backwards, we found the little schooner up in Chieke Bay, about twenty miles south of Killisnoo, a place where steamers plying between Juneau and Sitka stop. She was anchored in front of the Indian village of Chieke.

We found Schell and Hubbard taking life easy. Here they had a friend by the name of Hicks, a re-constructed Missourian, from his looks. He was married to "Hias" Jennie, the richest Indian woman in the village, her wealth being in the form of blankets. She had tons of them. They have no other kind of wealth. "Hias" means big, and Jennie was indeed a large Indian woman, but we found her to be a pretty good old sister, after she became acquainted with us and our Canadian rye.

Hicks had saved up some money and had recently gone into the stock business. He had sent his money to a stock-dealer in Seattle, Wash., on one of the steamers, and wrote him to send a start of hogs, chickens and cattle. They were finally unloaded at Killisnoo, and Schell and Hubbard brought them from there to Chieke in their schooner.

The stock consisted of a razor-back barrow hog, one dozen Leghorn hens, no rooster, and a black muley cow which had a papoose shortly after her arrival. Many of these Indians had never seen or heard of cattle before, and they regarded old muley and her black papoose as evil spirits. Even "Hias" Jennie wouldn't go near them or drink the milk, so muley and her calf were turned out on the tall grass to rustle for themselves. But while we were there, they were kept pretty busy fighting flies and mosquitoes.

The big barrow hog was the most contented animal in the village, for he had the leavings of all the fish caught by the several hundred Indians, but no doubt Hicks is out of the hog business ere this, as there was no chance for an increase.

The chickens were kept scratching for sea-fleas along the water edge, both day and night, to keep body and soul together. These sea-fleas are the size of mustard seed, and the hens seemed to like them, but it required so many to make a mess. The hens had twenty hours of daylight to scratch in. No telling what became of the poor "biddies" the following winter when there were but three hours of good daylight.

We didn't tarry long in Chieke Village, but went on up to the head of Chieke Bay, three miles distant, to look for the "Lost Rocker" gold mine, which tradition says is near a water-fall which falls over a cliff about 2,000 feet high. In Killisnoo we had heard of such a water-fall being at the head of Chieke Bay, so this was our excuse for going there. We found the water-fall to be grand and near it we pitched our tent. Then we began prospecting for the gold that never was there.

Here is where the bait we brought along proved a winner, for Charlie Hubbard liked the bait and put in most of his time in our camp. He thought our Canadian rye was fine. At first he had to pay for it, same as other Indians, but when he became one of our family, it was free to him.

14

In selling whisky to the Chieke Indians, we stirred up
a hornet's nest. One night a crowd of drunken bucks
made a raid on our camp and tried to force us to sell them
more whisky. We had to stand them off with firearms,
and Sayles and I had to sit up all night, as they were out
in the brush around our camp singing weird songs and
howling like coyotes. The next day the chief of the tribe
gave us orders to sell no more liquor to his people, as
some of them had nearly beaten their wives to death
during the night. We promised, of course, for we were
ready to quit, as our reputation as whisky peddlers was
established. Besides, we needed what whisky there was
left as bait for Hubbard to keep him in our camp.

Days ran into weeks, and while Sayles and I were out
hunting for the "Lost Rocker" mine, we would come
back to camp and find Hubbard and a warm supper. Hubbard knew where the whisky was cached out in the
timber, therefore he helped himself during our absence.
He had a small canoe of his own, and he could go and
come to and from Chieke at his pleasure.

Sayles and I were always testing rock for gold. We
were both posted on assaying, and we talked a good
deal on that subject.

Finally, Hubbard asked us the best treatment for chlorination gold. We told him, and now we were satisfied
that we were on the right trail, for the $10,000 worth of
gold stolen from the Treadwell mill was chlorination
gold taken from the bottom of a tank.

One evening Hubbard came from a visit to Schell in
Chieke, where no doubt they had both talked matters over,
and confessed that they had stolen $10,000 worth of gold

from the Treadwell, and he offered us $400 to melt it into pure gold for them. Of course we had to swear secrecy. We explained that it would be necessary to expend some cash for material to build a furnace to treat the gold.

That same night after the sun went down about 10 o'clock, Hubbard took me and a quart bottle of rye-juice to where they had the gold cached. It was across Chieke Bay from the Indian village, three miles, and about four miles from our camp. On arriving at the place, Hubbard dug up a frying pan, the inside of which was coated with at least $200 worth of gold. This was as far as he and Schell had got with their treatment. They succeeded in melting the stuff, but on trying to pour it into a mold to make a brick, it would cool and stick to the frying-pan. He also showed me their bellows, made of a cracker-box and a rain-coat. They had used bark for the fire. He designated the place where the rest of the gold was cached, but wouldn't tell me the exact spot, nor did I press him to know.

We got back to camp about 2 a. m. and woke Sayles up to get a drink out of his bottle, which was kept under his head, as ours was empty.

Hubbard and I were soon in the "Land of Nod," and my dreams had a gold lining, as I felt sure we were on the road to final success.

For several days following, we three discussed the subject of melting the stolen gold.

I had previously told Hubbard of scrapes which I had been into down in Texas and New Mexico, and how officers of the law had chased me out of that country. Therefore, he seemed to place confidence in me.

It was agreed that I go alone to Juneau and secure material to build a furnace, and the chemicals and crucibles for melting the gold.

Leaving Sayles in camp with Hubbard, I started in a canoe with an Indian, whom I had hired to take me to Killisnoo, a distance of twenty miles. Arriving in Killisnoo, I put up with the superintendent of the big fishery there. He kept a boarding house for the hired white men. The place was nothing but an Indian village. The passenger steamers, the Topeka and Queen, made weekly trips between Sitka and Juneau, and next day I caught the Queen for Juneau.

At Superintendent Durkin's residence on Douglas Island, I met Mr. Bordus and Durkin and told them of our plans.

After securing some clay to make a furnace, and material to melt the gold, I returned on the Topeka to Killisnoo. Before leaving, I arranged for Deputy United States Marshal Collins to be on board a United States man-of-war which was spending the summer at Killisnoo, on a certain day two weeks later, so that he could help us make the arrests, for fear the Indians might assist the prisoners.

Next day after my arrival in Killisnoo I hired an Indian to take me and my freight to Chieke. He had his family with him in the canoe, and in order to buy some food for his family he requested that I pay in advance. This I did, but whisky was bought with the money. By the time we were ready to start there were several drunken Indians, and they had a regular "Kilkenny" fight in the sand on the beach, the women folks joining in. After the "scrap" there was hair enough on the ground to make a nice hair-bridle, but not a drop of blood in sight.

On starting we found the canoe loaded to the guards. Besides the freight, there were three Indian women, two bucks and one sixteen-year-old girl, besides myself. The girl and I sat in the stern, she steering the canoe. The wind was in the right direction, so that the sail could be used. The Indians kept passing the jug of whisky, around, against my protest.

When out on the big strait, a storm blew up from the shore and the water became rough. One unruly Indian man wanted to steer the canoe and the others were trying to hold him. In doing so, they came very near turning the canoe over. I became desperate and knocked the unruly fellow down on his back in the bottom of the canoe. I then pulled "old Colt's 45" and threatened to kill the first Indian who got up on his feet. Then the women, including the girl, began crying. The girl was afraid to sit with me, so she joined her mother and they sat down on the unruly buck so he couldn't get up. Soon he fell asleep. We landed at our camp about sundown, and on unloading the grub and other stuff brought along, I dismissed the Indians and they started to Chieke.

I then walked up to camp 100 yards from the shore and found Sayles cooking supper and Hubbard sitting by the fire. I could see that something was wrong, but pretended not to notice it.

The camp-fire was outside and Sayles stepped into the tent to get something and while in there he wrote on a scrap of paper, "It's all off. They are suspicious of us and say they won't dig up the gold." This was slipped into my hand the first opportunity. Later I read it in the tent, but I continued to look cheerful against my will. There are times when a detective earns his salary, deep down where the public can't see.

By the time supper was over it was dusk. I then asked if the kiln of charcoal which I had helped start before leaving for Juneau had been burnt, as though I knew nothing about the deal being off. Hubbard spoke up and said: "No, Lee (I was then going by the name of Lee R. David), the fire has gone out and we haven't started it up again." As though surprised I asked the reason. Hubbard replied: "Let's walk up there, Lee, I want to talk to you."

We then started up the heavily timbered gulch for the charcoal kiln, a distance of several hundred yards. Nothing was said on the question at issue until we reached there. Then Hubbard straightened up to his full height, six feet one inch, and facing me said: "Lee, that partner of yours is a d——d policeman and Schell and I have concluded not to dig up that gold now."

I asked in surprise, what he meant by a policeman. He replied: "I mean he is a fly-cop—a detective." I said: "D——d if that ain't news to me. If I thought he was I wouldn't sleep until I had him anchored out in a deep place in the bay where no one would ever find him, for he knows things about me that would put me in the pen the rest of my natural life."

Then Hubbard asked: "How long have you known Sayles?" I replied that I had never met him until a few months previous, in Juneau, when an old Arizona friend of mine introduced us; that this friend lived in Juneau and knew all about my past history; that he knew enough to send me to the pen, and that I knew sufficient to hang him, and that he assured me Sayles could be trusted even with my life, as he had seen him tested when they were partners in the smuggling business between Canada and Montana. I assured Hubbard that if he was a detective my friend didn't know it, but that he may have turned to be a detective since my friend and he separated a few years previous, and if he had, I wanted to know it. So I asked Hubbard on what grounds his suspicions were based. He answered: "D——n him, he just looks like a policeman, and he has traveled over the world too much. He has told me all about his travels." I laughed outright and told Hubbard that he was foolish for getting suspicious on those grounds, and that I felt relieved, as I supposed that he had discovered good grounds for his suspicions.

I then told Hubbard how my friend had met Sayles in Canada on the line of Montana, at a time when Sayles' wealthy relatives in the old country had quit furnishing him any more money, as he was wild and reckless; that then Sayles joined my friend in the smuggling business and that they turned a few other tricks besides smuggling.

I told Hubbard that unless he felt perfectly safe that I would advise him to let the gold stay where it was; that, of course, it would hurt me a little, as I had spent some money on the trip, on the strength of the $400 they were to give us for melting the stuff.

After studying a moment with his head down, Hubbard grabbed my hand and shook it, saying: "Lee, I never doubted you for a minute. We will call the deal on again and go ahead; but I am only going to bring about one-fourth of the stuff at a time. When we melt the first batch you can take $100 worth out for your part. Then I will cache my part and bring in more; then there won't be any danger of us losing it all if he is a policeman." This I told him would suit Sayles and me.

We then returned to camp and had a round of drinks, and I told Sayles to bring some fire on the shovel and we would start up the charcoal kiln so it would be ready by the time the furnace was finished. Sayles wore a satisfied smile the balance of the evening. We all three went back and started up the kiln in good shape.

How quickly dark, threatening clouds can be banished with the proper use of "soft soap" or "taffy"; in other words, good hard innocent lying.

Next day after Hubbard had returned from an interview with Schell, we selected a place for the furnace and started to build it. The site chosen was in a grove of timber on a knoll, about 200 yards from our camp, a place where no one would ever think of visiting. Sayles bossed the job of building the furnace, as he took a great interest in such matters. Hubbard and I played the part of hod-carriers, though we held no card in any Union; consequently we were "scabbing."

When the furnace was completed, we figured it would require several days to dry, so as to be fit for use, and during this time I concluded to visit Killisnoo and buy a few luxuries as well as a bottle of Carter's Little Liver Pills, as I pretended to need some medicine.

I went to Killisnoo in a canoe, and on arrival there

consulted with Deputy United States Marshal Collins on board the man-of-war. I set a day when we would aim to have the first batch of gold melted. On that day it was agreed that Collins be at the extreme head of Hoods Bay and camp on the south side in the open, so that we could find him. I described the place that he should camp at. Before finding Hubbard and Schell, Sayles and I had been to the head of Hoods Bay. We knew by the maps and the lay of the country that the heads of Hoods Bay and Chieke Bay were only about five miles apart, and my aim was to travel this five miles afoot after Collins, when matters were ripe for arrest.

I then returned to camp and found the furnace and charcoal ready for business.

One night after dark, Hubbard brought in what he thought was about a fourth of the gold. It looked just like black mud and was very heavy. Next day we made experiments and melted some of the stuff into fine gold nuggets. This was the day Collins was to go to the head of Hoods Bay and remain there until one of us came. The day following, the furnace was kept going, and some nice nuggets were turned out. Hubbard worked hard, as he was anxious to get this batch finished so that he could get the nuggets cached in a safe place. But Sayles and I had agreed that we wouldn't quite finish the batch, so we worked with that end in view, although we had not planned a mode of action. That was left to my two by four brain, to act whenever I got a "hunch" that the time was ripe. The main point was not to let Hubbard recache this gold.

Towards sundown I had a fine supper cooking,—clam chowder and pies. I went out to see how the boys were getting along. Hubbard was sweating like a "Nigger" at election, in his haste to finish the batch before supper time While I was out there we weighed the nuggets and made an estimate of the value of the gold, including that just put into the crucibles to melt. This would make $1,900 worth. Here I went back to see that my clam chowder wasn't burning. I knew how long it would take to melt the stuff now in the furnace, so I regulated the cooking accordingly.

Hubbard and I slept together on one side of the tent, while Sayles slept on the other. Hubbard kept his rifle under the head of our bed, buried out of sight in the grass which we slept on. I secured this rifle and was looking for a safe place to hide it. Near the camp there was a deep hole of water not less than ten feet deep. All of a sudden I got a "hunch" that this would be a good place to hide it, so out the rifle went in the pool, which was quite wide, and no doubt it is there yet, as we never looked for it. Then I cached my Winchester rifle, so I could get it without Hubbard seeing me.

Now supper was ready, and I began to call the boys, Ten minutes passed and they didn't come. I called with an oath attached, to let them know I was getting angry. After another minute's wait I ran out to where they were at work. They had just emptied the crucibles and Hubbard was insisting that they fill them up with the last "mud" on hand, as he would rather finish than go to supper. As he had agreed to stay and keep the fur-

nace hot, Sayles had to give in, as he had no excuse.
So I found them preparing to put the last "mud" in
the crucibles. I began swearing and said my nice supper was getting cold. Hubbard began to make his talk
about finishing, but I told him that there would be another day, to-morrow, to work in, and so saying, I
grabbed the crucibles and "mud" and cached it behind
a log near by. I then picked up the can containing the
nuggets and started out in the brush to cache them.
Hubbard followed me and helped dig a hole in the
moss by the side of a log, where the can was deposited.
This was quite a distance from the furnace, so that
Sayles couldn't see us.

We then went to supper. Hubbard didn't feel good
until after we had taken a couple of appetizers before
sitting down to the nice meal.

My supper didn't agree with me, for I began to have
cramps in my stomach an hour afterwards; this, of
course, being a blind. I went to bed the same time Hubbard and Sayles did, but I couldn't sleep. In the course
of an hour or more, when I thought Hubbard was
asleep, I got up and put on my boots and clothes, but
Hubbard was awake and asked where I was going. I
told him I was going to make a hot toddy and see if
it wouldn't help my stomach-ache. After putting on
water to heat, I made the toddy and went back to bed.
Another hour passed and I got up again to make another toddy. This time Hubbard was asleep. Still, the
toddy was made and I sat by the fire awhile. Finally,
with my Winchester on my shoulder I slipped through
the brush to where the gold was cached. Securing the

nuggets and the balance of the "mud," I struck out for the northeast through the timber. Half a mile from camp I recached the gold, then continued up an open glade covered with skunk-cabbage, on which the hundreds of bears feed. Sayles and I had been to the head of this open glade where the heavy timber and underbrush started in again. From the head of this glade over to Hoods Bay, was an unexplored territory to me.

By this time it was quite dark. I could see the bears running into the timber at the head of the glade, just where I had to go. This made me feel a little ticklish, as I had heard it said that Alaska bears were dangerous when they had young ones, or if surprised by a person coming on to them suddenly.

Since pitching our tent here on Chieke Bay, one night a large bear stuck his head under our tent and grunted as though something was hurting him. Sayles and I woke up at the same time. While I was figuring whether to shoot Mr. Bear or invite him to walk in, Sayles gave a yell that caused the poor bear to nearly break his neck getting away We could hear the brush cracking for half a mile.

At this time of year these bears were unfit for use. They were poor in flesh and their fur was no good. Their habit was to come to the coast from the high mountain range in the center of this large island, and live on skunk-cabbage and berries until the salmon began to "run" up the fresh water streams. Then Mr. Bear would get fat on fish and return to his winter quarters in the high mountains.

From the head of the glade I found it hard navigating,

owing to the fallen timber and "devil-clubs,"—a tough briar bush with thorns like an eagle claw, which is poison to the flesh. They take hold of one's clothes and hang on like grim death to a dead "Nigger." I had to follow the bear trails. Often I had to crawl on my hands and knees for a hundred feet or more, under fallen timber. During all this time I would whistle or sing to scare the bears out of my path. Judging from the sound of the brush cracking ahead and up the sides of the mountains, there were a great many of them.

On top of the mountain range I came to a lake. There were no bear trails around it, and to go through the brush was too slow and tiresome, so I waded around the edge of the timber in the lake, up to my waist in water. Reaching the opposite side of the lake I found myself going down a creek, and by keeping in the middle of it half-knee deep in water, I could make pretty good time. In going down this creek I couldn't resist the temptation of firing my pistol twice, once to kill a large dog salmon, and the other, at a large bald eagle. I cut the eagle's claws off as relics.

It was after daylight when I woke up Deputy United States Marshal Collins in his tent. While he was dressing I made some coffee. Before starting, he gave orders to the two Indians to take his camp outfit back to Killisnoo.

We returned the way I had come.

On reaching the top of a high hill overlooking our camp, we saw Sayles and Hubbard getting breakfast. We slipped down through the brush and reached the tent on the opposite side from the camp fire. Stepping around the tent we advanced towards Hubbard. Collins pointed his pistol at him and demanded that he throw up his hands, as he was a prisoner. I had cautioned Collins not to shoot Hubbard under any condition, unless he should break to run or pull a gun. I explained that he had no gun as I had thrown it in the waterhole.

I was standing still, smiling, with the butt of my rifle resting on the ground. Hubbard paid no attention to Collins' demand, but straightening himself up to his full height, with both thumbs under his suspenders, he walked up to me and looking me square in the face said: "Davis, how in h—l can you ever face the public again, after the way you have treated me?" I laughed and told him that my business was mostly with individuals, not the public, hence my conscience wouldn't bother me on that score.

Poor W. Roxward Sayles felt relieved. Hubbard had gone out when they found me missing, and discovered the gold gone. Then he raised h—l with Sayles who assured him that I would be back soon; that I might have heard Indians prowling around while sick and sitting by the fire, and had recached the gold to keep them from finding it. Hubbard had then searched for my tracks on the beach, but failed to find any. Both canoes were on the beach, so he was satisfied I would return.

The matter wound up by Hubbard and Schell being taken back to Juneau in the Lucy, a steam launch. The Deputy Marshal, Sayles, and myself accompanied them. Arriving in Juneau, Mr. Schell was put in jail, while Hubbard remained in my company. He had given me his word that he wouldn't attempt to escape. I believed him, my object being to "job" him by having him make a written confession of the theft, so that Sayles and I wouldn't have to stay there as witnesses until court sat late in the fall.

For a week Hubbard went everywhere that I did, free from handcuffs. We slept together over in my cabin on Douglas Island, Sayles remaining in Juneau.

After Hubbard had confessed the robbery and agreed to testify to the theft in court, I had to turn the poor fellow over to the jailor to be locked up. This hurt me worse than it did him, but I made arrangements for him to receive better treatment than the other prisoners were getting.

This ended our work. The company got back their $10,000 worth of black "mud," as it had all been found and dug up where Schell and Hubbard had cached it. The gold-plated frying pan was also taken along, as it was worth a few hundred dollars, there being that much gold sticking to it.

When the United States Court convened late in the fall, Hubbard and Schell were sent to the penitentiary. Hubbard received a sentence of only one year in the Sitka Pen. Schell received a longer sentence, so I heard.

During his stay in the Sitka Pen, Hubbard used to correspond with Sayles and me regularly. The last letter received was after his sentence had expired, and while he was preparing to start for the Dawson City gold diggings to make his fortune. We only hope that he has become rich, for the world is full of worse men than Charlie Hubbard. Whiskey was the cause of his downfall.

After serving his term out, Schell became a desperado. Last account I had of him through the newspapers, was where he and a gang had killed a Deputy United States Marshal, and I believe one or two other men, and were in a stronghold not far from Juneau, standing off an army of men. The papers stated that the outlaws couldn't escape, as they were surrounded, but I never learned how the fight came out. The chances are, Schell was caught and is now serving a life sentence, if not dead.

While in Juneau one day, I ran on to my old friend and boss, W. C. Moore, with whom I had worked for three long years on the L X ranch in Texas, when a cowboy. While chasing the "Almighty Dollar" in the American Valley in western New Mexico in the early '8o's, he murdered two men and became an outlaw, with a big reward on his head. I was not surprised to see him in Juneau, as a cowboy friend had written me that he was in Alaska, and gave me the name under which he was going. I had also read a letter once, written by himself, under this same assumed name, to Mr. W. L. Dickenson. In this letter he told of being camped with the noted Tascott, the murderer of Millionaire Snell, of Chicago, and of how he would deliver him over to the authorities for part of the fifty thousand dollar reward which had been offered in all the papers. Here was a case of one outlaw trying to turn up another bad man for money.

Even had I not known the name under which Moore was sheltered, I would have known his poor handwriting and bad spelling.

In connection with the Moore letter, I learned a new lesson in high finance, to the effect that the fifty thousand big silver "plunks" offered for Tascott's arrest, was a fake, the truth being that he was not wanted, owing to the fear of a scandal in high life.

I had poor Bill Moore Badly frightened, although I had no intention of having him arrested. He wouldn't recognize me or acknowledge that he was Moore, and as soon as I left him he pulled out for "tall timber." Friends told me that he was known as a trapper, and only came into Juneau about once a year. Therefore, he must be living a "hell on earth," which should be a warning to others not to commit murder for the sake of the "Almighty Dollar."

No doubt, I had previously been pointed out to Moore as Lee Roy Davis, the Dickenson detective who helped capture Hubbard and Schell. The local papers had been full of news about the great detectives, Sayles and Davis, who recovered the stolen gold.

After receiving the blessings of Mr. Durkin and Mr. Bordus, for getting back their black "mud," Sayles and I boarded the steamer Queen for Sitka, so as to take in the Capital of Alaska before returning to civilization.

On the return trip from Sitka, we visited the great Muirr Glacier, one of the wonders of the frozen north.

At the Muirr Glacier I did a little stunt which should forever brand me as a fool.

The tourists on the Queen had climbed the hill and mounted the glacier. Most of the people had rented sticks with spikes in the end to keep from slipping on the ice, but I didn't, as I regarded them a foolish fad to make one look like a "globe-trotter."

15

We finally came to a natural ice bridge across a chasm hundreds of feet deep and about thirty feet wide. The bridge was only two or three feet wide with a slippery surface.

A nice looking young woman bantered some of the men to show their courage by crossing this bridge. No one responded. Then she gathered up her skirts with the independent air of a Boston school mar'm, and went across. On the opposite side she laughed, and dared one of us men to come across. Instead of complying with the dare, most of them got further back as though the mere thought of crossing the chasm gave them the shivers. I told Sayles that if some one else didn't go I would, as women are not built for holding as much courage as men, and for that reason, I couldn't stand to see the whole male population of the world disgraced by one little woman.

Finally I plucked up courage and started, but before getting half way over I wished to be back on the starting side. If my hair didn't stand up on end, it surely felt like it. I dare not shut my eyes, and with them open I could see too far below, where there seemed to be no bottom.

On reaching the lady's side, she gave me the "glad hand," which helped some, but it didn't relieve the strain on my mind as to how I should get back, for I was on an icy island with chasms all around. I followed the lady back, but it required every ounce of courage in me to make the start. Hereafter when a foolish girl wants to test the courage of men, she won't get me for a tool, no matter if she is a "good-looker" with a form like a "two-time winner."

I enjoyed the trip from Alaska immensely, for it gave me my first chance to study nobility at close range. We had on board a Duke from Italy and a Prince from Germany. The Prince's name was Bismarck, he being a nephew of the "Heap Big Chief" Bismarck, ruler of the German Empire.

The Italian Duke was a nice sociable gentleman with sense enough not to be a Duke, if it wasn't for the graft there was in it.

But with the other rooster, his Royal Princeship, he didn't have a thimbleful of brains. He wouldn't speak to anyone on the boat but the Captain, and he wouldn't stoop so low as to eat with the common herd. He got up on his highhorse once because I called him partner. He asked the Captain what that "bloody American" meant by calling him partner. He had taken the wrong route to see an Indian village, when I called and said: "Say, partner, you are on the wrong road." His Royal 'Iness was on a trip around the world.

One jolly soul on the Queen was a Mrs. Lane, the wife of Millionaire Lane of Angels Camp, California. And Dr. Bean and his lively wife of Pocatello, Idaho, were passengers. Also Mr. John Brown, of Blackfoot, Idaho, a member of the Idaho Legislature. In fact, the steamer was full of live, jolly passengers, which made the week's trip a pleasant one.

In Portland, Oregon, Sayles and I laid over a day to visit with Supt. Wooster, Capt. Jas. Bivens, Mr. D. G. Doogan, and Philip Berne, of the Dickenson Agency. We then boarded a train for Denver, and en route home I found a Dutchman who had a wonderful memory for faces and the human voice.

Sayles and I had got off the train to get a cup of coffee in a lunch room. The place was crowded. When I asked for the coffee, a man with his back to me said: "Hello, I know that voice." Then turning around to face me he said: "Hello partner, don't you know me?" I replied "No." He then said: "I'm Dutchy, the fellow who put up the turkeys for you fellers to shoot at, in Tuscarora, Nevada, several years ago. You are the feller who had the pretty Colts pistol."

I then remembered "Dutchy." No doubt he would make a good sleuth, providing he could harden his conscience and learn to look wise and keep his mouth shut at the proper time.

On arriving in Denver, Supt. McCartney gave Sayles and me the "glad hand" for our good work in Alaska, and the operation was closed after an absence of six months.

CHAPTER X

CHASING LEON CARRIER THROUGH THE REPUBLIC OF
MEXICO—RUNNING DOWN BAD MEN IN ARIZONA—
BIG ORE ROBBERY ON BULL HILL—GOLDEN FLEECE
ORE STEALING CASE—HOBO OPERATION—BIG MINING
SUIT IN ARIZONA—RUNNING DOWN BANKER'S SON
IN BRITISH COLUMBIA.

My next big case was chasing Leon Carrier, a noble
son of a noble member of the Canadian Parliament, from
one end of Old Mexico to the other.

Carrier had stolen thirty carloads of merchandise from
the Westerly Pacific Railroad Company, and the Dickenson Agency was employed to run his noble "nibs"
down.

In Mexico, Carrier changed his name often.

This operation afforded me a chance to visit my friend,
Daniel Turner, Supt. of the Wells Fargo Express Co.
in the City of Mexico, and to see the sights of that ancient
Capital once more.

I never heard what they did with Mr. Carrier on
getting him back to Canada. But the chances are, his
noble father paid the bills and put the young man on
the stool of repentance.

Soon after this, Mr. McCartney sent me to Arizona
to run down the noted, John Zillman.

The big insurance companies of New York had been
trying to locate John Zillman since 1879, when he was

supposed to have been killed and buried, in Barbour County, Kansas. The insurance people who had insured his life a short time previous to 1879 for $75,000 in favor of his wife, had what they thought was good proof that a drunken cigar maker had been murdered and buried for Zillman, so as to beat the companies out of the insurance money.

Mrs. Zillman, backed by her friend, Levi Baldwin, a rich cattleman, had sued the insurance companies in several courts, and always won their suit. But the companies would just as often appeal to a higher court, in hopes of finding Zillman. The case was due to come up in court again soon, and the insurance people felt sure that if they could run down two men, Fletcher Fairchild and Bill Herendon, one of them would prove to be the much wanted Zillman.

Supt. McCartney informed me that all I had to work on, was the fact that Bill Herendon was a desperado who smuggled between Arizona and Old Mexico, and was always on the jump to avoid arrest. In the case of Fletcher Fairchild, no one knew where he was living. The last account had of him was a year previous, when he left the Levi Baldwin cattle ranch in the Datil mountains of western New Mexico, riding a bob-tail horse, and headed west towards Flagstaff, Arizona.

After being given a description of Zillman, with a photo taken when he was a young man, I started.

In Holbrook, A. T., a cattle town on the Atlantic and Pacific Ry., I bought a horse and saddle, and later another horse. Then followed hard rides over deserts and mountains. My work led me through the wildest parts of Arizona. Part of the time I was in the Superstitious Mountains where "Apache Kid" and his cutthroat band of Indians were in hiding, my only companions being the two saddle ponies and "Phoenix," a Scotch terrier dog stolen for me in the territorial capital. The "chambermaid" in the livery stable stole this high-toned dog with a brass collar, because he needed a silver dollar to quench his thirst.

Both of my men were finally run down. Bill Herendon and his two outlaw chums who were well mounted gave me the liveliest chase. They were arrested in the Salvation Army mountains on the border of Old Mexico. As neither man proved to be the muchly wanted Hillman, "Phoenix" and I boarded a train for Denver. I had been on the operation three months, and used the name of Lee R. Davis.

My next Big case was for the Spion Gold Mining Co., of Cripple Creek, Colorado. I built a cabin on top of Bull Hill among the Western Federation dynamiters and sweated much blood for fear of being blown up at night.

A Coeur D'Alene member of the Miners Union, Oscar W., recognized me as the C. Leon Allison of Gem, Idaho. He had figured in the killing of Johnny Kneebone and had fallen heir to that "scab" blacksmith's pistol, after his murder at Gem, Idaho, in 1894. Oscar W. promised not to disclose my identity to the dynamiters, and he kept his word.

My several months hard work in the Cripple Creek district disclosed a big steal wherein our clients J. A. Hill, Horace Union, Dr. J. T. Remy and James Cownors, had lost about half a million dollars through the theft of rich gold ore. The superintendent of their mine, the Pikes Peak, and three of the directors in the Union Gold Co. were in the steal. I had to appear on the witness stand in Colorado Springs.

My next operation was a big ore-stealing case for Geo. Lakes, D. K. See and Attorney Dobbs of Denver. They were being robbed blind in their Golden Fleece mine at Lake City, Colorado, though their superintendent, Mr. Aker, was an honest man.

My work disclosed the slickest system of daylight robbery that was ever carried on in a civilized country.

I became one of the thieves after taking lessons in an assay office run by one of the gang.

W. O. Sayles helped me wind up the operation, which lasted a couple of months. In the eruption, 150 miners on the Golden Fleece lost their jobs. Twenty to thirty thousand dollars worth of rich ore had been stolen each month; hence the clients were happy over the stopping of this leak in their fat incomes.

Here another tramp hobo job fell to my lot. McCartney gave me $150 of expense money, and sent me south to roundup Tim Corn, the afterwards noted stock detective hung in Cheyenne, Wyoming. He was needed to testify in court, hence I was instructed to finish his bum operation, which he was doing for private parties.

At Coolidge, New Mexico, I found Corn early one morning with a tough gang of hobos. They were holding a council of war as to how they were all going to eat on the quarter of a dollar which one of them had.

Corn had lost his $100 expense money a few days previous, gambling in Albuquerque, hence he was really "on the hog." He was ashamed to wire home for more expense money so soon after leaving Denver. I finally got a chance to slip Tim Corn a few dollars to take him to Albuquerque, from whence he could wire for more money.

When ready to start, Corn gave a brakeman one dollar to take him to Albuquerque. It was a cattle train loaded with steers, and the "brakey" opened the trap door on top of the car, through which the hay is put into the racks which hang on the inside of the car. Horn being a big six-footer it was a tight squeeze for the "brakey" to shove him through the small hole. When inside, the trap door was fastened by the "brakey" and poor Horn couldn't get out if he wanted to. He was a Horn among horns, as he had to lie in the hay rack above the clashing steer horns.

Just then a red headed hobo came and sat down by me on the depot platform and said: "Say, Cully, did you see de 'brakey' shove dat tall guy in wid de steers?" I replied "yes," as he had seen me watching the proceeding. He then continued: "Dat guy is a fly cop for de Dickensons. De gang was goen to do him up tonight and get his big gun and watch. He said he didn't have no rocks (money), but I bet he did. If he didn't, where did he get dat big plunk (silver dollar), dat he give to de 'brakey?'"

I asked the hobo how he knew that he was a fly cop. He replied that the fellow had made a confident of an old Indian scout from Arizona, who now lived on a ranch at a spring near Coolidge; that they were drinking together in the saloon the night previous, and that the scout had told the secret to the barkeeper who gave it out to his friends on the quiet. Then one of these friends put "de gang next." I was worried for fear the train crew might know the secret and kill Corn, but my hands were tied, as the train had pulled out, so that I could do nothing to warn him. Had the train crew killed him, he would have avoided the trouble of being hung in disgrace. Besides, many lives which he snuffed out for pay, while acting as stock detective for the cattlemen of Wyoming, would have been saved. He told me of killing two of these supposed cattle thieves, one of them being a cowboy named Matt Rash.

I never think of Tim Corn but that his bulky form and big ears loom up in my mind's eye as he was being shoved into the roof of that cattle car.

I tramped it all the way to Los Angeles, California, and back through Arizona and New Mexico. The work was being done for the S. T. & G. Ry. Co. On this tramp job I saw enough of life in box cars and under water tanks to write a large sized book.

In Denver, a couple of months later, I put on my good clothes and was transformed from a hobo to a city gentleman.

I was finally sent to Minas Prietas, a large mining camp in the State of Sonora, Old Mexico. Howell Lines, who was a third owner and manager of five gold mills in Minas Prietas, had sent to the Denver Agency for a good mining detective who understood the Mexican language and customs, to run down $20,000 worth of amalgam which had disappeared mysteriously from one of his gold mills.

TIM CORN.

After spending over a month in Minas Prietas, eating fresh oysters on the half shell every meal at the Hotel Colorado, and enduring the heart-rending cruelties to the poor horses and mules which hauled the freight and ore, the $20,000 worth of amalgam was found where it had run off with the quicksilver into the tailings dump. Carelessness on the part of employes had caused the loss. It was recovered, and my fun, drinking mescal and dancing with pretty Mexican girls, was cut off.

While on this operation, I had made one trip out into the wild mountains with a saloon man and a blacksmith, who were suspected of being into the supposed steal. We went to examine a mining prospect which the blacksmith owned. Of course, we took along a good supply of mescal, a Mexican liquor which makes drunk come quick, for snake bites.

I also made one trip to Guaymas, a seaport city on the Gulf of California, to work on an old man who was suspected, and while there, I came within a hair's breadth of crossing the dark river of death, from whence there is no awakening. Still, our old mythical devil would, if he could, have awakened me to scorch my whiskers for hopping around on the face of the earth and sipping more than my share of the honey of life between hops.

On the train, en route to Guaymas, I met my Bull Hill friend, Mr. M., one of the Union Gold Mining Co. directors, who had been mixed up in that big ore-stealing case. He gave me his hand and assured me that he held no ill-will against me, as I had done only my duty and had told the truth on the witness stand in Colorado

Springs. He was accompanied by a friend whom I suspected of being mixed up in this same steal, though I had never met him before. Of course, he knew all about me.

On arriving in Guaymas, we three went to the same hotel, the Alameda, I think it was called.

That night we took in the sights, and hired an Indian to take us out into deep water in the Gulf, so we could catch barracuda, a large, slender, deep-water fish. We were to start at daylight next morning in a small sailboat. I felt that it might be a "job" on the part of M. and his companion to drown me in revenge for the part I had played against M. in the Cripple Creek district.

After midnight we three climbed the broad stairs to our rooms, which fronted on an open court. I had a separate room adjoining my two companions, and Mr. M. agreed to wake me at daylight.

In going to bed my corduroy pants were put under the pillow, and then noticing that my old Colts 45 was lying on the center table, I placed it on top of the pants.

Next morning while the room was still dark, a loud rap came on my door. I jumped up, half asleep, and grabbing the legs of my pants which hung over the side of the bed, with the intention of putting them on before going to the door, I jerked them out from under the pillow. In doing so, the pistol landed on the floor and struck on the hammer, which rested on a loaded cartridge.

The report of the shot in the close room was deafening, and the powder smoke and dust from the falling plaster almost choked me. I stood still, with the pants in my hand, wondering if my friend M. had thrown a bomb into the room. Just then I saw the silver mounted pistol on the floor, and realized the truth.

M. and his friend were at the door trying to get in to see if I had committed suicide, rather than get up so early to go fishing. I let them in and the smoke and dust out, by opening the door.

The only damage was a few yards of torn plaster from the ceiling, and a red streak across my forehead, where the bullet had barely stung me. Luck again gets in her fine work in my behalf.

We went out in the Gulf about ten miles, and had a fine day's sport catching fish and drinking something which was not sea water.

Finally I landed back in Denver, Colorado, to wait for some other exciting operation to turn up. But I didn't have long to wait, as a hurry-up call came from Arizona for a good sleuth.

This operation was for N. V. Parke, owner of the United Birdy Copper mine, of Jerome, Arizona, and now a United States Senator from Montana. And while on the work, I got a peep behind the curtain of "Frenzied Finance."

In Arizona a big fight was on over the ownership of the Equator mine, five miles south of the great United Birdy.

I was sent to Jerome and Prescott a month or two before the case was to come up in court at Tuscon. No one was to know me but Asst. Supt. Allen and Supt. Joseph Giroux, of the United Birdy mine, also Eugene Giroux, brother to the superintendent.

Later, poor Mr. Allen got an overdose of "Frenzied Finance" mixed with high wines and corn juice, and shot his head off. I adopted the name of Lee Roy Davis.

In Prescott I met some old-time friends who knew my right name and occupation, but I had no fear of them giving me away. They were Mr. and Mrs. Goldsworthy and their son, the railroad agent at that point, and Mr. Johnny Kinney, with whom I got on my first champagne "drunk" in Las Cruces, New Mexico, in 1881, while a cowboy, and on trail of cattle stolen in Texas by the notorious "Billy the Kid." Up to that time I had never tasted champagne.

The A. T. & S. F. Ry. was then building down the Rio Grande river, and had reached Rincon, forty miles above Las Cruces, and La Mesilla, the twin towns. I was working on Johnny Kinney secretly, so as to get in with the noted "Hurricane Bill" and his gang of cattle rustlers and desperadoes. Kinney then owned a butcher shop at Rincon, the terminus of the railroad, and much of his fresh beef came through "Hurricane Bill" and his gang.

In Las Cruces I was invited by Kinney to accompany him to La Mesilla, and attend a wedding in a wealthy Mexican family. I did so, and champagne flowed like water, giving me my first taste of high life, and a champagne headache.

Of course, on being recognized by Kinney, in Prescott, we had to "hark back" to that wine supper and dance in La Mesilla. We did this between drinks at Mr. N. V. Parke's expense.

In Prescott I made the acquaintance of Mr. Duke,

the big man on the opposing side, so as to work on him at the trial in Tucson. I also made the acquaintance of many of his witnesses and thereby learned some of their secrets.

At the trial in Tucson, Parke's and Duke's money flowed like water down a duck's back, swift and easy. Money was crowned King for the time being, Justice being hog-tied and losing her scales in the shuffle.

Albert Ezekiel, a Deputy United States Marshal, who afterwards joined the Dickenson force, was Duke's secret man.

As I was supposed to be a tough cowboy out of a job, Duke got me to do a little extra detective work for him. He had me watching Joseph and Eugene Giroux, so as to find out their plans. Often I would report of hearing conversations between the Giroux brothers at the Xavier Hotel, which indicated an important meeting after night at a certain place. I would then have the Giroux brothers help carry out my scheme as a blind, and Duke would help me "shadow" them, which convinced him that I was working faithfully for his interest.

It was a puzzle to Mr. Duke as to why I refused to meet and consult with his leading attorney, Mr. V. E. Block, now a United States Congressman from Colorado; my excuse to him being that my cowboy friends would mob me if they knew I was acting as a detective. So for that reason, I wouldn't trust anyone but himself. The truth of the matter was, I had met Attorney Block in Colorado Springs, Colorado, while with Dr. J. T. Remy, on the Spion Gold Mining Co. operation, and feared being recognized by him.

The Duke crowd won the suit. The jury was bought outright, after being locked up. An additional $10,000 of the slush fund drawn out of the bank at the last moment did the work. A county officer, who was on the jury, told each juryman who was sticking out for N. V. Parke, to go out in the toilet room, which would be to their advantage. The bailiff, who was into the scheme, would accompany the stubborn juryman into the toilet room where a man was planted with the cash. There the bargain was arranged for high stakes, and our side was left floundering in the "soup." I was on the "inside" and knew what took place. My particular friend on the jury held out until the last one. That night when they were dismissed from the jury after bringing in a verdict for the Duke side, this fellow almost shed tears over the fact of going back on us, but he said he couldn't resist the temptation of the fancy price offered him in the toilet room.

The only consolation I could get was in helping him spend some of this "tainted" money.

The next suit came up in Prescott, and it was rotten to the core. My friend Johnny Kinney assisted me here.

Robt. and Joe Morrison, Prescott attorneys, were assisting Attorney Block at this trial, and Joe Morrison recognized me as C. Leon Allison whom he had met in Santa Fe, New Mexico, when he was in the United States Land Office there, with his father, Judge Morrison. This affected my work, as he was suspicious of me working against his client, Duke.

In Prescott I had two operatives from Denver assisting me.

Albert Ezekiel had come from Tucson to work for Duke.

Thousands of dollars of Parke's and Duke's money were squandered every night on "Whiskey Row," where a dozen saloons stood in a solid row fronting the Plaza and Court House. The "girl" singers and the music on the raised platforms in the rear of some of the saloons, had a tendency towards making the old "Hasayampa" sinners forget that they were born with Nature's full allowance of manhood, and that the courts are intended to deal out justice, regardless of the amount of "dough" (money) in sight.

After another hard fought monied battle, the Duke side won again. Of course, Duke had an even "break" from a legal and just standpoint, but without their big slush fund to act as sauce for the roasted gander, they never could have won.

The case went to the higher courts, and was later settled mutually, so I was informed by Congressman Block, whom I met under false pretenses many years later, in Yampa, Colorado.

On this operation I had gained valuable lessons in high finance and the ease of committing perjury, by otherwise good men and citizens.

Another operation on which I was detailed about the year 1897, was the running down of a banker's son. He had gotten away with large sums of money in a north-middle State, to save his old father in a middle State, from going to the wall financially. After putting the father on his feet with the stolen money, the young man crawled into a hole and pulled the hole in after him so

16

far as any trace of him remained. From a former chum of this banker's son,—whom we will call Get-there-Eli,—our clients received a "tip" that he was somewhere up in British Columbia. Then I was sent to run him down.

After I had located Get-there-Eli in Greenwood City, a new mining camp on the Kettle river, in British Columbia, I proceeded to make his acquaintance and to win his friendship, which I did finally. I found that Get-there-Eli was the manager of a mine in Greenwood City, and he was making piles of money selling stock at fifteen cents a share in his new company, which had as officers some of the "big guns" of Canada. He was going under an assumed name, but looked exactly like his photo which I carried, and answered the description to a dot. On investigation I found him to be one of the solid men of this new mining country. He was considered an expert on mines, though on getting acquainted with him, I found his knowledge on mining was of the "graft" kind picked up from books, etc., as bait to catch "suckers" and I soon found that the country was overrun with "suckers" ready to grab any kind of bait which smelled of dividends.

In Prescott, A. T., I once asked my friend, Johnny Kinney, how he managed to make such an easy living, and as to how Prescott prospered as a mining center with so few pay mines tributary to the little city. He replied: "You must remember that we get many English capitalists to look over our country every year. Englishmen are like those fish with the big mouths, called suckers. Their mouths are always open ready to receive a bait that looks like a dividend. Of course, they get hooked, but then new ones are coming out all the time."

I found Greenwood City swarming with this kind of fish. The king fish of the bunch was a fine fellow named Germain. He was past middle life and had accumulated a nice little fortune in the drug business in London, England. Hearing of the great Boundary Mining District, he sold out his drug business and came to Greenwood City, arriving there a couple of months ahead of me.

The snow lay deep on the ground, and he found many old "stove-warmers" at the saloons, who had rich prospects to sell *cheap,* though they were covered with several feet of snow which would prevent a prospective purchaser from examining the veins until the snow melted in the late Spring. So, for that reason, they would sell *cheap* for *cash.* When Spring came, poor old Germain had most of his fortune invested in these kinds of mines.

On the Queen's birthday, Get-there-Eli had got me to sell some of his mining shares. On that day the English "suckers" bite better than any other time. Of course, I wanted to make myself solid with Get-there-Eli, by selling a good bunch of his stock. It was "wild cat" stock then, but the mine, which I examined, had the ear marks of a possible producer in the future.

I have always been a good fisherman when I didn't have to wait too long for the bite, and the larger the fish the better. Therefore, my hook was baited and thrown towards Mr. Germain. His mouth was open and I landed him for $600 in cash, my commission being $80. During the day I hooked a few smaller "suckers" and made good wages.

Shortly after the Queen's birthday, Mr. Germain informed me that he had started two men to work on one of his mines, as the snow had gone off in that neighborhood, a few miles north of town. He said he had great confidence in my judgment on mining matters, and would like for me to advise him as to the best way to develop this mine quickly, so as to make a dividend payer of it.

He and I walked up to the mine one morning. We found the two "Micks" down in the six-foot holes working like Turks to keep warm. On our arrival the two miners stopped work and Germain jumped down into the open cut. He asked me to come down into the hole so as to get a better look at the fresh ore. I told him that it wasn't necessary as it was all alike, just a big blue limestone ledge. The two miners looked daggers at me, as I was taking the bread and butter out of their mouths by knocking them cut of a job.

The smile faded from Germain's face like the dew from a sun-kissed rose. With a look of despair, he asked if I meant that he had no mine there. I told him such was the fact. He then said: "What if my other mines turn out like this one? If they do, I am a ruined man." I advised him not to take my word for it, but to hire a certain mining expert who lived in town and who had a good reputation, to come up the next day and examine the property. My advice was taken and the two miners lost their jobs.

Germain's other mines were examined by the same expert and when I was leaving Greenwood City, poor Germain was packing up to leave the "bloody swindling country" to return to his family in London, England, a poorer but wiser man. I was truly sorry for the poor fellow, and the $80 of his money which was in my pocket seemed to be hot. I felt like giving it back to him, but didn't dare to, as it would have placed me on the fool list.

Germain was not alone in his misery when the snow went off; the woods were full of the same kind of sick "suckers."

When the time came for swooping down on Get-there-Eli, our friends sent an agent from the east to pick the poor fellow's financial bones. On the arrival of the agent I steered Get-there-Eli to his room after supper, as the agent was a supposed friend of mine from Texas, who wanted to invest in mines. He and Get-there-Eli were old friends, and to see the look on Get-there-Eli's face when I shut the door and locked it and introduced him to his former friend under his own name, was worth a trip to British Columbia.

After shaking hands with the agent, poor Get-there-Eli sat down on the bed, and with pale face, told me that I had played my cards splendidly.

A deal was made to return the stolen money,—many thousands of dollars,—if we would promise to not expose him in British Columbia, where his reputation was above par, and his chances of becoming a millionaire good.

Our friends wanted their money back, and I had been playing my hand with that object in view.

The agent started right back to the boyhood home of Get-there-Eli to get the money from his parents, while I remained to keep an eagle eye on G. T. E. We became bedfellows and greatly attached to each other.

He was a fine, portly young man, with more than the average allowance of brains.   He and I kept up a correspondence for a couple of years, and he reported good fishing and schools of new "suckers" arriving, eager to take the hook.   Since then I have lost all trace of him.

Finally I received a letter to discontinue and return to Denver, as matters had been settled.

On this trip in British Columbia, I met two of the old Coeur D'Alene dynamiters, Jack Lucy and "Spud" Murphy.   The latter threatened to kill me, but my friends Geo. Mimms and Millionaire Jim Clark, in Grand Forks, persuaded him out of the notion, as I was pretty handy with a gun myself.   I had helped send "Spud" Murphy to the pen in 1892 from Coeur d'Alene City, Idaho.

I reached Denver after an absence of about three months.

CHAPTER XI

My next operation out of the city was of a "Frenzied Finance" order, wherein a man whom we will call Bill Blank, a cattleman whom I had known by reputation all my life, had swindled Kansas City money brokers out of large sums of money through shady transactions.

This William Blank had come from a noted family of Texas cattle raisers, and in a cattle deal Bill was "foxy" and could out-fox a fox. It was also said that he had nine lives like a cat. During the '80s, in New Mexico, Curly Bill's outlaw gang shot him seven times through the body and left him out on the desert for dead, so the story goes. But he wasn't dead by a jugful, as a couple of days later he crawled into his camp and soon after began figuring on a big cattle deal in Montana.

Some Kansas City money brokers had furnished cash to buy steers in San Antonio, Texas, the Spring previous to my being detailed on the case, taking a mortgage on the steers for security. The steers were to be driven to the Indian Territory and there fattened for the fall market on buffalo grass.

As a precaution against loss, and so the money brokers could identify their property in case of trouble, the tip of one horn of each steer was cut off.

247

The cattle were taken to the Comanche Indian Reservation in the western part of the Indian Territory, and there turned loose to fatten. They were kept within a certain range by Blank's cowboys riding lines. Late in the Fall Bill concluded he didn't want to ship the steers east for "feeders." Therefore he turned them over to the brokers to get their money if they could, he himself withdrawing from the scene. When the brokers sent cowboys to gather up all steers with the tip of one horn cut off, they failed to find any but a few of the original number. They were not in the country, and Blank said he couldn't account for them being gone unless the Indians had killed them. Then I was detailed to unravel the mystery.

From Denver I started on the Denver & Ft. Worth Ry. for Amarillo, Texas, there to buy a horse and saddle and ride to the range where the Blank steers had been kept during the summer.

I arrived in Amarillo, Texas, at three o'clock Christmas morning. A blizzard was raging and the weather was very cold. Knowing that my old cowboy friend of early days, Jack Ryan, kept a saloon in this town, I concluded to go there and warm up. On entering Ryan's place I found Jack behind the bar.

After shaking hands, Jack asked if I could recognize any of my old friends among the drunken men sleeping on the floor, chairs and tables. Casting my eyes over the bunch I picked out my friend Burkley Howe sleeping in a chair and dead to the world from over-indulgence in "firewater." In looking at him my mind drifted back to 1878, when he, then a fine looking, sober young man of high education and wealthy parents, came to the Panhandle of Texas, then a wild, unsettled country, to learn the cattle business. He came from Massachusetts, the former home of David T. Beals, Erskine Clement and Mr. Bates, for whom I was then employed. As I was then boss of an outfit on the staked plains where the little city of Amarillo now stands, Howe was turned over to me to be taught the cattle business.

Now, here sat that same Burkley Howe on this Christmas morning, over 20 years later, a total wreck and aged beyond his years from that greatest of all evils, liquor.

Slapping him on the shoulder I said: "Hello there, Burkley Howe, old boy!"

Before opening his eyes he yelled: "Well, I'll be d——d if there isn't Charlie Siringo!" He had recognized my voice. He then jumped up and began hugging me and declaring to the other drunken men who had awakened when he yelled that I used to be the best wild-horse rider in the United States. He had seen me ride some "bad" horses and he couldn't brag on me enough. In order to choke him off, I called the crowd up to take a Christmas drink with me.

Ryan then informed me that my old friend, John Hollicott, the manager of the L X ranch, which I had helped establish, was at a saloon across the street celebrating Christmas. Running across the street I found Hollicott dancing a jig and having a rattling good time, as he called it. He almost choked me as he dragged me up to the bar to take a Christmas drink "on him." The whole crowd of a dozen men were called up to drink. I was the hero of the moment with Hollicott. Finally we went across to Jack Ryan's place and Howe joined in the celebration.

At daylight Hollicott's coachman hitched up the spirited team of mules and we started for the L X ranch on the Canadian river 20 miles north, to take Christmas dinner with the "boys" and girls there.

I left poor Howe laid out on the floor and I haven't seen him since, but I was informed through friends that he died a year or two later which proves what liquor can do in a twenty years' tussle with robust manhood.

We had a cold ride against the raging blizzard with the thermometer ten degrees below zero, hence the cork was pulled from the five-gallon jug several times before reaching the ranch.

It was about 10 A. M. when we reached the roaring fire in the large stone fireplace which I had helped to build over twenty years before. There was the identical hearthstone put in place by W. C. Moore, the outlaw murderer whom I met in Juneau, Alaska, and me.

Thoughts of bygone days flew thick and fast, and the flames from the log fire seemed to be playing hide and seek with other bright blazes of long ago. Possibly my familiarity with the jug en route from Amarillo had something to do with my imagination.

Hollicott introduced me to the Lee family who lived on the ranch. The head of the household was Mr. Garnett Lee, then came his good-looking, black-eyed wife and their two beautiful young lady daughters. The younger, a girl of 18, had just come from a college in middle Texas to spend the holidays. She was indeed a little "peach," and it was all I could do to keep from falling in love with her, even though I was old enough to be her father.

Several of Hollicott's cowboys from outside camps were on hand to sample the Christmas dinner. Two of them, Charlie Sprague and Johnny Bell, were former chums of mine and had worked under me when I was a "boss" on this ranch. The others I had never met before.

About 2 P. M. the fat gobbler and cranberry sauce, with the side "fixens" were set on the same old table from which the noted outlaw "Billy the Kid" and I ate meals together twenty years previous. It was a dinner fit for kings and queens, and we all did justice to it. When we got through Mr. Turkey-gobbler looked as though he had been to a bone-picking match.

The afternoon was spent "harking back" and sampling the contents of the jug.

At night, after supper, one of the boys got out his violin and the dance started. There being only three ladies present we had to make a girl out of one of the "boys" by tying a handkerchief around his arm, in order to fill out the set.

Towards morning the jug began to work on Hollicott and he wouldn't let me dance. He insisted on "harking back" to the early days of our cowboy lives. He and I first met in 1876 in Kiowa, Kansas, at which time he was a cowboy for the Hunter & Evans cattle outfit, and I was drifting around to give my mustache a chance to grow.

John Hollicott was a high-bred gentleman, born in bonnie Scotland. He was a fine-looking six-footer, with a heart like an ox. Being born tired was his only fault, especially when it came to getting up in the morning. At one time he had worked under me on a big roundup on the South Paloduro, and getting him up for the peep o'day breakfasts was my hardest work. That same year, 1883, Mr. Hollicott took a jump from a common cowboy to the manager of this big L X ranch, with its 50,000 head of cattle and the hundreds of fine horses. Hence the fact of his being born tired didn't seem to work to his disadvantage.

I had been considered as one of the candidates for this fat position, but was told that some of the stockholders in the company objected to me as not being tame enough for such a responsible position. Therefore, Mr. Hollicott won out, and years later, I was his honored guest.

Towards daylight the dance broke up and the coachman drove Hollicott and me and our Christmas "jag" up to the mouth of Pitcher Creek, a couple of miles, where Hollicott had his private home.

We retired together in the same bed, and Hollicott was soon fast asleep. But not so with me—I couldn't sleep for "harking back" in my own mind to the day when Mr. Bates and I slept at this very spot, and chose this as the headquarters camp of the future L X ranch. That was in the early fall of 1877, and "Deacon" Bates, Mr. David T. Beals' partner, had brought me along into this wild unsettled country to help him select a cattle range for a new company which Mr. Beals had formed.

The country was then alive with buffalo and Indians. Across the river from the mouth of Pitcher Creek, only a mile, three hundred half naked and painted Apache

Indians were then camped. Hence Mr. Bates and I didn't know what moment our scalps might be lifted. We selected a range forty miles square. The grass was fine and not a single cow-brute to eat it, until after the first L X herds arrived from the north.

Now, as I lay by the side of my old cowboy companion, the thoughts of those good old free and easy days came back. But finally my brain felt like scrambled eggs—a jumbled up mess of woolly buffalo, painted Indians, yelling cowboys, bucking broncos, long horn cattle, fat turkey gobbler, two pretty girls and a big brown jug; then I fell asleep.

About 10 A. M. I was awakened by Hollicott, who was up and holding the jug and a glass, ready to give me a morning "bracer."

After a hearty breakfast I asked Hollicott to take me back to Amarillo so that I could buy a horse and saddle for my journey to the Indian Territory. He replied that I had to lay over another night and "hark back," this being a favorite expression of his. When I insisted that it would take me at least a day or two to buy a horse and saddle and that I was in a hurry to reach my destination, he said: "Now, Charlie, don't mention horse and saddle to me again, when you get ready to go the best horse on this ranch will be brought up to the door, saddled and ready to mount, and if that don't suit you, I'll send my team and coachman to take you wherever you want to go."

I remained, and in the afternoon we followed the pack of hounds in lively chases after wolves and jack rabbits. After breakfast next morning, a five-year old brown horse, sixteen hands high, and in every respect a model piece of horse-flesh, was brought to the door of the stone house at the headquarters ranch, where lived the Garnett Lee family. On his back was Johnny Bell's saddle.

This horse had just lately been broken, he having run wild on the range all his life. I had known his sire and his grandsire on his dam's side, and they were of the best blood. The sire was Glen Alpine, a four-mile running horse, and the grandsire on the dam's side was a high-priced trotting stallion which Mr. Beals had shipped from Boston, Mass., when the L X ranch was first established. Mr. Beals had once presented me with one of old Glen Alpine's colts, the pick of about fifty head, but like many other fool cowboys I got short of cash in a poker game and sold him for $200. Hence this big snorting brown was the second gift-horse from the same blood.

On mounting Glen Alpine, Jr., after bidding everybody,' including the two pretty Lee girls, goodby, Hollicott told me never to sell this horse, but to shoot him when I had no further use for his horseship. I promised that he would never be sold.

Some of the "boys" rode a few miles with me and they said that Hollicott and the girls were no doubt disappointed at my horse not bucking, as they expected a free show, with me as the star actor. They said this horse was a hard bucker and was always ready to show his skill. They couldn't account for him not bucking that morning. But he made up for it the next morning and on many occasions afterwards.

Two days later Glen Alpine, Jr., was left in a livery

stable at Panhandle City, and I boarded an A. T. & S. F. Ry. train for Woodward, Oklahoma, one of the new boom towns in the recently opened-to-settlement "Cherokee strip."

In Woodward several former cowboy friends were met, among them being two cowboys who had worked under me on the range. One, Billy Bell, was a brother to Johnny Bell who gave me the saddle. The other was Jim Goeber, late sheriff of Potter County, Texas, in which county the L X ranch and Amarillo are situated. Here I also met Temple Houston, a son of the Lone Star State hero, Sam Houston. He was a bright lawyer, and through liquor, had become a man-killer, so I was told. But whiskey soon put him under the sod, judging from later newspaper accounts.

After investigating matters connected with my operation, I returned to Panhandle City, where Glen Alpine, Jr., was mounted, and a start made south.

One night was spent at the Charlie Goodnight ranch, where next day I rode out in the pasture to see the Goodnight herd of buffalo and some half-breeds.

Mr. and Mrs. Goodnight were not at home, therefore I didn't get to see them. In the early days I had eaten meals with them both in cow camps, and on one occasion, Mrs. Goodnight, a good-hearted little lady, divided the wild berries which she had gathered, with me. For this I have always held her in high esteem, as in those days women in the Panhandle country were scarce and far between.

My work lay mostly in Greer County, Oklahoma, Mangum being the county seat, and across the north fork of Red River, on the Comanche Reservation in the Indian Territory. This brought me onto ground gone over by Tim W. in the Tuscarora, Nevada, operation.

Finally I rode to Vernon, Texas, on the Fort Worth Railroad, to work on Mr. C. T. Merrick, a big cattle king, now a banker in that town. From him I gained much valuable information about the Bill Blank cattle, without his knowing my object. I visited at his home and became acquainted with his lovely wife. He is a Prince and she a Queen, of the American kind.

In Vernon, Glen Alpine, Jr., was left in a livery stable and I boarded a train for the cities of Fort Worth, Dallas, Austin and San Antonio.

In Austin, the capital city, I made the acquaintance of the noted Robert G. Ingersoll and his good wife. We rode in the same car to San Antonio, and I had the pleasure of a private talk with this great man.

In and around San Antonio I found out all about the steers purchased by Bill Blank. Trips were made out on the range where the steers had been purchased, and the end of one horn cut off, and I also found where a man whom we will call Capt. Dash had bought a herd of steers with the same ranch-brands as the ones bought by Blank, and the tips of both horns of these were cut òff, and thereby hangs the tale of this plot.

In the course of time I got back to Vernon and found Glen Alpine, Jr., seal-fat, so that he bucked like the old Harry when I mounted him.

Finally I bade goodby to my friends in Vernon and started on a six hundred mile ride for New Mexico on trail of a herd of cattle driven to New Mexico by Bill Blank the previous summer.

On reaching the staked plains my road was as level as a floor for about two hundred miles. It was indeed a revelation to me how these plains had settled up with a hardy race of small ranchmen, with windmills to furnish water. In former days I had scouted all over these plains in search of L X cattle which were in the habit of following the buffalo south, and at that time there were no settlers at all. Now, windmills could be counted by the hundreds in a day's ride.

West of Plainview, near the eastern line of New Mexico, I stopped with a gentlemanly young nephew of Bill Blank's so as to work on him and find out on the sly about the herd of cattle driven to Arizona by his wide-awake uncle.

Before reaching the Pecos River my good name saved me from losing supper and sleeping out in the cold without bedding. The ranches here were far between.

Night had almost overtaken me when I rode up to a Mr. Taylor's ranch. Tying Glen Alpine, Jr., to the gate-post I knocked on the door. It required several knocks to bring results. Finally the door opened just a little and a nice-looking young woman who proved to be Mrs. Taylor, asked what was wanted. I requested to stay all night. She was sorry but had to refuse on account of her husband being absent, and she and Miss Alice Littlefield being alone. I asked if Miss Littlefield was related to Jim and Geo. Littlefield, and to my friends, Phelps and Tom White. She answered yes, that Alice was a daughter of Jim's. Then I gave my true name and Miss Alice opened the door wide and gave me a hearty welcome, after introducing me to Mrs. Taylor.

17

Miss Alice and I had never met, but knew each other by reputation. I had worked on the cattle trail between Texas and Kansas for her uncle and father before she was born.

The two ladies had a big laugh over their plans to fight me to a finish in case I insisted on stopping. Their guns were primed and cocked for my benefit, as they supposed I was a desperado, from the fact of my having a Winchester rifle on my saddle and a pistol strapped around my waist, for people in this country had become civilized and quit loading themselves down with firearms.

I spent a pleasant night and found Mrs. Taylor to be a jolly good little woman, and Miss Littlefield was a lovely and highly educated young woman who seemed out of place in this desolate country.

Two days later I put up for the night at the Lewis ranch on the Pecos river, forty-five miles above the lively town of Roswell, New Mexico.

I got an early start from the Lewis ranch next morning, as the distance to the next water was about 90 miles across a desert country, without roads or habitation.

A lunch was put up for me by Mrs. Lewis, and with a full canteen of water I started. I had made a trip over this desert country once before in 1881, with Lon Chambers, when we rode from the L X ranch in Texas, to Lincoln, New Mexico, there to meet Deputy United States Marshal John W. Poe, and act as witnesses in the noted "Billy the Kid" cattle stealing case. On the trip we came very near perishing for want of water, as our horses played out.

Recalling my past experience in crossing this desert,

I couldn't help feeling a little shaky, starting out alone, though I had great faith in my horse not playing out this time, for I had come to the conclusion that there was no getting tired with this son of that great horse, Glen Alpine. With faith in one's horse the battle is half won.

We headed for the Capitan mountains, which were in sight. There being no road and the ground being rough and soft, we made slow headway. Often "Glen" would go up to his knees in the soft gypsum soil, which is full of caves. At noon I stopped an hour to let "Glen" graze and to eat my lunch. I had water, but poor "Glen" had none. By sundown we had traveled about fifty miles, which was equal to seventy-five over a good road. "Glen" was beginning to act tired, though I think it was more from the lack of water, as the day had been very hot. There was one small drink left in the canteen and I had been saving it for the past couple of hours as a life-preserver.

Just at dusk I dismounted to fix the saddle tightly on "Glen's" back for the thirty-mile night ride to water. The front cinch was tightened and I was pulling up the flank one, when "Glen" went to bawling and pitching. He bucked 'round and 'round, taking me with him. I hung onto the bridle reins for dear life. Finally I had to turn loose, and "Glen" was soon only a streak of brown in the twilight. At last the streak disappeared entirely. He had gone back the way we had come, at a clip which did credit to his ancestors. I swore a blue streak for not drinking the last water in the canteen while I had the opportunity.

I stood still for a few moments, wondering what to do. There to the southwest lay the dim outlines of the Capitan mountains, a walk of thirty miles to the first water. And towards the east, nothing but a desolate-looking stretch of darkness. I could still see "Glen's" tracks, and my mind was finally settled on following them so long as they could be seen. Therefore I struck out in a trot "all same" Comanche Indian on trail of his supper when following a wounded deer.

A run of about one mile brought me to where I could no longer see the tracks. There I stopped to go back, rather than risk the sixty mile walk to the Pecos River without water. I began to wish that I had given up the detective business before starting into it, for the future looked a little scaly to me then. My tongue was already swollen slightly, and there was no guessing how it would be by morning.

I could see a dark object which looked like a clump of bushes, off to the east about a quarter of a mile. A faint hope sprung up in my heart that this might be "Glen" who had gotten his foot in the bridle reins and had to stop. Finally I concluded to investigate this dark object and when within a hundred yards of it a loud snort reached my ears and away he flew. My heart beat with joy at being so near water, even though it was out of reach. "Glen" was soon out of sight again, but I ran in the direction he had gone. In a few moments the dark object hove in sight again. Here I concluded to use my brain against common horse sense. I walked leisurely around the dark spot until I was east of it. Then I began to whistle favorite tunes, now and then sitting down to give "Glen" a chance to get used to me. When within a few yards of him he began to snort. I sat down and pulled grass, speaking to him all the while. On getting hold of the broken bridle rein I felt just like I did when the soldiers arrived in Wallace, Idaho,—like shouting hurrah for America.

The canteen and rifle were still on the saddle. The water was gone—out of sight, just as soon as the canteen could be put to my parched lips.

On mounting "Glen" I gave him to understand, by tickling him with the spurs, that he couldn't lag back and pretend that he was tired, as he did an hour earlier.

About midnight we reached the slope of the Capitan mountains. Then "Glen" was unsaddled and staked out to a bush, and I lay down on the saddle blanket with the saddle for a pillow, and went to sleep.

Next morning at 8 o'clock we filled up with water out of a large reservoir on the wagon road between White Oaks and Roswell, and at 10:30 A. M. we ate a square meal in the town of White Oaks.

As this town had been my headquarters during the winter of 1880 and '81, when in charge of a squad of cowboys on trail of the noted "Billy the Kid" and his desperate gang of outlaws, I was soon shaking hands with old friends. Among them were Attorney John Y. Hewett and his partner, Wm. Watson, then the well-to-do owners of the rich Old Abe gold mine, of White Oaks.

Of course, Judge John Y. Hewett and I "harked back" to the winter of 1880 when I gave him his first law case. He had drifted into this new mining camp and had put out a shingle as a lawyer.

During the winter one of my "rangers" as they were called by the natives, got into a shooting scrape with Sheldon, the town schoolmaster, and I hired Lawyer Hewett to defend my man, "Big-foot Wallace," whose right name was Frank Clifford.

The trial came off before Judge Frank Lea, Justice of the Peace, and Hewett won his first case by freeing "Big-foot Wallace."

But poor big-hearted "Big-foot Wallace" became an outlaw after quitting my outfit in Texas· the following summer. I still retain the tintype photo of him sent to me from Old Mexico after he had shaken the dust of Uncle Sam's domain from his number ten boots. In his letter he bade me goodby, saying that in all likelihood we would never meet again.

He and Ethan Allen, of White Oaks, had just held up a store and secured money and jewelry, at Los Lunas, New Mexico, on the Rio Grande River. At Socorro a posse of officers surrounded them. Young Allen was captured, but "Big-foot Wallace" made his getaway by swimming his horse across the raging Rio Grande. The officers dare not follow as the river was up and dangerous for man and beast.

Young Allen was held at Socorro, the scene of the robbery, and placed in the town jail along with a negro criminal, and the same White Oaks schoolmaster, Sheldon, whom "Big-foot Wallace" had the shooting scrape with. Mr. Sheldon had been on a drunk that day and was put in jail to sober up.

That night a mob of Mexicans broke open the jail, liberating the negro and hanging Mr. Sheldon and

BIGFOOT WALLACE.

Ethan Allen. They did this to spite the white "gringos" for hanging the Baca brothers in Socorro a short time previous. Of course, this was tough on the well-educated eastern schoolmaster, whost worst sin was a love for "fire-water." Had "Big-foot" been captured, he too would have met the same fate, and he and Sheldon could have buried their hatchet of bitter hatred while the ropes were being adjusted about their necks. Such was life in the untamed west.

In White Oaks I also met other old friends, among them being Jones Taliaferro and his wife. Also Dr. M. G. Paden and Paul Mayer. The latter owned the livery stable of the town and his brother was the "City" Marshal.

Marshal Mayer had a complicated case on his hands, and knowing me to be a Dickenson detective, he asked that I solve it for him.

A miner with a sauerkraut brogue had been paid off the day before, and put the $300 in a trunk in his cabin, and while he was up town that night, some one with an axe broke in the door, then broke the trunk open and skipped with the money. I told Mayer that I was too tired to do my best as a sleuth, but that if he would bring "Dutchy's" partner, Williams, of Irish extraction, to my room at the Hotel Ozane and leave him locked up with me, I would do my best to recover the money.

Williams stood on his dignity for awhile, then first on one foot, then the other, until he became tired and broke down. The $300 was turned over to poor "Dutchy," who took the first stage for the railroad. He wanted to pay me for my trouble, but I refused it, something out of the ordinary for a detective.

This gave me a local standing as a sleuth, and quieted my nerves after that hard ride, by swelling my head, thus giving the blood more room for circulation.

Two days later I started north, continuing on trail of a young Texan whom I will call "Cunny" for short. He had been a cowboy for Bill Blank at his White Mountain ranch in Arizona, and had helped drive the cattle which I thought might be some of the stolen steers from the Indian Territory to Arizona.

One hundred miles north of White Oaks I found "Cunny" in the mining camp of San Pedro. We soon became warm friends and I worked him for all he knew, without his knowing who I was. But later I told him my business, and our friendship continued.

My investigation showed that none of the steers had been driven to the Arizona ranch. They had been stolen in a more honorable way, a way that few old-time Texas cattlemen would call stealing. It was on the order of horse trading in Texas,—to the sharpest trader belong the spoils. In fact, many Texans would have patted Bill Blank on the back with "well done, Bill old boy."

The scheme was well carried out from start to finish, as follows:

Bill Blank and Capt. Dash had laid the plot together, so I was informed, and my whole work indicated that it was true.

In the early Spring both went to San Antonio, Texas, and bought each a herd of steers from the same ranch-men, so that the cattle would have the same brands on them. The herds were put up at the same time. Capt.

Dash cut the tip of both horns off, while Bill Blank cut the tip of one off. This was done supposedly, to tell them apart, should they ever become mixed together. as both herds were bound for the Indian Territory. On the Comanche reservation both men had secured leases of a certain stretch of range, adjoining each other. Bill Blank had borrowed the money with which to buy his steers, giving a mortgage on a certain number of cattle with designated ranch brands, and the end of one horn cut off. Being on adjoining ranges the two herds naturally became mixed, and the summer and fall was spent by the Blank and Dash cowboys in cutting the remaining horn off the Bill Blank steers, thus transferring them from Blank to Dash.

As the steers waxed fat in the Fall Capt. Dash had many feeders to sell on the eastern market, and the cowboys were kept busy gathering to ship. When Capt. Dash was through shipping, Bill Blank concluded to let the brokers in Kansas City, who had loaned him the money, foreclose the mortgage, but they couldn't find anything to foreclose on. Bill Blank had taken a back seat from whence he could, with a broad smile, view the windup. And then your humble servant came onto the scene and took a front seat, playing one of the last acts in the drama.

In order to keep in touch with "Cunny" in case we needed him as a witness, I hired him to take charge of my Sunny Slope ranch, a couple of miles from Santa Fe, New Mexico, which I was fixing up for a "hobbyhorse" to ride in my old age. I really needed a man to run the place, and by hiring "Cunny" I could kill two birds with one stone.

It required two days of my valuable time to get "Cunny" pulled away from his Mexican sweetheart in San Pedro.

Santa Fe is only forty miles north of San Pedro, therefore we didn't have far to go. "Glen" was left on my ranch in "Cunny's" care, while I returned to Denver and discontinued the operation, after being on it about four months.

I have never heard what action our clients took against Bill Blank. They may have exposed the scheme to Blank and got a partial settlement, and again, they may have concluded to pocket their losses and in future lock their stable door before the horse is stolen, especially if old-time Texas cowmen of the tricky horse-trading kind are prowling around.

"Cunny" was never called on as a witness against Bill Blank. He had charge of my ranch for two years and then went to mining on a prospect in which I was interested. Thus he swore off being a wild and wooly cowboy, and is now a prosperous mine expert in the booming gold districts of Nevada.

Glen Alpine, Jr., lived a retired easy life on my Sunny Slope "hobby-horse" and died at the age of fifteen, though he never quit the habit of bucking, even in his old age.

On one occasion he gave a "bloody" Scotchman a "touch of high-life," which was bloody in fact, at the windup.

John Hart, a friend of mine from Denver, but now living in Albuquerque, New Mexico, wanted the satisfaction of riding a good horse once in his life, so I let him ride "Glen."

We started from the Sunny Slope ranch to take a forty mile ride to Bland. I was on my pet mare, Lula.

Now, Hart was an expert as a carpenter and contractor, but as a bronco buster he proved a total failure before we had gone ten miles on our journey. Saying, "Come on Hart," I started Lula off in a swift gallop. In a moment I looked back just in time to see poor Hart in the air and "Glen" running towards me. Hart swore he didn't do a thing but dig the "bloody hold 'orse" in the side with his heels, after I had started. Having some sticking plaster in my pocket, Hart's face, hand and elbow were patched up. He said the hard stony ground had come up and struck him before he was ready, for he figured that one-half of a somersault more would have saved his face by landing him on the fleshy part of his pants.

Hart rode Lula the balance of the trip.

CHAPTER XII

KANSAS DAISY AND BUTTERFLY MINE-SALTING CASES—
TRAMPING ON THE OREGON SHORT LINE RAILWAY
COMPANY'S SYSTEM—A BIG ORE-STEALING CASE IN
SALT LAKE CITY, UTAH—TRIP TO BRITISH CO-
LUMBIA—PLAYING OUTLAW IN CRIPPLE CREEK,
COLORADO.

During the next couple of years I led a strenuous life
unraveling ore-stealing and mine-salting cases.

First came the Kansas Daisy case, of Prescott, Arizona.
A Mr. B. of that enterprising town had put out a bait
and caught some big fish in England. When the aforesaid big fish, who were organized as the Anglo-Continental Mining Co. began to smell a "mice," they called
on the Dickenson Agency to investigate and see if their
corn-crib really contained rats. Hence, I was sent to do
the cat act.

While in Prescott, and after satisfying ourselves that
the Kansas Daisy mine had been salted, some mine ex-
perts, with Detective Willis A. Loomis (now Chief of
Detectives in Denver) to guard the samples of ore until
safely in the Wells Fargo Express office, arrived from
Denver to sample the property. On these samples being assayed in Denver, they showed an average value of
$1 per ton of ore, instead of the $8 per ton as reported
by the German expert sent from London by the com-

pany, and on whose advice the mine was bought at a high price.

The Denver law firm of Thornes, Bryan & Wye had charge of the work, and they gave orders that I dig up evidence as to how the trick was done.

Finally, I went into partnership with a saloon man named Joe Hobbs, a brother-in-law to the noted Deputy United States Marshal Joe La Fors, of Cheyenne, Wyoming (whose testimony hung stock detective Tim Corn), and with a miner named John Forbes, in the mining business. We bonded a gold claim on Groom Creek and started a shaft down on the vein. I had made the acquaintance of Joe Hobbs while working on the John Hillman operation in Jerome, and he knew me only as Lee Roy Davis. He had a brother-in-law, Jeff La Fors, in Prescott, who gave me much assistance without knowing it.

One day in March when the streets of Prescott were covered with a deep snow, Alex G. and I boarded a train for Los Angeles, California, there to prepare for a trip to Alaska, as Mr. G. thought.

Before departing from Prescott, I shook hands with my many newly-made friends, among whom was "Bucky" O'Neil, afterwards a Captain in Roosevelt's Rough Riders, who was killed by a bullet through his head in the charge up San Juan Hill in Cuba.

Next morning Alex G. and I awoke in the land of roses. The contrast was indeed great, from deep snow to roses in bloom on nearly every vacant lot. In Los Angeles we settled down to a life of ease, at the expense of the Anglo-Continental Co. I had been to this city before, but as a bum tramp only.

Alex G. and I made pleasure trips to all places within reach of Los Angeles. We even went to Tia Juana, Old Mexico, and spent a week or two at San Diego.

After I had secured a full confession from Alex G. as to how he and Mr. B. had salted the old German expert's samples as they were being taken from the Kansas Daisy vein, and also after being hoisted to the surface and there sacked and sealed, Attorney Bryan arrived from Denver to assist me in closing the operation; that is, as far as my work was concerned.

Attorney Bryan and I met to arrange for the windup. I had already planned most of it in my reports which had been read by Mr. Bryan.

At 10 A. M. one day, an officer of the United States Commissioners Court arrested Alex and me in my room. I was indignant at the arrest, while Alex G. was frightened. On the way to court Alex whispered to me not to give anything away which he had told about the Kansas Daisy.

When brought before the United States Commissioner I was put on the stand first. Attorney Bryan went at me as though he thought I had worked on the Kansas Daisy at the time of its sale, and finding that I had not, he asked if I had ever heard any one say that the Kansas Daisy had been salted. I kept avoiding the question and wouldn't give a direct answer, as though I didn't want to give Alex G. away. He frowned at me once, as much as to warn me to "stand pat." But finally Mr. Bryan pinned me to the wall so that I had to answer yes or no. Then I had to admit that Alex G. had told me all about the way he and Mr. B. had salted the samples. When I started to tell the truth, Alex turned pale and became nervous.

After finishing my testimony, Alex was put on the stand, and just as I had guessed, he confessed the whole crime rather than make me out a liar and ruin his chances of the trip to Alaska. He made a sworn confession, which implicated Mr. B. and made the German expert an "easy mark."

Soon after my return to Denver, this same old German expert got caught with another salty fish-line, which caused the Anglo-Continental Mining Co. a heavy loss. Mr. A., of Denver, had baited the hook, and the Swede saloon keeper, Knute Benson, of Silverton, Colorado, who owned the Butterfly mine, did the rest. When the $20,000 mill was completed and started up, it was found that they had no mine.

The honest, easy-going old German expert had been salted again, and I was sent to Silverton to work on the saloon man, Benson. He and I became chummy and made several trips out in the mountains. He said that he went into the deal so as to get a $20,000 mill put up free; that he knew the company would forfeit it according to the contract, rather than pay the balance of the purchase money, and then he and Mr. A. would develop a pay mine to furnish ore for their mill.

We failed to secure evidence enough to convict any one, so the Anglo-Continental Co. lost what they had invested, unless they possibly squeezed something out of A. and Benson, on the strength of my reports. I never learned how the matter came out, except that I heard the mine and mill fell back to Mr. Benson, and that the German expert washed his hands of the whole American continent.

I had been on this case a couple of months, and on the Kansas Daisy about four or five months.

About this time another tramp operation fell to my lot. It was on the whole system of the Oregon Short Line Ry. in Wyoming, Utah, Idaho, Montana and Oregon. The work was being done for the manager of that company. Mr. Roycroft of Salt Lake City, Older Galvan, and Mr. Vanderman, officials of the road, also had a hand in the operation.

On this work I had several narrow escapes from death, once from a wreck, when the end of a box car in which I was riding was smashed in, and another time in Idaho an angry brakeman came very near kicking me off a freight train while running twenty-five miles an hour. It was a cold night, and I was lying face down on top of a box car to shield myself from the cold wind that was blowing. He slipped up on me and gave me a kick in the ribs which nearly sent me rolling off the car. In an instant my hand was on old Colts 45, and I thought seriously of shooting the fellow, but satisfied my wounded feelings by calling him all the pet names in the cowboy dictionary which has never been printed.

He slowed the train down so that I could get off, but I made him stop it to a standstill. We were both standing on top the car, and he was kept at a distance by threats of killing him. I didn't propose to have a wrestling match in a place of that kind.

A week or two later, I caught this same "brakey" by being with a squad of bums. He didn't recognize me, and we all paid him for a ride to the end of his run.

While I was on this bum operation, deals were made for whole box car loads of sheepshearers, and often I would be one of them. We would be packed like sardines when the crowd was large, so as to get us all into one box car, then the door would be fastened from the outside. A fine chance for a jumbled-up mess of human hash, in case of a bad wreck. With the freight crews this traffic in sheepshearers was fine "picking" from a financial standpoint, for they traveled from place to place in droves, a mixture of all nationalities, even to the chili-eating sons of old Montezuma. The fares were $1 apiece for each division.

While on this operation I visited the great Mormon Jubilee, the fiftieth anniversary of the settlement of Utah in Salt Lake City. It was a free show which beat anything I had ever seen. Every Mormon in the State who could raise the "price" was there.

On the day of the big street parade I had the experience of knowing how a hobo feels when he falls in love.

I was standing on the sidewalk in the hot sun, trying to get a view of the parade in the middle of the street. Directly in front of me stood a beautiful young lady. She was small, and I could have seen the parade over her head if it hadn't been for her silk umbrella. I finally became impatient, and tapping her on the shoulder, asked if she wouldn't let me hold her umbrella so that I could get a view. She turned square around and faced me. Then was when Cupid first got in his work. Up to this time, I had not seen her pretty face. She looked me in the eyes, then glanced down at my dirty and ragged

18

clothes. I smiled and said: "You need have no fear of me stealing your umbrella. All I want is to make the umbrella do double duty by shielding both of us from the sun, and at the same time allow me to see the parade."

She gave me the umbrella. Soon she became talkative, and explained some of the interesting sights in the parade. Among them being her aunt, Mrs. Watson, sitting on the deck of the Brookline—a ship that represented the one that brought her aunt over the ocean. Hence, I concluded that this pretty little lady might be named Watson. I had made up my mind to ask her name, but just then a "Weary Willie" chum of mine stepped up saying: "Say, Cully, drop dat rag—meaning the umbrella—and I'll steer you to a joint where they sell two whopping big schooners (glasses of beer) for a nickel."

Turning around and seeing my unwashed and ragged chum the lady reached for her "rag," and at the same time gave me a look with her pretty dark eyes which froze little Cupid to a "stand still."

That night while riding in a box car loaded with hobos I vowed this would be my last tramp operation, for I had had more than my share of that kind of work. I had made one hobo test on the D. & R. G. Ry. system, in addition to the ones recorded herein.

I arrived in Denver after being absent about two months.

Later, I was told of how on the strength of my reports, every freight brakeman between Salt Lake and Butte City, except one who was in the hospital, got "fired" from the Oregon Short Line service. Also many freight conductors and engineers "got it in the neck."

Tramping on a railroad is a fine schooling for a detective, but very tough on one's sensitive nature; hence only one in twenty operatives make a success at playing hobo.

These train crews had been "coining" money, and they had become so greedy that often a poor hobo who was known to be sick and out of money, would be put off the train between stations on the desert, just because he refused to give up some little relic, such as a ring, watch or pin, possibly remembrances from dear ones at home. The "brakeys" would even take pocketknives for fares. It seems that greed for the "almighty dollar" is planted in some bosoms, be they high up in the social swim or low down in the muddy pool. But in my tramp work I have found hundreds of "brakeys" whose hearts would melt at my pitiful tale of woe of being flat broke. Some have even offered me money to buy a square meal, besides giving me the free ride.

Next I was detailed to go to Salt Lake City, Utah, to assist operative Billy S. on an ore-stealing case which he had been working on for a couple of months. Billy S. had made himself "solid" with one of the leaders who were stealing ore by the wholesale, but as yet he had no positive evidence.

I landed in Salt Lake City, the big town with wide streets and pretty swift girls, as an outlaw from New Mexico and Texas. My name was Lee Roy Davis. As on outlaw I didn't go to killing men, but I soon had some of the gang afraid of me. Once when I had filled up on "puss cafe" in the New Resort saloon, with Billy Best as mixologist, I made the gang think I was on the warpath. I pulled out my old Colts 45, and striking the table with it, declared I was a wolf and that that was my night to howl. The result was, Billy S. had to help pull Joe Buttinski out from under the table and assure him that I wasn't as bad as I looked

To illustrate the splendid memory of some men, I will cite the case of an ex-cowboy by the name of O. D. Brown, who is a trusted official in the Salt Lake City postoffice. On first arriving in the city, I called at the postoffice to ask for Lee Roy Davis' mail. Brown stuck his hand through the window and said: "Hello there, Charlie Siringo, shake." I told him my name was Davis. He replied that he would remember the name and forget my right one. He then told where we had run cattle together in Texas, over 20 years before. Then I remembered him and shook his hand.

We were together many times during my couple of months stay, and he thought because I had committed a crime, was why I had changed my name. Of course, this didn't sit well on my pride, but I thought it best to let matters remain as they were.

Brown finally secured me a fine job to take charge of a mule train for a friend of his in Peru. I was to accompany the mules on the ship and become one of them, as it were. In introducing me to this friend, Brown told him that I was just the man he wanted, as I could ride anything that wore hair, talk Mexican, and could be trusted. Both were greatly disappointed when I declined the position at any price. Brown took me to one side and said I was making a mistake by leading a wild life and remaining here where I might be captured any time. I told him that I would rather be in the penitentiary in America than associating with mules in a Peru, South America, mining camp.

In the course of a month or so, Billy S. and I began to note results from the tons of beer and liquor consumed while with the gang. Often Billy S. and I would make night raids on a sampler or a smelter to get samples of the stolen ore-pile, which was called the "Jessie," by the ore thieves. Then again, we would break the seals on cars loaded with stolen ore, so as to get samples as evidence.

On one of these night raids into a carload of stolen ore, I flim-flammed our client, Banker Z. B. James, a reputed millionaire, who also owned mines and a smelter. We would notify Mr. James on what nights these raids were to be made, and he would sit up at his residence waiting for us. In his presence, the samples would be marked so that we could identify them in court.

In order to mark a chunk of ore different from the rest, I asked Mr. James for a silver dollar to mark it with. He gave me the dollar, and when through with it I put it in my own pocket, and on reaching the street Billy S. remarked that I was the slickest daylight thief he had ever seen. We had a big laugh over the matter, and at the New Resort saloon the dollar was blown in for mint juleps, and they tasted sweeter "all same" stolen watermelons.

Of course, there was no necessity of my stealing this dollar from Banker James, as he was a liberal client, and allowed us to spend "all kinds" of money for drinks and high living. But I wanted to play "foxy" and flim-flam a millionaire banker before his own eyes, and it was done so easily I told Billy S. that next time I would get a $5 gold piece out of him.

A couple of nights later we made another raid, and I asked Mr. James for a $5 gold piece to mark a certain piece or ore, so that the marks would be yellow. He gave me the gold piece, but when I had finished, his strong right hand was extended ready to receive back his five gold "plunks." Of course, it was returned as though I had no intention of keeping it. I caught Billy S.'s eye and he was grinning like a 'possum eating yaller-jackets. This time it was "foxy" James instead of "foxy" yours truly. No doubt he had noticed me put the silver dollar in my pocket, hence concluded to keep a string on the gold piece.

After a couple of months' work, we had sufficient proof to land half a dozen men in the penitentiary, one wealthy man among them. This big fish had a nice family who swam in the same social pool with Banker James, and Mr. James hated to injure the family. Therefore, he concluded to make out a bill for the many thousands of dollars' worth of ore stolen, and for the expenses incurred by Billy S. and me, and present it for payment, the bill to be backed up with the proof of guilt. If paid, matters would be dropped with a warning to sin no more, especially against the James' family. But if he failed to toe the mark, then the services of Billy S. and myself would be required longer. A settlement was no doubt made. Mr. James told us with one of his broad-gauge smiles, which denoted victory, that our work was ended and we could return to Denver.

In this case one big fish instead of swallowing the little fishes saved a lot of little ones from going to the "pen."

On arriving in Denver, I got a jolt which shook my globe-trotting desires to the very foundation.

I had been receiving letters from Supt. McCartney for the past three weeks, asking if I couldn't crowd the Salt Lake City operation and finish it up soon, so as to return to Denver, as he needed me. I would answer back that the work couldn't be hurried, which was a lie of the deepest dye. The truth was, we could have closed the work two weeks sooner than we did. But I didn't know but that he had another tramp operation for me. I didn't believe in dropping a good thing so long as it could be held onto without injuring the Agency.

Mr. McCartney informed me that my friend, W. O. Sayles, had started two days before for New York City, there to ship for London, England, to meet our clients, and from there go to South Africa to work up a big ore-stealing case, which would take a year or two, and that the New York office and Mr. Roy J. Dickenson had selected me for the operation and had been waiting on me for nearly a month, but that the clients in London got tired of waiting, and then Sayles was detailed to go. He was allowed to take along another operative, Hiram Oker, to help him.

My bones ached for a week on account of losing this trip to Europe.

Next, I was sent to British Columbia to run down a George H., who had salted a mine in Old Mexico. Mr. Wheezer being the victim, and Thornes, Bryant & Wye being our clients.

It would require too much space to record my many ups and downs in British Columbia trying to find a trace of Geo. H.

On the way to Ft. Steele after leaving the head of Lake Kootenai, I had a tussle with a blizzard when the thermometer registered forty degrees below zero. It was December. I was in an open cutter and for twenty-eight miles the wind kept whistling a tune through my whiskers, which sounded like: "Say, old boy why didn't you save your summer's wages and buy an overcoat?" I had on only a light leather frock coat. This pure and innocent new-born blizzard from the frozen north would never have asked the question, had it known of the many inducements for spending a summer's wages in Salt Lake City. It may have frolicked behind the curtains in an Eskimo Indian village, but that isn't sporting by gaslight in the Mormon capital.

Finally I decided to end this wild goose chase in the region of the North Pole, and start right by going to California and working on the relatives of Geo. H's wife. This had been tried, without success, but not by yours truly.

At the foot of Mt. Shasta, the snow-capped mountain of northern California, in Siskiyou county I landed in a sleepy little town called Gazelle. I put up in an old fashioned country hotel with a large fireplace and plenty of wood to feed the fire which was kept burning night and day. This country hotel was the home of the Edson brothers, wealthy cattlemen. It was here that Geo. H. formerly lived and married one of Siskiyou county's pretty daughters. The parents of Geo. H.'s wife lived on a ranch in this county and so did a married sister.

I spent a couple of days roasting my shins before the log fire and getting my breath after those cold rides in the north. And while doing so, I hobnobbed with English royalty in the person of a royal son, or grandson, of Lord Nelson, the Dewey of England. He was a fine young man, and was on a bear hunt around the world. I happened to see him kill a neighbor's pet coon by mistake as he swore to the enraged rancher; but whether he mistook it for a bear or a wildcat, I never knew.

Finally I put spurs to my two by four brain and started out to work on the sister of Geo. H.'s wife.

A short ride on the train brought me to the town of Montague. Two miles from that town was the ranch of the lady's husband. He owned a valuable ranch well stocked with cattle. We will call him "Huze," for short.

The night was dark, and it was 8:30 P. M. when I stood at the front gate of "Huze's" residence in the country. I aimed to get there late so they would have to keep me over night. The only light in the house was in the kitchen in the rear of the building. My mind was so taken up with the operation that I forgot about dogs. In slipping around to a man's back door, I generally have one hand on old Colts 45, but not so this night. Just as I turned the corner of the house and was within 10 feet of the kitchen door, here came a Siberian bloodhound, which loomed up like a mustang in a fog. She was as large as a good-sized colt. She had sprung out of a dog house in a corner of the back yard. I did a double stunt with lighting rapidity,—sprang for the kitchen door, turning the knob with my left hand and pulling old Colts 45 with the right. The door was slammed in the dog's face, just in the nick of time to prevent a tragedy. The dog had thrown her weight against the door, and it was all I could do to close it. She was growling and raving.

As soon as the catch snapped in the door, my pistol was back in its place out of sight, and I faced the big fat man and his small young wife. Both were on their feet and thunderstruck. I begged their pardon for intruding so suddenly. The lady replied that it was lucky I did, as the "doggy" would have eaten me up alive, as she had pups and was more vicious than usual.

After introducing myself as a Texan who had made a little fortune in mining, and who was in search of a good cattle ranch, I told of how people in Montague had referred me to them as wanting to sell out. "Huze" replied that he would sell if he could get his price, which was 'way up into the thousands. I informed him that if the place suited I wouldn't stand back for the sake of a few thousand dollars, more or less.

Then I was invited to stay all night and examine the ranch and stock next day. By 10 P.M. the fat man was dozing after reading a newspaper, and the little lady and I were going over the family album which I had picked up from the table. She pointed out her two sisters' photographs, one being married and the other single. The single sister was actually pretty, and I told her so. I asked where she lived and she hesitated as though not wanting to answer. I broke the strain by asking if she was now in California. She replied no, that she was with her other married sister up in British Columbia. I looked her in the face and asked what part of British Columbia, as I had made my stake mining up there. She replied: "Oh they live near Victoria." I said: "Why that's where I'm going to close up my mining deal. Maybe I'll see them up there. What's their names?" The names were given, then I questioned her as to the particular place they lived at. She acted as though she didn't want to tell, but the questions were so pointed that she couldn't avoid answering without taking chances of insulting me, and thereby losing a possible sale of their ranch and stock.

After finding out that Geo. H. and his wife and her pretty young sister lived in Alberni, an Indian village on the Alberni canal, a couple of days' travel by steamer from Victoria, the Capital of British Columbia, my day's work was finished and I was ready for bed. The fat man showed me to my room upstairs about II P. M., and I was soon stretched out between white sheets, dreaming of my coming trip to Vancouver Island, British Columbia.

The next day Mr. "Huze" and I rode over the ranch, and I expressed great delight in everything and declared that I would purchase the place providing my brother liked it; that we were going into partnership in the stock business, hence I would have to wait a few weeks for this brother to join me.

A week was spent at Gazelle and Montague, and I made the acquaintance of Mrs. Geo. H.'s parents. They were nice folks and had one son who has attained distinction in South Africa as a mining engineer.

A few days before Christmas, "Huze" and I took a trip to San Francisco, and I have never seen him since we separated in that city.

Finally I took passage for Seattle, Washington, by rail, thence by steamer to Victoria, British Columbia. In Victoria I took passage on a dumpy little steamer which was loaded to the guards, for Alberni. On the ocean along the southern border of Vancouver Island, we experienced rough seas and squally weather. About half of the time the little steamer was almost standing on end, and I expected to see her turn upside down any moment. Seasick, did you whisper? Well, I reckon yes! The few hours sail up the Alberni canal was delightful, after the rough ocean trip.

There was a "white folks'" hotel in the Indian village of Alberni, and my headquarters were established in it. There were only two star boarders at the hotel until my arrival, then there were three of us who could order eggs for breakfast without danger of raising the roof from the house. One of the star boarders was Judge Keenie, and the other his "niece;" "quien sabe," as a Mexican would say, for who knows.

The Judge was a tall, preacher-looking old gentleman, and evidently he was a fine man. I used him for a cat's paw to pull my chestnuts out of the fire. I soon learned that he was a particular friend of Geo. H., who was operating a mine about twenty miles from Alberni. Judge Keenie had practiced law for years in Socorro, New Mexico, hence he and I found much to talk about, as I knew many of his friends and a few of his enemies.

Finally Judge Keenie took me on a visit to Geo. H. and his family. They had a nice home near the mine, in which quite a force of men worked, and the mine which Geo. H. had bought, no doubt with the money secured from our clients, had the ear-marks of being a good one. Some ore was being shipped every week or two on a steamer to the smelter in Tacoma, Washington.

Several visits were made to the Geo. H. mine during the next few weeks. Finally he and his family moved to Victoria and put up at a swell hotel there. Of course, I followed suit and made my home in Victoria also. I had never told of my visit to their old home in Siskiyou County, California. In fact, I wasn't supposed to be the same man who met "Huze," as I had adopted a new name.

Valuable real estate belonging to Geo. H. in California was located, and with the valuable mine on Vancouver Island, our clients felt safe, so far as getting their money back when the time came for bringing suit, and until that time Geo. H. would be kept track of by our Agency, who have "correspondents" in all cities and towns where they have no regular offices.

Finally, towards Spring, I returned to Denver and its glorious sunshine. During my stay on Vancouver Island, I saw the sun only a few times. But while Denver beats on sunshine, Victoria holds the winning hand on lack of graft and political corruption, and for just laws, rightfully administered.

I never heard how Geo. H. came out in his war with our clients.

My next important out-of-the-city operation was an ore-stealing case.

One morning Supt. McCartney called me into his private office and told me that he had a hard nut for me to crack, and that he would depend on me cracking it, although one of his good operatives had already failed.

A Mr. R. B. Bursell had become tired of paying our regular rates of $8 per day and all expenses for the services of an operative, with no chance of success. Hence he wrote to Supt. McCartney advising that the operation be called off. But Mr. McCartney asked for a chance to try yours truly for a week or two.

With old clothes on, I landed in Victor, one of the big towns in the Cripple Creek mining district, and in just one week I had secured a confession from Geo. Shaul and Young Wilson, as to how they stole Mr. Bursell's $2,000 worth of rich ore which was in sacks ready for shipment.

Geo. Shaul was an expert safe blower and bad man generally. He was known to be one of the worst ore thieves in the Cripple Creek district, but he was too slick to get caught.

In order to make myself solid with Shaul and Wilson and their associates, I "shot up" the town of Victor one night. I supposed that I had made my "getaway," but towards morning my castle was stormed by the got-rich-quick Mayor, Millionaire Jimmie Doyle, and his mob of policemen. My door was broken down and I landed in jail.

Before arresting Shaul and Wilson, the Sheriff of El Paso County, "Win" Boynton, secured permission from my Supt. J. S. Kaiser, and Gen. Supt. McCartney, to let me unearth a murder case in Goldfield, wherein a saloon proprietor and one of his guests were shot down in cold blood one night in an attempt to rob the place.

I put in a month on this murder case, and associated with Shaul and his gang of cut-throats constantly.

A few days before I was ready to close the operation, a blackmailing detective by the name of Hawkins gave me away to the gang, on the sly. He and I had done some work for Attorney Goudy, of Colorado Springs, several years before. He had recognized me.

"Baldy Bob" and his gang had a plan laid to murder me and throw my body into an old abandoned shaft; but Nelly Taylor, a tough dance hall "girl," put me on my guard, as she couldn't believe me low down enough to be a detective. Thus my "bacon" was saved by a scratch.

At the trials in Colorado Springs, with me as the star witness, Geo. Shaul and Wilson received a sentence to the penitentiary of six years each for stealing the Russell ore, and "Baldy Bob" got a life sentence for the murder of the two men in Goldfield.

After being sentenced, Geo. Shaul jumped out of a two-story window at the jail and with a broken leg made his way back to Cripple Creek where two days later he was found almost at the point of death in an old cabin. He got well and served his sentence out.

CHAPTER XIII

A Lawsuit in Bent County, Colorado—A Big Murder Case in Benkelman, Nebraska—Ernest Bush Sent to the Penitentiary for Life.

Soon after arriving back in Denver I was detailed on a coal case to be tried in Las Animas, Colorado. Our clients were the Colorado Matte and Ore Co., and my work was against the Victor Fuel Co.

I was especially instructed to get in solid with the sheriff of the county, Las Animas being the county seat. This I did in fine shape, through playing myself off as a Texas cattleman who had a herd of steers on the trail for Las Animas.

The case had been fought in this and other counties of the state before, and the population were more or less divided as to which company was right and which was wrong.

Mr. Delos A. Chapelle, the president of the Victor Company, was a popular man and had many friends among the ranchers.

Judge Beaton, a noted fisherman, was the leading attorney on our side, and he and Mr. Keeble, President of the Colorado Matte Company where the only ones supposed to know me. But towards the last I heard that the secret had been given away to District Attorney Ross of Trinidad, Colorado, and other friends of our side.

In this way the Sheriff no doubt found out who I was, though he never said anything about the way I had played him, except to give me a hint, and to give me a wide berth.

One day he met me coming from an artesian well with a small tin-bucketful of water, when he said: "Say, Mr. Le Roy, is that water for your herd of cattle?" With a smile I answered "Yes," and he passed on. I knew then that he was "onto" me, but my work was already finished. He was a nice fellow just the same, even though he did feel a little "sore" towards me.

My next was a complicated murder case in Benkelman, Nebraska. The county attorney Mr. Goodehart, in that sleepy little county-seat town, wanted a good detective, as none other could make a success the way matters stood. Gen. Supt. McCartney informed him that he had a cowboy detective who would succeed if any one could. Therefore I was detailed on the case.

Arriving in Benkelman, Nebraska, in cowboy attire, I met Prosecuting Attorney Goodehart and County Commissioner, L. Morse, at night in a secluded place. They explained the case of how Ernest Bush, a nineteen year old boy had come into their county that Spring, broke, and asked to work for his board at County Commissioner Morse's ranch, a few miles out of Benkelman, which request was granted.

Mr. Morse "batched" at his ranch, and had working for him an old Grand Army man by the name of Baily. This honest old soldier who had fought for his country took a deep interest in the poor homeless "kid," and let him sleep with him in his bed.

19

A few days later Mr. Morse drove to town in his buggy, giving Mr. Baily orders to fix a hay rack that morning. On returning in the afternoon Mr. Morse asked Ernest Bush where Mr. Baily was. He replied that he hadn't seen him since noon. That night Bush worked hard and fed the stock himself.

As Baily didn't show up by morning the whole country turned out to search for him. The only clue found that day was the old man's false teeth on the trail leading to the river, about a quarter of a mile distant. They had been broken and trampled into the mud by the cattle going to water, where a hole had been cut in the ice for that purpose.

The next day Mr. Baily's body was found lodged in a fallen tree a few miles down the river. It was found through the ice having melted and exposing one gloved hand protruding above the water. In the top of the head were several buckshot wounds. This indicated to the angry men that Baily had been cleaning the stable when shot from the loft window above. Mr. Morse had a shot-gun in the house, but no buckshot cartridges for it.

Bush was arrested as the guilty party, but cool and unconcerned, he protested his innocence.

Finally Bush had a preliminary trial and the court room was full of people. When Prosecuting Attorney Goodehart cross-questioned the poor boy too severely, some of the audience hissed. They thought it was a shame for a big prosecuting attorney to impose on a boy whose face was plastered over with a coating of innocence.

Bush's parents in Council Bluffs, Iowa, had sent an

attorney from Omaha, and also hired a local lawyer to defend him.

When the Judge dismissed the case and freed Bush for want of evidence, some of the ladies in the Court room threw their arms around the boy's neck and kissed him.

Of course this hurt the Prosecuting Attorney's feelings and then he was determined to prove the truth with the help of the Dickenson Agency and the County Commissioners to back him up with funds, for it takes cash to employ the big Agency, as they never work for rewards. They must have a good guarantee to insure their pay of $8 per diem and all necessary expenses. They rightly contend that a detective working for a reward will often stretch the truth in order to convict, whereas, with the per diem plan, there is no incentive for an operative to perjure himself.

After the trial Bush's local attorney took charge of him and cautioned him against talking to strangers or picking up with any one, as detectives were liable to be put on his trail to get a confession. His attorneys also advised that he not leave the country, as that would look as though he was trying to run away. He was also told to keep in touch with his Benkelman attorney. Our clients had found out the above through a friend of the boy's. Therefore I was told that my work would have to be pretty slick in order to make friends with the boy, as being a stranger he would naturally be suspicious of me, and if he were not, his lawyer would be.

The lawyer had got the boy a job with a Mr. Scott across the river, two miles distant.

To make a long story short, I won the boy's friendship in a hurry, and persuaded him to run away with me and not even let his lawyer know what had become of him.

About a week after my arrival in Benkelman, Bush and I were on the way to New Mexico.

In riding through town on our horses on the morning of our departure, a fat boarder at the hotel, who no doubt had a large criminal bump in his makeup, called the boy off to one side and told him that I might be a detective trying to get a confession out of him. I was told this after we got out of town.

I had played myself off as an ex-outlaw and chum of the noted train robber and desperado, "Black Jack," who, at the time was in his glory, though a year or two later he was hung, at which time the rope pulled his head off. I had told of owning a ranch in New Mexico at Santa Fe, and of having quit the outlaw business. But I had promised to get him into "Black Jack's" gang.

On this operation I used my own name.

On arriving in New Mexico I kept Bush hid out at my ranch near Santa Fe, by telling him that as he was going to become a member of "Black Jack's" gang it was best that no one in Santa Fe make his acquaintance, or see him with me; and furthermore, that it would be best for him to lay low for fear the Nebraska officials should try to locate him.

I had an old man by the name of Atwood working on my ranch and taking care of my pets, and of course I posted him to not tell anyone that the boy was there.

Bush and I made several trips out into the mountains on my pet horses, and on two occasions it was all I could do to prevent him from murdering poor Mexicans for what money they might have. He would beg me to ride on and let him do the job alone; that he would hide the body and overtake me. He had bought a pistol and was anxious to try it on a man, but I argued that it wouldn't do for me to allow a murder committed so near my home. I told him that he would get his fill of murdering when he got in with the "Black Jack" gang.

I had told Bush that one of "Black Jack's" main chums was now at Bland, New Mexico, in the Cochiti mining district, and that I would have him come and meet him (Bush). Therefore, I wrote to my friend "Cunny," the Texan whom I followed in the Bill Blank case, and who had worked on my ranch about two years. "Cunny" was then mining in the Cochiti district. I wrote him that I would want him to visit me on the ranch soon, and I wrote a letter for him to copy and mail to me in Santa Fe. In this fake letter, he agreed to take my "kid" friend with him when they started on their next big raid. Of course Bush read this letter, and after that he kept me busy buying pistol cartridges so that he could practice shooting. He was then a happy boy.

One day a gentleman named Goeble, said to be a brother to the murdered Governor Goeble of Kentucky, who was a guest at Attorney Thomas B. Catron's residence in Santa Fe, rode out in a buggy to see our fine poultry. Bush thought he might be an officer from Nebraska after him, so he loaded my double-barrel shotgun with buckshot cartridges, and set it in the bedroom clothes closet, to be used in case of an emergency. When the visitor drove up to the gate and alighted, I raised the trap cellar door in the kitchen and advised Bush to hide there until the fellow left. He did as directed. I then went out into the yard to talk with the man, and while we were standing talking, a large hawk began to soar overhead. I ran in to get the shotgun, but found the closet locked from the inside. I began pushing to force the door open, when Bush said: "If you push open this door I'll let you have both barrels of this gun. What in the h——l do you want?"

I explained that it was me, and I wanted the gun to shoot a hawk. When he opened the door he had both barrels of the gun cocked and pointed towards me. He said he thought I was the other man. He hated to give up the gun though, for fear I was putting up a job to capture him. But I laughed at him for losing confidence in me so easily. On reaching the back yard the hawk was gone and I returned the gun to Bush. This cheered him up and he begged my pardon for doubting me.

Soon after this my friends, Mr. Alois B. Renehan, one of the prominent attorneys of Santa Fe, and his pretty young wife, came out to the ranch to visit me, and I wanted Bush to meet them, but he wouldn't hear to it, though they got to see him from a distance, while he was skulking in a hollow amidst the growing corn and sorghum.

Bush and I slept together in a separate room from Mr. Atwood, and one night, after the boy had gone to sleep, he began dreaming and talking to himself. He finally climbed upon me with both knees on my stomach, and both hands clutched about my throat. He was strong for his age, and to prevent him from cutting off my wind, I ran the fingers of one of my hands along my neck under his hands. Then I waited patiently for developments. Soon he released the hold about my neck, and looking and pointing up to the ceiling said: "Oh look, look, see him, he's got wings!" Then he collapsed and fell over on his side, asleep.

Next morning I told him of what he had said in his sleep and asked what he meant by it. He laughed and said: "Why, I was dreaming about that old———Baily, who is now pushing clouds in hell. I could see him just as plain, and he had wings too!"

Here I got a full confession of how he murdered poor old Baily, which was as follows:

After Mr. Morse had driven away from the ranch, Baily began working on a hay rack out in the cattle yard. Then Bush made preparations to carry out his plan to murder the old man for his money. He had noticed that the old soldier carried a large fat pocketbook in his vest pocket. He had loaded a shell with buckshot for the purpose. While Baily was working on the hay rack Bush got Mr. Morse's shotgun and placed the buckshot shell in one barrel,—the other barrel already contained a shell, loaded with birdshot. Bush then crawled into the hogpen and stuck the gun through a hole in the fence. Baily was facing him, but had his face turned down, as he was sawing a two-by-four inch scantling, which caused the top of his head to be pointed towards the concealed gun.

The distance was about thirty yards, more or less.

Both barrels of the gun were fired at the same time. Baily gave a scream and fell over. Then Bush ran to the house and got two cartridges loaded with birdshot. These he put in the gun and then ran to where Baily lay struggling with death. He asked the old man if he was much hurt, intending to fire both charges into him, in case he had life enough to answer. But he only groaned a few times and was dead. Then Bush went through his pockets and found a few five and ten dollar bills and a little silver. The fat pocketbook contained nothing but mortgages and pension papers. Then the young murderer put a harness onto his own horse in the stable and tied the tugs together behind the animal. Then one end of a rope was tied to the tugs, while the other end was fastened to the old man's neck. Now the horse was mounted, so as to drag the body to the river, but the horse became frightened and bucked all over the corral, dragging the corpse behind his heels. Finally he ran out of the open gate and Bush headed him towards the river, a quarter of a mile distant, over the cattle trail made in the deep snow. At the river the body was thrown into the hole, cut in the ice where the cattle watered. It drifted with the current under the ice and was soon lost to view.

In going back over the trail the boy picked up one of Baily's mittens. This he burned in the stove.

Then the cattle were rounded up and put in the corral and driven to water over the trail, so as to obliterate all signs of the body dragging in the snow.

After the horse was put up, Bush put away the saw, which he had had great difficulty in getting out of the corpse's hand, and he hid the scantling which was partly sawed in two. Then he found some buckshot and bird-shot holes in a post which stood directly behind Baily, in line. These shot had missed the old man's head. With his knife he made the buckshot holes look like spike holes, and the marks of the small shot were scratched and obliterated.

The money he hid by burying it at the foot of a telegraph pole in the pasture. Later its hiding place was changed to the lining of his clothing, where a few bills still remained. These he ripped out and gave to me, so that they could be spent in the natural course of business. He said I could just give him credit for the amount and pay him back later.

While I was in the kitchen getting breakfast and Mr. Atwood was out milking the Jersey cows and feeding the stock, Bush imitated to me how the murder was committed. He got the shotgun and had me put a stick on a chair, then put my knee on it and use the fire poker for a saw. Of course I made sure the gun was empty. When he pulled the trigger I gave a scream and fell over on the floor groaning. Soon he stood over me and asked if I was hurt much. A few more groans and kicks and I was dead. He said my part was played to perfection. Then we both laughed and I complimented him on his courage and said he was made out of the proper stuff for a member of the "Black Jack" gang.

He then told of how slick he played County Attorney Goodehart, and of how nice it was to have the ladies kiss and caress him in the court room.

During the next few days Bush told me of all the

crimes committed by him. They were many, and some of them heartless. His first crime was stealing a lot of money from his own mother, and the next was earning $50 from his uncle for setting fire to the uncle's residence, while the family were absent on a visit. The uncle got the $3,000.00 of insurance money and afterwards became well-to-do.

One of his crimes was, where he and two men in northern Nebraska, made a raise of a lot of money, then went out into the woods and played cards to see who should have it all. One of the men won the "boodle." Then Bush and the other loser put up a job and killed the lucky player and buried his body where it no doubt remains to this day.

In the course of a week after confessing to me, I noticed for several days that Bush was sullen and seemed to be brooding over something. Finally one evening, when I returned from town, where I had gone to get meat for supper and to write a report, Bush was in a good humor. He showed me a key which he had made to unlock my valise. It was a good piece of work. He then confessed going into my valise and reading the letters, etc, therein. I had put these letters into the valise for just such an emergency. I asked why he wanted to read my letters. He said: "Now Charlie, I'm going to confess to you that I have been worrying for several days, because I told you that I killed old Baily. I was afraid you might be a d——d detective, so today I made a key to fit your valise, for I thought if you were a detective you would have something in there that would give you away. If I had found anything that looked suspicious, I was going to kill you to-night and then get on Lula and hit the road. I might have killed old Atwood too, but I had it all fixed how you were to be killed so as not to wake up Atwood."

I asked if he had intended to kill me quick so I wouldn't suffer. He replied: "Yes, I had a hatchet sharpened for the purpose."

Then he went and pulled a sharp hatchet from its hiding place and showed me just where he had intended to split my head open, as I slept. He said he was going to play he was asleep until he knew for sure that I was not awake.

I asked if he was out of the notion of carrying out his plan; if not, I wouldn't let him sleep with me any more. He replied: "Oh you needn't be afraid of me now, Charlie, for I have made up my mind that you are all right. What convinced me the most after I got to thinking the matter over was the way you always leave your pistol where I could get hold of it. Often when you and I were here alone you would walk down to the well, or to the garden, and leave the pistol lying on the table or bed. I concluded a detective wouldn't do that."

From now on, I carried out the Dickenson Agency motto: "We never sleep." Previous to this I had been sleeping with part of one eye open, figuratively speaking.

As I wanted a witness to the boy's confession, I wrote to my friend "Cunny" in Bland, to come over at once.

When "Cunny" arrived Bush was happy, as I had told him that "Black Jack's" chum was coming and I advised him to try to make a good impression on him, so that he could go on their proposed raid.

I went to town and left "Cunny" and Bush together the first day. "Cunny" put in his time "loading" the "kid" with the bloody deeds of "Black Jack" and his gang, and of the money they made.

On my return I found Bush happy and in love with "Cunny." I asked if he had told "Cunny" of how he had made his killings. He said no, and asked me to tell him about it as it would look too much like bragging for him to tell it. I agreed to start the subject and then he could go on and finish it. So after supper I got the boy started and he repeated the whole story of Baily's murder, and next morning while Atwood was doing the outside work, I had Bush get the shotgun and show "Cunny" how it had been done. I played Baily by sawing the scantling with the poker.

As this was all the evidence needed, I put up a scheme to get Bush to Denver before making the arrest. I had a letter come from our office in Denver purporting to come from a Wyoming horseman who had arrived in that city with some cheap horses. In the letter a price was given on fifty head, with a promise that he would hold them until I could get there. Of course this letter was shown to "Cunny" and Bush, and "Cunny" told Bush that he would have plenty of time to help me drive the horses to Santa Fe as the "Black Jack" raid would not start for a month yet.

Therefore, next day Bush and I got ready to start on the A. T. & S. F. train at 11 o'clock in the night. I suggested to Bush that he and I walk from the ranch to the depot, which was about two miles, so as to save hitching up a team so late in the night. "Cunny" sat up with us until we started at 9:30 P. M.

The night was dark and on going half a mile Bush balked and wouldn't budge another step. Said he: "Charlie, d—d if I feel right. I am not going any further."

I laughed and told him to come on, that he must be crazy. He continued: "I've got a hunch that you are a detective and have got officers hid between here and the depot to arrest me. Now I want to tell you one thing, if you do turn out to be a detective and I have to go to the 'pen,' you can figure that your life will end just as soon as I get out. If I go up for five years or ten years, you can figure on living just that long and no longer."

I laughed and told him that I would want to die if I was low down enough to be a detective. I assured him that there were no officers hid in the arroyos between there and town. Then he said: "All right, we will see. You take the lead and I'll walk behind you with my pistol cocked ready to shoot. Then if any one shows up on the trail I will empty my pistol into you." I told him to go behind and if he saw any suspicious men to cut loose at me, but to make a death shot so that I wouldn't suffer. He then got out his pistol and carried it in his hand. He walked about twenty feet behind me.

After going half a mile he stepped up to my side and slapped me on the shoulder saying: "I reckon you are all right, Charlie. If you were a detective you wouldn't take such chances of being shot by me. I could have killed you and got your money, then slipped back to the ranch and got on Lula and hit the trail for Mexico."

He put up the pistol and we walked side by side the balance of the way to the depot. There we boarded the train.

At Lamy, the junction of the main line, I telegraphed to my horse man in Denver, stating at what time we would arrive there. We arrived in Denver during the afternoon and went to a restaurant to eat a square meal. Just then a couple of our men and a city officer came and arrested Bush. I protested and they threatened to arrest me if I didn't keep quiet.

Bush was taken to a room in the St. James Hotel, where County Attorney Goodeheart and one of the County Commissioners from Benkelman, Nebraska, were waiting. In about half an hour I went to the St. James to see if I couldn't go on Bush's bond till morning.

Bush hated for me to leave when I bade him goodby. He didn't seem to suspect me of having a hand in his arrest.

Next day he was taken back to Benkelman and a surprise sprung on his lawyer, who never knew what had become of the "kid."

Shortly after, I had "Cunny" meet me in Denver and we went together to Benkelman, Nebraska, to appear against Bush in the District Court, which was in session there. Bush's same two lawyers were on hand to defend him, and a noted criminal lawyer from Lincoln, the Capital of the State, was there to assist Mr. Goodeheart in the prosecution. He was a large man with a very large bump of self-importance sticking out of his head. But he made the mistake of bumping up against my stubborn bump. He tried to force me to be drilled as to my testimony. He said he had had lots of experience with railroad detectives and they generally made a bad impression on the jury, so for that reason, he wanted to put me through a drill. When he demanded it, then my stubborn bump got to working and I read the riot act to him. I informed him that I was going to tell the truth, and that truth needed no drilling, and that I held the winning hand in this game, hence he couldn't make me do anything. His dignity then got down off its high horse and collapsed.

The scantling which was sawed partly in two was found where the boy said it was, and the buckshot and small shot were cut out of the post.

After I had testified the Lincoln lawyer was so pleased that he advised against putting "Cunny" on the stand for fear of weakening my evidence. Therefore "Cunny" was not used.

Of course Bush's attorneys gave me an awful "roasting."

The court house was packed with people from the whole county. The jury were out a short time and brought in a verdict of murder in the first degree. There was no kissing in the courtroom this time. Bush looked daggers at me. He received a life sentence in the penitentiary, and it was sustained by the State Supreme Court.

Naturally I was quite a hero in the little town of Benkelman, and had many invitations out to dine.

I had hard work pulling "Cunny" away from a pretty little corn-fed girl who was waiting on our table at the hotel.

The chances are that Ernest Bush will be pardoned
out of the penitentiary before he is an old man.   Then
he will choose a wife from his own class and go to breed-
ing degenerate criminals like himself. Thus the devil
work will go on while society sleeps.

Oh, what fools we mortals are to allow it.

CHAPTER XIV

On Trail of Union Pacific Train Robbers Through Utah, Colorado, New Mexico, Kansas, Indian Territory, Arkansas, Tennessee, Mississippi, Montana and the Republic of Mexico.

After the Bush operation, I was detailed on several small cases in near-by towns, and also did some city work in Denver.

Finally I was put to work for the Colorado Matte & Ore Co. on a long operation to find out the feeling of their coal miners. This was not pleasant work, as my associates were coal miners of every nationality.

I started in at Trinidad, Colorado, and worked all the coal towns tributary to that city. Then I changed to Florence, and worked the coal camps around there.

Finally, during the early summer, I was detailed with my friend W. O. Sayles, who had just returned from South Africa, to go on trail of train robbers for the Union Pacific Railroad Company. One of their passenger trains had been held up at Wilcox, Wyoming, and a large amount of unsigned money stolen, and in a fight which followed, Sheriff Hazen was killed by the robbers.

From the best information obtainable, the Hole-in-the-wall gang had committed the robbery.

In Denver, Sayles and I bought a "30-40" smokeless powder Winchester rifle each, also blankets and camp outfit. Supt. John S. Kaiser instructed us to go to Salt

Lake City, Utah, and there buy horses and saddles and ride into Brown's Park, Colorado, just over the line of Utah which is a haven for criminals. In Wyoming some of the robbers had been seen driving a bunch of horses south, headed for Brown's Park. These were the particular men we were going after, but anyone who looked suspicious of ever having robbed a train, was to be "spotted."

A 500 mile ride over the continental range of mountains on the D. & R. G. Ry. brought us to the Mormon Capital. The first thing we did was to hunt up our friend "Doc" Shores, special agent of the Rio Grande Western Ry., and tell him of our proposed man hunt, for he was in a position to help us.

Sayers and I then bought a good saddle horse apiece, and a pack animal, also saddles, grub, etc., and a good supply of rifle and pistol cartridges.

Just as we were ready to start "Doc" Shores received a letter from one of his confidential men in Hanksville, Utah, stating that two men supposed to be Union Pacific train robbers had just passed there going south; that they were driving thirteen head of good horses. Shores let us read the letter and we felt confident these were the men we were after, as they had the same number of horses as seen in Wyoming.

We arranged with Mr. Shores to furnish us a stock-car on the narrow gauge D. & R. G. Ry. so that we could ship our horses and outfit to Marysvale, Utah, and from there we could make a fast ride and reach Dandy Crossing on the Colorado river about the same time as the robbers. The letter had stated that they were headed for the Dandy Crossing ferry. We telegraphed in cipher the contents of the letter and our intentions to Supt. Kaiser, and asked for his advice. Soon we got an answer to follow our first instructions, which meant to "hit the trail" for Brown's Park.

We selected our route through Emigration Canyon to Park City, a large mining camp, thence 'to Heber and east over the range of mountains to the head of Strawberry Creek on the Duchesne Indian Reservation and down that stream to the Duchesne river. On Strawberry Creek we had good fishing, although Sayles didn't enjoy the sport on account of the mosquitoes. They had his face and hands chewed to pieces. His face was swollen so badly that he looked like a breweryman. I was too tough for common mosquitoes, as I had been hardened with Texas gallinippers chewing on me from the cradle to early manhood. A gallinipper is larger than two northern mosquitoes.

On arriving at Ft. Duchesne, a U. S. Military post on the Indian Reservation, after a five days' hard ride, we found a telegraph message from Supt. Kaiser in Denver, stating that the two men and thirteen loose horses seen in Hanksville en route to Dandy Crossing were undoubtedly the train robbers that we were after, and for us to give up the Brown's Park trip and turn south on trail of these men.

It was evident that someone had made a blunder by not letting us ship our stock to Marysvale and thereby reach Dandy Crossing the same time as the robbers, if not before, and also have saved us a tiresome 500 mile horseback ride. We were not mad but the cuss-words hurled over towards Denver left a sulphuric taste in our mouths for a week.

From Ft. Duchesne we headed south for Price, Utah, on the Rio Grande Western Ry. En route to Price I learned from a rancher that my Wyoming friend Tom Hall, who had so kindly prevented a rope being placed about my neck, and who made the crutches for me to walk with, now lived in Price and ran a saloon there, although he was now going by his right name, Tom Nichols, the old murder charge in Texas having been canceled.

Not knowing that I was acquainted with Tom Hall, this rancher gave me his history. He told me of how he and his two brothers "Mid" and George Nichols, had conducted a saloon at "Hogtown" on the edge of Ft. Duchesne, and of how George had killed a man and skipped out to wear the brand of an outlaw.

A ride of three days brought us to Price early one afternoon. My first desire was to get a good look at Tom Hall, to see if he had changed from of old. I didn't dare enter his saloon for fear of being recognized by him, in which case my work might be spoiled by our indentity being made public. Furthermore, I didn't know but that our meeting might end in a fight, for the chances were a bitter feeling aginst me existed on his part, and in that case he wouldn't hesitate to use his gun.

When directly opposite the Nichols saloon, Tom walked out in his shirt sleeves and seated himself in a chair facing me. He was the same Tom, tall and good looking, but a little older and fleshier.

I stepped into the newspaper office at my back and

asked for some exchange papers to read. These were furnished and I sat looking out through the glass-front at Hall, and wondered what his life had been since we held the Irish wake over the corpse of poor Mrs. Howard.

The next morning Sayles and I pulled out for the south in a driving rainstorm, which had been falling since midnight. About five miles out we came to a raging creek which couldn't be crossed without danger to ourselves and horses. Therefore we started back to Price only to find ourselves cut off from that place by another swift creek which had risen over its banks in the past half hour. There was nothing for us to do but wait in the rain for this creek to go down. This it did towards night. On arriving back in Price, we put up at the same hotel where we had stopped the night before, and while in our room upstairs, a knock came at the door, which was opened and the visitor invited to enter. He introduced himself as the editor of the local paper, and explained to us that we were virtually under arrest as Union Pacific train robbers; that he had been sent up by the sheriff of the county to advise us to surrender peacefully. Of course we laughed and told him that we were prospectors on the way to the Henry mountains south of Hanksville. The editor then told us that the sheriff and a posse with Winchester rifles had the hotel surrounded, and to verify his assertion we were told to look out of the window. This we did, and saw men with rifles. The editor told of how the sheriff had been fixing to go on our trail, when we rode back into town.

We gave a history of how we had outfitted in Salt Lake for a prospecting trip and that we had pick and shovel, gold pan and other prospecting tools in our pack. He said there was no doubt in his mind but that we were all right, and he would so report to the sheriff. Thus the matter ended, and the "dogs of war" were called off.

The next morning when ready to make another start a photographer took our pictures.

For the next three or four days we had a wet ride, swimming creeks and traveling in sticky mud up to our horses' knees at times. We went through several Mormon towns to Emery, thence over a desert to Dirty-devil Creek, and up that stream to Hanksville, where the two supposed train robbers had been seen.

In Hanksville we made the acquaintance of Charlie Gibbons who ran the only hotel and store in the place. In a general talk with him and his brother and other men, we found out that two suspicious characters with thirteen head of horses had crossed the Colorado river at Dandy Crossing about ten days previous, and that nearly a week later, a third man with five head of horses crossed. He made inquiry for the first two men. Charlie Gibbons' brother helped this last man swim his horses across the river, and from the description given us he was evidently the notorious "Kid" Curry. He told Gibbons and Johnny Hite, who had charge of the ferry, that he would go where the grass was good and camp until he heard from his friends.

After Sayles and I crossed the river, we trailed this man up White's Canyon. We found where he took his horses up a rocky bluff several hundred feet high, which looked like an impossible feat. By this time it was late in the evening so that one of us had to return to Dandy

The Author and W. O. Sayles.

Crossing after some grain for our horses. It was agreed that Sayles go back and follow till dark. It was all I could do to get my horse up the steep bluff.

When on top of the mesa the country was level. I followed the trail to a wide rocky arroyo where all traces of the horses' tracks were lost. They had evidently gone down this rocky canyon. I searched the canyon for two miles down and then gave up the chase to get back to camp before it became too dark to see my way down that steep bluff.

A year later I found out through Mr. John Duckett, of Bluff City, Utah, that I was within half a mile of this lone outlaw's camp when I turned back. Duckett was working a mining prospect across White's Canyon and could see every move made. Duckett said the fellow camped there two weeks. They were only a couple of miles apart, but couldn't visit each other without traveling ten to twenty miles, owing to bluffs and canyons. So, the chances are I came very near running into my game. In that case there would have been "something doing." And it is possible that this outlaw saw me trailing him. In that event he would have had the best of the fight.

All is well that ends well.

Owing to the fact of my losing the trail of the lone outlaw on the rock-bottom bed of the canyon, Sayers and I concluded to follow the tracks of the two men and their thirteen head of loose horses. The tracks still showed plainly in the valley of White's Canyon, as there was no travel to speak of in that country.

To recite our ups and downs in finding water and keeping the dim trail and of having our pack horse killed by a rattlesnake bite, would require too much space. Suffice it to say that we reached Bluff City, a little Mormon settlement on the San Juan river, in good health, the distance being about 120 miles with not a habitation on the route.

In Bluff City we learned of the two U. P. robbers being there two weeks ahead of us; also two of our operatives. Alvin Garman and Alvin Darkbird. had arrived a couple of days ahead of us and had taken up the trail of the robbers who were headed east.

By this time we knew they were Union Pacific train robbers, as they had passed some of the unsigned bills stolen in the Silcox, Wyoming, train holdup. They had passed one $20.00 bill with a merchant in Thompson's Falls and another with Charlie Gibbons of Hanksville.

Darkbird and Garman had been sent by Supt. Kaiser to Flagstaff, Arizona, there to buy outfits and cut across the country to Bluff City, Utah, so as to assist Sayles and me, or to intercept the robbers in case they headed south for Arizona.

Sayles and I figured that we were born leaders of men, hence we didn't like the idea of bringing up the rear, three days behind the other two operatives. Therefore, in Mancos, Colorado, on the Denver & Rio Grande railroad we put our jaded horses in a pasture and stored our camp outfit, taking our saddles along with us, and boarded a train for Durango. Here we overtook Garman and his chum. From Durango, Sayles and I led the chase by riding on trains, in buggies, and on hired saddle horses. We left the other two boys far in the rear, and they finally lost the trail entirely and returned to Denver.

In Lumberton, New Mexico, my friend J. M. Archuleta, who was one of my chums in the Archuleta, Colorado, uprising, had seen the two robbers and the thirteen head of horses, two of them being very noticeable, one being a pretty cream color and the other a large dapple iron gray. After leaving Lumberton we lost the trail, but we heard of two men and a bunch of horses headed south towards Bland, New Mexico. It was agreed that I follow this clue, while Sayles searched the country around Pagosa Springs, Colorado.

By riding on a Denver & Rio Grande train about 500 miles, I landed in Santa Fe, New Mexico. There I went out to my ranch and saddled up Glen Alpine, Jr. He was fat and bucked like a wolf.

A forty mile ride brought me to Bland in the Cochiti mining district, where lived my friend "Cunny." He had seen the two men and bunch of horses, and they proved not to be the robbers.

While I was riding in the heavy timber on the head of Peralta Canyon, I ran onto a sister of the Polk brothers. She was alone in a new cabin just built, and recognized "Glen" before she did me. We had both put up at their place in the Wichita mountains, Indian Territory, when on the Bill Blank operation. They had lately moved out into this wild country. No doubt the lady thought "Glen" and I were inseparable, and that I had been riding him ever since she last saw us. I was in a great hurry and couldn't give an account of myself.

On returning to Santa Fe, I received a telegram from Sayles, saying that he had found the right trail, going through Pagosa Springs, and over Mosca Pass into the

Wet Mountain Valley. Shortly after rejoining Sayles
south of Canyon City, Colorado, we lost the trail again.
He then went to Cripple Creek on a false scent, while
I went east and picked up the trail by tramping
afoot ten miles from a little railroad station where there
was no horse to be hired. In Cucharas Junction the trail
crossed the railroad and headed for Rattlesnake Buttes,
towards the Arkansas river.

Of course I kept the Denver officials of our office
posted by wire.

Sayles was called in and sent to Montana to work on
a clue as to where some of the stolen money which had
been sent to the City of Washington had come from. I
continued to follow the trail down the Arkansas river.

In Lamar, Colorado, I met my friend Newt Parrish
who was in a bank there. He and his lovely wife and
I had become acquainted out in the Wet Mountain
Valley several years previous, when I was chasing a
tough character for Henry Tompkins, the hardware
merchant prince of Colorado. I had spent two months
on that operation playing outlaw, cowboy, and miner,
but I overlooked giving an acount of it in the proper
place herein.

Finally I landed in Dodge City, Kansas, and found
that my men and horses had passed through there on
their way down the Arkansas river; but I concluded to
lay over a half day and note the changes in this the
toughest of all early-day western cattle towns.

In looking over the prosperous town I found many
old landmarks in the way of buildings, etc., but only one
live one, the live one being old "Dog Kelly," the early-

day mayor of Dodge City. He was nicknamed "Dog Kelly" because in the early days he always had a pack of greyhounds following at his heels; and the strange part of this story is that the dogs were still with him, though not the same dogs, of course.

After Kelly and I had a few drinks we began to "hark back" to 1877 when my friend Jim Kennedy, son of the Texas "Cattle-King" shot at the Hon. "Dog Kelly" and killed his "lady" companion, and how Bat Masterson and a gang waylaid Jim Kennedy by hiding behind an old well dump at Mead City and shot him as he rode by.

This brought to my mind how near I came to being put out of business by this afterwards noted Bat Masterson. It happened in July, 1877. Dodge City was then one year old, and she had a graveyard with 81 men sleeping their last sleep. One of these had died a natural death and the other 80 with their boots on, in other words, were killed. A fine record for a year old town.

I had landed in Dodge City with one of the Littlefield cattle herds from Texas. One night "Wess" Adams, a cowboy chum, and I rode into town to have a good time. There were several dance-halls in full swing, but we settled on the Lone-Star dance hall as the "girls" there seemed better looking and the name had a Texas flavor. Bat Masterson was the night bar-keeper.

About 11:00 P. M. "Wess" Adams called me outside and told me how he had been insulted by a big long-haired buffalo-hunter by the name of Jim White, and he said this fellow ought to be taught a lesson to show him that the killers of buffalo are not in the cowboy class.

He then asked if I would stay with him in a fight. Being a fool boy, and realizing the disgrace of a cowboy quitting a chum in time of danger, I told him to go ahead and start the ball to rolling; that I would stay with him.

Our horses were taken out of the livery stable and tied in front of the Lone-Star dance-hall. Of course we both had on Colts 45 pistols. The hall was filled with cowboys and buffalo-hunters. When the fight started, Bat Masterson, who was behind the bar, gathered a lot of heavy beer glasses together and began throwing them in the direction of my head. One glanced from the side of my head and hit the wall nearby. Pieces of the broken glass struck me in the face, drawing blood. This was the only blood lost by yours truly. When Bat had no more glasses to throw, he came running from behind the bar with an ice mallet. He started in on a big dutch cowboy who had no hand in the fight, which was then raging between a dozen cowboys and buffalo-hunters. It was a shame the way that poor Dutchman got his face mashed. The blood flew every time Bat struck with the ice mallet. I was too busy helping my chum, to go to Dutchy's assistance, though I would have liked to.

There wasn't a shot fired, but in two instances pistols were used as clubs to knock men down.

After long-haired Jim White was lying on the floor apparently dead, with blood flowing from wounds in the head, and I had seen a buffalo hunter stab my partner in the back, I dragged "Wess" to the door and out to the sidewalk where we both mounted our horses. Just as we did so, an officer, I think Joe Mason, ran up and demanded our arrest, but we didn't surrender worth a cent. We just jumped our horses towards the sidewalk and with drawn pistols made the policeman get back into the little hallway from whence he had come.

We then put spurs to our horses and rode east out of town on the run, and yelling cowboy fashion. Of course we were both half drunk on the poisonous liquor passed over the bar by Bat Masterson, now one of President Roosevelt's pet revenue officers of New York state.

On reaching the stock yards a mile east of town, we dismounted and went into the little board shanty to examine "Wess" Adams' wound. Laying him on his stomach I pulled his shirts over his shoulders and found a horrible knife-wound under the right shoulder blade. The knife had been thrust in and then brought around in a semi-circle in the shape of a large horseshoe. The open part of the shoe is where the flesh was not cut, and the other part of the wound the flesh stood out several inches from the body. The clothing was saturated with blood. Lighted matches had to be used in order to see. I told Adams that the wound was serious, and for him to lie there until I could ride back to town and get some medicine and a needle and thread to sew up the wound.

Getting on my pet horse, Whisky Pete, I rode fast, but on nearing town I became "foxy" and thought possibly the officers might be watching for our return, and this "foxy" part of my makeup saved my bacon. For, about fifteen years later, Supt. Jas. McCartney, in Denver, introduced me to Bat Masterson, and in telling him of my part in the fight at the Lone-Star dance-hall, he told how he and a gang of officers had followed us to the edge of town and there on each side of the road, concealed themselves from view, thinking we would take a notion to return. He said they were armed with rifles and shot-guns and intended to make angels of us if we returned. He said they stood guard till morning. They were no doubt anxious to increase the size of the cemetery, at that time the pride of the town.

By riding south in a deep arroyo, I struck the railroad track and followed this into town. Riding up to the rear of a drug store I kicked on the door till the angry old Dutchman in his night-shirt opened the door. After purchasing needles and thread, sticking plaster and a candle, I returned to the stock yards the same way I had come.

I found poor Adams groaning with pain, but he kicked like a bronco steer when my knee was put on the wound to force the swollen flesh back in its place so that it could be sewed up. The horseshoe shaped protruding flesh could not be pushed back in place on a level with the rest of the body, therefore I had to discard the needle and thread and use sticking plaster.

We had an 18 mile ride to make to the Bates & Beals cattle camp, and towards the last part of the ride I had to hold Adams on his horse, he was so weak from loss of blood. We arrived in camp long after daylight. We had both hired out to this firm to drive a bunch of steers into the wild Panhandle of Texas, and there help to establish a new ranch.

From "boys" who went into Dodge City next day,

we learned that long-haired Jim White, who was the boss of a large gang of buffalo-hunters, was not dead, though very low. His skull was cracked in several places and a lot of sewing had to be done on his many wounds. He finally recovered. It was one of White's men who had stabbed Adams.

Our "boys" reported that the officers had no suspicion as to who Adams and I were.

In the course of a couple of weeks, Adams was able to ride.

This little scrape illustrates what fools cowboys were after long drives over the trail. Had a shot been fired that night in the dance-hall as a starter, the chances are several new mounds would have been added to that fat graveyard.

I continued on the trail of my two train-robbers, on horse-back, in buggies and on trains. They passed through the outskirts of Wichita, where I spent one night visiting old friends and acquaintances. Among them were Bedford Wood, ex-city marshal of Caldwell, Kansas, now a city detective in Wichita, and "Dynamite" David Lahey, a brilliant newspaper writer of early border days; also Jack Davis, proprietor of a white bull dog and the swell Club Saloon of Wichita.

After retiring for the night in this prosperous little city of 25,000 people, my mind naturally drifted back to a summer night in 1876 when I entered the place, then a village of the wild and woolly kind with about 2,000 population.

I had just arrived from a three months' cattle drive up the Chisholm trail from Southern Texas, and during the night I was arrested by policeman Mike Meagher, who afterwards became town marshal of Caldwell, Kans. and was shot and killed in the bloody Talbot cowboy raid on Caldwell, when the streets were made red with human blood. But Mike Meagher was a kind-hearted officer and on account of my youth liberated me after a few words of friendly advice.

Another cowboy and I had tried to play smart by scaring the old fellow who kept the toll bridge across the Arkansas river, and at the same time beat him out of the toll which was 25 cents each. We cared nothing for the money as our pockets were bulging out with a summer's wages. We were on our way from the town proper, to the Red Light dance-hall across the river. When the bridge man came out of his shanty to collect the toll we both put spurs to our horses and pulling our pistols began shooting into the air. The old man jumped into his shanty and came out with a double-barrel shot-gun. By that time we were nearly across the bridge and our pistols were empty, but the old fellow turned both barrels loose at us and we could hear the buckshot rattling along the bridge at our horses' feet. One shot struck me in the calf of the right leg, leaving a mark to this day as a reminder of the hurrah cattle days of Wichita, where the noted-"Wild Bill" Hecock made his first record as a man-killer, while marshal of that town.

From here I followed the trail south to Caldwell, Kansas.

In this former hurrah cattle town, where I once made my home for about two years, I met many old-time friends, too numerous to mention. Among them were only two ex-cowboys, Jay Willis and "Dick" Malone, and a solitary ex-cattle king, Sol. Tuttle.

My friend "Dick" had drifted to bleeding Kansas with a herd of longhorns from Southern Texas. And his inclination then was to help paint towns red. But now he does his painting with a brush instead of with "red licker" and a six-shooter. He is following his trade of painting houses and ceilings sky blue, and in living happily with a pretty wife and sweet little daughter, Katherine.

From Caldwell the robbers followed the Indian Territory and Kansas line to Arkansas City, Kansas. Here I continued on the trail to Winfield, thence to Coffeeville and into the Indian Territory through the towns of Wagner and Tahlequah to Ft. Smith, Arkansas.

Before reaching Ft. Smith I was joined by operative Darkbird who had been sent from Denver to assist me. We trailed the men and horses through Pine Bluff and to Hot Springs, Arkansas. Here we lost the trail. We split up and searched the surrounding country. Soon I received a telegram from Darkbird in Tennessee telling me to meet him in Nashville, the capital city of that state, as our men had got rid of their horses and boarded a train for there. I hurried to Nashville by way of St. Louis, Missouri, where I spent one night with my sister and her family. In Nashville I met operative Darkbird and found he had followed a wrong trail. The men he had followed were evidently desperadoes, but not the ones we wanted.

Here Darkbird became sick with malaria and returned to Denver.

21

A couple of years later in looking over correspondence on this operation, I found one of Mr. W. L. Dickenson's letters to Gen. Supt. McCartney. It was dated Chicago, Dec. 22nd, 1899, and stated:

"I note that operative Siringo has picked up the trail of these men at Benton, Arkansas, and that operative Darkbird has returned home, being very sick with malaria. I am very sorry to hear of operative Darkbird's illness. The swamp country through which he passed has evidently knocked him out. I fear it may do the same with Siringo, but he is as tough as a pine knot and I never knew of a man of his size who can endure as much hardship as he does."

It gave me much satisfaction to know that I was considered tough, in more ways than one.

In Nashville I saw more pretty girls to the square inch than I had ever seen before or ever expect to see again. I sat at a dinner table with about a dozen college girls and each one was a beauty of the first water, and on the streets my neck was almost disjointed looking around at pretty young women. I was glad to get away so as to give my eyes and neck a rest.

Arriving back in Hot Springs, Ark., I hired a saddle horse and searched the mountains for a trace of my men. This brought me among a queer class of people, some of them moonshiners. One old moonshiner assisted in putting me on the right trail of the robbers. Their trail led through Little Rock, the capital of the state, thence down the Arkansas river through the swamps to a wild unsettled country 25 miles south of Stuttgart. Here the loose horses were turned over to a long-haired old man, who had outlaw sons, by the name of La Cutts, who lived in De Witt, not far from the mouth of the Arkansas river.

The robbers mounted the pretty cream colored and the dappie iron-gray horses and headed north to White River, thence down that stream to Clarendon, then due east to Helena on the Mississippi river. Crossing the "Father of Waters" they passed through Glendale and Lula, Mississippi, thence east one hundred miles through the "Black Belt," where in some places negroes are thicker than flies on a syrup keg in August. They then rode one hundred miles south, thence back west to the Mississippi river at a boat landing above the town of Rosedale. Here both robbers hired a man to ferry them across the Mississippi to the mouth of the Arkansas river, after their horses and saddles had been turned over to a strange negro man who disappeared in the swamps.

At the mouth of the Arkansas river one robber, whose name I had reason to believe was Owens, and who was a desperate outlaw, went up the Arkansas river in a skiff, while his companion boarded a little tramp steamer and went down the "Father of Waters." They had agreed to meet in two weeks, but I couldn't find out where. This put me up a stump with no chance to proceed.

I went to the City of Vicksburg, Miss., and posted officers to be on the look out for my men; also did likewise in the large towns of Indianola, Greenville and Cleveland.

While trailing these men through the swamps of Mississippi among the negroes, I had more fun than a bushel of monkeys over the comical antics of these green black men and women and their kinky-headed pickaninnies.

Often I had to walk through the deep mud when a horse or vehicle couldn't be hired. And my feed was mostly corn bread, sorgum syrup and fat bacon.

Finally I received orders to give up the chase and return to Denver, as my services were needed in Montana on the same operation.

On quitting the chase I was about three weeks behind the two train robbers.

In Denver I was informed by Asst. Supt. "Rank" Curran, who had charge of the U. P. Ry. train holdup operation, that W. O. Sayles had run into a brother, Loney Curry, and a cousin, Bob Curry, of the noted outlaw "Kid" Curry, in Harlin, Mont.; that Loney and Bob owned a saloon there and had sent some of the unsigned bills stolen in the Silcox, Wyo., robbery, off to be cashed. In this way they were located, but sold their saloon and skipped out before Sayles had a chance to arrest them. They had become suspicious of Sayles, so for that reason he could not work on their friends secretly.

Sayles had found out that the right names of Kid and Loney Curry were Harvey and Loney Logan and that they were born and raised in Dodson, Mo., near Kansas City, and that for years they had been making their headquarters in the Little Rockies, a small range of mountains 50 miles east of Harlin, the railroad station where Bob and Loney had owned the saloon. Therefore, I was instructed to meet Sayles in Helena, the capital of Montana, and then buy a horse and saddle at some point and ride into the Little Rockies and get in with the friends of the Logan brothers.

So finally, with several hundred dollars in my pocket I started for Helena, Mont. I took along instructions for Sayles to hurry on direct to San Francico, Cal., there to start in as Asst. Supt. of the Dickenson office in that city. There was to be a change of superintendents in the San Francisco office, and they wanted Sayles to learn the office work by starting in as an assistant. He was appointed superintendent soon after arriving in San Francisco.

General Supt. of the Western Division, Jas. McCartney, had tried to induce me to accept the position of Asst. Supt. of the San Francisco office before it was offered to Sayles, but I refused it. I told him that if he should ever die and the Dickensons should offer me his position I might consider it, but wouldn't promise that I would accept it. The truth is, I didn't want to be tied down in an office, even with an advance in salary and a chance to swell up with self-importance.

In Helena, Mont., I visited with W. O. Sayles and detective M. B. Wilmers a couple of days. Sayles gave me much information about the Little Rockies, although he had not been there himself, but he had talked with many men who had.

It was thought best for me to outfit in Great Falls and ride about two hundred and fifty miles across the "bad lands," to Landusky, the small cattle town in the Little Rocky mountains.

Bidding Sayles goodby I boarded a train for Great Falls, Mont., where I bought a bucking broncho mare and started east for Lewiston, Mont., about three days' ride. In Lewiston a severe blizzard was raging, it being about the latter part of February. I waited two days for it to moderate, but it seemed to grow worse. Therefore, a start was made one morning when the thermometer registered about 20 below zero, and with the wind blowing a gale. The people at the hotel advised me not to start, and I wished before night that I had heeded their advice.

My route lay over a flat country north to Rocky Point on the Missouri river, a distance of about 80 miles, and only one ranch on the route. It was this ranch that I aimed to reach before night. After traveling against this cold wind about 15 miles I could stand it no longer. My mare could hardly be kept headed towards the blizzard. I had a woolen hood over my face and head and even then my nose and ears were about frozen. I could see the mountains off to the east where I had been told the mining camp of Gilt Edge was situated, so for there I headed, not caring to return to Lewiston. About night I struck the wagon road between Gilt Edge and Lewiston, and then I was happy.

A long climb over this mountain range brought me into the live camp of Gilt Edge about four hours after dark. I felt like a half frozen fool for ever having undertaken such a journey. But after I had gotten on the outside of a large porterhouse steak and the trimmings, which included two hot whiskies, I began to thaw out and felt better.

Next morning I concluded to take a different route to the Rocky Point crossing of the Missouri river. Therefore I obtained a sketch of the route to the "Red Barn" on the south border of the "Bad Lands." A hard, cold ride brought me to the "Red Barn" ranch, where I found a crowd of cowboys congregated waiting for the weather to moderate. From here it was 30 miles across the "Bad Lands" to Rocky Point, and I was advised to lay over a few days and wait for a "Chinook" wind to melt the snow so that the dim road could be followed. I did so, and while waiting, I gained some information about the "Kid" Curry gang. Loney Curry had stopped here before and after the Silcox train robbery on the U. P. Railway.

I started one morning after a "Chinook" had been blowing all night, so that the snow was almost gone, but the sticky mud on the "Bad Lands" was something fearful. It would stick to the mare's feet till the poor animal could hardly gallop. I had seen many kinds of sticky mud in my life, but nothing to equal this.

The warm wind was blowing a gale, and soon after leaving the "Red Barn" I had a race after my broad-brim cowboy hat which made me swear and laugh by turns. The country was level, and when my hat blew off the wind took it "a sailing" across the country. It went like a wheel, on edge, and I tried to keep up with it, but my mare was handicapped in the race on account of the balls of mud sticking to her hoofs. After a mile and a half run I outwinded the hat and caught it, but in getting off in the mud to pick it up after I had made the mare step on it, I found I couldn't get my foot in the stirrup, owing to the mud which was stuck fast to it. Here my early cowboy training in the art of fancy swearing came in play, as it seemed to relieve my mind, while the mud was being scraped off my foot with a knife.

I had been told of the many dim wagon roads leading in different directions, which were liable to lead me astray, and this gave me much worry when I came to the forks of a road. The thoughts of a blizzard striking me on these "Bad Lands" where there is no wood or habitation, caused cold shivers to run down my back whenever the dim trail seemed to be bearing away from a north course. It was a cloudy day so that I couldn't tell for sure which was north.

Just as night was approaching I found a piece of glass from a telegraph pole. This satisfied me that I was on the right road, hence I was happy. I had been told that in the early days the government had a telegraph line on the road to Rocky Point, but that the line had been moved away years before. I still keep that piece of green glass, as it had brought good cheer to my drooping spirits.

I arrived in Rocky Point on the south bank of the Big Muddy river three hours after dark. Here I found old man Tyler and his son running the ferry and keeping a small Indian trading store.

My mare had only traveled 30 miles, but she had carried about 75 pounds of mud across the "Bad Lands," hence she was almost played out on arriving at Rocky Point.

I had often heard of the "Bad Lands" and wanted to visit them, but now that desire has vanished.

Before reaching the Little Rockies, I learned that outlaw Harvey Logan, alias Kid Curry, had a half in-

terest in a horse ranch 'with one Jim T.; that they owned
about 500 head of good horses which ranged in the
Little Rockies.

As luck would have it, on reaching Landusky, the
small village in the Little Rockies, I made the acquaintance of Jim T. through an accident. In riding by the
saloon in front of which were a crowd of rough looking
men, my mare shied and I spurred her in the flanks.
She began bucking and old Colts 45 flew out of the
scabbard, striking a rock in the street. When the mare
quit bucking, Jim T. gave me the pistol which he had
picked up. This meant a treat for the crowd, and I
became acquainted with the partner of "Kid Curry," the
slickest and most bloodthirsty outlaw of the age.

To recite all my ups and downs and the valuable information about outlaws and tough characters secured
for my agency would take up too much space. Suffice
it to say that I played myself off for an old Mexico
outlaw and became "Solid Muldoon" with the worst
people of the community. I had adopted the name of
Chas. L. Carter.

Harvey Logan had killed old Pike Landusky, the man
for whom this town was named, several years previous,
which first started him on the road as a genuine desperado. Jim T. informed me that he advised Harvey
to kill Landusky, and for that reason he will always be
his friend through thick and thin.

Pike Landusky's widow, Julia, still resided on their
ranch two miles out of town. The family consisted of
two boys and three girls. One of these girls, Elfie, 20
years of age and good looking, had a three-year-old son

by Loney Logan. They had never been married by law, which seemed no disgrace here.

In trying to capture Loney Logan at Dodson, Missouri, where he was in hiding with his aunt, Mrs. Lee, mother to Bob Lee, alias "Bob Curry," by officials of the Dickenson agency (my friend Tom F. Kipple being at the killing) he was shot through the head and killed.

I had made myself "solid" with Elfie Curry, as she was called, hence read all of her letters and was told all of her secrets. She had stacks of letters from her husband, as she called Loney, and also from Mrs. Lee and her daughter, and during Bob Lee's trial in Cheyenne, Wyo., she received letters from the lawyers whom Mrs. Lee had sent from Kansas City, Mo., to defend her son. As I had free access to Elfie's trunks I could read these letters at any time.

The Kansas City lawyer came to Landusky after evidence to prove an alibi for Bob Lee, and while he was working with Elfie and Jim T., I was introduced to him, and learned all of his secrets. Jim T. would meet him at Elfie's house in town.

During the round-ups and horse branding trips I showed my skill in throwing a rope. This made me solid with Jim T. who lived with his common-law wife on a ranch a few miles south of Landusky. They had a bright little three-year-old boy named Harvey in honor of the outlaw Harvey Logan. This little fellow felt at home with a small pistol buckled around his waist,—then he would go wild. A high picket fence had to be built around the house to keep him from running away.

One evening during the past winter when the ther-

LITTLE HARVEY T. AND HIS DOG.

mometer was hovering about zero, little Harvey struck out for "tall timber" with his pet dog, a large yellow cur. They tramped the hills all night. Next morning the whole population of Landusky, in the male line, about twenty-five men, were out searching for the child's corpse, as it was thought impossible for a boy of his tender age to endure the bitter cold night. But the little fellow proved to be tough like his daddy. He was found in the afternoon many miles from home, huddled up by the side of his pet dog, fast asleep. The warmth from the dog's body had no doubt saved his life.

This boy is pretty good material for a future train-robber. He says that will be his occupation, and his father encourages him, as he says he would like to see him prove as brave a man as his namesake, Harvey Logan.

"Like begets like" is a true saying. There is no doubt but that Jim T. was a hard case and landed in Montana under an assumed name.

Mrs. Julia Landusky gave me many inside facts of Jim T. and his actions when he first landed in the Little Rockies as a slender young man. Now he is a middle-aged, large, heavy man.

Judging from the time he came to the Little Rockies and his description as given by Mrs Landusky, Mr. W. L. Dickenson is confident Jim T. is no other than "Dad" Jackson of the noted Sam Bass gang who robbed the Union Pacific train near Ogalalla, Nebraska, in the early '70's. Most of this gang were killed or sent to the penitentiary for this hold-up, "Dad" Jackson being the only one who made his "get-away." Mr. Dickenson, who was then an operative in the agency, worked on the case.

Shortly after my arrival in the Little Rockies I received a ducking in the cold icy waters of a branch of Milk river. I was going to Harlin on the Great Northern railroad, with Puck Powell, the ex-cowboy postmaster of Landusky. We were the only passengers in the open stage coach drawn by four horses. On reaching the swollen stream which was full of broken ice, we persuaded the kid driver to swim the team across. When out in mid-stream the large chunks of ice struck the stage coach, carrying horses and all down stream. The spring seats were all that showed above water, and Puck, the driver and I, were upon these. We were having a free ride with the poor horses trying to swim up stream. Something had to be done to save the horses from drowning, so with all my clothes on I jumped into the icy cold water. On reaching the bank in a bend of the creek the driver threw me the lines. The lead horses were pulled ashore and the vehicle swung around against the steep clay bank, so that Puck and the driver could step off without getting wet.

Undressing in the cold wind to wring the water out of my clothes, gave me a taste of old-time cowboy life. We didn't reach the stage station until dark.

During the month of June, I came within an ace of losing my breath, which would have put me out of business for all time.

I was at Jim T.'s ranch and he got me to drive a bronco team to Rocky Point on the Missouri river twenty-five miles. This team of four-year-old browns had only been hitched up in harness a couple of times. The broncos were hitched to an old buckboard and a bottle of water put under the seat, as the weather was hot and no water en route.

Before starting at 7:30 A. M. Jim T. cautioned me to be careful as this team had run away and smashed up a vehicle the past fall, since which time they had been running wild on the range.

The twenty-five mile drive to Rocky Point was over a broken, rocky country, with a very dim wagon road to follow, and there was not a habitation on the road.

Jim T. opened the gate and I started with the browns tugging at their bits. For the first few miles the horses made several efforts to run, though I managed to get them checked up, but when about five miles out, business started. As we flew over the rocky road as fast as the horses could run, I remember seeing something black, which must have been one of the tug-straps, hitting the broncos on the hind legs. I also remember seeing a deep gully ahead, and to avoid it, I threw my weight onto one line to turn the team around the head of the short gully. I cannot account for my not jumping and letting the out-fit go to the d—l, for I've been in runaways before, and I generally sprout imaginary wings and fly out of the rig. I am all right on a horse's back, but a rank coward in a vehicle.

When I woke up the sun was about two hours high, it being about 5 P. M. I was lying flat on my back with the hot June sun shining in my face. I couldn't move or open my eyes, and I wondered what was wrong. Finally, by making a strong effort, I got my right hand up to my eyes,—the left arm couldn't be raised. I discovered that my face and eyes were covered with a baked coating of some kind. This was scraped from my eyes when they opened. Still, I couldn't think what was wrong. Soon I became deathly sick at my stomach and started to vomiting. I managed to turn over on my left side so as to vomit on the ground. Then I discovered that I was throwing up blood. Raising up my head I saw the hind wheels and the bed of the buckboard upside down, and only a few yards from me lay my Colts 45 pistol and the bottle of water which was put in the buckboard on starting. Then it all came fresh to my mind of the runaway, but I didn't remember of the vehicle turning over. The last that I could recall was turning the team around the head of the gully.

As I was dying for a drink of water after lying in the hot sun for eight or nine hours, every nerve in my body was strained to crawl to the bottle of water.

A little of the water was used to wash the blood out of my eyes. In vomiting, while on my back with my head slightly down hill, the blood had run over my face and eyes and when dried, had formed a hard crust.

The water and the crawling had revived me so that I could sit up. On feeling the top of my head I found that my high stubborn bump had overflowed and filled up the hole where the religious bump ought to have been, according to phrenology rules. In fact, the top of my head was badly swollen, which showed that I had landed on the ground wrong end up. My back pained the worst, and it was like pulling a tooth to try to get onto my feet. Therefore I started out to crawl back to the Jim T. ranch about five miles. After crawling a few hundred yards I managed to gain my feet. Several times en route I was on the eve of giving up and lying down to rest, but the fear that I wouldn't be able to get on my feet again, kept me pushing ahead.

When within a mile of the ranch, after the sun had set, I saw a man afoot running towards me. I was reeling from one side to the other like a drunken bum, and this had brought Jim T. to my rescue. He saved me from a fall by grabbing me in his strong arms just as I was falling. I had given up and couldn't have walked another step. I was carried to the house and put to bed. Jim T. kept a good supply of horse liniment in the house and he used this on me with a lavish hand as though it was water. There was no doctor nearer than the railroad fifty miles, so I wouldn't consent to T. going after one.

Two days later the bronco team were found, still dragging the front wheels of the buckboard.

While recovering, I had a good chance to get information about the "Wild Bunch," from Jim T., but he would never give a hint as to where "Kid" Curry was, though I found out enough to convince me that they kept up a correspondence through the post office in the prosperous town of Chinook, on the railroad, not far from Harlin, but under what names, I couldn't tell. He informed me that his mail addressed to Landusky was watched when it left the railroad station of Harlin.

In talking, Jim T. showed a very bitter spirit against the Dickensons for killing his friend Loney Logan, and for sending Bob Lee, alias "Bob Curry" to the pen.

Our agency had lately captured and convicted Bob Lee for his connection in the Silcox, Wyo. U. P. train hold-

up.   He was caught in Cripple Creek, Colo., and convicted and sentenced to the pen for ten years, in Cheyenne, Wyo.

Jim T. assured me that Loney's brother "Kid Curry"
would soon get even with the U. P. railroad company
and the Dickensons by robbing another U. P. train; that
the "Kid" was then in the south making preparation for
a deal of that kind.

It was three weeks before I had fully recovered from
the runaway, and even to this day I can feel the effects
of the fall in my head and arm.

I had found out many secrets of past crimes in the
west.

We knew that Flat Nose George Curry (who was not
related to "Kid" and Loney "Curry") was one of the
robbers of the Silcox, Wyo., train hold-up, and deputy
U. S. Marshal Joe LaFors of Cheyenne, had written the
officials of the U. P. railroad that he had learned through
a reliable source that Flat Nose George Curry was with
a tough character named Henry Smith, somewhere in
the northwestern part of the state of Chihuahua in Old
Mexico.   Therefore I received orders by mail to meet
LaFors in Denver and go with him to Old Mexico in
search of Flat Nose George Curry.

We had decided that "Kid" Curry, Jim T.'s partner,
would steer clear of the Little Rockies where every one
knew him, but in this we were mistaken, for not long
after I left he slipped back and killed Ranchman Winters
who had killed his brother Johnny.

Winters was a prosperous stock raiser and he told
me that he expected to be waylaid and killed by "Kid"
Curry.

In the latter part of August I slipped out of the country on my red roan horse for which I had traded the bucking mare. No one knew I was going but my supposed sweetheart Elfie Curry. I told her that my partner was to be executed for a crime we had both committed in Old Merico, and that I feared he would confess and give me away; that if he did she would never see me again as I intended to cut my suspenders and go straight up, where my friends would never hear of me. Otherwise I would return. She was given a certain address in New Mexico from whence letters would be forwarded to me.

Nearly a year afterwards a letter from her reached me through that address. In her letter she wrote that poor little Loney, her four-year-old boy, was heartbroken over my long absence, and kept asking: "Mamma when is Mr. Carter coming home?" The little fellow was pretty and bright, and we had become greatly attached to each other. Of course, the letter was not answered, and I heard no more of them.

In Harlin my horse and saddle were sold and I boarded a train for Denver.

On reaching home Joe LaFors met me and we went to El Paso, Texas, together. In El Paso LaFors located until I could run down Henry Smith and his chum who was supposed to be Flat Nose George Curry.

It had been agreed by Mr. Morris Butt, the president of the West Pacific Railway Company, that LaFors could stay in El Paso until I ran the men down. Then I was to notify LaFors and he would come to me to identify Flat Nose George Curry, whom he had seen.

22

In El Paso I boarded a train for Casas Grandes, Mexico, at the foot of the Sierra Madre mountains. There I secured a horse and saddle and the strenuous part of my work began.

About 100 miles northwest of Casas Grandes, in Janos, a large Mexican town, I got on the trail of my men. But in the wind-up two weeks later, I concluded that Henry Smith's chum was not Flat Nose George Curry.

In the Mormon Colony of Dias I wired to Joe LaFors, in El Paso, Texas, that we were on the wrong trail— hence he could return home to Cheyenne, Wyoming.

Soon after this Flat Nose George Curry was shot and killed in Utah, while trying to resist his capture. This confirmed my decision that Smith's chum was not the man wanted.

While resting a few days in the Mormon colony of Dias, Mexico, I saw some queer sparking. The pretty eighteen-year-old hired girl at the place I was stopping made love to the sixty-year-old proprietor, and married him. This made his fourth wife, all living within a stone's throw of each other.

On this trip into Old Mexico I recognized several former cowboy chums, but I didn't make myself known Among them was one who was outlawed from Texas. He was going under an assumed name and was living with a native woman. They had a house full of little half-breeds of all sizes, from the cradle up into the teens. So, why disturb him when he was faithfully assisting Mother Nature to improve the human race.

From Dias I rode on a stage coach to a station on the Sierra Madre railway, and arrived back in Denver after an absence of over a month.

CHAPTER XV

A 1,000-MILE HORSEBACK RIDE FROM GRAND JUNCTION, COLO., TO ALMA, NEW MEXICO—IN WITH "KID" CURRY'S "WILD BUNCH" CROWD, IN COLORADO, UTAH, ARIZONA, NEW MEXICO AND WYOMING.

Arriving in Denver, Colorado, I found out the particulars of a late train hold-up on the U. P. railroad at Tipton, Wyoming.

Our Asst. Supt., Mr. Goddil, had been on the ground investigating this late robbery and had decided that "Kid" Curry, Bill Cruzan and a man who might be Longbough, did the job.

Jim T. of Landusky, Montana, had told me that "Kid" Curry was planning to rob the U. P. Ry. again to get revenge for the Dickensons killing his brother, Loney, hence I concluded that Jim T. knew what he was talking about.

Our agency had just received a "tip" through an ex-convict in Grand Junction, Colo., that he talked with "Kid" Curry and a tall companion at their camp on a Mesa twenty miles south of Grand Junction, and that they told him they were going south where the "climate would fit their clothes," and that they had just broken camp and started south on horseback. Therefore, I was hustled right out to get on the trail of these two men.

I was instructed to pick up their trail if possible, and stay with it wherever it might lead, and should the trail not be found, then I was to drift southwest through Utah and Arizona and into New Mexico to Alma, in western Socorro county, where some of the stolen unsigned U. S. bills from the Silcox, Wyo., robbery had been passed.

A 300 mile ride over the Continental Divide on the D. & R. G. Ry., brought me to the little city of Grand Junction where my friend "Doc" Shores and his lovely wife—she who fed my face so well while I was a prisoner in the Gunnison jail, years before—have a beautiful home.

While purchasing horses and getting an outfit ready for the trail, I made my headquarters at the Shores residence, but on the sly, so no one would see me coming and going, as every man, woman and child in that town knows Shores as an officer.

During my stay I made the acquaintance of Charlie Wallis, the sheriff of this, Mesa county. He was an ex-cowboy from Texas, and New Mexico, and an old friend of Tom Hall's, now Tom Nichols, of Price, Utah; hence we had some pleasant chats of old-time cowboy days.

I started south with a blue-roan saddle horse and a red-roan pack horse, and they were both good ones for such a trip, more especially the saddle animal which could make a meal on greasewood or any kind of rubbish when it came to a show-down during deep snows when the feed played out.

Before reaching the Paradox Valley, the home of the notorious Young boys who are known far and wide as "bad" men, I made the acquaintance of a Mr. Elliott and his brother-in-law W. B. Moss, and found out for sure that my men had passed their ranch only a week ahead of me. I showed Mr. Elliott the photo of "Kid" Curry and he was positive that the small dark man was the same as the photo. Before making a confidant of young Elliott, I satisfied myself that he was all right and could be trusted. Of course I had to trust to my judgment in human nature.

From Elliott's ranch the two train hold-ups were trailed into the Paradox Valley and right up to Ed Young's ranch, and from Ed Young's father-in-law, who had no idea that I was a detective, I found out that the two robbers had gone south with Lafe Young, who was an outlaw and dodging the officers. He had last seen them in the La Salle mountains where they had a bunch of range horses rounded up with a view of stealing a fresh mount.

I remained in the Paradox Valley about a week and became quite "chummy" with Bill Young and met his mother and pretty black-eyed young sister.

There was a store in the valley, and from the proprietor Thomas Swain, I gained much valuable information. He was an honest old Englishman and I made a confidant of him.

I had got on the wrong trail by following two men into the La Salle mountains, and through Thomas Swain I found out that one of them was my friend "Cunny" of New Mexico. They were on a prospecting trip to Utah and Nevada. Seeing "Cunny's" handwriting where he wrote to have his mail forwarded, convinced me that I was on the wrong trail, but I soon got on the right trail and headed south through a wild unsettled country, for the Blue Mountains of southern Utah.

In the Blue mountains I got in with a tough gang, one of whom was Bill G. the manager of the Carlisle Cattle Ranch. He was an outlaw from Oklahoma and New Mexico, and gave me the secrets of his past life. From him I found out that my men "Kid" Curry and his tall chum, who was a stranger in that country, had left the hidden haystack the morning previous to my arrival, Lafe Young being with them. The two train robbers he said were broke, as they had failed to get any money from their last train hold-up at Tipton, Wyoming, hence he gave them a supply of grub. They told G. that they were going where the climate would fit their clothes. He figured that meant Arizona or New Mexico, as their clothes were light for cold weather.

Every fall Bill G. put up a stack of hay for his outlaw friends so that they wouldn't have to feed their horses at his ranch. This haystack was hidden in a heavy grove of piñon and cedar timber a couple of miles from the ranch. My men camped one night at this hidden haystack and then pulled out for Indian Creek where Bill G. visited their camp next day to recover a Winchester rifle which they had stolen by mistake from one of his cowboys. He had just returned when I arrived.

I drifted over to Indian Creek, a place noted for tough characters, and got in "solid" with an outlaw named "Peg-leg." His chum "Kid" Jackson was afraid of me for fear I might be a detective.

"Peg-leg" had been to the camp of my two men, and Lafe Young had told him that they were Union Pacific train-robbers making their "get-away," but he didn't learn their names. His description of the small dark man tallied with that of "Kid" Curry to a dot.

"Peg-leg" informe me that just previous to my arrival on Indian Creek, these men broke camp. Lafe Young returned north while the two train-robbers drifted south down the Colorado river.

One day "Peg-leg" and I rode into Monticello, the Mormon county seat of San Juan County, Utah, a distance of twenty miles. It was a small town of 200 people, presided over by Bishop Jones of the Mormon church.

En route to Monticello "Peg-leg" and I rested for an hour on top of a high mountain ridge from whence we could view the whole country around for a hundred miles or more. It was a clear sunshiny day. Looking to the westward beyond the Indian Creek settlement, the great Colorado river could be seen with its jagged cliffs and canyons, which made a beautiful sight. And beyond the Colorado river "Peg-leg" pointed out the "Robbers' Roost," which "Butch" Casiday and the "Wild Bunch" used as headquarters for several years until Joe Bush and a posse of Salt Lake City officers made a raid on the "Roost" and killed some of the gang.

Beyond the "Robbers' Roost" was the Henry mountains, a mere bluish blotch on the lovely blue sky. The distance to them from where we lay, as the bird flies, was about seventy-five miles, but in order to reach them one would have to travel about 200 miles, as the country between is almost impassable and devoid of inhabitants.

"Peg-leg" told of secret trails to the Colorado river, and of the "Wild Bunch" having a boat hidden in the rushes at a certain point so they could cross the river and reach the Henry mountains quickly. He said that "Kid" Jackson used this boat a week previous.

Southwest from where we were there is not a human habitation for about 300 miles down in Arizona, and it is a very rough country with a scarcity of water, therefore it can be realized what a haven of rest it must be for the "Wild Bunch" and their kind.

"Peg-leg" and I aimed to reach Monticello after dark, so that he wouldn't be seen until he found out if the coast was clear; in other words, if there were any outside officers in the county looking for criminals. After we had put up our horses and had a lunch in a cabin on the outskirts of town, "Peg-leg" borrowed my pistol so that he would have two, leaving his Winchester rifle with me, and struck out in the dark to find the sheriff of the county. He had told me that the sheriff stood in with the outlaws and kept them posted as to when there was danger in the air, but I didn't know whether to believe it or not. To satisfy myself I followed "Peg-leg" in the dark, keeping my rifle hidden under my coat.

"Peg-leg" found the sheriff at a dance and they met under some trees in a dark place and had a long pow-wow. This seemed strange considering that the sheriff had warrants in his pocket for "Peg-leg" and at least half a dozen for "Peg-leg's" chum, "Kid" Jackson.

On returning to the cabin "Peg-leg" reported to me that the coast was clear and that no outside officers or detectives were in the county. We then put in a few hours with "Peg-leg's" sweetheart and her mother.

"Peg-leg" told how the past winter two officers left the railroad with a team and buggy to search for "Kid" Jackson in the Indian Creek country, there being big rewards out for his arrest; that these officers wrote to the sheriff asking that he meet them. The sheriff then sent for "Kid" Jackson and told him to "hit the high places" until these officers left. But instead of hiding out, "Kid" Jackson and "Peg-leg" went to these officers' camp one night, running off their horses and shooting into their tent, the result being the two sleuths had to "hoof it" back to Moab where they secured transportation to the railroad.

I found out that Bill G. had been sheriff of this county two terms, and when he couldn't hold it any longer he selected a man who was a member of the Mormon church whom he could trust to protect his friends among the outlaw class. I got this from "Peg-leg" and Bill G. himself. No wonder the Blue Mountains have been an outlaw's paradise for many years.

During my three weeks' stay in the Blue mountains I gained much information about past crimes and the names of noted outlaws. I found out that a "bad" outlaw of Texas had married a Mormon girl on Indian Creek, under an assumed name, but after they had been married a year or two he confessed the truth to his wife. She then fixed it with the church so that they could be married in his own name in a way that the secret wouldn't leak out. This was done to place their children on the shady side of Heaven; otherwise they would be on the sunny side of Hades. Bishop Jones of Monticello performed the church ceremony in secret, so that the man's true name wouldn't leak out. I got this from Bishop Jones' own lips after I had made a confidant of him. I also met this ex-outlaw from Texas and found him to be a nice fellow, apparently.

After making a confidant of Bishop Jones, a fine law-abiding citizen, he gave me some valuable "tips;" but he was very angry when I gave him the secrets of how his Mormon sheriff was standing in with the "Wild Bunch." He assured me that a law-abiding sheriff would be put in at the next election, and no doubt he kept his word, for I heard that Bill G. was sent to the Utah penitentiary soon after election.

After leaving the Blue mountains I drifted south to Bluff City on the San Juan river, thence west 120 miles over that uninhabited, rocky, desert country, over which Sayles and I passed, to Dandy Crossing on the Colorado river.

On reaching the foot of Elk mountain a deep snow covered up all trails and the clouds and falling snow prevented my seeing familiar landmarks to guide my way. The result was that I was lost for a couple of days and nights; and one dark night I saw the campfire of Jim Scorrup down in a deep canyon. I was then twenty miles off my road to the southward. Jim Scorrup of Bluff City was camped all alone under a ledge of rock, and had a whopping big fire burning. The sight of this fire raised a cowboy yell in my throat that startled Scorrup and his shepherd dog. I was wet, tired, and hungry.

Scorrup was out hunting lost stock. Next day the sun came out and Scorrup put me on the right trail to Dandy Crossing. He went with me as far as White's Canyon and we camped together that night. We bade each other goodby next morning and I haven't seen him since, but there will always remain a warm spot in my heart for Jim Scorrup, as he knows how to put new life into a lost sinner.

On reaching Dandy Crossing about night, during a severe rain storm, Col. Hite, formerly a wealthy politician of Springfield, Illinois, helped to swim my two horses across the Colorado river. In doing so the Colonel got his 250 pounds of flesh wet to the skin. We had trouble making the horses "take the water," and Hite let me do all the swearing, as he said he had been brought up a Christian and felt better to do his swearing by proxy.

From Dandy Crossing I rode north through the Henry mountains to Hanksville, two hard days' ride. As Sayers and I had been in Hanksville, I felt at home here with Charlie Gibbons and his family, with whom I put up. I made a confidant of Mr. Gibbons and told him my business. He gave me some new pointers about "Butch" Casiday and the "Wild Bunch." He had first become acquainted with Casiday after he helped to rob the Montpelier, Idaho, bank out of a large pile of gold. This gold was turned over to Gibbons for safe keeping, he not knowing of the robbery. Later it was taken to the "Robbers' Roost," fifty miles east of Hanksville, where the "Wild Bunch" used twenty dollar gold pieces for poker chips.

Bill G. had told me of going into the "Robbers' Roost" while sheriff of San Juan County, Utah, and of how his friend "Butch" Casiday and his gang kept him there two days playing poker for twenty dollar gold pieces, they staking him out of their pile of gold.

I had received orders from Asst. Supt. "Rank" Curran, through the mail, to drift over to the Sevier Valley, where "Butch" Casiday was born and raised, and find out all I could about that outlaw, for future use; and from there drift south through Arizona and New Mexico to Alma, in the latter territory, Alma being the southern rendezvous for the "Wild Bunch," while the Hole-in-the-Wall, in Wyoming, was their northern hangout. This of course meant a horseback ride of over 1000 miles through the most God-forsaken desert country in the United States.

On leaving Hanksville one morning a traveling photographer took a snapshot of me and my horses. This photograph I present herein to show what a cowboy detective looks like when on the warpath, with bedding, grub, and kitchen fixings tied to his saddle-pony's tail.

A day's ride due west up the Dirty Devil river brought me to the Mormon settlement of Cainsville. Here I put up for the night. On leaving the Dirty Devil next morning to cross an unsettled rough desert called San Rafael Swell, I bade goodby to civilization for a few days.

After the first night out I lost the dim trail and concluded to head due west over a high snowy range of mountains for the town of Emery, at the head of Castle Valley. Sayles and I had stopped there, hence I knew by the lay of the mountains where the little Mormon town was located on the opposite side of the mountains. This proved to be a bad mistake, for after camping out in the snow two nights I had to turn back as the snow became too deep for travel, and I was not yet to the top of the range.

That night I had no feed for the horses, and through kindness of heart I hobbled them out, that is, tied their front feet together so they could hobble around among

THE AUTHOR

N ROBBERS.

the rocks on a side hill and pick up a little dry grass. This was mistake No. 2, for next morning I had to shoulder my wrath and follow their tracks fifteen miles to the head of Starvation Creek, where there was a small spring. This was back in the direction of Dirty Devil river. In traveling these fifteen miles afoot I felt like swearing, but I realized the uselessness of uttering cuss words where they would have been wasted on the desert air. I contented myself by making a vow that hereafter one of the horses would be tied up to a tree, feed or no feed, as I would rather count their ribs than their tracks.

The next morning I found the dim trail over which Sayles and I had traveled. This was followed until dark, where camp was pitched without either wood or horse feed. And to make matters worse it was raining hard.

The following morning I pushed ahead to reach a ranch where Sayles and I had stopped nearly two years previous. At that time a Mormon lady and her pretty young daughter lived there alone, as their lord and master was absent trying to make a living, the soil on their homestead being too poor to grow sufficient food. But imagine my surprise on finding the place vacated and not a blade of grass for my tired and hungry horses in sight. It was about night and raining hard, which made the road slippery and hard on the horses.

About midnight we came to a ranch on the side of the road, which was considered as being only four miles from Emery. Dismounting, I went to the house and knocked on the door, and a dog inside made a terrible racket, as though he wanted to eat me up. Repeated knocks and loud calls failed to bring any one to the door. I thought seriously of breaking down the door, and if it had to be done, killing the dog and cooking a supper, providing there was anything to eat in the house. But on second thought I concluded it dangerous, as there might be someone inside with a gun. Thus was my well developed cautious bump getting in its work.

Finally I started in the cold rain, and the poor horses didn't want to go. A half-hour's ride brought me to a small raging creek which my horses wouldn't go into, despite the severe spurring received by my mount. Then we turned back with the intention of breaking down the ranchman's door, but to my great delight, on coming in sight, a light was shining in the window and before knocking I heard voices inside. On knocking I was admitted, and the frightened woman who was alone with her small children, explained that she didn't open the door the first time because she was afraid, and that after I had been gone quite awhile, she built a fire to make coffee to quiet her nerves.

By the time the horses were put in the stable and fed, the kind lady had a hot meal on the table and I ate dinner, supper, and a three o'clock breakfast all at one time. Then I lay down by the open fireplace to sleep.

But why waste time to chronicle the hardships of a fool cow-puncher who had started out as a detective to see the world and to study the phrenology bumps on the heads of other people, instead of living the "simple life" on a small patch of the earth's surface. So I will hurry on to Alma, New Mexico, the outlaws' Paradise, near the border of Old Mexico.

A ride of several days over mountain trails landed me in Circleville, the home of "Butch" Casiday before he turned out to be the shrewdest and most daring outlaw of the present age, though not of the blood-spilling kind like "Kid" Curry and "Black Jack."

A week was spent in the straggling village of Circleville, and I found out all about "Butch's" early life and much about his late doings. His true name was Parker, his nickname being "Sallie" Parker when a boy. This nickname of itself was enough to drive a sensitive boy to the "bad."

I had hard work to keep from falling in love with Miss Parker, the pretty young sister of "Butch" Casiday. She was the deputy postmistress in Circleville, and I made her acquaintance.

Hard, cold rides brought me to the town of Panguitch, thence due south to the Mormon town of Kanab, on the line of Arizona. Here I laid in a good supply of grub, as this was the last settlement for hundreds of miles.

A three days' ride over the Buckskin mountains and down the great Colorado river, brought me to Lee's Ferry on that stream. Not a habitation or a settler was seen between Kanab and Lee's Ferry, Arizona, and I found water scarce and "far between." But it was surely a treat to see this lone ranch down in the narrow valley of the Colorado. It was indeed an oasis in the desert. Here green alfalfa was a foot high and the flowers, and the combs on the chickens were in full bloom.

Another three days over an uninhabited desert country brought me to the Indian trading store at Willow Creek. From here I turned due east across the Navajo

Indian Reservation and through the Moqui Indian country, my object being to find out if any of the "Wild Bunch" had been seen lately. Therefore, for the next two weeks I was among Indians all the time, and I learned some interesting lessons, especially among the Moquis, who live on the very top of round mountains in the desert. At one of the big Moqui villages I took my horses up the steep trail and rode into the Chief's front yard. My horses were fed and the Indians made an idol of me. They dug up old rusty dried venison which had been buried for a coon's age, so as to give me a feast fit for the gods. I remained all night and was invited to take me a squaw and become one of them, but I told the Chief that I wasn't ready to settle down, as I wanted to settle up first.

On the Navajo and Moqui Indian Reservations I visited the Keams and the Hubbell trading posts. Both Captain Keams and Mr. Lorenzo Hubbell treated me royally and gave me valuable information about "Kid" Curry and his gang, when the previous spring, they left a trail of blood behind them in making their "getaway" from southern New Mexico. They had killed two officers near here, and killed other men before reaching Wyoming.

Finally I crossed the Atlantic & Pacific railroad at Gallup, New Mexico, thence south through the Zuni Indian country to a salt lake a few miles east of the Arizona line. Here I found a settlement of Mexicans putting up salt for the markets in far off towns. And here I saw a great curiosity in the form of a bottomless lake on the top of a round mountain. To reach it one has to climb to the top of the mountain on the outside and down a trail on the inside. I went swimming in it, as the water is warm in winter, it being out of reach of the wind. It is said that the Government tried to find the bottom of this salty body of hidden water, but failed after putting down a line 3000 feet. The lake from whence the salt is gathered lies at the foot of this round mountain.

From here I went to the line of Arizona, where a few days previous two of Pete Slaughter's boys murdered William Beeler, the brave officer who had trailed "Kid" Curry and his gang to Baggs, Wyoming, the spring previous. The two seventeen-year-old boys murdered Beeler in revenge for the killing of Monte Slaughter not long before.

From here I drifted south to the American Valley ranch, where my friend W. J. C. Moore, the outlaw cowboy whom I saw in Juneau, Alaska, killed two men, which set him adrift with a big reward on his head.

From American Valley I rode south to Luna Valley and made the acquaintance of many tough characters. Here I made a confidant of a ranchman by the name of James G. Smith, and found out that he had known me in Texas years before. He gave me valuable information about the "Wild Bunch," and his good wife filled me up on civilized food.

Finally I reached the sleepy little town of Alma, New Mexico, and my thousand-mile horseback journey was ended.

The town of Alma supported one store and one saloon, both being well patronized by the wild and wooly population thinly scattered over the surrounding country.

23

I started in to make myself "solid" with the tough element of the district, so as to find out more about the "Wild Bunch" and as to who passed a lot of that unsigned money stolen in the Silcox, Wyoming, train holdup. This stolen money had been passed in Alma a few months after the train holdup, and when the matter leaked out Asst. Supt. "Rank" Curran, of our Denver office, was sent there to investigate. There being no deputy sheriffs in this western part of Socorro county, it being about 120 miles from the county seat of Socorro on the Rio Grande river, Mr. Curran had no local officers to assist him. I was told that the sheriff couldn't get a man to accept the deputyship in the western part of this county, as it was too tough and dangerous, being overrun with outlaws and desperados.

Mr. Curran had to take someone into his confidence, so he used bad judgment by selecting the two leading business men and citizens of Alma. One of these was the storekeeper and the other the saloon proprietor, Jim Lowe. Of course Curran went into detail of how he was on a hot trail of the Union Pacific train robbers who had passed some of the stolen money in Alma. This was enough. That night Mr. Curran was driven out of town and would have been killed had it not been for saloonman Jim Lowe.

Curran was not a western man, he having formerly been Superintendent of our Chicago office before being taken down with that dread disease, consumption, and coming to Denver for his health. Hence he was glad to get out of Alma alive, and of course he naturally felt grateful to Jim Lowe.

After getting in with the tough gang, I learned the truth of how Jim Lowe saved Murray's life, and how next morning Lowe sold his saloon and "hit the trail" with outlaw "Red" Weaver, for "tall timber;" that Jim Lowe was none other than the notorious "Butch" Casiday of the "Kid" Curry gang.

Among the men whose friendship I made was Jesse Black, one of Jim Lowe's warmest friends, who had figured in the raid on Frank Murray. He was considered a hard case, but no one seemed to know who he was or where he came from.

Part of my time was spent out in the mountains in the Mogollon mining camp and at the mining town of Graham, where there was a gold mill; also at the cattle town of Frisco, near the Arizona line.

In Frisco I got in with a bronco-buster and "bad" man, who told me the spot in the mountains, about forty miles southwest, where Jim Lowe had established a "Robbers' Roost" or rendezvous, and at that very time was there with eight outlaw companions, but who these companions were he didn't know, as they were from the north. He was only acquainted with Jim Lowe. He pointed out the particular mountain in the distance where they were camped, and getting ready for some kind of a raid. This bronco-buster had been to their camp lately.

On learning of this, I at once wrote to Asst. Supt. Curran, telling him of Jim Lowe's rendezvous and of my plans to visit their camp and try to get in with the gang.

Soon I received a reply by mail saying that I was mistaken about Jim Lowe being "Butch" Casiday, as he ("Rank" Curran) had met Lowe and found him to be a nice gentleman. In the letter he instructed me to sell my horses and return to Denver as he wanted me to join a tough gang in western Colorado and southern Wyoming, who stood in with the "Wild Bunch."

So this ended my work in Alma during the late spring. Putting a stop to my visiting Jim Lowe and his gang may have been a godsend, as they might have killed me; but still, it may have terminated in the killing or capture of the whole bunch.

After selling my horses in the Mogollon mining camp I boarded the stagecoach for Silver City, the county seat of Grant county, New Mexico, a distance of about eighty miles to the southward, this being the nearest railroad.

Blake Graham, a warm friend of Jim Lowe, was a passenger on the stage with me. We had a good supply of liquor along and he told me the whole secret of Jim Lowe being "Butch" Casiday. He told of how when Asst. Supt. Murray was run out of Alma, Jim Lowe sold his saloon and skipped; that he (Blake Graham) rode several miles with Lowe and "Red" Weaver when they were leaving, and of how Lowe said he didn't have the heart to see Frank Murray killed, and for that reason he helped get him out of town in the night.

This outlaw "Red" Weaver was killed in a pistol duel with Jim Hollman in the street of Alma just before my arrival.

The driver of the stagecoach was Bill Kelly, who claimed to be the original "L. S. Kid" of the Panhandle, Texas. I had known the "L. S. Kid" as a wild smooth-face boy, hence Kelly and I became quite "chummy." Young Graham and I and the two traveling men aboard kept Kelly loaded with liquor so that he would make good time, and amuse us with his western songs. He claimed to have originated one of these songs while a cowboy in the Panhandle, Texas, and he sang it half a dozen times en route. It had a lovely tune and seemed to strike me just right. It ran thus:

My lover is a cowboy,
  He's kind, he's brave and true;
He rides the Spanish pony
  And throws the lasso, too;
And when he comes to see me
  And our vows we have redeemed,
He puts his arms around me
  And then begins to sing:

CHORUS:

Oh, I am a jolly cowboy,
  From Texas now I hail,
Give me my saddle and pony
  And I'm ready for the trail.
I love the rolling prairie
  Where we are free from care and strife,
And behind a herd of long-horns,
  I will journey all my life.

We rise up in the morning
  At the early dawn of day,
We vault into the saddle
  And quickly ride away.
We rope, brand and ear-mark,
  I tell you what, we're smart,
We get the herd all ready
  For Kansas, then, we start.

Chorus.

When lowering clouds do gather
  And livid lightnings flash,
And crashing thunder rattles
  And heavy rain-drops splash.

What keeps the herd from roaming
　And stampeding far and wide?
'Tis the cowboy's long, low whistle
　And singing by their side.

Chorus.

And when in Kansas City
　The boss he pays us up,
We loaf around a few days,
　We have a parting cup.
We bid farewell to city,
　From noisy marts we come
Right back to dear old Texas
　The cowboys' native home.

Before reaching Silver City about night, the liquor began to work. Then Graham and I pulled our pistols and emptied them through the canvas-covered top of the stagecoach. This set fire to the canvas top and the wind carried the fire to my roll of bedding in the rear; then we all became fire-fighters. We drove into Silver City without a buggy-top and the liquor all gone.

As my daughter Viola lived in Silver City with her aunt and uncle, Mr and Mrs. Will F. Read, I laid over the next day to visit them. Viola had grown to be a pretty young lady and was just finishing her education in the Territorial Normal College in Silver City.

I also visited with my old White Oaks (N. M.) friend, Jim Brent, who was now City Marshal of this town; also with Sheriff Goodall and ex-Sheriff J. K. Blair, both model officers.

I then boarded a train for Denver, stopping off in Santa Fe one day to visit my pets.

On arriving in Denver, Asst. Supt. Curran sent me

at once to Grand Junction in the western part of Colorado, there to purchase a horse and locate one Jim F. who had been run out of Dixon, Wyoming, by the vigilantes, as he was known to be in with the "Wild Bunch." It was reported that he had taken his family and settled somewhere near Grand Junction.

I finally located Jim F. through my friend Sheriff Charlie Wallis. He had bought a small patch of land in an out-of-the-way place on Grand River near Palisade, twenty miles above Grand Junction, and lived there with his young wife and two pretty little girls.

After much planning and scheming I got in "solid" with Jim F., although he had received a letter of warning from his friend Tom T., in Dixon, Wyoming, to the effect that the Union Pacific Railroad Company had a Dickenson detective on his trail. I brought him this letter from Palisade, as he had given me orders to get his mail. On reading it he swore the most wicked oaths against all detectives and swore to cut out the heart of any detective who undertook to win his friendship. He let me read the letter.

I had been cautioned to watch Jim F. as he was a wicked fellow and would kill a man without mercy. He had cut his own brother-in-law's throat in a fit of anger, and he had once served a term in the South Dakota penitentiary, while his brother Charlie, whose friendship I won later, was an ex-convict from Utah.

To show what a temper Jim F. had, I will cite a case wherein he came very near drowning his own child while sitting at the dinner table. The door was open and a swift irrigation ditch full of water flowed by the

door. The eldest girl, eight years old, cried for more
fish when there was none left. Jim grabbed the child
and threw her with all the force of his makeup,—he being nearly six feet tall, 190 pounds in weight and thirty-
two years of age,—into the irrigation ditch. It was only
a few hundred yards to the treacherous Grand River,
and Jim had to run fast to catch the half drowned girl
before she reached the river. Of course this broke the
child of wanting fish after it was all eaten.

Jim F. and I became fast friends after he had seen
the newspaper accounts of my shooting scrape in southern New Mexico, and of my being an outlaw who was
badly wanted by the officers of Grant county, New Mexico. Of course I had these accounts put into the papers
and marked copies sent to me.

I was going by the name of Lee Roy Davis. The
Palisade paper once referred to me as "mysterious white-
horse Davis," my saddle horse being white.

During the month of August, Jim F. and I pulled out
for "tall timber." We put in a couple of weeks at the
head of White River above Meeker. We lived on venison and fish and camped out alone. From here we
drifted to Hayden, Colo., where Jim F. had friends;
thence to Dixon, Wyo., to show Bob Meldrum the "man-
killer" town marshal and the vigilantes, that Jim F. was
not afraid to come back. I had promised to help fight
his battles, and we came within an ace of having a shooting scrape with Bob Meldrum on reaching Dixon.

To recite how Jim F. and an ex-convict friend of his
by the name of Ed. Muirr made the blood flow one night
when they beat up and robbed a gang of telephone com-

pany workmen who had been paid off, would take up too much space. I didn't care to take a hand in the robbery. Still, I got $60.00 of the tainted money from Jim F. in payment for a loan made in Meeker.

On the Snake River, above Dixon, at the foot of Black Mountain, is where Jim F. lived on his ranch when run out of the country by the Cattle Association, as it was known that he was a cattle rustler and used his ranch for a rendezvous for tough characters.

It was at this Black Mountain ranch that Jim F. furnished horses and grub to "Kid" Curry and his gang when they started out to rob the Union Pacific train at Tipton, Wyo., about 100 miles north, the fall previous, and after the robbery Jim F. kept them hid on Black Mountain until the officers quit searching for them. I was shown the exact spot where they camped high up on the timbered mountain. Here Jim F. carried grub to them and kept them posted as to the movements of the officers. From him I learned that "Kid" Curry, Bill Cruzan and the "Tall Texan," whose right name was Kilpatrick, held up the train at Tipton, Wyo. And I found out that after leaving the Black Mountain they drifted south to the Blue Mountains in Utah, thence further south into New Mexico. But before reaching Utah, Bill Cruzan turned back on his mule and later was met by Bert C. south of Grand Junction, Colo. Bert C., Jim F. said, was a go-between and kept the "Wild Bunch" posted by getting mail or word to them.

Jim F. also gave me the secrets of the Silcox, Wyo., train holdup, and many other noted cases. Also told how he assisted in a bank robbery in Nebraska, and of his many cattle stealing and fighting scrapes in the Black Hills of Dakota.

Jim F. and I were fixing to pull out of Dixon and go to Rawlins to meet friends of Jim F's, when Ellis, a merchant of Dixon, called Jim to the rear of his store and advised him not to go to the Union Pacific Railroad as Pinkerton detectives were on his trail and would arrest him. At this Jim F. concluded to "hit" the road back to Grand Junction, Colo. He sold me his packhorse and outfit and gave me a letter of introduction to his friend Jack R. who stood in with the "Wild Bunch," and who had two saloons in Rawlins, Wyo.

On leaving the Grand River at Jim F's home, my name had been changed to Harry Blevins, so that the New Mexico officers couldn't get track of me. Jim F. selected my new name, and in this name he gave me the letter of introduction which was short and to the point. It merely stated: "This will introduce to you my friend Harry Blevins. He is righter than hell." Among the "Wild Bunch," "right" meant that a man is all right and can be trusted.

After seeing Jim F. off and headed south for Colorado, I pulled out for the north. I put up one night at the Twenty-mile ranch owned by Jim H., a friend to Jim F. and the "Wild Bunch." He was a wealthy stock man and had furnished one of the horses to "Kid" Curry for the Tipton train holdup. I let him read the letter to Jack R. and he told me to come to him and he would find me a hiding place should the officers ever get on my trail. He told me about the Tipton and Silcox robberies and said he had helped "Kid" Curry out more than once.

I arrived in the hurrah little city of Rawlins, where half the men are railroad employes and the other half, with the exception of the gamblers and saloon men, smell sheepy. Even the cattlemen get to smelling like sheep from the constant chasing of sheep off their ranges. Rawlins is the center of a great sheep country.

Jack R. welcomed me with open arms on the strength of Jim F's letter, and it wasn't long until he told me of the "Wild Bunch" and their doings. He had made his first stake through "Butch" Casiday and his gang, after they robbed the Montpelier, Idaho, bank out of about $30,000 in gold. At that time Jack R. owned a small saloon in Baggs, on Snake River near Dixon. The gang was headed for the "Robbers' Roost" in southern Utah and stopped over a few days to rest in Baggs, and while there they threw enough twenty dollar gold pieces over Jack R's bar to give him a stake, so that he could open a good saloon in Rawlins. Jack R. told of how "Butch" would shoot an old widow's chickens just to hear her swear. Then he would have the old lady smiling by giving her a twenty dollar gold piece for every chicken killed.

During the winter in and around Rawlins, I led a hurrah drinking life, and made friends among the tough element. Among those met was Bert C., virtually one of the "Wild Bunch," but who was slick enough to keep out of the law's clutches. His home was in Grand Junction, Colo. He and I became "chummy," but he kept his secrets to himself. He was noted for being "close-mouthed" and no doubt that is why "Kid" Curry and the "Wild Bunch" put such confidence in him. But

I played my cards so as to open Bert C's mouth and get his secrets.

In the Spring he and I went to Grand Junction, Colo., where we hobnobbed with his tough cowboy friends. Among them was our friend Jim F.

During the summer Bert C. and I rode from Grand Junction to Rawlins, a distance of about 300 miles, on horseback.

While in Grand Junction, I received a fake letter from my supposed attorney, Ex-Governor L. Bradford Prince, requesting that I come to Santa Fe, New Mexico, and sign some papers in order that certain property could be sold. This letter was on Attorney Prince's letter head and looked genuine.

Jim F. asked me to visit his friend Bob McGinnis in the Santa Fe penitentiary, and if I got a chance to give him a "Wild Bunch" cipher code, so that they could communicate with each other through the mail. The code was each fourth word, in a friendly letter on general news; that is, each fourth word to be written down which would convey the secret. And I was instructed to tell Bob McGinnis to hold a stiff upper lip, as his friends would bribe the officials of New Mexico and have him out before many years.

Jim F. and Bert C. had told me confidentially who Bob McGinnis was, that he was a Utah chum of "Butch" Casiday's, whose right name was Elza Lay. This was a secret which hadn't yet leaked out.

Jim F. gave me certain words to say to Bob McGinnis which would convince him that I was all right. He and Jim F. had been in the cattle stealing business together several years previous.

In Santa Fe, New Mexico, I took Ex-Governor Prince, Attorney General E. L. Bartlett, and Warden H. O. Bursom, of the penitentiary, into my confidence, so that I got to visit McGinnis and gave him Jim F.'s secrets.

I found McGinnis to be a pleasant fellow, but a hard looking "mug" He acted as though he felt that a job was being put up on him when the guard was called away for a few minutes. It was then that I imparted the secrets to him.

Bob McGinnis was one of "Black Jack's" gang and helped kill my warm friend Ed. Farr, sheriff of Huerfano County, Colo., also Ed. Farr's deputy, Mr. Love. In this fight Bob McGinnis was shot three or four times through the body and then made his "get away." Several months later he had a hand to hand fight with the sheriff of Eddy county, New Mexico, and shot two officers before being overpowered and captured. He had just recovered from his previous wounds. He and "Franks" were camped out in the sand hills east of the Pecos River, when the sheriff and his posse surprised them. "Franks" made his "getaway."

McGinnis was tried for the killing of Sheriff Farr and his deputy, Love, after robbing a Denver & Ft. Worth train. He received a life sentence in the penitentiary at Santa Fe.

About the time of my visit with Bob McGinnis in the Santa Fe pen "Butch" Casiday, Bill Carver and Harry Longbough robbed the Winnamuca, Nev., bank and secured $30,000 in gold. It was plain to me now, that some of this money would be used to free McGinnis from prison.

On rejoining Jim F. in Palisade, Colo., I gave him a hair bridle and steel bit made by Bob McGinnis, the bit being made from old files, as McGinnis had learned to be a blacksmith and electrician. I had also brought from the Santa Fe pen a hair bridle and bit for my own use. This is now kept as a relic.

It was early summer when Bert C. and I started, in company with his young brother, across country for Rawlins, Wyo. We each had a saddle horse and I had a pack animal to carry the grub and bedding.

On reaching the Green Cattle Company's headquarters ranch on the edge of Wyoming, we learned of the Denver & Rio Grande train holdup east of Grand Junction, and from now on we were suspected of having had a hand in the holdup. Bert C. gave me to understand that Bill Cruzan was in this last holdup. It seems that Bert knew it was billed to come off.

Before reaching Dixon, Wyo., we met many of Bert C's and Jim F's tough chums.

In Dixon, Bert C. got a tip from someone, whom I suspected to be merchant Ellis—knowing that he had given Jim F. a friendly tip—that the Dickenson agency had a cowboy detective by the name of Charlie Siringo working in with the "Wild Bunch," so as to get their secrets. This worried Bert and he became sullen for awhile, as though suspicious of me. He questioned me as to whether I had ever heard of Charlie Siringo. Of course I hadn't. I felt confident that Ellis had gotten the secret from either Asst. Supt. Goddil or Curran, as they had told me of what a fine man he was and how he could be trusted with any secret. This goes to prove that it is unsafe for a detective to trust his life in the hands of any man, and this very knowledge is the cause of much sweating of blood by detectives.

From Dixon, Bert C. and I visited Baggs, where his sweetheart, Miss Maud, a respectable girl, lived. We remained in this little hurrah town a few days drinking and visiting with Bert's friends.

Bert C. had, previous to our arrival in Dixon, given me many secrets of the "Wild Bunch." He told of how they kept a system of blind post offices all the way from the Hole-in-the-Wall in northern Wyoming to Alma in southern New Mexico, these post offices being in rocky crevices or on top of round mounds on the desert. In passing these post offices he said members of the "Wild Bunch," who were on the inside, would look for mail or deposit notes of importance. Also late news of interest would be clipped from newspapers and deposited in the post office by passing members.

Bert C. also told me the whole secret of "Butch" Casiday's "getaway" from Alma, New Mexico, when he ran a saloon there under the name of Jim Lowe. He told of how a Dickenson detective named "Rank" Curran came there in search of the men who had passed some of the stolen unsigned bills from the Wilcox train holdup, and that "Butch" Casiday happened to be the man who had passed these bills; that after the gang had run Murray out of the country "Butch" sold his saloon, and in company with outlaw "Red" Weaver, drifted west to the Arizona line to join "Kid" Curry and his gang. He told of how "Butch" and "Red" Weaver were waylaid and captured by William Beeler's posse who were on trail of

"Kid" Curry and gang, they being headed north after committing bloody crimes, but that in the night "Butch" made his "getaway" from the officers on a bareback horse, without firearms or grub; that in riding north, "Butch" overtook the "Kid" Curry gang, and thinking them officers of the law he kept out of sight by hiding in daylight and riding in the night, but when he came to one of their blind post offices he found news which convinced him that he had been hiding from friends, with nothing to eat but crackers.

On reaching Baggs, Wyo., "Butch" was kept hid by "Mid" Nichols (brother to my friend Tom Hall) in his residence. "Mid" then owned a saloon in Baggs.

Finally Beeler and his Arizona posse arrived in Baggs and took "Mid" Nichols into their confidence, telling him of how they were on the trail of the "Kid" Curry gang.

That night "Butch" left the Nichols home riding a good horse and saddle and armed to the teeth. He had to cross a bridge where two of Beeler's men were on guard. They supposed he was a rancher leaving town, and gave him a friendly salute.

"Butch" then remained hidden in the mountains near by until the Beeler posse left Baggs. Mrs. "Mid" Nichols kept "Butch" supplied with grub and liquor, as she was in the habit of taking a horseback ride every day for exercise.

On reaching Rawlins, Bert C. and I boarded a train for Wolcott, there to meet Jack R., "Chip" Reed, and other friends. Jack R. also owned a saloon in Wolcott. From Wolcott we all returned to Rawlins. Then champagne corks flew thick and fast for several days—then several days of agonizing headaches.

One of the "Wild Bunch" secrets given me by Bert C. disclosed the fact that my friend Jesse Black, of Alma, New Mexico, was a hard "hombre" whose right name was Byron Sessions. He had been brought up in Utah and went to New Mexico with "Butch" Casiday after the Montpelier, Idaho, bank robbery.

I spent the whole fall in and around Rawlins and had the pleasure of riding "Butch" Casiday's pet mule "Ikey." I had gone with Jack R. on a wild horse hunt into the Haystack Mountains, where Jack R. kept a hired man and a pile of grub to feed the "Wild Bunch" when passing through the country. On his last visit here, after our Asst. Supt. Frank Murray had scared him out of Alma, New Mexico, "Butch" had left "Ikey" to be cared for by Jack R. I found "Ikey" to be a "peach" of a mule, easy riding and as limber as a cat, and he could run like a scared wolf. But he had one fault—he was afraid of shooting. He left me on the desert once afoot, when I got down to shoot at game.

On this trip Jack R. showed me outlaw Bill Cruzan's rendezvous, a rock cabin built high up in the bluffs overlooking the Laramie River, but I found out that Bill Cruzan had quit living here since the Dickenson agency had got on his trail for the Tipton train holdup; that now he kept moving from place to place, since "Kid" Curry had given him the shake.

During the summer "Kid" Curry and his gang had robbed a Great Northern railroad train up in Montana, securing a large sum of new unsigned U. S. Government bills, and I found out that "Kid" Curry had been in Rawlins where he met Jack R. and Jim H. of the Twenty-mile ranch.

24

The Dickenson agency was employed to run down these West-Northern train holdups, and, of course, all the information secured by me was used in tracing up the robbers.

Finally, during the fall, the "Tall Texan" (Kilpatrick), who was with "Kid" Curry when I trailed him into the Blue Mountains, and who assisted in the Tipton, Wyo., Union Pacific train holdup, was arrested in St. Louis, Mo., along with "Kid" Curry's sweetheart. "Kid" Curry and one of his chums made their "getaway" and Curry came direct to Rawlins to dig up some of the stolen Great Northern money which he had cached on Jim H's Twenty-mile ranch. He wanted this money to hire lawyers to defend his sweetheart, who had been passing some of the stolen bills in St. Louis.

"Kid" Curry only remained in the vicinity of Rawlins two days. He then boarded a train for the east. I didn't know of his being in Rawlins until two days after he had gone. Then I got the secret from Jack R. and Sid. J. The latter told of how "Kid" Curry had seen me in a saloon one night when he was watching the crowd through the rear door. He singled me out as a suspect, saying that I looked too bright and wide-awake for a common rounder; but Sid. J. assured him that I was all right, though "Kid" Curry wouldn't believe it until told so by Jack R. They called Jack R. out of his saloon into the alley. Then Sid. J. said he asked Jack R. if Harry Blevins was "right;" that Jack replied "yes." Then "Kid" Curry was satisfied. I considered it quite a compliment to be called bright by such a wide-awake judge.

"Kid" Curry and His Sweetheart.

But poor "Kid" Curry ran up against a live issue on this trip east. In Knoxville, Tenn., he was arrested after shooting two officers. He finally had a trial in the United States Court, for passing money stolen in the Great Northern train holdup. He was convicted on several different counts and was sentenced to the pen for a total of 130 years, so it was said.

During the trial I was told that my friend Jim T. of the Little Rockies in Montana, was on hand with a good supply of the "long-green" which makes the mare go. The result was that "Kid" Curry made his "getaway" from the high sheriff before reaching the penitentiary walls, and the supposition is that the aforesaid "long-green" and Jim T. were the lifting powers which placed the "Kid" on the smooth road of freedom.

The sheriff was arrested for liberating the "Kid," as it was said he received the snug sum of $8,000.00 for being asleep at the proper time. But I never heard how this honorable official got out of the scrape. The chances are though, that he had to use some of his tainted money to get himself out of the law's clutches.

Kilpatrick, the "Tall Texan," received a sentence of 15 years in the pen, and "Kid" Curry's sweetheart got a long sentence behind prison walls.

Early in the spring another one of the "Wild Bunch," Bill Carver, was killed in Texas while trying to make his escape. Bert C. informed me confidentially, that Bill Carver was the notorious "Franks" of "Black Jack" fame.

I put in a lively fall in Rawlins and the towns adjoining, including Grand Encampment, the big mining camp, and I drank poison liquor enough, against my will, to kill a mule.

In Rawlins I was considered an ex-outlaw, though no one but my friends knew where I came from. Sheriff McDaniels wrote a full description of me to the Dickenson officials in Denver, and in the letter he said I was the toughest looking fellow he had ever seen, and he knew that I must be an outlaw from the way I stood in with Bert C., Jack R. and their gang. McDaniels even went to Denver and had Asst. Supt. Curran look into my case to see if something couldn't be dug up against me, but Mr. Curran couldn't find any one in the agency's rogue's gallery who would fit my complexion.

During the fall I was arrested in Rawlins and paid a $20 fine for carrying a pistol. Judge Smith gave me the full extent of the law on the strength of my tough looking face and the company which I kept.

There was a big machinists' and boiler-makers' strike under headway on the Union Pacific railroad, and Rawlins was the hot-bed of slugging matches on "scabs," and of course, I was in a position to give valuable tips on the matter in my reports. My friends, the city marshal and his policemen, all stood in with the union sluggers.

Among my friends who stood in with the "Wild Bunch" gang was Charlie I., a saloon man of Ft. Steel, Wyo. As boys, he and I had run cattle together in the Panhandle of Texas. He would have known me had I been going under my own name.

Another tough "hombre" whom I knew in Caldwell, Kans., when he was a wild and woolly cowboy there, was Newt. Kelly, the man who stabbed my friend Tim Corn to the point of death in Baggs, Wyo. Once when drunk he felt sure that he had seen me in the Indian Territory or Kansas, but I made him forget the idea.

Early in the winter U. S. Deputy Marshal Joe LaFors came to Rawlins and Jack R. asked if he knew a Dickenson detective by the name of Charlie Siringo. Not knowing that I was in the country, LaFors replied "Yes," and described me to a dot. Later Jack R. introduced us. We pretended to never have met before, and LaFors insisted to Jack R. privately, that I was not Charlie Siringo, although the same size and complexion, etc. LaFors and I met to talk the matter over later.

I could see a coolness on the part of Bert C. and Jack R. which showed that they were suspicious of me, although they tried to hide their true feeling.

A couple of days later I boarded a train for Salt Lake City, Utah, thence to join my friend Jim F. in Palisade, Colo. My horse was put in a pasture in the Ferris Mountains, and my saddle and camp outfit were stored in Jack R's saloon to show that I intended coming back. Several years later Joe LaFors found out that Bert C. had left the country with my saddle and outfit and that my horse was killed and used for wolf bait in poisoning wolves.

After visiting a week with Jim F. in Palisade, I started for the Big Horn Basin in the vicinity of the Hole-in-the-Wall in northern Wyoming. I had received instructions from Asst. Supt. Curran to go up there and get in with friends of the "Wild Bunch," and learn their secrets.

In order to reach the Big Horn Basin and the Wind River country I had to go by rail through Denver, Colo., and Sidney, Neb., thence to Cody, Wyo., at the edge of Yellowstone Park, thence by stage coach 100 miles south to Thermopolis, Wyo. Thermopolis I found to be a small town with the largest hot water springs in the United States. Her hope for the future was also large.

Here I registered at the Keystone hotel under a new name—Chas. Tony Lloyd—so that my associates further south wouldn't learn of my being here.

The Keystone hotel was run by an ex-cowboy, Emory, who was friendly with all the tough characters in the surrounding country, therefore I courted his friendship and led him to believe that I was a hard case. Mr. Emory was a law-abiding citizen himself, but having been a cowboy he naturally sympathized with other cowboys and cattlemen who were in trouble. In fact, I found the general sentiment here to be on the side of the "Wild Bunch" and their class. Those who didn't sympathize with them didn't dare express themselves; that is, with the exception of a few men, among whom was a Dr. Hale and an ex-deputy sheriff by the name of Cameron. But the latter had been put out of business a few weeks previous to my arrival. He now lay at the Keystone hotel shot full of holes and at the point of death. He had been shot by Fred Sted, a young tough. Cameron was the worst shot up man, to be alive, that I had ever seen. He was shot in different places through the arms and body with soft-nose Winchester rifle bullets, which generally tear a hole big enough for a cat to crawl through. He finally recovered though, but was disfigured and crippled for life.

In Thermopolis and the surrounding mountains, I put

in the winter and made friends with all the hard cases, among whom were Fred Sted, the fellow who shot Cameron, Jim McCloud, an ex-convict who escaped from the Leavenworth, Kan., penitentiary, and Tom O'Day, one of the original members of the "Wild Bunch," who had helped "Kid" Curry and his gang rob a Belle Fourche, S. D., bank, besides many other crimes.

I also made friends with Mike B., a well-to-do cattleman who stood in with the "Wild Bunch," by furnishing them grub, horses and money, and going on their bonds when in trouble. He had gone on Fred Sted's bond for the shooting of Cameron, and before the trial came off, Sted jumped his bond and "hit the road" for "tall timber." He waited until green grass came in the spring, of course.

Tom O'Day hung out at Lost Cabin, about 20 miles out in the mountains, while Jim McCloud made his headquarters with ex-convict Shaffer and a bad "hombre" by the name of Frank James at the Mike B. cattle ranch a few miles down the Big Horn River. Before the winter was half over, I had become "chummy" with O'Day and McCloud.

One morning O'Day came to town and we met in Skinner's saloon. As O'Day was hungry he sat at a table with Fred Sted in the rear of the saloon, where there was a restaurant, to eat a lunch. Before doing so he unbuckled his big Colts 45 and belt of cartridges from his waist and gave them to the bar-keeper to lay behind the bar. After he had sat down to eat, an enemy walked up in front of him and pulling a pistol shot six times at O'Day's head, but the fellow was excited and didn't take time to aim. Each bullet went over O'Day's head, just missing him by a scratch. After the pistol was empty the fellow broke to run out of the door. As he did so O'Day threw his coffee cup at him with such force that it struck the door knob, shattering it into a hundred fragments. Then O'Day put on his pistol and swore he wouldn't be so foolish as to play law-abiding citizen by putting it behind the bar again.

This excitement started O'Day to getting drunk earlier than usual, and of course, I joined him. At the Beals bath house, where we had gone with a crowd, tougher than ourselves, we came very near getting into a pistol war with the Beals family, who ran a respectable place. We ran the place to suit ourselves, and I had to endure the agony of hearing O'Day call Mrs. Beals all the foul names in the cowboy language, and furthermore, I had to tell the good lady to keep her mouth shut and to keep her hubby hid out if she didn't want to become a widow.

O'Day and I had agreed to paint the town red and stick to each other in spite of hades and high water, hence I couldn't follow the dictates of my conscience, as that wouldn't be business. Of course, if it had come to a matter of saving the life of a good citizen, business wouldn't have been considered.

It was 3 o'clock next morning when O'Day became too drunk to navigate. Then we retired to our virtuous couches.

For several days after, I received lectures from the preacher and two civilized·school mar'ms who boarded at the Keystone hotel. They thought it a shame that a man like me should throw himself away by associating with such men as O'Day and his lewd female companions. These good people had been trying to reform me ever since my arrival, and this last carouse seemed to be the straw which broke the camel's back, hence the lectures. Of course, these were bitter pills for me to swallow, but I had to gulp them down as though they were sweet, for it wouldn't be policy to make a face showing they were bitter, for fear of offending O'Day and his gang, should they hear of it.

This hurrah life was kept up until late in the spring, when I shook the dust of the Big Horn Basin from my feet. I hadn't been gone very long when my chums, O'Day and McCloud, were arrested for holding up a stage coach and stealing a bunch of horses.

While awaiting trial in the Cheyenne City prison, Jim McCloud and the noted stock detective, Tim Corn, broke jail, but both were captured before getting out of the city, and soon after Corn was hung. Both McCloud and O'Day were sent to the Wyoming penitentiary for six years each. My friend, Joe LaFors, helped to land them in prison, where they both belonged. Of course, it was tough on me to thus lose two dear "chums."

Having finished my work in Wyoming, I was hurried to Arizona to find out the whereabouts of a certain "bad" man, who was supposed to be in with the "Wild Bunch," so that our agency could keep track of his movements. I had nothing to work on but the fact that he was getting mail at Flagstaff, Ariz.

From the postmaster in Flagstaff, I found out that this "bad" man had left for parts unknown and left instructions that his mail be forwarded to Gunnison, Colo.

I had also been instructed to locate a brother-in-law of the late outlaw, Bill Carver, alias Franks, and get some secrets from him.

A trip to Phoenix, thence to Douglas on the Mexican border, put me on trail of my man. I had found my old cowboy chum, Jim East, in Douglas, and he assisted me.

Up in the mountains near Rodeo I found Bill Carver's brother-in-law, and got all the information wanted. Then I made a little jump of over 1,000 miles to Gunnison, Colo. Here I located a sister of my "bad" man. She had a pretty 18-year-old daughter whom I had to fall in love with, in order to find out the whereabouts of her "bad" uncle. For about two weeks I did some swift courting and learned new lessons in human nature, and the power of wealth.

I had made a confidant of Mr. George Holmes and his lovely wife, who owned a large store in Gunnison. They introduced me into the upper crust of Gunnison society, so that I could take my girl to the club dances, and Mr. Holmes gave the young lady a tip that I was a wealthy timber man. That settled it; she did the courting after that. She actually proposed to me one night when we were out buggy riding. If I blushed she couldn't see it as the night was very dark. Of course, I tried to reason with this tender bud by telling her that I was too old to marry a young creature like herself, but she argued that age "cut no ice" where there is love and plenty of money to keep the pot boiling. I managed to put off the wedding until I could give the matter mature thought, and in the meantime I advised her to figure out about how much she would need for a swell wedding gown with the necessary trimmings. She thought $250.00 would cover the bill nicely.

After getting the information wanted, I cut my suspenders and went straight up, so far as the poor girl was concerned. But in reality my confidants, Mr. and Mrs. Holmes and Sheriff Watson, were bade goodby. Then the train carried me home.

On reaching Denver, I closed the Union Pacific train robbery case after having traveled more than 25,000 miles by rail, vehicles, afoot and on horseback, and after being on the operation constantly for about four years.

The "Wild Bunch" during these four years were pretty well scattered, many being put in their graves and others in prison. The only two really "bad" ones who escaped were "Butch" Casiday and Harry Longbough. But through my work on Jim F. we found out for the first time who Longbough was, and where his relatives live. Jim F. had first known him as the "Sundance Kid" up in northern Wyoming.

And "Butch" Casiday would no doubt have been caught had my hands not been tied by Asst. Supt. Curran, who insisted that he was not Jim Lowe, whose rendezvous I wanted to visit; but before his death Mr. Curran acknowledged his mistake. Also Mr. W. L. Dickenson confessed to me that there was no further doubt about "Butch" Casiday and Jim Lowe being one and the same person.

And if Sayles and I had been allowed to use our own judgment in hurrying to Dandy Crossing instead of going to Ft. Duchesne, matters might have taken a different turn, although it might have caused one or both of us being planted on a Utah desert.

During these four years of strenuous life along the West-Pacific Railroad lines, I secured much valuable information for the Dickenson agency. That is, information not connected with train holdups, the agency having a system wherein matters of importance are put on record, for immediate or future reference.

CHAPTER XVI.

A Big Railroad Stealing Case in Texas and Old Mexico—A Bullion Stealing Operation in Salt Lake, Utah.

On returning to Denver, I was hardly allowed time to get my breath, when Supt. J. S. Kaiser detailed me on a railroad case which had been awaiting my return.

I was told that Mr. W. L. Dickenson, of Chicago, had been holding this operation for me, as the work was for one of his personal friends and one of the agency's best clients. Therefore I was advised to do my best.

The work lay in Texas and Old Mexico, and the general manager of the big railway system was not to know of the operation as the object was to get at the bottom of big steals and crookedness.

I landed in a twin city on the Texas-Mexico border with my saddle and cowboy outfit, and pretended to be a horse buyer. In the course of a few weeks I had made myself solid with the brother of the railway manager. He was a high Mason and a swell sport. He stood at the top notch for honesty and business ability. He was a fine looking, large man of middle age.

During the progress of this operation I made two trips into San Antonio, Tex. On the first visit to the Alamo City, I was taught a new lesson in how clothes really do make the man.

I made the trip from Old Mexico to San Antonio in

rough cowboy clothes. It was late Saturday night when I arrived, so that I couldn't buy clean clothes. Next day being the Sabbath, I concluded to ride out to the Hot Sulphur wells and take a bath so as to pass off the time. An electric car dumped me off at a swell place a few miles out of the city. The bath house and hotel were connected. They were grand and must have cost a million dollars, and were grand new buildings.

After taking a Turkish bath and geting back into my old clothes I went into the office to pay my bill. The new manager of the new institution waited on me. He was a fine looking, dark-complexioned man with winning ways. He asked me as a favor to go up to the new hotel and try their Sunday dinner, and that if I didn't say it was the finest meal served west of New York, it wouldn't cost me a cent. I begged to be excused on account of my rough clothes, but he argued that clothes don't make the man, that my face covered all the defects in the clothing. He finally offered to borrow some clothes for me to wear in the dining room, but this I wouldn't hear to. So to please the gentleman I agreed to go. It was then after the noon hour.

Strolling through the quarter of a mile of covered walk, I arrived in the hotel rotunda. After registering I made a bee line for the large dining room, which was crowded with fashionable ladies and gentlemen. Throwing my big cowboy hat on the hatrack I entered the dining room door, but here I was stopped by a black, shiny individual, whose forefathers way back in the dark and woolly past, fought their battles with cocoanuts from the tree tops. His face was so black that charcoal would have made a white mark on it. He said: "Hold on dah, mister, who is it you wants to see?" I replied that I wanted a square meal. He then said: "Dats all right sah, I'll show you whar you can fill up."

He then led me to a small side room fronting on the hallway. My head began to swell up for I thought he was going to put me into a choice, private dining room away from the common herd, so that I could verify the manager's promise that they served the best meal west of New York.

I was shoved into the small room where sat a lady and small child eating their dinner.

After a long wait a small negro boy came to get my order. He called off a few common articles and I told him to bring me the best in the house. The stuff he brought was "on the bum," and no doubt it tasted worse because the manager had screwed up my mouth for a fine meal. The meat was so tough I couldn't eat it.

After another long wait the boy came back and I ordered cake and preserved figs. The boy looked at me with astonishment and said: "No siree, you can't get no figs in dis room. You can hab de cake but de figs don't go." I asked why, and he replied: "Caus we don't dish out figs to de serbents."

Then my wrath which had been accumulating ever since the tough meat was laid to one side, broke loose. Things were said which were uncomplimentary to such a swell establishment. I left the room at once, with the intention of bending the barrel of my old pet Colts 45 pistol around the African's head for putting me into the servants' dining room. But on reaching the hallway I concluded that such a scene on Sunday would be brutish, as it might cause some of the ladies and children in the dining room to faint. It would at least have spoiled their dinner. Then I decided to go down to the bath house and give the manager a piece of my mind.

In walking through the rotunda the clerk called my attention to the fact that my dinner hadn't been paid for. He soon found out though, that he had stirred up a hornet's nest, so he allowed me to pass out.

On reaching the bath house, I learned that the manager had boarded a car and gone to the city. I then did likewise, and in a cafe got a square meal.

About two weeks later, on finishing my work in Old Mexico and the western edge of Texas, I spent another Sunday in San Antonio. This time I wore good clothes and made another trip to the Hot Sulphur Wells. I found the manager absent, but nevertheless I tried his Sunday dinner, and found it fine. The big African usher didn't know that he had ever seen me before. He was all smiles when he turned me over to the head waiter, who, no doubt, thought I was good for at least a twenty-five cent tip, but he was mistaken, as I hadn't gotten over my disappointment of the previous visit. All "coons" still looked alike to me.

This experience convinced me, beyond a doubt, that clothes do make the man, especially among people who cannot judge human nature through the face.

Asst. Supt. "Hank" Geary, now superintendent of our Denver office, came to Old Mexico to assist me in closing the operation.

The wind-up was a success, as I had caught the brother

of the general manager stealing money from the railway company outright; also caught many of his friends among the passenger conductors.

I arrived back in Denver after an absence of about two months, but only to remain over night as an operation had been awaiting my return for nearly two months. Mr. Z. B. James, the Salt Lake City, Utah, banker and smelter man, was the client and he wouldn't have any one but me to do the work. Of course, I was anxious to get back to the swift little city by the great Salt Lake, and it was a pleasure to know that banker James had overlooked my sin of having "flim-flammed" him out of that silver dollar the night that operative Billy S. and I had the stolen ore in his residence.

A five hundred mile ride on the D. & R. G. Railway, over the backbone of the American continent, landed me in Salt Lake City. Mr. James was met in his private office in the Z. B. James' bank, and the work discussed. He explained that his large smelter at Murray, six miles east of the city, had been sold to the smelter trust, hence this work was to be done for them under his supervision. He explained that bars of bullion had been missed from the smelter and also from sealed cars after their arrival . at the eastern refinery, so he wanted me to get in with the tough element of Curran and Salt Lake City and find out who were doing the stealing.

In the smelter town of Murray I secured a cheap room, and with "bum" clothes on, I loafed in the toughest saloons in the town.

In the course of a couple of weeks I was in solid with the toughest thieves and cut-throats ever allowed to go

25

unhung. Some of them were married men, and when not on raids, they were at home with their families, bringing up a new set of criminals for the future. Some lived in Murray and others in Salt Lake City. Of course, I visited freely among them and became one of the gang, though I refused to assist in their petty thieving and robbing, as I claimed to be holding my energy in reserve for large deals.

My two months' operation showed up big steals wherein cars of bullion were broken into. Also where bullion was stolen direct from the smelter.

A Mormon, whose brothers were high up in the church and in with county officials, was the leader of these steals. And to save their good name the small caliber superintendent of the Rio Grande Western Railway, Welby, and his Mormon Special Agent, John Brown, did underhand trickery which would have been a disgrace to a Piute Indian.

My work, though, put a stop to future steals and banker James was satisfied. Several of the smelter employes, who stood in with the steals, lost their jobs. My friend "Cunny" helped me to close the operation.

"Doc" Lockredge and the Author.

CHAPTER XVII.

A Mining Case in Alma, Colorado—A Prospecting
Trip with a Half-Breed Mexican — Taking
Prisoner to Kansas City, Missouri—Working
on United States Senator Smoot.

After returning from Salt Lake, I was detailed on many different kinds of operations, some of them taking me out of the city and state for a few weeks at a time. On one of these trips to Gunnison, Colo., and other places, I looked up evidence against the noted English mine promoter, Whittaker Wright.

Another operation was for a very prominent financier, of Denver. On this work I spent about a month in the mining town of Alma, Colo., and of course, I had many visits with my old friend "Doc" Lockridge. I found him living alone high up in the mountains on the edge of timber-line.

Strange to relate, I saw in the Alma livery stable "Jacky's" bronco, which I broke to ride about fourteen years previous. He was now a swell driver.

This operation proved a success, but I hated to face one of the financier's mining partners who had in confidence given me the secrets of a crooked deal.

This partner was a nice fellow, and he and his lovely young wife had treated me royally at their nice home in Alma. I had passed myself off as a rich mining man from New Mexico.

While with this financier, in his private office in a certain firm of Denver, I had the pleasure of meeting Mr. ———, one of the high officials of this firm. This brought back memories of my first winter in Denver as a detective, over fifteen years previous.

He was then a young man trying to sprout a mustache. For one whole month they had me shadowing this young man, who held a minor position in the said business firm, so as to find out his habits, which were model, and of the Sunday School order. But I prayed that he would get "bad" and spend his evenings down town. Twice a week he would visit his sweetheart out on Capitol Hill, which was then a howling wilderness, with the exception of a few new residences scattered here and there, and no sidewalks.

I had to remain out in the bitter cold while he did his courting in the parlor. One bitter cold night I got warmed up by peeping under the window curtain at the bright fire and the red-hot love-making. They were pure and innocent, and kept a bright light burning in the lamp. About midnight he would depart for his room down town and he would whistle every step of the way, which made it easy for me to follow.

No doubt my favorable reports started Mr. ——— to the high position he now holds.

About the time that this operation was finished I was detailed on a case at Hastings, Colo. The Wonder Fuel Company there had one of their large barns full of horses burned up, and I was sent there to find out who did it. No one but the president of the company, Mr. Delma B. Capilla, and the local manager, Mr. Johnson, were to know me. But later I found out that Mr. Johnson became frightened for my safety and confided in the two town marshals, Hightower and King.

In the course of a few weeks I was positive that Joe Johnson, a half-breed man-killer, who lived with his Mexican family there, had committed the crime with the help of his brother-in-law and a half-breed Mexican by the name of Wilford H.

But the question was to get evidence sufficient to convict. Therefore, it was decided that I hire Wilford H. and go on a gold prospecting trip through the mountains of Colorado and New Mexico. The idea was to get him off by himself in hopes that he would confess.

After a few days spent in the little city of Trinidad, on the border of Colorado, Wilford H. and I boarded a north-bound D. & R. G. train for Walsenburg, where we bought our saddle animals and outfit.

In Walsenburg, Wilford had many Mexican friends. I had two friends in the town to whom I confided. They were the sheriff, Jeff Farr, brother of sheriff Ed. Farr, who was killed by Bob McGinnis of the "Black Jack" gang, and undersheriff Jack McQuerry.

Not having my rifle with me, Jeff Farr loaned me the Winchester rifle, owned by his brother Ed. before his death, for the trip.

` On Wilford's and my leaving Walsenburg, our first camp was pitched at the foot of the Spanish Peaks about two miles from the Staplin ranch, a tourist's resort. We camped here about a week or ten days and prospected the Spanish Peaks from one side to the other, even up to the extreme summit of the highest peak.

From the Spanish Peaks we drifted into New Mexico and camped in many wild spots where a human being would not be seen for days at a time.

At the once prosperous boom mining camp of LaBelle, New Mexico, we rested a couple of days. In this town there were buildings enough for several hundred inhabitants, but only one lone Dutchman lived in the place then. I had visited LaBelle once years before, when the "boom" was on, and the town was overcrowded with people from every corner of the earth; hence I couldn't help but notice the great change. On my former visit while on trail of a "bad" man from the Wet Mountain Valley in Colorado, I arrived in the town after midnight and at that late hour the saloons were filled with drunken life.

That operation was for Mr. Hiram Wilkins, a big hardware merchant of Colorado, and while on it I had many ups and downs and hard rides.

From LaBelle we went to Elizabethtown, thence crossed the big mountain range to Taos, the home and burial place of the noted Kit Carson. Here Wilford had some Mexican relatives, as he was born and partly raised in Taos. For the time being, he dropped his Colorado name of Wilford H. and took up his right name of Wilford W. Of course, I was cautioned not to give it away that he had been using another name.

After a few days' rest in Taos, we drifted south twenty-five miles into the high mountains where no one lived, and where we didn't see any one for a whole week. Here I did my best to get a full confession out of Wilford, but failed. He gave the full details of how the stable was set afire in revenge for the company running an opposition hack and stage line to ruin the business of Joe Johnson, and he gave me to understand that Joe Johnson, with the help of others, set fire to the stable and that he (Wilford) saw the first blaze and could have saved the horses from burning up had he desired to do so.

The fact is, he wanted me to know that he knew all about the crime, but he didn't want to say enough to incriminate himself and Joe Johnson. He proved to be a pretty foxy half-breed.

I had received orders from our Asst. Supt. P. P. Berriman, now superintendent, who had charge of the operation, to "shake" Wilford H. as soon as I felt satisfied that sufficient evidence to convict could not be secured, and come home.

As Wilford wanted to remain in Taos with his relatives, I shook him and then started down the Rio Grande river, two days' travel to Embudo, where my outfit was sold. It being only a few hours run on the D. & R. G. railway from Embudo to New Mexico's ancient capital, Santa Fe, I went there to visit my ranch and put in one day and night with my pets.

Then I returned to Denver and discontinued the operation after being on it about two or three months.

Soon after this, Joe Johnson shot and killed a prominent man by the name of Fox in Trinidad, Colo. Mr. Fox was writing a letter in the post office when Joe Johnson stepped up to him and blew out his brains with a shot from a large pistol, and for this Johnson was hung by the neck until dead. Thus society got rid of one "bad" man, even though I had made a failure of sending him to the penitentiary.

Soon after my return to Denver, I was detailed to work on the Gratton case in Colorado Springs, for the Gratton Estate.

Millionaire Gratton, the lucky carpenter who had discovered the rich Independence mine in Cripple Creek, had died and his son was trying to break his will, through the courts. I was sorry when the contending forces compromised their differences, as it knocked myself and several other Dickenson operatives out of leading a high-life in the lovely little city of Colorado Springs.

Soon after the Gratton case ended, I had a pleasant trip to Kansas City, Mo., with a man who had no suspicion that I was a sleuth. Had he suspected me he would have jumped off the train and possibly broken his neck. We wanted to get him into Kansas City to save extradition expenses. The moment he stepped off the train in Kansas City I pointed him out to Mr. Williston, the superintendent of our Kansas City office, who was at the depot to meet me. Then he had a local officer arrest the man without his ever knowing that I was in the game.

I boarded an early morning train for home.

My stay in Denver was short, as Asst. Supt. "Rank" Curran hustled me off to Utah in company with operative J. V. Marke, now an assistant superintendent of the Denver office, and operative B., our work being to dig up evidence against a distinguished citizen of Provo, Utah, to prevent him taking his seat in a public place, our clients being boss workers in the Lord's vineyard, who didn't like the taste of the sour grapes coming from the corner of the same vineyard where this gentleman worked.

We operatives were divided into different districts, mine being the beautiful little city of Provo, the home of the quarry. In Provo my headquarters were established though some of my work was done in Salt Lake City, where I knew one church leader, Mr. Cannon, whose acquaintance I had made while on my first operation for Banker James.

I had adopted the name of Charles T. Lloyd in Provo, and passed myself off as a well-to-do mining man from New Mexico

I had been instructed to run down a certain young lady of Provo, who was supposed to have married this citizen and was living in one of the church colonies of Old Mexico, as one of this man's plural wives. No one in Provo seemed to know what had become of this young lady after her supposed plural marriage to him, as she had promptly dropped out of sight as though the ground had swallowed her up.

I worked on the high and mighty, the low, leading people of Provo, and others, who had more wives than the law allows, and I secured "cinch" cases against some of them.

I found out that Miss Bessie Johnson had been a schoolgirl chum of the young lady who was supposed to be in Mexico as the wife of the hunted one. Therefore I started out to win the friendship and acquaintance of Miss Bessie. A Mr. Moran, who owned a barber shop in Provo was used as the cat's paw to pull my chestnuts out of the fire. He was a fine fellow and a friend to the Johnson family.

I had made up my mind to pretend to be in love with

Miss Bessie, no matter how homely she might be. But these pretentions turned into facts the moment that Mr. Moran introduced me to the young lady at her home. It was one of my many genuine cases of love at first sight, and even to this day little Cupid gives me a dig in the ribs with his dart, when I think of her, which is quite often, although she is now married to a Salt Lake City business man.

During the balance of my stay in Provo, not a day passed without my meeting Miss Bessie, who was just as sweet as she was pretty. She used to play the piano for me while her pretty young sister Marie sang, and they made a team hard to beat.

From Miss Bessie I found out all about the supposed young plural wife of Mr. ———. She was then in a college at Logan, Utah, finishing her education. She and Bessie, who was twenty-one years of age, corresponded with each other, and Bessie had the young lady's photo which was shown to me.

After nearly a two months' stay in Provo, during which time much of the honey of life was sipped by yours truly, my tent was folded and a start made for Denver, Colo.

As my reports showed, the intended victim came out with flying colors. He lived a happy contented life with a lovely wife whom I talked with, and a house full of nice, bright children, and if he had other than this lawful wife, I failed to discover it.

Mr. ——— owns a business in Provo, and I failed to find one individual who had a bad word to say against his moral character.

CHAPTER XVIII

THE WENTZ KIDNAPPING CASE — EIGHT MONTHS
AMONG THE MOONSHINERS OF KENTUCKY AND VIR-
GINIA.

My next operation was an educator, as I was thrown
among a strange class of people who think nothing of
taking human life.

It was about the middle of November, 1903, when
manager of the Western Division, Mr. Jas. McCartney,
called me into his private office to inform me that I had
been selected for an operation after every agency office
in the United States had been scoured for a suitable
operative to do the work. He then gave me an outline
of the operation which was to be conducted through the
Philadelphia office, our client being Millionaire Dr. Wentz
of Philadelphia, Pa., whose young son Edward Wentz
had lately been kidnapped in the mountains of Virginia
and was supposed to be held a prisoner in Kentucky for
a ransom, although it was feared that the young man
had been taken to Kentucky and murdered for revenge.

Mr. McCartney informed me that it was a very dangerous operation and asked if I were willing to undertake it. Of course I replied yes, as I was itching to have
some new experiences and to see new country. Then
Asst. Supt. "Hank" Geary gave me the large pile of correspondence which had taken place between the different
offices on the subject to read over.

Mr. McCartney's letter to the head officials of the New York office caused my head to expand several inches, for he gave me a great "send off," and the replies to this letter were equally flattering. I was thought to be the only man in the agency who could go among the "moonshiners" of the Kentucky mountains and stay there in spite of danger and threats.

On short notice I boarded a train on the U. P. Ry. for Chicago, Ill. Arriving in the smoky city by the lake, I called at our agency office to see the "boys," including Mr. W. L. Dickenson, Gen. Supt. F. V. Taylor and Supt. Schaumwort.

At night Charlie S. saw me off on the Cannon Ball train for Buffalo, New York, by way of Detroit, Mich., and through Canada to Niagara Falls.

From the train I had a fair view of Niagara Falls and other sights. In Buffalo, New York, I laid over one night. I enjoyed the ride from Buffalo to Philadelphia, as everything seemed different from "out west."

In Philadelphia I found the cleanest, most good-natured city that I had ever been in, but holy smoke, to use a cowboy phrase, she is slow. Even the girls and the "hurry-up wagon" are not so swift as in other cities. And I found that same graveyard slowness prevailing in our office, from the superintendent down to the office boy.

I turned myself over to the superintendent, Mr. A. M. Pierce, and he turned me over to Asst. Supt. E. E. Eslin, who had charge of the Dr. Wentz kidnapping operation.

When not busy working in the office to familiarize myself with the operation, I was taking in the sights of the city, the most interesting being the building where the Declaration of Independence was signed; also the art galleries were interesting to me.

Chief Clerk Dailey kindly acted as pilot in showing me the sights of the city.

After spending a week in the city of Brotherly Love, I was called to New York City by Mr. Roydel L. Dickenson, who wanted to consult with me about the Dr. Wentz operation. Of course, this just suited me as I wanted to see that city of sky-scrapers.

The day was spent with Mr. Dickenson, he taking me out to lunch with himself and Gen. Manager Mr. Geo. E. Langston.

In advising me about my future work in Kentucky and Virginia, Mr. Dickenson said I was taking my life into my own hands and that he didn't expect to see me come out of those mountains alive. He said I had no idea of what kind of people inhabited those mountains; that they are a different class from those of Texas and the west; that they think nothing of shooting a man in the back on the least provocation; that they are not the kind of men who will fight it out face to face with an opponent; that the records of the Dickenson agency since 1850 prove this. Therefore, in a serious manner Mr. Dickinson advised me to expect death at any moment. He said it was almost impossible to get an operative located in those mountains, from the fact that strangers do not go in there unless they have business, and in that case they are known by the merchants or have letters to some one there stating the nature of their mission.

He said the main object was to find Edward Wentz if still alive and held a prisoner, so as to get soldiers in there and clean out the country, or if dead, to recover the body. He thought it would be almost out of the question to convict any one in the courts of that country owing to the fact that the Virginia Coal & Iron Co. of which Dr. Wentz is president, had many enemies among the ignorant and lawless element, and because the people are all mixed up and related to each other, so that it is difficult to get an unbiased jury. He felt sure that I wouldn't be in there away from the railroad twenty-four hours before they would have me "spotted" as a detective in the revenue service, to run down "moonshiners," or on the hunt for young Wentz, and in that case I would have to use my own judgment as to whether to get out of the country or stand my ground. He insisted that I must not feel backward about leaving the moment that I realized my life to be in immediate danger. But I told him that my stubborn phrenology bump wouldn't allow me to leave after I once got in there.

I was instructed to leave the number of my watch, a description of my pocket-knife, key ring, pistol and the prominent marks on my body, including the fillings in my teeth, so that my body in case of death could be identified. I sent these to the Philadelphia office after arriving on the ground, as I had received a reminder to do so from Asst. Supt. Eslin, through the mail.

Before parting with Mr. Dickenson he tried to get me to promise that I would, after finishing this operation, accept the position of assistant superintendent in one of the western offices. It caused a smile when I told him that I didn't consider there was much honor in being an assistant superintendent. He replied that it was necessary to start as an assistant so as to learn the office work, before becoming a superintendent. He cited the case of my friend W. O. Sayles becoming superintendent soon after being made an assistant, and he said it was through his request that I had been offered the promotion, ahead of Sayles. I finally told him that the position of operative suited me.

During the day I met Mr. Jay Cornbush, manager of the Eastern Division, and Supt. C. D. Hornybill, also young Alman Dickenson and the many assistant superintendents.

It was agreed by Mr. Dickenson that I take an early morning train back to Philadelphia, and that when my operation was finished I could come back and see the sights of New York City. So bidding Mr. Dickenson goodby, he turned me over to operative G. J. H. who had instructions to take me to dinner or to one of the theaters or anywhere else that I might want to go, at the agency's expense.

A pleasant evening was spent, and after midnight a ferryboat landed me in "Jersey" where a train was boarded for the slow City of Brotherly Love.

Soon after my return to Philadelphia I started for Winchester, Kentucky, with about $400.00 in my pocket and a small trunk containing my cowboy boots, hat, etc. It had been decided best that I go into Letcher County, Kentucky, which borders on Wise County, Virginia, where Edward Wentz was kidnapped, by way of Jackson, in Brethitt county, Kentucky, as if I left the railroad in Wise county, Virginia, where the trouble occurred I would be suspected at once.

In the little city of Winchester I put up with Mr. Hays, who ran a hotel. Here I rigged out in my old cowboy clothes and boarded a branch train for Jackson, the trunk with my good clothes being left with Mr. Hays until further orders. Of course Hays didn't know where I was headed for.

I found Jackson to be a drunken tough town. The militia were just pulling out after having been there for a long time, on account of the trouble over the assassination of lawyer Marcum, which had ended in many killings.

The next day after my arrival in Jackson, I saw something which convinced me that the human race is slightly mixed with the pig family of animals. An old man on a mule started out of town with two jugs of whisky tied across the back part of his saddle. He hadn't gone but half a block when the string broke and the jugs fell to the ground and broke. The street was quite muddy and the whiskey lay in pools on the ground. The old man got down on his knees and hands and began to drink from the fiery pools. Soon others came and followed suit. They put me in mind of a drove of human swine.

In Jackson I bought a mule and an old light spring wagon. Then it was two days before I could get the mule shod, as all blacksmiths in town were drunk. The mule stood at one shop all day while a pair of shoes were being fitted. In the meantime I was taking in the dives with a young man from Rock House Creek, up in the country where I was going. On returning to the shop to get Mr. Donkey I found that the smith had made a mistake and put the mule shoes onto a sleepy old grey horse tied to a tree outside the shop. The feet had been rasped down to fit the shoes. That night my mule got out of his stable and "hit" the road for "tall timber." Next morning I followed his tracks into the mountains and found him shut up in a log stable down in a field. The woman and boy didn't want to give him up until their lord and master came back from town, but he was taken back to town just the same, as I felt sure they were thieves.

Finally I got started for Whitesburg, the county seat of Letcher county, about 150 miles east.

The first day out I was compelled to wait an hour at a narrow bridge where several wagons had the road blocked, while the drivers were in a saloon near by drinking. I was told that this was a game the saloon man played every day to make business for his place, and that it often caused serious fights.

My route was up Lost Creek through mud up to the mule's knees in places.

The road was in the bed of the creek most of the way, as the small patches of level land upon the banks were needed by the poverty-stricken people for farming purposes. Even the sides of steep mountains were used for crops. This applies to the whole mountain regions of Kentucky, as I found out later. I soon discovered my mistake in having started with a vehicle, but I supposed the country was unsettled in places so that I would have to camp out. On that account camp outfit

26

and bedding had been brought along. The whole country is thickly settled, especially along the main roads and creeks. Some days the best I could do was twelve or fifteen miles, owing to the deep mud and large rocks in the bed of the creeks.

Before reaching Hazzard, the county seat of Perry county, I found a man by the name of Pat N., who was a brother to Ashford N., a "bad" man in Wise County, Virginia, who was suspected of having a hand in the kidnapping of Ed. Wentz, as he had been seen near the scene and as it was known that he was a bitter enemy of the Wentz brothers, Ed. and Dan, who had charge of the coal properties in that country. I put up with Pat N. until I had secured a letter of introduction to Ashford N. in Virginia.

Pat informed me that his brother "Ash" had spent three years in Texas, therefore I expressed a desire to meet him.

Pat N. kept a small saloon and store with about $50.00 worth of goods on hand. He had about eight children and I had to sleep with three of the boys. The whole family slept in one little room the size of a Utah chicken house. So with about eleven of us in one room, the purity of the air can be imagined. This is another kind of a bitter pill that a detective has to swallow.

On reaching Hazzard, which is on the Kentucky river, I found court in session, and the little burg was full of drunken men, though no saloons were allowed to run as it is a local option county.

I was advised in Hazzard by many not to undertake the trip alone over the mountains to Whitesburg, as the road was almost impassable for a vehicle, and the country inhabited by an ignorant and vicious people who had been known to murder travelers for their money and valuables.

After leaving Hazzard the road led up the Kentucky river for several miles east, then turned to the north up a rocky, muddy creek, and now my misery began. The higher up the creek we got the worse the road became, and the wilder and woollier the people appeared.

The water in the creek was frozen over, so that in following its bed the mule and rig would break through, causing the air to become impregnated with swear-words. Ten miles of this and "Donk" and I were ready for supper at one of the "shacks" called houses, along the road.

My patience had been tested between Jackson and Hazzard by the fool questions asked me by every man, woman and child met, but it was at the bursting point before reaching Whitesburg, for here even small boys carrying pistols or squirrel rifles would stop me in the road to ask fool questions. They all started out in the same strain: "Say mister, wha'r mought you be goin?" and "Say mister, what mought your name be?" A fool girl about eighteen years old who was wading in mud up to her ankles, got in the seat beside me before she asked any questions. I had invited her to ride to the little store two miles ahead, where she was going. After getting on the seat she turned her good-looking face towards me and said: "Do you live in these parts, mister?" I replied no, that I lived in Texas.

The blood could be seen rushing into her face after it got past the dirt around her neck. Most girls in these mountains keep the dirt washed from their faces, which leaves a dark ring around the neck. Some hide this ring by wearing a high collar, but it's a safe two-to-one bet that it's there just the same.

Here the frightened girl begged me to stop the mule and let her out, which I did, though I told her that she need have no fear just because I was from Texas.

The girl beat me to the store by a quarter of a mile. Then the dozen or more men, women and children at the store turned out on the road to see the wild man from Texas, and they wore me out asking fool questions.

This is the part of Kentucky where preachers dare not come on account of the men and boys getting drunk and shooting off their guns, and mouths, too.

In going over the mountain I had to hire two white men and a half-breed negro to help me, as the road was blocked with ice so that we had to climb the side of a steep hill. Two men had to hold the vehicle up to keep it from tumbling over the mountain cliff, while the other man and myself kept "Donk" on his feet, and here "Donk" proved himself sure-footed and a stayer.

Here a small settlement of half-breed negroes lived. A full-blood negro is a curiosity to the natives of these mountains of Kentucky, though they are plentiful in the coal mines over the line in Virginia.

On driving down to the Rock House Creek, which is noted for "moonshine" whisky and tough men, about night, I found everything in an uproar. Most of the people were drunk and on the warpath. A celebration had been held in the schoolhouse. The blood hadn't begun to flow until nearly night, though the "moonshine" liquor had been flowing all day. The row started over a man cutting a mule's tail off almost up to his ears. Several men were badly hurt, so it was said. The fight continued far into the night at the house where I had intended to stop, owing to it being a tough place. As a rule I selected the toughest places to put up at, but this night I was advised by two men not to stop at this house or I would be killed before morning, on account of being a stranger, and this house being the head-quarters for the drunken gang. So I stopped on the adjoining farm.

Next day a severe snowstorm was raging, and about 3 :00 P. M. a man who was on his way from Rock House to Whitesburg where he lived, gave me a couple of drinks out of his jug of "moonshine" whisky, which he had bought at a still. He gave me his name as Sol Holcomb, and invited me to come and put up with him in Whitesburg, as his wife sometimes kept private boarders. He described the house so that it could be found easily.

After dark I drove up to the log mansion owned by Sol Holcomb. Then I had another drink out of the same jug, but now the bottom had to be tipped high up in the air in order to squeeze a drink out of it.

At the supper table I told Mrs. Sol Holcomb, who tipped the scales at 250 pounds, and her pretty twenty year old daughter Lizzie, who weighed only an even hundred pounds—that Sol had saved my life by stopping me on the road in a blinding snowstorm to let me sample his liquor.

I didn't tarry long in Whitesburg, but continued on up the Kentucky river, eighteen miles to Craftsville, where I had had some "fake" letters sent from Galveston, Texas, by my cousin, Miss Jeanette McKay.

In Philadelphia we had selected Craftsville post office as a good point for me to head for, as it was in the heart of the tough district where the Potter-Wright feud has been going on for years, until nearly all the male members of both parties had been killed.

On reaching Craftsville I was somewhat surprised, for I expected to find a little town or one store at least. There was nothing here but old widow Bee Craft's house and farm, and the young wife of old lady Bee Craft's son Tom was the "whole cheese" in handling Uncle Samuel's mail. Once a week she would have to strain her nerves in going over about one dozen letters and a few dozen papers, mostly Fireside Companions from Portland, Maine. The mail sack would be dumped out on the floor and sorted over there. All mail addressed to Craftsville would be put in the garret until some one called for it.

The next day was Christmas eve, and "Nels" Craft, a son of the widow Bee Craft, came from his place half a mile below on the river, to find out who wanted to send for Xmas "moonshine," as he was going to a still that day. Tom Craft and I both sent for a supply. That night we all, including the old lady and her adopted daughter Miss Lou, rode down to "Nels'" place to eat supper and drink "moonshine." "Nels" and his brother-in-law, Tilden Wright, had returned from the still with the liquor.

On the way home after midnight Tom Craft made the air ring with his shouts and yelling. He was loaded

Emma S., "Donk" and the Author.

with "moonshine" inside and out. Miss Lou rode behind me on "Donk" and helped to hold me on, as I was a little bit loaded myself, though my early training in Texas prevented me from yelling in the presence of ladies. The cowboy "Comanche yells" were almost choking me though, in their eagerness to escape, but by force of will-power they were held back.

Next morning was Christmas, and young Wiley Craft rode down from his father's place half a mile above, to tell me that he had caught the fat 'possum for which I had offered a reward of fifty cents the day before.

On the previous day I had gone up to John Craft's with Tom to see the pretty girl from Donkey, Virginia, who had just arrived with her father "Doc." They were taking tin-type photos and canvassing for a life insurance company in Detroit, Michigan. This seventeen year old girl, Emma, was certainly a "peach," when it came to the bloom of youth and beauty painted on her cheeks.

In Philadelphia, Donkey, Va., had been given to me as the toughest little spot on earth, and a likely place to get some information about young Wentz. Therefore I concluded to fall in love with Emma, even though I was old enough to be her father, so as to have an excuse for visiting Donkey, Va.

The 'possum was part of the scheme. I returned with Wiley Craft to see Mr. 'possum and have Emma take his picture before I got on the outside of him, for Mrs. John Craft had agreed if one was caught, to cook him with sweet potatoes for my Christmas supper.

I found the opossum to be young and fat. His picture was "took" and he then went into the pot.

Miss Lou had gone up to John Craft's early in the day with her sweetheart, Bennie, who had a bad case of lovesickness, to join the crowd of young folks who had congregated there.

After helping Mrs. Craft put the 'possum into the pot I went into the large front room to drink "moonshine" with "Doc," John Craft and others, and to watch the young folks play a new kind of a kissing game.

A large number of couples would form a circle by holding each other's hands. This circle of young men and women would revolve round and round until one of their number snapped his or her fingers at some one in the audience. Then the one snapped at would jump up and catch the snapper and by force kiss him or her. I noticed that the kissing was always on the cheek, and when Miss Lou snapped at me, while I was talking to "Doc" about "Donkey" town, I warned her not to do it again, if she did it would wind up in a western kiss which is generally planted where it will do the most good. I also told her that I was a little too old to get into their game, although this was a lie, as at that very moment I was dying to get into the game just long enough to kiss Emma once, and thereby lengthen my life about five years.

In passing, Lou snapped at me again, and the tussle began. I went at it in a systematic manner and when her head rested on my left arm and her face was turned up towards the ceiling, the kiss was planted on her lips where it did the most good, to one poor sinner at least. Then I had to get inside the ring and choose a girl from the circle. Of course Emma was the victim and it was

soon over, as sweet things seldom last long, at least
not long enough.

As Mrs. Bee Craft and Tom's wife were getting up
a fine turkey dinner, I had promised to be back there at
noon. I felt sure of finding a drunken crowd there on
my return, as they had begun to arrive before I left.

On getting "Donk" to start, Lou insisted on riding
behind me in spite of the protests from her lover Bennie.
I tried to persuade her to let Bennie take her home, as
he had brought her, but she wouldn't have it that way,
so there was nothing for me to do but be "blooded" and
take the chances of an assassin's bullet later.

On reaching home the mule was put into the stable
and fed, after Lou had been helped off at the front gate.

Loud swearing could be heard in the house, which
showed that the "moonshine" was getting in its work.

On stepping onto the porch, Tilden Wright, one of
the noted feudists whose father and older brothers had
lately been killed by the Potter gang, came out of the
dining room and met me face to face. With his right
hand resting on the handle of the large pistol strapped
to his waist, he said in an angry and insulting voice:
"Say, Lloyd, how would you like to have your ——brains
scattered all over this floor?"

I knew there was war in the air from the way Mrs.
Tom Craft, who had followed Wright out of the dining
room, looked. She was pale and trembling. Therefore
my hand went up to my breast to the shirt front which
was open, before answering. Then looking Wright in
the eyes with a good natured smile I said: "Why, Tilden,
it wouldn't feel very nice to have my brains scattered on

the floor, and besides it would cause a lot of extra work to clean them up."

Then I asked the cause of his anger and found it to be the Virginia girl, Emma, whom he said I was acting a fool over, when there were prettier girls in Kentucky than she; that his sister-in-law, Miss Victoria Craft, was a prettier girl than Emma. I asked him why he didn't trot out Miss Victoria so I could get a look at her and decide the matter for myself. He replied: "Why damn it, you saw her last night at Nels' party," I told him he was mistaken as Victoria's mother was sick so that she couldn't attend the party at "Nels'." He studied a moment and replied: "That's so, her mother was sick last night. I'll bring her up tomorrow and you'll say she's a prettier girl than Emma."

Then Wright took his hand from the pistol and started staggering into the large front room where the gang were.

Had Wright pulled his pistol he would have been surprised when old Colts 45 came out from under my left arm where it was concealed in a "Wess Harding" shoulder scabbard. The day being warm, I was in my shirt-sleeves, hence he could see no pistol and thought me unarmed. My shirt was kept unbuttoned from the collar down, in order that my hand could reach the pistol quickly. At nights I slept with it under my arm.

On going into the dining room I found a crowd of strangers eating at the table. Most of them were drunk and noisy, and eyed me with suspicion as the old lady seated me at a vacant place.

"Mose" Craft who owned a "moonshine" still, and who

had run "moonshine" stills all his life, was at the table eating, while two men kept him in his seat as he wanted to go into the other room to renew the fight with "Nels" Craft, his cousin. "Nels" was being held by other men in the front room. Broken dishes and blood were scattered over the dining room floor. The fight had been a fierce one; and others besides the cousins had taken a hand. Pistols and knives had not been used owing to the efforts of the women folks and old man Joe Craft, who was quite sober and acted as peace-maker.

On finishing my dinner I concluded not to go into the front room where the drunken mob were, but to "hike" back to Emma and the 'possum and sweet 'taters.

I was just leading "Donk" out of the stable, which was a hundred yards from the residence at the foot of a mountain, when I heard Tilden Wright calling: "Lloyd, you —— where are you?" Then looking towards the house I saw Tilden Wright and "Mose" Craft searching for me. They staggered around back of the house and when out of sight I led the mule back of the stable and let down a rail fence. When inside the pasture the fence was put back in place. Then "Donk" was mounted and a run made up a small gulch, thence a short climb up the mountain side to a thicket of timber and brush. Here I dismounted and lay down to watch developments. I was high up above the house and could see Wright and Craft searching for me. When they searched the stable and found my mule gone, they began calling me all kinds of names. Then they began shooting down the timbered lane through which I was supposed to have gone. They then went to the house and I had a good laugh all by my lone self, at the way they had been fooled. Had they found me the chances are it would have ended in bloodshed, for later "Mose" Craft, who is a fine fellow when sober, apologized to me and said they had got it into their heads that I was a spy from the revenue office in search of "moonshiners," hence he and Tilden trying to find me to raise a "racket."

A climb over the mountain and the letting down of two more rail fences and the fording of the Kentucky river, brought me to John Craft's where I joined the lively crowd and had my nerves quieted with a few more young kisses. This time one of John Craft's daughters started the ball to rolling by "snapping" her fingers at me. She wanted no doubt, to try the experiment of a western scientific kiss.

During the middle of the afternoon, Joe Craft and four other men brought "Mose" Craft and his fighting "jag" up to our place so as to get him away from "Nels." They had been fighting again.

Here I received some new lessons in human nature, which differed from anything which I had ever seen before.

The house was full of young ladies, and some who were not so young. "Mose" Craft stepped into the door and opened up with the most vulgar language that the human tongue is capable of uttering, and he topped it off with a vulgar song. In my native state, he would have been filled so full of lead by angry fathers, brothers, and sweethearts, that it would have required an extra team to have hauled his body to the graveyard. The girls and women all ran to the kitchen as soon as pos-

VICTORIA CRAFT.

sible. Mrs. John Craft soon had "Mose" in bed and asleep.

Gee, but I did enjoy that 'possum and the sweet potatoes.

I returned to Mrs. Bee Craft's late at night and found the old lady and Miss Lou sitting by the kitchen fireplace. The balance were in bed or had left for their homes.

Mrs. Bee Craft had drunk her share of the "moonshine," hence she was in a talkative mood. She told me all about her oldest son, who is now married and living a peaceful life in another part of the state, having lived an outlaw life for years in these mountains, on account of killing revenue officers who were trying to stamp out "moonshining;" and of how her husband was burned to death while drunk in the house of two "bad" women.

In speaking of her enemies, the old lady used language which caused me to blush on acount of Miss Lou, who was present. But Lou didn't seem to mind it, so from that time on while in these mountains, I did not waste any more blushes.

Old Lady Bee Craft turned out to be, in my estimation the most honest and motherly woman in this mountain region. I had a chance to learn her true nature.

The next day Miss Victoria, Tilden Wright's sister-in-law, came to the widow Bee Craft's, and I took her and Lou up to John Craft's and had their pictures "took."

Miss Victoria was a nice, good-looking girl, but as a beauty she couldn't travel in the same class with Miss Emma.

A couple of days later I bade the Crafts goodby for

the time being, and started for Whitesburg in my spring wagon. Tom Craft advised me not to start as the river was frozen over at two of the bad crossings, and if the mule and rig broke through the ice I couldn't get them back onto the ice, as the water was belly-deep to a horse. In the eighteen miles to Whitesburg the river had to be crossed about a dozen times. I thanked Tom for his advice, but told him that out west we never crossed a bridge till we got to it, and then if the bridge was gone, we crossed anyway.

At one of the crossings my mule and wagon broke through in deep water, and I scared "Donk" by yelling and whipping so that he split the ice wide open. He would make a jump up on the ice, and then when it broke through, he would try, try again. Finally he was on the run, splashing water all over me until I was as wet as a drowned rat. Once he slipped on the ice and went down into the water on his side, but he came up running.

Soon after this, we passed Monroe W.'s house by the side of the road, and being wet, I concluded to make an effort to stay all night. I wanted to make Monroe's acquaintance anyway, as he was one of Wentz's bitterest enemies and suspected of having a hand in kidnapping young Wentz. He had been in the "moonshine" liquor business all his life and was considered a king-bee among the "moonshiners."

The hired man informed me that Monroe W. was down in a pasture after some cattle, and wouldn't be back for an hour. He also informed me that Monroe W. was not in the habit of taking strangers in to put up all night. This I took as a hint that I had better be going on as it was late in the evening.

Just about dark, after I had started up a steep grade to go over a high ridge into Whitesburg which lay two miles further down the river, a 250 pound piece of middle-age humanity rode up behind me on a large bay horse and commanded me to stop. I did so, then he rode up by the side of the wagon and in an angry voice asked: "What in the h—l are you doing in this country?" I told him that we were going to Whitesburg, providing the Lord was willing and the mule held out. He replied:

"We don't want your kind of people in this country, so you had better hit the road and go back where you came from, and you want to go d—d quick, too. You will be lucky if you get back."

I asked why they didn't want me here. He replied:

"You are a d—d detective that's why." I asked what a detective would be doing in such a country as this. He replied: "That's all right, we've had your kind of people here before, spying around to catch moonshiners. You had better turn that mule around and hit the road back if you know what's good for you."

Here I looked back down the road and saw two men on horseback coming in a slow walk. They were a quarter of a mile away, at a turn in the road. I concluded that they were into this scheme to run me out of the country, so I started to get mad and my stubborn bump began to work.

The mule was started ahead, and I told the big mountaineer that I was going to Whitesburg in spite of h—l and highwater. He replied: "Well by God if you do, you and your d—d outfit will go into the river."

Here I became mad "proper," and said: "You cut-throats may shoot me from behind a tree up on the mountain side, which I am told is your favorite way to assassinate people, but you can't scare me. I'm going to Whitesburg, so turn your wolf loose.

He put spurs to his horse and started up the steep grade on a trot ahead of me saying: "Well by God if you do, I'll have you thrown in jail till we can investigate you."

I hallooed back: "All right, you'll find me at Sol Holcomb's" At this he jerked his horse up and said: "What in the h—l do you know about Sol Holcomb? You have never been in Whitesburg!" I replied: "The d—l I havn't; I just left Whitesburg two days before Christmas."

He then started off again, saying: "All right, I'll just have you thrown in jail anyhow."

As it soon became dark, I lost sight of Monroe W. and the two men following behind.

It was plain to my mind now, that this big man who proved to be Monroe W. had never heard of me being in the country, and when his hired man described me and told him I wanted to stay all night at his place he concluded that I had just come from Virginia, from whence they had been looking for detectives. And a month later, after I had become "solid" with his mother-in-law, Lottie H., I found out that my guess was right, for she said that Monroe W. thought I was a detective sent from Virginia to work on the Wentz case, but that when he found out I had already been to Whitesburg and had driven overland from Jackson, Ky., he tried to pass it off as a joke as though he just wanted to frighten me.

It was over an hour after dark when I drove into Whitesburg, and when I went into the little "shack" of a post office, Monroe W. and a man whom I later found was one of his chums, were there ahead of me.

I asked for my mail and a letter was handed out. It was just the one I wanted, and I knew no others would come at that time. Just as I received the letter Monroe W. stepped up and asked to see the post-mark on it. I replied, certainly, if it would do him any good; so the letter was handed to him. He then took it to an oil lamp in one corner where he and his chum examined the post-mark which was Galveston, Texas. This was one of the "fake" letters which my cousin Jeanette McKay had copied from one I sent her. Later, after I had taken Monroe W. into my confidence, I let him read the contents of this "fake" letter.

Had I not mentioned the name of Sol Holcomb, showing that I had been in Whitesburg before, there is no telling what might have happened, for if the two riders seen following behind were into the play they could have taken a cut-off bridlepath after getting over the high ridge, and have joined Monroe W. without my seeing them. Then if so disposed, they could have way-laid me and thrown my body and the outfit into the river, far below to the left.

Thus did Christmas of 1903 pass into oblivion, along with the one spent on the L X ranch with Hollicott and his demijohn.

27

CHAPTER XIX

A Hurrah Life Among the "Moonshiners"—I Escape Possible Death by a Scratch—The Body of Ed. Wentz Found.

After becoming settled in Whitesburg at the Holcomb log mansion on the main street, I began to study the people. I found that those living in town were an improvement over those of the country.

My spring wagon was discarded never to be used again by me. It was put under a shed for Mrs. Holcomb's chickens to roost on. I concluded to stick to the hurricane deck of a mule or horse in future.

On making inquiry I found that Ashford N., whose brother lived on Lost Creek, was in the Whitesburg jail serving out a six months' sentence, by order of the much hated Republican District Judge Morse, who tries to enforce the laws. "Ash" had been convicted of selling liquor in this prohibition county of Letcher, Kentucky. At the jail through the steel bars, my letter of introduction from his brother Pat was presented, and we became fast friends. He let me read his love letters and I furnished the "moonshine" to revive his drooping spirits.

Ashford N. had lived three years in Greer County, Texas, now part of Oklahoma; and I happened to be acquainted in that country which cemented our friendship.

The jail was filled with men, the worst looking and

418

most confident one being Shepard, who murdered a
man in cold blood, at the same time wounding a woman
and baby, on Big Cowen Creek, a few miles south of
Craftsville, on Christmas day, just past. He had shot
the man, Riley Webb, while he was warming his hands
at a fireplace. Still he was confident of coming clear at
his trial, as he had given Attorney Dan D. Field a horse
to defend him.

After becoming acquainted with the situation as exist-
ing in Letcher County, I could see good grounds for
Shepard's confidence in acquittal, for Mr. Field is a
bright lawyer and is related by blood or marriage with
nearly every one in the county. Besides, whisky is
cheap. I myself with a pint flask of "moonshine" as a
weapon, faced a dignified Democratic judge and had a
shooting scrape virtually annulled. I showed good judgment though, by presenting the flask of liquor before
stating my case, and I assured this acting district judge
that my intention was not to bribe him with this flask of
corn juice, which was an open lie that could be seen by
a less learned man than this Honorable Court.

I did the job to save Birdie H's sweetheart a trip to
the penitentiary.

I made frequent trips to Collins' still in Knott County,
on the head of Rock House creek, after liquor for myself and friends.

I knew the date when "Doc" and his daughter Emma
were to be at Collins' still to take pictures, so my plans
were arranged accordingly.

On that date "Donk" and I marched up to the Collins
residence with two empty jugs to be filled, one for my-

self and the other for Ashford N. who had sent the cash to pay for his gallon of firewater. Miss Emma greeted us at the gate, and my spirits soared upwards. We had come twelve miles over a rough mountain. I made pretense of having to hurry back, but Emma and her father insisted on my remaining all night. So "Donk" was put into the stable and the good time commenced.

We first emptied "Doc's" bottle of corn juice; then I bought a full one for "Doc" and me, and another of apple brandy for Emma.

The woods were full of rough looking people who came to get liquor and to have their pictures "took."

After supper "Doc," Emma and I had the front room all to ourselves. We had started in for the night with two full bottles. Toward bedtime I began to feel the effects of the corn juice, and on the spur of the moment did a foolish trick, which ended all right, though.

"Doc" suggested that I take out a policy in his insurance company for $1000. I told him that I had left Texas suddenly, under a cloud, therefore didn't dare to have my life insured in favor of any of my relatives there; my idea being to give the impression that I had committed a crime in Texas and had to skip out. Then "Doc" asked if I didn't have a relative or friend outside of that state who would appreciate $1000 in case of my death. I answered "No." Here Emma with one of her sweet innocent smiles, asked me to have the policy made out in her name.

I was never known to be a "piker," or to show that I was not a "dead game sport" when it comes to dealing with pretty girls, so consent was given and the policy was made out with Emma as the holder of the stakes in case I shuffled off this mortal coil.

The danger soon flashed across my addled brain that when I visited the tough town of Donkey, Virginia, I might be considered worth more to Emma dead than alive. Still, I was too "blooded" to "crawfish" now, at the commencement of the game.

There was one redeeming feature in the transaction, it was an accident policy, so that if they tried to kill me and failed, I would get paid for the wounds, myself. The premiums were paid up for two months.

About midnight "Doc" and I retired in the broad-gauge bedstead, while Emma occupied the narrow gauge one near our feet. "Doc" slept next to the wall, so I acted as barkeeper, the full quart bottle being on a chair near my head.

I had just fallen asleep, when "Doc" dug me in the ribs saying "Lloyd are you asleep? If you ain't, hand over that bottle." Then we both took a drink. Soon sleep began to creep over me, but for fear of being awakened again, I thought it best to give "Doc" another drink in hopes of filling him up. But I didn't know then that trying to fill "Doc" up would be like pouring sand in a rat hole with the other end in China. The bottle was emptied just as day was breaking, then we both got our first good sleep.

When breakfast was called I got up feeling good—no sign of headache which follows the free use of liquor, not pure.

It was agreed that I join "Doc" and his daughter at John Craft's and accompany them home to Virginia.

Before leaving with my full jugs for Whitesburg, I gave Emma a quart bottle of apple brandy to keep up her spirits on the way home.

Arriving in Whitesburg I made preparation to start next morning for Craftsville.

The Holcombs and other friends begged me not to risk a visit to the head of the Kentucky river in the Potter neighborhood and to the tough town of Donkey, Virginia. They cited countless cases of murders and robberies committed in those places. Miss Lizzie Holcomb especially pleaded with me not to go. She and I had become a little "sweet" on each other, though we did our courting on the sly, as I told her that she was too nice to be seen at public gatherings and out riding with me, as I hadn't finished sowing my wild oats, and that I might be seen at any time drunk and in company with bad women, which would be a reflection on her character if she kept company with me.

The poor innocent girl couldn't understand why a man of my age and apparent intelligence should want to scatter wild oats over the country. Miss Lizzie was a pure Christian girl, and she had never had her eye teeth cut in the ways of the world. She tried hard to reform me, but the more she preached reform, the worse I seemed to get. Of course it pained me to act against my conscience in this way, but it was "business." I had started out to graduate in the big Dickenson College, therefore I didn't propose to be branded as a "quitter," just for the sake of upholding goodness and purity.

That night the county jailer, Boney Isum, a nice fellow, who had won his spurs and been elected county jailer through the fact of having recently killed a U. S. revenue officer near Whitesburg, brought Ashford N. from the jail to my room at Holcomb's, and with the assistance of the two jugs of liquor we made "Rome howl" until the roosters crowed for day. Boney Isum loved liquor, and he was a good judge of its purity, as he and his forefathers before him had conducted "moonshine" stills in the face of Uncle Sam and his standing army.

During the early part of the evening, Sol Holcomb spent his time in my room with Boney, Ashford and me, and in order to be in the "swim," Mrs. Holcomb, Lizzie, the little girl Alberta, and the fifteen-year-old boy Andrew, drank what they called "stugh," made of whisky, sugar and hot water.

Next morning with two quarts of liquor in my saddle pockets, I started for Craftsville, where the night was spent with the widow Bee Craft and her family.

Early next day I joined "Doc" S. and his pretty daughter at John Craft's, and we started up the river for Donkey, Va.

The girl rode behind her father on the large white horse. I carried the photo outfit on "Donk."

We passed through the noted Potter settlement and put up for the night at Bentleys.

During the forenoon next day, some pictures were "took" as per advertised schedule; that is, advertised by word of mouth, as there were no newspapers in the county.

After dinner we left the extreme head of the Kentucky river and began to climb up the western slope of the

Black Mountain range, the top of which is the dividing line between Kentucky and Virginia. On reaching the highest point of the range, "Doc" pointed out the lay of the country. From this black mountain of the great Cumberland range, flow four large rivers, the Kentucky to the west, the Cumberland to the southwest, the Sandy to the north and the Pound river to the eastward. The heads of all these rivers were now in sight and at our feet. It was certainly a grand view of a heavily timbered country settled only on the streams, except in certain spots.

Then we rode into the noted Pound Gap, where two houses, one a residence and the other a saloon, stand. They are on the line of Kentucky and Virginia, and are owned by the notorious "man-killer" Britt Potter, whom I found later to be a nice fellow, though a little bloodthirsty at the mention of the Wright family, who had reduced the male members of the Potter fireside with hot lead.

The saloon had been closed by law since both Letcher County, Kentucky, and Wise County, Virginia, had adopted local option. Then Britt had moved down the river a few miles to where his father Abraham Potter lived. Here Britt is training his little boys to shoot. One of them became impatient one day because there were no Wright boys in sight, so killed his own brother, by shooting him in the head while he slept.

Just after passing through Pound Gap we came to the spot where a few years previous, the whole Mullens family, all but one boy, who was fleet of foot, were ambushed and killed for their money, the old man having just sold his land and was leaving Kentucky.

"Doc" and I climbed the large rock behind which the five assassins were concealed.

As soon as the boy, whose suspenders were cut in two with a bullet where they crossed in the back, spread the news, "Doc" S. was one of the first to join the officers and go on trail of the assassins. They came together in a house, and when the smoke of battle cleared away "Doc" was branded for life with a bullet through his face from one side to the other. In the flight one of the officers crossed the dark river of death, and so did some of the outlaws. The balance were captured and sent to the pen.

A few miles down the mountain side through the tall timber, we came to the first house, owned by "Doc" S's brother-in-law, Brennan. Here we "liquored up" and warmed by the fire.

About three miles further, we came to the only Donkey town on earth. It contained only one store and about one dozen houses. "Doc" owned the two story frame house across the street or road from the store, and a farm south of the swift flowing Pound river.

Mrs. "Doc" S. and the five small children were happy over Miss "Mousie's" return, she being the oldest child, and her mother being an invalid. In Donkey I found that Miss Emma was known by the name of "Mousie," although not ratified.

The older boys took our saddle animals to the stable across the river, while "Doc" and I walked a few hundred yards down the river to old man Eli S's. Here I was introduced to "Doc's" father and mother, his brother Gregg and his wife and his pretty black eyed sister Lillie, whose age was twenty-six. The old man being an invalid, spent most of his time propped up in bed in the front room which faces the main road.

After the old man had been assured by "Doc" that I was "true blue" and all right, the different kinds of liquors, apple brandy, mint brandy, blackberry wine and doctored "moonshine" which would kill a mule as it was full of "lye-ball," were pulled from under the bed which was the old man's "blind tiger" and his way of making a living. Then the drinking began and ended when "Doc" and I were called home to supper.

Before leaving old man S's I had to promise to be their guest the following night. Here the thought of the insurance policy in favor of "Mousie" came flashing through my memory, and I wondered if they would try to kill me by poison or bullets. I hoped they would use the bullet method, for then I could bring old Colts 45 into play and stand a chance to win some of the insurance money by only getting wounded. Many in Whitesburg and at Craftsville had warned me to steer clear of old man S's "blind tiger" which they said was a death trap. Therefore my mind was in shape to expect anything.

We retired early at "Doc's," and I slept soundly as the door to my room was locked so that no one could get in to play for that thousand dollar prize.

Next day I put in my time horseback riding with Miss Lillie S., and buying sweets, calico and ribbons for the S. kids, including Miss "Mousie."

That evening I became the guest of Eli S. and his family.

After the chicken supper we all congregated in the front room where the liquor was stored, and where a fire blazed in the old fashioned fireplace. "Doc" had joined us. Soon Miss Lillie got out her guitar and commenced to play and sing. One of her songs worked me up to a high pitch; it set me wild. It ran thus:

"Oh meet me in the moonlight
 When all alone,
For a story I have to tell
 And it must be told alone."

Her sweet, low voice seemed to fit the song to perfection. I couldn't buy the drinks fast enough to suit myself and to encourage her to play and sing the same song over and over again. I was in an earthly Heaven. The different kinds of liquor helped matters along, and so did Miss Lillie's meet me in the moonlight glances. Music and singing had not had such an effect on me since 1882 in St. Louis, Mo., when I cut up a fine parlor chair.

I had just landed in St. Louis and bought a new suit of "hand-me-down" clothes. The Jew who sold them couldn't induce me to discard my cowboy hat and high heel boots, nor could my sister or her up-to-date husband.

One day while walking down Fourth street a well dressed Southern gentleman gave me his hand and asked if I was not from Texas. Then we had a few rounds of drinks. This gentleman proved to be one of the wealthy ex-slave-owning Terrys of Wharton county, Texas, adjoining the county of Matagorda where I was born. I had heard of the great Terry plantation when a small boy.

Nothing would do Mr. Terry but that I visit his residence. He said that he had just married a young lady
and wanted to show her what a real Texas cowboy was
like. I went. On our arrival the elegant parlor was
filled with elegantly dressed ladies, but no gentlemen.

After being introduced to the ladies, a plush mahogany
chair was given me to sit in. I was very cautious and
sat down gently so as not to spoil the delicate thing.
Here Mr. Terry asked his beautiful young wife to play
a few of her favorite pieces on the piano, as I would no
doubt enjoy music of that kind after so many years of
sleeping and eating out doors. The lady's sweet singing
is what upset me. My mind was centered on the pretty
singer, while no doubt many eyes were centered on me.

When Mrs. Terry quit playing and wheeled around on
her stool to see what effect her singing had had on me,
I came back to my right senses. I found myself sitting
on one foot, which was under me on the plush-bottom
chair seat. The other foot was up on one of the chair
rounds, and in my right hand was a sharp I. X. L.
pocketknife with which the chair had been whittled to
ruination. The brussels carpet was strewn with mahogany shavings.

I didn't realize that there was anything wrong until
Mr. Terry began to yell and laugh. Finally Mrs. Terry
broke into a laugh. The older ladies were too much
mortified to even smile. I insisted on paying for the
chair, but Mr. Terry wouldn't hear to it. He said this
was worth more than a dozen chairs to him, as his wife
had been begging him to round up a real live Texas
cowboy and bring him home so she could see what they
looked like.

THE AUTHOR AS HE APPEARED WHEN HE WHITTLED
THE CHAIR.

After getting over my blushing, I confessed that it was Mrs. Terry's pretty face and sweet voice which did the damage.

Whittling on boxes and ranch benches had become a fixed habit with me, hence cutting the chair.

"Doc" went home early. Mrs. Gregg S. had gone to bed in another room, and the old lady had gone to bed by the side of her husband in the room that we were celebrating in.

About 1:00 A. M. Gregg and I were pretty well "loaded," under the influence of the mixed drinks.

Finally my head began to swim and I became deathly sick. The thought of having been poisoned flashed through my mind. I asked to be shown to my room, so that I could lie down, but my real intention was to slip out of the house and try to find Mr. Gibson's place in the upper end of the town.

"Nels" Craft had told me that if I got into trouble in Donkey to hunt up his friend Gibson, who was a square man. He had described the house to me.

Gregg conducted me into the adjoining front room and insisted that he was going to sleep with me. This settled the matter in my mind,—it was a sure case of poisoned to get the $1000 life insurance and the money I had with me.

I started to the front door, telling Gregg that I was going outside to sit down and get some fresh air. He said that he would go along too. Then I got mad, and with my hand on the handle of old Colts 45 which was sticking in the waistband of my pants, I told Gregg to stay right where he was and to keep away from me. No doubt if he wasn't too drunk he could see the fire flashing from my eyes, for I meant business. When I opened the door and stepped out into the darkness, he called to me saying he would leave the door open so I could find my way back by the lamp light.

It had been raining, and the road which followed the bank of the river was very muddy, almost knee deep in some places. It was too dark and my head was in too much of a whirl to see the footpath on the side of the hill, so I kept the middle of the road, and twice fell down in the mud, but I strained every nerve to reach Gibson and tell him that I had been poisoned.

About two hundred yards above "Doc's" house I came to a place answering the description of Gibson's. I knocked on the door and a rough mountaineer in his night clothes admitted me to the inside. He informed me that his name was Gibson and that "Nels" Craft was a friend of his. Then he was told my suspicions of being poisoned. He replied: "I saw you out riding this evening and I'm not surprised. You ought to have known better."

Mr. Gibson held the candle while my muddy boots and outer clothing were being pulled off, and when the pistol was jerked out and placed under the pillow, he gave a jump as though startled.

I then fell over on the cot and he pulled the cover over me. In a moment I was dead to the world.

Soon after daylight, the noise of Gibson's building a fire in the front room woke me up, and on finding myself not dead from the supposed poison administered by the S's, I was ashamed of myself.

My outer clothing was a sight, with the mud still adhering to them, but they were put on.

Before leaving, Mr. Gibson promised that he would not tell of my poison suspicions. He was told that I intended to fix up a story about getting lost and finding his place by accident.

In passing "Doc" S.'s house on my way to the old man's "Mousie" who was outside splitting kindling for the morning fire, spied me. She came running out to the fence saying: "Oh Mr. Lloyd, where have you been? They are all crazy down to grandpa's. They have been up all night searching for you in the river and everywhere. Uncle Gregg came after papa to help find you. They thought you fell into the river."

I explained to "Mousie" of how I got drunk and went outside to get some fresh air, and sitting down on a rock fell asleep, and that when I woke up I took the wrong direction and found myself at Gibson's house, and was put to bed.

There was great rejoicing on my arrival at old man S.'s place. They felt sure that I had fallen over the bank into the river and was drowned. Their greatest worry seemed to be over the chance of the story getting out that I had been robbed and murdered, and if my body was never found, of people thinking that it had been concealed to hide the crime.

I made up for my misconduct by going to bed like a gentleman that night.

About midnight Gregg and I opened the front door to go outside before retiring for the night. This woke up the old lady and in an excitable voice she called out:

"Oh, Gregg, come back here, don't you take Mr. Lloyd off and lose him again."

The chances are the S.'s don't know to this day the true story of my getting lost in Donkey.

It shows how a man's mind can be worked up by hearing false tales about people. While the S.'s were handling liquor contrary to law, I had no fear of being harmed by them after learning their true natures.

After this I made other trips to Donkey, and Gregg and I rode out to "moonshine" stills in the wildest part of the mountains, and so far as the S.'s were concerned, I felt perfectly safe.

On one of these trips to Donkey I saw "Doc's" courage and "Mousie's" cooking tested.

"Doc" and I had walked down to old man S.'s to "liquor up" a little when we heard much shooting up at the store. Soon a man came down to tell "Doc" to keep hid out as his most bitter enemy was drunk and hunting for him to kill him on sight. It was this enemy who was doing the shooting at the store. He and his partner had just come down from their "moonshine" still on the Black Mountain with the intention of wiping Donkey off the face of the earth, just because "Doc" S. lived in the place.

"Doc" had left his pistol at home and he couldn't get to it unseen without a long walk over the hills. He asked for the loan of mine so that he could face this enemy and give him the opportunity of putting him out of business. I loaned "Doc" my old Colts 45 as I was anxious to have her tested in a hand-to-hand battle by some one else besides myself.

With the pistol in his hand held behind him under his coat, "Doc" started for the store and I with him. In front of the store there were several men. One of them stood on the edge of the store platform facing "Doc's" house. In his hands he held a Winchester rifle, and around his waist was strapped a large pistol. He had been firing the Winchester rifle into a dirt bank just under "Doc's" door yard, so as to bring "Doc" out of the house.

The wild and woolly "moonshiner" had just reloaded his rifle magazine with more cartridges when "Doc" and I stepped upon the store platform behind him. Just then "Mousie" stepped into the side yard and the "bad" man fired a bullet near her. "Doc" stepped up almost to the fellow's side and in a cool, low, voice told him that if he shot again he would kill him. The fellow turned his head slowly around and saw "Doc" by his side, but he made no effort to bring the rifle around towards his bitter enemy. There both stood like statues, neither saying a word. The suspense was a strain on my nerves, as I wanted to hear old Colts 45 talk while a brave man's finger was on the trigger.

At this moment Ike Potter and four companions from Kentucky, rode up, and seeing the situation, Ike Potter called the "bad" man by name and asked him to step out to him. This he did. A few words were spoken. Then the "bad" man walked in the mud by the side of the horsemen and all disappeared down the road. When below old man S.'s the shooting began again. Two days later we heard that this "moonshiner" was in jail for shooting up the county seat, Wise, Va.

28

When "Doc" handed me back old Colts 45 after we had entered his home, I imagined that I could see the poor pistol shedding briny tears over the chance she had missed of showing her abilities, when it came to puncturing human flesh; for I had been a cruel master and for twenty odd years had kept her in restraint.

Now about "Mousie" and her cooking; I had been to the railroad towns of Glaymorgan, Wise, and Norton, Virginia, and I had promised Miss "Mousie" to be back in Donkey on a certain day, sure. She had agreed to get me up a swell supper with her own hands.

On my way back to Donkey on the appointed day, I stopped at Pound, two miles below Donkey, where there is a postoffice, and there found "Doc's" oldest boy and the fat white horse. The boy and I rode home together. He could talk of nothing else but the good things "Mousie" was cooking for my supper. He said she had been baking pies and cakes all day.

But holy smoke and little fishes, what a deceitful world this is. I had to look pleasant and pretend that "Mousie" was the best cook in the world. Besides, I had to fill my stomach with pie, cake and biscuits which would have taken a week to digest, had it not been for the goodnight kiss received before retiring. Still, the poor girl did her best, which couldn't have been worse from an indigestion standpoint.

I felt satisfied that the people around Donkey, Craftsville and the Potter settlement had nothing to do with the kidnapping of young Wentz. Furthermore, I was satisfied that he was dead, as I had got it from Ashford N. and Mrs. Lottie H., both of whom no doubt knew what they were talking about. Ashford had assured me that he was dead and would never bother Kentuckians again, and Lottie said she knew that he had been killed for the cruel way in which he and his men had treated her and Birdie, and for killing her half brother Daniels, though she didn't know what had been done with the body. She said the parties who had done the job kept the matter to themselves; that all she cared to know was that he had been killed.

On top of Black Mountain, at the head of the Cumberland river, on the road leading from Whitesburg to Stonaga, Va., several citizens of Letcher County, Ky., had owned saloons which were run in defiance of the laws of Wise county, Va., and Letcher county, Ky. These saloon buildings were built on the line of the two states, half in Kentucky and half in Virginia, so that when officers of one state would try to make an arrest the saloon fixtures and goods were moved into the opposite end of the building over the state line.

One of these saloons had been run by Lottie H., her sixteen-year-old daughter Birdie, and her half brother Daniels, with the help of her nineteen-year-old son Jim.

Another saloon at the same place had been run by my fat friend Monroe W. who had lately married Lottie H.'s oldest daughter.

The other saloon had been run by Ashford N.

The Wentz Company owned the coal mines at Stonaga, Va., about three miles down the mountain side from these above mentioned saloons. Dan and Ed Wentz, sons of millionaire Dr. Wentz, of Philadelphia, Pa., were in direct charge of these mines, and they objected to these saloons being located so near, on account of their employes being made drunk.

One night a raid was made on the saloons. In the fight which followed the town marshal, King, of Stonaga, was shot and killed, an so was Lottie H.'s half brother, Daniels. The liquor was destroyed and the buildings sawed in two. The half in Kentucky was left standing while the other part was hauled away or burnt up. Lottie H. and her daughter Birdie were marched through the mud afoot, and placed in jail at Wise, Va. And for this crime against blue-blooded Kentuckians, Ed. and Dan Wentz were doomed to die, though after Ed. was kidnapped Dan kept out of the way, so that he couldn't be caught unawares.

This is the story told me in confidence by Lottie H. She gave me the full details of the fight from beginning to end, all except the manner in which Ed. Wentz was put out of the way, and this she claimed not to know, as her friends who had the matter in charge kept it a secret.

While Lottie didn't confess it as a fact, she gave me to understand that Monroe W. and his money were leading factors in the plot, and that was why he tried to run me out of the country; that he supposed I had just come from Virginia to run down the Wentz mystery, and that when he found that I had come from Jackson, Ky., he thought maybe I might be all right, though she said he was always suspicious and uneasy and advised her not to associate with me for fear she might let something drop, as I might be a detective on the Wentz case.

I had become so "solid" with Lottie H. that Monroe W. and his gang couldn't break our friendship. I had confided in her as to a killing of two men in Texas in which fight I took part, and I had let her read all my Texas and New Mexico letters on the subject. While I had hoped that she would let the secret out of my being an outlaw, she didn't do it. She was just as true as steel to me and kept her promise not to give me away.

Lottie H. had a farm two miles below Whitesburg on the Kentucky river. She was a fairly good-looking middle-aged woman of more than the average intelligence. With her lived Birdie and Jim with his young wife Ollie, and a younger son and a daughter Mary.

Lottie H. was a sister of Sheriff Ed. Callihan of Brethitt county, Kentucky, who soon after was arrested for bloody murders committed in and around his home town of Jackson.

Many were the murders committed through this honorable officer of the law, as told to me by Lottie H. He had formerly been a member of the noted Hatfield gang of the McCoy-Hatfield feud notoriety.

I was given the details of a late cold-blooded murder committed through sheriff Callihan of Brethitt county. He owned a big mercantile establishment in the country east of Jackson. A man started a store in the same neighborhood, and in order to get rid of this store sheriff Callihan hired his brother-in-law S. to kill the owner.

One day S. with some picked witnesses drove up to the opposition store in a wagon and raised a fuss about a log hook which had been borrowed. S. shot the man dead.

There being some uncertainty about the result of the trial in Jackson, the jury had to be bought at quite a cost to Lottie H.'s brother. S. came clear, and later appeared on the scene in Virginia where Ed. Wentz was kidnapped. After the kidnapping of Wentz he married Lottie H.'s daughter Birdie. He had "shook" her and returned to Brethitt county just previous to my arrival. From what I could learn he had a hand in getting away with Ed. Wentz.

I put in much of my time at Lottie H.'s drinking, dancing and having a big time. I also kept up my carouses with Ashford N. in my room in Whitesburg, through the assistance of the jailer, Boney Isum.

In order not to disturb the sleep of the Holcomb family, I had Mrs. Holcomb fit me up a room in a log cabin away from the main residence. Here Ashford N. kept his jug of liquor and often slept with me, the deputy or jailer coming after him in the morning.

Ashford told me all about young Wentz passing him in the road near Kellyville, Va., on the morning of his disappearance, but he wouldn't say that he had a hand in getting away with him, though he indicated as much and seemed to want to impress me with the fact that he did.

A good deal of my work now was over on the head of the Cumberland river, where I used to get "moonshine" fresh from the illicit stills. I had gained a "foothold," and "moonshiners" were not afraid of me now.

On one of these trips to a "moonshine" still with Ashford N.'s chum, Brown, who lived over on the Cumberland river at the foot of the southern end of the Black

Mountain near where that bunch of saloons were cut in two, I secured some information about Ed. Wentz. I learned that he was dead, and that he had been taken from his horse alive by three men.

Brown and the few people in his wild out-of-the-way neighborhood were very bitter against the Wentzes and their company for having gobbled up vast stretches of valuable coal and timber land, and their interference with the liquor traffic.

In riding over the mountains with Brown in search of pure "moonshine" I was told many blood-curdling tales of murder in which Brown had figured, and from others I found he had told the truth. He was honest enough though to acknowledge that the people of these mountains didn't give enemies a chance to fight for their lives; hence they are generally shot from ambush, which he thinks is the proper way. He himself has been shot clear through the body, and he showed me the wounds.

I traded my mule off to Brown on this trip. While on the way to a "moonshine" still he pulled out $40 and offered it as boot between my "Donk" and his small three-year-old blue roan pacing stallion. I accepted and saddles were changed.

In this trade I won a prize, for he was the swiftest natural pacer and the best piece of young horseflesh that had ever been straddled by an ex-cowpuncher.

As to searching for pure "moonshine," I will state that much of the "moonshine" in these mountains is doctored by adding "lye-ball," pure concentrated lye. With one gallon of pure "moonshine" liquor and one ball of lye, about three gallons can be made, and only an expert can tell the difference, though one's stomach soon finds it out.

Through the teachings of the S. boys, in Donkey, and Ashford N., I had become an expert in knowing the difference between the pure and the adulterated liquor.

Towards spring, Ed. Wentz's body was found by accident in a wild heavily timbered country three miles from where his horse and saddle had been found on the night of his disappearance. It was found near Kellyville, Va., on the eastern slope of the Black Mountains directly over the mountain from the head of the Cumberland river in Kentucky.

Our Asst. Supt. Estin of the Philadelphia office hurried to the spot to view the body before it had been moved. He found that young Wentz had been shot through the heart and placed on top of some logs in a reclining position. Down the hill from the body lay his pistol with one chamber empty, to give the idea of suicide, and also his eye glasses, hat, etc. Mr. Estin informed me later, that it would have been impossible for Wentz had he shot himself, to have reached the spot where the body was found, he having been shot through the heart. Estin also said that the body had no doubt been placed where it was found at least a month after he had been kidnapped; for when he disappeared the forest leaves had just begun to fall, and under the body the leaves were plentiful, showing that his body had been put there after the leaves had fallen.

Furthermore, after the young man's horse had been found, Dr. Wentz and his son Daniel had hired hundreds of men who scoured the woods for ten miles square in the neighborhood of where the horse and saddle were found. The coal mines at Stonaga had been closed down and all the men turned out to search for the missing man. They were divided up into gangs and walked abreast through the thick woods, so that every foot of ground could be searched. It was done systematically. Mr. Estin says that men who were in this searching party claim that they remember going over the spot where the body was found, and had it been there they couldn't have helped seeing it.

The body was in good shape, with the exception of the right hand being cut off. The hand was never found, and here hangs a tale.

Shortly after young Wentz's disappearance his father began to receive mysterious letters offering to free Ed. Wentz for certain sums of money up into the hundreds of thousands of dollars. Finally a letter came from San Francisco, Cal., that if a large sum of money was not put in a certain place and an advertisement put in the personal columns of the San Francisco Examiner, stating that all was O. K., his son would be killed and his right hand sent to him to prove that their threat had been carried out.

The chances are that young Wentz had been held alive for a month or so in hopes of a ransom from his father, and when their scheme failed they took him to the spot where the body was found and fired a bullet from his own pistol into his heart. Then laid the body on the limbs of the dead tree where it was discovered by men hunting cows. The hand may have been cut off with the intention of sending it to Dr. Wentz, but later decided to be a dangerous thing to do, as it might lead to detection. Again, the hand may have been lost before the time came for sending it.

I found out that Lottie H. had relatives living thirty miles from San Francisco, Cal. She kept up a correspondence with them. I had seen their letters; hence if Monroe W. and his gang had young Wentz secreted in the mountains they could have had that threatening letter mailed in San Francisco by their relatives. One of these male relatives came to Whitesburg from California after my arrival on the scene, and I became well acquainted with him.

There is one thing sure,—if the gang above referred to didn't commit the crime, then Lottie H. and Ashford N. wanted to leave the impression on my mind that they did, and were therefore revenged.

Dr. Wentz would have paid any amount of money for the return of his son alive, but he had received other mysterious letters which had been run down and found to have been written by "cranks." Besides, the time allowed in the letter referred to above was too short, considering the great distance from San Francisco to Philadelphia, to meet the demand before the time set for the killing and the cutting off of the hand.

After the body of Ed. Wentz had been taken to Philadelphia for burial. I made frequent trips into Virginia along the railroad which skirts the foot of Black mountain, from Stonaga, through Appalachia, Kellyville and Norton, and Wise, the county seat.

Near Kellyville lived a man named Hubbard, and his family, and they were thought to know something of the crime, as young Wentz's horse and saddle had been found in the road leading to Kellyville by two young men who were stopping at the Hubbard place.

Hubbard was known to run a "blind tiger," selling liquor against the law and keeping a hard gang around him. Therefore I worked on Hubbard and his two daughters; and here I became acquainted with one of Ashford N.'s brothers who was in the "moonshine" liquor business.

I satisfied mself that Hubbard and his family had nothing to do with the murder of Wentz, but not so with the brother of Ashford N.

In working on the Hubbard girls I bumped into some more cooking of the M. S. brand.

Ashford N. was always glad at my return to Whitesburg, for it meant a jolly time with plenty to drink in my log cabin.

Finally, Ashford longed for liberty. He still had about two months to serve behind the bars. He decided to break jail, and my influence was used where it would do the most good in pushing matters along.

The night for the escape was planned. It was agreed that I leave some liquor at Dicie F's on Big Cowan Creek, as "Ash" might be dry when he reached there on the way to Brown's place.

Dicie F. was the woman wounded Christmas day by Shepard when he shot and killed Riley Webb. She lived in what was called a tough neighborhood. Jailer Boney Isum had introduced me into society over there. A relative of his had one of his wives living next to Dicie F's. She was a tall muscular young woman with two healthy babies and the regulation low water mark on her neck. She split her own rails and put in her own crops. All she asked of her lord was that he visit her once in awhile to see how the crops were getting on. Her lord's main wife and half a dozen children lived eight miles from this girl, therefore no danger of hair pullings.

·Boney Isum had only one wife anchored, and she lived at the jail.

In these mountains nothing is thought of a man having half a dozen "wives." One fellow of the Brigham Young build, who lives at the head of the Kentucky river, has seven women, and all have raised large families, and all have the stamp of being chips from the old block. It would be a safe wager to bet that one-third of the population of these mountains are of illegitimate birth.

When Ashford N. broke jail he put in the first night down at Lottie H's, and the next night at Dicie F's, thence to Brown's place. No one suspected me of being on the inside. He could serve me better by being a free man. My plans had been laid for the future, when a full confession of the Wentz murder was almost certain.

During the winter I had made three trips out to civilization, once to Bristol, Tenn., once to Knoxville, Tenn., and the other time to Huntington, West Va. These trips were made to meet Supt. Bearce, or Asst. Supt. Estin to get a new supply of money. My horse would be left in a livery stable at Norton, or Appalachia, Va.

While in Knoxville I went to see the saloon building which is now used as a restaurant, where "Kid" Curry made such a brave fight, shooting two officers.

While in the mountains of Kentucky and Virginia I learned all the tricks of beating the Government in the licensed still business. I visited several stills so as to get onto these tricks, which are many.

I had made arrangements to start a licensed still in partnership with Lottie H's son Jim. The site was selected up in the head of a gulch on the Lottie H. farm. When this news leaked out Lottie said that Monroe W. objected and swore it shouldn't be started. After this I received private warnings through friends to keep away from Lottie H's or I would be killed; but I never could find out who made the threats, or whether they were made on account of the Wentz matter or love for Lottie H. and her daughter Birdie. A wealthy and influential citizen was "dead stuck" on Lottie, and since my arrival on the scene she had grown cold towards him. He often came to see her while I was at the house, and he wouldn't speak to me. His son R. was in love with Birdie. It wasn't known for certain which I loved the more, as I played "sweet" on both; therefore these threats may have come through jealously.

On two occasions I suspected a trap laid for me, but I was too "foxy" to put my foot into it.

A fellow known as "In the Woods" Brown had tried to lead me into the trap, so I suspected. He had once made an unsuccessful attempt to assassinate merchant Jim Fraser and when caught, confessed that he did it for $50. But it was said that all of his attempts had not proved failures.

While in Whitesburg my reports were all mailed to different addresses in the far west, and all my mail came from that country. We were lucky in having an honest intelligent young man, Samuel Collins, for postmaster in Whitesburg, otherwise my mail would have been tampered with, for he told of the inducements offered him for some of my mail. These inducements had been offered when I first came to the country, and I suspected Monroe W. as being the gentleman who had tried to "work" young Sam Collins. Of course the postmaster didn't say that he had been offered money, but that certain parties were suspicious of me and wanted him to let them have access to my mail.

During the month of May when my plans were ripe for starting the whisky still with Jim H., I had been requested by our Philadelphia officials to give my opinion as to whether convictions could be secured against the murderers of young Wentz, if convincing proof was secured. I gave it as my opinion that it was a waste of money to try to convict any of these people, owing to the fact that most of the settlers and their offspring are related either by blood or marriage, and of the further fact of the bitter feeling against the Wentz company.

A good deal of this hatred had been brought about through the Wentz's arresting men for cutting bee trees and trespassing on company land.

In the meantime while waiting for money to start the still, I was learning all the ins and outs of the still business.

It was Jim H.'s and my intention to establish our liquor warehouse on top of Black mountain on the lots owned by his mother. Then we would have Ashford N. and a few men of his stamp peddle liquor on the sly among the coal miners in Stonaga and the other coal camps nearby. I had also visited Middlesboro, Ky., to learn the licensed still business. The Ball brothers, there being four of them, were friends of Jim H. They owned a still and four saloons in that town. Since then, these Ball brothers have gained notoriety on account of killings, the state militia being called out to capture them in their mountain stronghold.

One day I had been up the river to Sam W.'s place, drinking "moonshine" and having a big time, Sam W. being one of the "bad" mankillers of the country.

I arrived back in Whitesburg about sundown. Lottie H. was in town on her mule. She asked me to ride home with her as there was a drunken crowd in town and she was afraid to go home in the dark. We started, and I noticed R. and some of his drunken companions watching us as we rode across the river, R. being a married man who was in love with Birdie H. and jealous of me, no doubt.

On reaching Lottie H.'s home I ate supper, after which Lottie and I sat on the porch talking. Birdie and her younger sister Mary had gone to bed. Lottie tried to persuade me to stay all night, but I refused under the pretense that I could sleep late in the morning in my own room and thereby get rested after my "big time" up the river. But the truth of the matter was, I smelled a "mice" from the way R. and his gang had acted when Lottie and I rode out of town.

It was about 10:00 P. M. when I bade Lottie goodnight and rode across the river into the main road. The night was cloudy and dark, and my route lay along the river bank in the shadow of tall trees.

After going a quarter of a mile I saw the outlines of four men afoot in the road coming towards me. On seeing me they jumped over a rail fence and ran to a clump of bushes in the field on my right, and hid. I rode slowly past this thicket with my hand on old Colts 45. A few hundred yards further up the road I met Lottie H.'s hired man Day, coming from town on a mule. I told him of the four men hiding in the thicket. Next day in court Mr. Day testified that he had met me, and of being told about the four men in the thicket, and of how he had just got to bed when R. and three drunken companions came into his room and wanted to know where Lloyd was. On being told that I had gone home R. said that must have been I who went up the road when they hid. That then, he said, the gang went into the room where Lottie H. and her two daughters were in bed, and demanded to know where Lloyd was. They were told that I had gone back to Whitesburg. Then the gang commenced raising Hades. Soon after this, Lottie H.'s nephew Jim D., who was a deputy sheriff, dropped into Lottie's on his way from his sweetheart's place down the river. Here a battle began, one against four, and when the smoke cleared away the deputy sheriff lay mortally wounded with a bullet through his body, while two of R.'s companions were wounded from bullets fired by Jim D.

Early that morning I was back to Lottie H.'s and did all that was possible to relieve the suffering of the wounded deputy sheriff. At midnight he died, and from that time until morning the scene was affecting to even calloused nerves like mine, for the dead man's brothers, Jesse and Bob, cried all night.

After we had all been singing religious songs around the bedside of the corpse, old grandma H. got me to one side and said: "I didn't think we would have to lay poor Jim out so soon, but I did expect your death before this. I know what I'm talking about. You have been marked for death quite awhile. You have been warned several times but you won't leave. Now you take my advice and get out of this country just as quick as you can. I can't tell you all I know, but I don't want to see you killed."

Grandma H.'s oldest son was the father of Lottie H.'s children. He had been dead a couple of years.

One of R.'s wounded companions made a confession on being arrested, and said that R. had furnished him with a pistol to go down to Lottie H.'s and help raise a fuss with me, so as to "do me up;" that he went by R.'s house to get the extra pistol as he had none of his own, while R. had two.

I continued to visit at Lottie H.'s as though grandma H. had not given me the friendly warning.

Soon after, I received instructions from Asst. Supt. Estin to sell my horse and outfit and meet him at a certain hotel in Washington, D. C. In the letter he stated that the operation would be closed as it was decided that a conviction could not be had, no matter how strong the proof.

After selling the horse and outfit, my friends were bade goodby for a short time, as it was pretended that I was going to return after a short visit to the World's Fair in St. Louis, Mo.

I had made many warm friends in Whitesburg, among

29

them being Sam Collins the postmaster, and a young lawyer, Wilson Field.

There are some good people in these mountains, and others not so good. Their worst fault is their reckless regard for human life. They think no more of killing a man than of killing a wild beast. At least twenty murders were committed in these mountains during my short stay.

They also need education in their mode of living, especially in their home life, wherein one wife is not considered sufficient for one man. Also, they need bath-tubs. I failed to see one bath-tub in the counties of Letcher, Perry and Knott. Possibly they are afraid of wearing out should they wash too much.

One morning Mr. B. whose weight is 300, and who is said to never have done a day's work in his life, although past middle-age, he being a king-bee of the "moonshiners'" brigade, and I were to start early on a squirrel hunt. On reaching his house he informed me that he couldn't go hunting as this was his bath day; that his wife kept track of it and was now heating the water. He said he always took a bath regularly every six months; that some people didn't believe in bathing so often, but he did. Out in the back yard his little delicate wife had two large kettles on the fire, as though it was hog-killing day.

Another curse of this country is the marrying of first and second cousins.

I was glad to get away from Whitesburg, for two reasons one of which was to get beef to eat. I had not seen or tasted a piece of beef in Kentucky during my over seven months' stay, that is, away from the rail-roads. I was also anxious to get away from the sound of banjos. Nearly every household has from one to half a dozen of these instruments, and nearly every child can pick the same tune. Some few can pick as many as three or four tunes.

Regardless of my wild-oat sowing habits, pure-hearted virtuous Lizzie Holcomb gave me a goodby kiss, with a hope that I would reform and quit scattering oat-seed broadcast over the land.

Before shaking the dust of the Kentucky mountains from these pages, I will state that should any reader of this book wish to see a dying man smile, he or she ought to be present when the last breath is just leaving me, and then mention Mrs. Sol Holcomb and the first four-legged monkeys which were ever in Whitesburg.

A couple of Italians brought two trained monkeys to Whitesburg. They were dressed up in human rigging and performed on the main street which contained only five stores and the overgrown court house. The town turned out to see the monkey show. It was a circus sure enough, but all the monkeyshines were not per-formed by the little "monks." There were others.

There were old gray headed men and women who had never seen a monkey before. When it was all over Mrs. Sol Holcomb came into the sitting room of her house, perspiring like a "nigger" at an election. She said: "Lor' bless my soul, I didn't know befo' that mon-keys was human beins! I jess wouldn't of believed it."

Good-natured, easy-going little Sol Holcomb smiled and said: "Why Bess, they ain't humans, they are jest animals."

Here Mrs. Sol got up on her high horse and with her strong right arm bared to the elbow and pointed towards her hubby said: "Now look a here Sol, don't you dare tell me them ain't humans, for I knows better. They are jess as much humans as any black nigger or you either, Sol!"

I spent three days in Washington, D. C., on leaving Kentucky, and there took in the sights. In Philadelphia I stayed two days settling up the affairs of the Dr. Wentz operation. Then Mr. Roy L. Dickenson phoned for me to come down to New York City. I arrived in New York City on that morning, and most of the day was spent with Mr. Royder Dickenson. He showed me through every nook and corner of the large block owned and occupied by the Dickenson agency. I also visited with the other high officials, and the many assistant superintendents, too numerous to mention. That night I went to a theater at the agency's expense.

Next day my old Denver friend, executive clerk Mr. C. K. Hibben, showed me some of the great sights of the city, and I took in Coney Island on an excursion steamer.

Mr. Dickenson gave me permission to take in the World's Fair in St. Louis, en route to Denver. But he requested that I go from St. Louis to Chicago to visit Mr. W. L. Dickenson, as he might want to see me, though I suspected this was done for my own pleasure to give me a rest.

En route to St. Louis one night and part of one Sunday were spent in Pittsburg, Pennsylvania, which gave me an opportunity of seeing part of that smoky city.

In St. Louis I took in the World's Fair with my sister and her family.

While in that city I also visited the Dickenson agency under the supervision of Mr. Wooster, whom I already knew.

Then I took the back track for Chicago to meet Mr. Wm. L. Dickenson. He had no business for me, except a desire that I go out to his residence and ride his new $500.00 saddle-horse and give my honest opinion about him, also that I take a look at his half dozen fine bull terriers. The horse I found to be a "dandy." He was certainly the finest gaited large horse that I ever straddled, but for real heavenly delight he couldn't hold a candle to the little blue-roan sold in Kentucky by me for $60.00.

While in Chicago I enjoyed the visit with Mr. Dickenson and the superintendents and their assistants.

Shortly after my return to Denver, Supt. J. S. Kaiser received a letter from Mr. W. L. Dickenson requesting that I make out a bill for my personal expenditures while taking in the World's Fair several days, and the agency would pay it. I did as requested, and it pleased me, as this is something employers seldom do.

Thus did the most interesting operation of my eighteen years' connection with the Dickenson agency end. I had been gone from Denver eight months.

CHAPTER XX

A Mining Case in Kelly, N. M.—Big Robbery in
Prescott, A. T.—Incendiary Case in Wyoming—Mrs. Shaw Kidnapping Case in Pueblo,
Colo.—Chase After "Bad" Man in Sonora,
Mexico—Cattle Case in Wyoming and Montana—"Frenzied Finance" Operation in Roswell, N. M.

Soon after my return from the Dr. Wentz case in
Kentucky and Virginia, I was hurried south to Magdalena, New Mexico, on the A. T. & S. F. Ry. From
there I went to the mining camp of Kelly to meet Mr.
Cochran, the manager of the Kelly mine, on a stagecoach.

Mr. Cochran started me to work on certain mining
men of the camp to gain certain information for the
benefit of him and his associates.

My name here was Chas. T. Lloyd. I remained over
a month and did the work successfully.

En route back to Denver, Colo., I stopped off a few
days in Santa Fe to visit my pets at the Sunny Slope
ranch. Two of my pet horses, Lulu and "Glen" had
crossed over to the happy hunting ground where, if the
Indians' religion is correct, they may be ridden by the
noble red men on buffalo hunts. I felt grieved over their
death.

A few days spent in Denver and I was off for Cheyenne, Wyo., to meet U. S. Marshal Hadsell and his deputy Joe LaFors, and the client who is a high-up statesman.

The Warren Live Stock Company had had their home ranch on Pole Creek, twelve miles north of Cheyenne, burnt along with a lot of stock, causing a loss of about $40,000.00. It was known to have been set afire, but there was no clue as to who did it. Joseph LaFors had worked on the case and found suspicious circumstances connected with an ex-convict named Bert H. Hence it required that I win the confidence of cowboy Bert H. and get a confession from him if he committed the crime. Bert H. was known to be somewhere on the Laramie plains about seventy-five miles north of Cheyenne.

In order to hail from the adjoining state, Nebraska, I went there on a U. P. Ry. train, and from Sidney, Nebraska, I took a B. & M. train to Torrington, Wyoming, near old Fort Laramie, where years before I had attended dances on crutches. Here I bought a horse and saddle and rode west for the Laramie Plains, several days' ride distant.

Bert H. was found at the Jim K. ranch. He had a contract to put up some wild hay for Jim K. He did the hay-cutting all alone in the gulches and low places far from the ranch, the country being wild and unsettled.

Bert H. and I became fast friends and we made trips into the settlements. He told me all about himself and we planned big horse-stealing raids into Nebraska. He had been sent to the Wyoming pen for stealing horses, and he now kept a small band running on the range as a nest-egg to drawn on.

During this fall of 1904 while working on Bert H. I took in the great cowboy tournament at the Frontier Day Celebration in Cheyenne, and while there I was kept jumping sideways to avoid running into Bert C. of "Wild Bunch" fame and others whom I knew.

This cowboy tournament was a great treat to me, especially the "bronco-busting" contests. The riders did fine, but in the roping contests the ropers, as a whole, were "on the bum," which would have been considered disgraceful to the early-day cowboy. But this can be accounted for by the fact of the present-day cowboy not getting much every-day practice.

One day when Bert H. and I were five miles from the Jim K. ranch we saw a streak of flying calico in the air. As it drew nearer, we discovered it to be Mrs. Jim K. sitting clothespin fashion on an old horse who was running his best. As soon as the frightened lady could get her breath she informed us that her only child, a twelve year old boy had shot himself in the leg with a pistol.

She and the boy were the only ones at home, as her husband had gone away on a week's trip and their hired man Joe Cruelty would not be back until night.

As the wounded boy had been left lying on the kitchen floor alone, I put spurs to my horse and galloped to the ranch while Bert H. followed with the team and wagon, so as to take the boy to Chugwater station on the Cheyenne Northern Railroad about twenty miles west.

The boy was found on the floor badly frightened. I discovered that the bullet was lodged deep down in the calf of his leg. After bandaging the wound with wet towels, first cleansing it with diluted carbolic acid, I began to cheer him up, by laughing and telling him of the value of bullet-marks in the making of a good cowboy. He had a great desire to be a wild and woolly cowpuncher.

By the time Mrs. K. arrived I had the boy laughing.

Then I explained the foolishness of making the trip to Cheyenne, just to have the bullet cut out, at an expense of at least $200.00, in the face of the future honor to be derived from carrying lead in his flesh, as in old age he could tell his grandchildren that he was packing lead shot into him by wild Indians when the Laramie plains was a howling wilderness. I assured the mother that the boy would be well and on his feet in two weeks, whereas in Cheyenne hospital he would be kept just as long as she could be grafted out of the doctor's fees. The result was, when Bert H. arrived there was no need for the team, as the proposed trip to the railroad had been given up.

I finally decided beyond a reasonable doubt, that Bert H. had no hand in the burning of the Pole Creek ranch; therefore, I went near the line of Nebraska to work out another clue which had been given by Senator Warren and Joe LaFors.

On leaving the Laramie plains the wounded boy, who was on crutches and out of danger, sold me one of his half-starved Russian wolf-hound pups. He was all legs and hair, and had never had a square meal, as the eight dogs on the ranch were fed once a day on mush by the hired man, Joe Cruelty, who only fed them half enough, the few table scraps all going to his own two shepherd dogs and Mrs. K.'s pet cats.

I named the pup "Jimmie Long-legs," as a name should always be founded on facts, and the fact of Jimmie having long legs was a reality.

On leaving the ranch one morning to make a hard ride without water, Jimmie played completely out and couldn't navigate.

I was uncertain as to whether the bronco which I had just traded for, would consent to carrying double, but it was a case of "pushincy,"—something had to be done to get Jimmie to water.

Riding up by the side of the pup I reached down and caught him by the nape of the neck. Then swinging him across the saddle in front of me, the bucking contest began. Here was a bronco-busting contest going to waste on the desert with no one to see but the Lord, and if His all-seeing eye gathered in any fun from this free show He failed to let it be known by slapping me on the back and saying: "Well done thou good and faithful bronco and dog buster." The pup was being "busted" too, or at least would have been had his stomach contained anything but the lingering memory of his last mush supper.

Every time the bronco came down on his front feet with his hind parts up in the air, my whole weight was thrown against the pup's empty mushbasket, and of course the air was full of yelps. I wanted to smile but didn't have time.

On reaching the creek where there was a small lake, I shot a mudhen for Jimmie. Then I had to pull off my boots and pants and wade out into the muddy lake to get the hen. While ripping the mudhen open preparatory to skinning the feathers off, the "purp" which was sitting on his long tail eyeing the operation, smelled the blood and made a grab for the hen. I tried to take it away from him but he held on, so turning my hold loose I told Jimmie to pick his own duck; but bless you, he ate feathers, bill, feet and all. It was filling that he was after, and not dainties.

Here I changed Jimmie's name to "Eat 'Em Up Jake" and he retains that name to this day.

Later in Cheyenne City, I put E. E. U. J. in a crate and expressed him to Santa Fe, New Mexico, there to join my other pets.

My next few weeks' work solved the fire mystery. The secret was locked up in the brains of two wealthy brothers who had cattle on a thousand hills. They were bitter enemies of Senator ———— and his company. I became quite chummy with one of them and he told me enough to satisfy me as to their guilt.

I spoiled one scheme which the brothers were using against the ———— Company. They had an extra 'phone instrument which was used to get the secrets passing between Senator ———— and his manager, Mr. Willson in Cheyenne City, and the foreman of the Pole Creek Home ranch. A wire would be attached to this private telephone line and then fastened to the extra receiver on the ground. My informant told me in confidence of how after the fire, he lived on this telephone line catching all the secrets of Joe LaFor's sleuthing work.

In Cheyenne city I met Senator ———— at his home and the case was discussed. We decided that it would require a long siege at great expense to secure evidence enough to convict, more so, as the secret was locked up in the heads of two "foxy" men who had money to fight the case to the bitter end.

The senator said that he would read the "riot act" to these brothers so as to let them know that he knew of their guilt and how they had stolen his secrets from the telephone line, and how they used to kill and cripple his fine range horses by running them into barbed wire fences, one of their favorite schemes being to raise the wires which fenced in a windmill and trough, so that the thirsty Warren horses could crawl through to the water. Then the wild animals would be stampeded through the wire, many being ruined and some killed. On the strength of this information from me, the senator disposed of his range horses.

It was agreed that the operation be discontinued, therefore I returned to Denver.

My next operation out of the city was to Salt Lake, Utah, to do secret work on a son of Banker O'Gormley of that city; also on his friends, all young "bloods" and "high rollers."

I passed myself off as a mining man and secured the information wanted, relating to a copper mine and new smelter in one of the southern territories. Then I dropped out of sight and returned home.

Soon I was hurried off to Prescott, Arizona, to work on a big robbery which had just taken place.

Jim S. was the treasurer of Yavapai County, Prescott being the county seat, and on the morning after election, his party being defeated, S. was found by his daughter bound and gagged, and locked in the vault of the court house. All the cash, many thousands of dollars, was gone.

Jim S. claimed that two strangers overpowered him after midnight and locked him in the vault, after which they took the cash and skipped. But his bondsmen had a suspicion that he did the job himself, hence the Dickenson agency being called into the case.

I arrived in Prescott, Arizona, about 10 P. M., and after securing a room strolled down "Whisky Row" fronting the court house, and there on the street my friend Joe Hobbs in company with the county treasurer Jim S. was met. Of course I was introduced to S. and we three went into a saloon to "irrigate."

This illustrates how good luck often helps a detective, though it would have been an unlucky meeting had I not previously played my cards right with Joe Hobbs. He and I had been partners in a mine when I was working on the Jersey Lillie mine-salting case. He had been used then as a cat's paw to pull my chestnuts out of the fire, and now I intended to use him again for the same purpose, as he and S. were bosom friends.

Joe Hobbs knew me by the name of Lee Roy Davis, therefore that name had to be used.

After midnight I invited Mr. Hobbs and S. to have a feast with me, and while we were in a cafe eating, two officers came in and arrested S. on a warrant sworn out by his bondsmen.

Hobbs and I accompanied the Texas gentleman to jail and saw him safely put to bed behind cold steel shutters.

Of course, my friend Hobbs was "hot under the collar" over the arrest being made at night when bonds could not be given for his friend's release.

At 8 P. M. next day, in Lawlor's office, I met the

bondsmen who had employed the Dickenson agency. They were: Mr. James Wardner, Mr. Tony Motts, Mr. John Lawson, Mr. Robt. Howe and his partners in the Palace saloon and theater, Messers Smith & Belcher. They gave me all the facts in the case, of how Jim S. on the morning after the election had been found by his daughter who was the assistant treasurer, locked in the vault and all the county funds gone.

My visits at the home of Mr. Hobbs were enjoyed, as Mrs. Hobbs was a nice little soul and had three sweet little children. Besides, she was a good cook and gave me an opportunity of testing her culinary art. She was a sister of my friend Joseph LaFors, the deputy U. S. Marshal of Wyoming. On this account I disliked using her and her hubby as cat's paws.

Of course it was impossible for me to stay in Prescott without being recognized by my old friend Johnny Kinnie, who still owned mining interests there. After we had come together, I found that he still loved "red licker," "all same" twenty-five years previous, when he and I went to a swell Mexican wedding in La Mesilla, New Mexico, and got "loaded" on champagne.

As Kinnie was a good Democrat, same as Mr. Hobbs and Jim S. and knew the inside workings of the Arizona brand of political whisky-soaked corruption, I used him also as a cat's paw, though with his consent.

Johnny Kinnie and I went to the strong Miners' union camp of McCabe where I did some secret work among old Coeur D'Alene, Idaho, dynamiters, who knew me well, but who failed to recognize me. Kinnie was fearful lest one particular rabid dynamiter from the Coeur

D'Alenes might know my face and voice; for only a few weeks previous he had told Kinnie of that Dickenson detective "Allison—Siringo" who had joined the Gem union and turned traitor. He said he would know me should we ever meet, but the fellow drank at my expense many times and told me all about the prospects for a man of wealth like myself, investing money in that camp.

Before court sat I made a trip to Phoenix, the capital of the territory, and to Tempe and other places. On these trips I was gathering evidence to be used against the schemes which Jim S's friends were manufacturing to clear the county treasurer.

Finally the day of trial arrived, and after the jury were selected I informed our clients that the defense would "fix" a few of the jurymen so as to be assured of a "hung jury"; and later our clients were given the names of the "fixed" jurymen, as I had got the information from headquarters, but it was too late now to remedy the evil, as the case had started.

During the trial a Catholic priest did a little stunt on a court official to save one of his church members of wealth and influence who might be sent to the penitentiary in case Jim S. was convicted.

As soon as the jury were dismissed the four "fixed" jurymen met Hobbs, Jim S. and myself in one of the saloons. Then drinking began, and these jurymen told of how they had worked for an acquittal. One of these "fixed" jurymen said he wouldn't have brought in a verdict of guilty had he been at an upstairs window in the court house and seen Jim S. carry off the county funds

Thus is Arizona justice blind-drunk sometimes.

Of course Jim S. was put under bond for a new trial, he being convicted at the fourth trial, and sentenced to the penitentiary for four years.

The next day I bade my friends goodby and pulled out for Denver stopping en route at Santa Fe, New Mexico.

I found a wonderful change in Eat 'Em Up Jake. He had grown to be almost as large as a young colt, and his ribs were covered with good solid fat. Mr. and Mrs. B. C. Volk who had charge of my ranch kept him filled up as per my request. E. E. U. J. knew me and seemed to take great delight in showing how easily he could pick up a jackrabbit. The pleasure of seeing him outrun a swift jackrabbit in a few hundred yards race amply repaid me for the trouble and expense of getting him to Santa Fe. Besides, he was a beautiful specimen of the Russian wolfhound breed, and it was a satisfaction to know that I had "brought him up" from a lanky half starved pup to his present lordly state. His hair was now long and curly and as white as snow, with the exception of a few cloudy spots. It was also a pleasure to think back to the time when he and I slept together and "busted" broncos on the sagebrush flats of Wyoming.

Soon after returning to Denver I was sent to Mt. Carbon, a coal mining camp in Gunnison county, Colorado, to investigate a fire which had destroyed a "tipple" and other buildings.

I found Mt. Carbon to be a desolate place on the snowy crest of the great rocky mountain divide. Here at midnight, with the snow from two to ten feet deep, I

EAT 'EM UP JAKE.

walked out into the hills and with old Colts 45 shot out the old year 1904, and ushered in the new year of 1905. It was a single handed New Year's celebration at a height of over 10,000 feet above sea level, with the whole face of nature wrapped in her purest robe of white, and with the large flakes of snow falling thick and fast. My mind naturally drifted back twelve months to when old Colts 45 and I smoked in the new year just dead, among the "moonshiners" of "Old Kintuck."

I finally decided that the fire which destroyed the tipple was an accident caused by defective electric wires.

Then I "hiked" back to Denver to await a new operation.

For the next few months my work was on short operations in the city or the nearby towns.

During this time I made one "big catch" in the person of Joseph Adams, alias many other names. He was a member of the noted Knox-Whitman gang of check forgers and had been chased all over the United States and Europe. In the crowded postoffice one Sunday morning I recognized him as resembling the Adams photo which was carried in my pocket. After this "foxy" gentleman had gotten a letter at the general delivery window he went out into the rainstorm and tried to cover up his tracks by going through out-of-the-way streets and alleys. On turning a corner he would stand concealed to see if any one were following him. Here my early training in "shadow" work came in play. He finally went to his room on 14th street. Then I stepped

30

into a nearby drug store and 'phoned to Assistant Supt. Geary that I had the muchly wanted bank forger located, giving the number of the street where his room was located.

Soon Asst. Supt. B. and operative "Dick" H. were sent to assist me.

When Asst. Supt. B. and one of the city officials arrested Adams in the afternoon, when he had finished a meal, I dropped out of sight, as we poor operatives are compelled to do in order to hide our identity. But not so with the assistant superintendents; they can swell up and look wise as though they are the whole "cheese."

Next morning the daily papers came out with glowing accounts of the great detective ability of our Asst. Supt. Mr. B. in the running down of this great criminal. Of course Mr. B. didn't "load" the newspaper reporters. He merely looked wise and they did the rest. I mention this to illustrate how an operative in the Dickenson institution is a dead duck so far as the public are concerned. Adams was sentenced to a long term in the penitentiary, so I was told.

During the early spring I was sent to Leadville and Cripple Creek to make an investigation on mining matters.

On returning to Denver I was sent to Pueblo, Colorado, to work on the Blanche Haws kidnapping case.

Mrs. Haws was the principal witness against Republican officials in recent election frauds in Pueblo, and she had just been kidnapped and spirited away to parts unknown.

On reaching the city of Pueblo I met our clients, District Attorney S. H. Grave, Geo. E. Lord and J. A. Boothly, both of the Daily Chieftain, the leading newspaper of the city.

A couple of days later Mrs. Haws was found in a wagon, being in the hands of her kidnappers en route to Canyon City.

Mrs. Haws and several men were thrown in the county jail. I had found out enough to convince me that Mrs. Haws "stood in" with the "play" and had been kidnapped by her own consent.

She was a good looking young woman of the free and easy kind, and swore by all that was holy that she had been kidnapped by force. A few days later in the same jail where I had been a prisoner with the cold-blooded murderers Dick Manley and Anderson, many years previous, I broke Mrs. Haws down and she made a full confession. Undersheriff Tim O'Leary assisted me.

While on the Haws case in Pueblo I had the pleasure of inspecting President Roosevelt's teeth without his knowing it.

He was returning to Washington from his noted bear hunt. He made a short speech from the rear of his private car. The chief of police, McCafferty, who knew my business, had given me a "tip" as to where the President's car would stop. Therefore the widow, on whom I was working, and who thought I was a rich mining man, and I, secured a choice place to stand. We stood within a few feet of "Teddy" the Great, and I could look into his mouth while he was talking, and see every tooth in his head, and a finer set of teeth I had never seen before. Every one seemed to be perfect, and they were set into jaws that were built for wear and tear.

While making his heart-to-heart talk to the great audience, the President showed his regard for the safety of others, and also the activity of his massive brain.

On the rear end of the coach dozens of children were hanging. The engine backed up to the train and the jolt knocked some of these "kids" off onto the track where they would have been run over had the coach moved a few feet further. With outstretched arms ready for action, the President sprang forward and grabbed at some of the urchins who were still hanging onto the car. The coach came to a standstill before any damage had been done, and quicker than a flash the President's whole countenance changed, and with a smile he said: "Look out boys, little apples always go to the bottom of the barrel!"

Of course this put himself in the big apple class, which caused a roar of laughter. But the point which struck me forcibly was the quick action of both thought and speech.

I had seen "Teddy" Roosevelt once before at Trinidad, Colo., when on his way to the Rough Riders' Reunion at Las Vegas, New Mexico. This was before he became President. At that time too, I stood near the end of his car, though dressed as a coal miner and being in company with a gang of striking miners.

Finally I returned home after doing all that could be done against the "Grand Old Party" of President Lincoln and Ben Butler.

I had found out enough to satisfy me that the Republican party had corrupted decency and the sacred franchise in the city of Pueblo, but that is not saying that the Democrats wouldn't have done the same had they been in control of the political machinery.

In Denver, where the Democrats had been in power for many years, they had carried corruption with such a high hand that even a Pattersonian anarchist of the sic-em-tige kind ought to hang his head in shame, and blush every time he sees a statue of the Goddess of Liberty.

At one of these corrupt elections in Denver, I was instructed to put on "bum" clothes and join the hobo gang in the slums, so as to secure evidence. I only voted a few times,—eight in all,—three times before the same judge of election. Others of my hobo chums voted all day as they needed some "easy" money.

The notorious Jack Hall of the old Clifton Hotel had charge of the Democratic slush fund, where I did my voting that day. My earnings for the day only amounted to $1.75, at 25 cents a vote, as the paymaster skipped out with the funds after my last vote was deposited, just before the polls closed. On finding out that the "money-guy" had vanished, there was much swearing and gnashing of teeth among these poor downtrodden American citizens who help make our laws.

Denver has made great strides though, in the matter of buying votes, since the time that Wolcott put up his good hard cash to become a Republican senator of these glorious United States, where every man is a king, with the sacred right to vote. At that time the Republicans had control of the city, it being about sixteen years ago. But at that time they had no "scab" voters; they paid union prices,—a new two dollar bill for each vote.

My next operation was trying to run down a hard case in the State of Sonora, Old Mexico.

Operative J. V. Marke, now one of the Asst. Supts. of the Denver office, had just worked up a big steal in Colorado City, Colorado, and this man was wanted in connection with that case. He had been seen by a traveling man at a *fiesta* in the town of Magdalena, Mexico, and had told of owning a placer mine out in the La Briesa mining country, about 100 miles east of the railroad town of Magdalena. But as to the name he was using down in Mexico we were ignorant; therefore I had only his description to work on.

In Magdalena, a small city, I failed to get a trace of my man, as at the time he was seen there the city was full of strangers attending the *fiesta*.

From here I went overland by stage, private conveyances and on horseback to the La Briesa mining camp owned by Col. W. C. Green. From La Briesa I scoured the wild mountain regions for fifty miles around, wherever gold had ever been found. I did this on horseback and had some trying experiences with the half-starved Mexican ponies breaking down.

I concluded that my man had never been in this La Briesa country.

On returning to Magdalena I boarded a train for the south and scoured the country through to the city of Guaymas on the Gulf of California. In Hermosillo, the capital of Sonora, I enjoyed life for a week, and also took in the dives and tough places where my man would naturally hang out, as he was a gambler by profession.

There was great excitement throughout the State of Sonora over the Yaqui Indian war, Indian prisoners were being brought into the capital and shot, then their bodies hung up to trees to rot down, it being a crime to remove a corpse from its necktie swing. I could have seen five of these warriors shot and hung up about five miles north of Hermosillo, but I had no desire to witness the scene.

In Nogales, Arizona, on the Mexican border, I found a hotel proprietress who had seen my man as he was leaving Mexico. He had stayed at her hotel while waiting for the northbound train.

From here I went to Naco on the train, thence back into Old Mexico to the large mining camp of Cananea; thence back to Bisbee and Douglas, Arizona. In Douglas I met my old cowboy friend Jim East and his good wife.

After putting my case in the hands of the Arizona Rangers, I returned to Denver, stopping off a few days at Santa Fe, New Mexico.

Soon after my arrival in Denver the Captain of the Arizona Rangers wrote me that they had my man located and asked if they should arrest him. This letter was turned over to our clients in Colorado Springs so they could make their own terms with the Arizona Rangers. This ended my connection with the operation. I had gone under the name of Chas. Tony Lloyd on this trip.

I reached Denver just in time to see the State Legislature seat Peabody in the Governor's chair for a second term, in spite of the protests that his opponent Alva Adams had been elected and was entitled to the seat.

It was predicted that Governor Jas. H. Peabody would be assassinated if the legislature confirmed his election; therefore the Dickenson agency was called on to furnish two bodyguards for the governor, who could shoot straight and were not afraid to die. Yours Truly and old Colts 45 were selected as one of these bodyguards and we were itching to plant six 45 caliber bullets where they would do the most good for society. Mr. Pace, one of Capt. John Howard's patrolmen, was the other bodyguard.

After the legislature had seated Governor Peabody, a big reception was held at night in the Peabody mansion on Capitol Hill, and there I experienced a touch of high-life, and at the same time had a couple of years added to my life by the governor's pretty daughter, Miss Jessie, pinning a carnation to my coat and smiling her sweetest while doing so.

In order to keep peace in the Republican household, Governor Peabody resigned his office later, and the legislature appointed Jesse McDonald, a good Republican from Leadville, as the new executive. Thus did I lose my job and the chance of high living, also the opportunity of killing members of Western Federation of Dynamiters, or the spilling of my own Texas blood for the benefit of society and the corrupt politicians.

A few days later I was en route to Sheridan, Wyoming, to work on cowboys and cattlemen to secure secrets of a "Frenzied Finance" nature for a live stock commission trust of the east.

I was given a letter of introduction to Chas Long, a cattle inspector and deputy sheriff at Sheridan. Mr. Long was a cowboy of the old school, and assisted me in my work.

In Sheridan I made the acquaintance of an old Texas cowboy by the name of George Carroll. He was now a prosperous cattleman. I went with him and his young son to their cattle ranch on the Rosebud river in Montana, and while on this trip I lived my old cowboy life over again by eating fine fat beef stuck on a stick and roasted over a campfire.

After about a month spent in and around Sheridan, I secured the coveted sworn affidavit from the McKinley brothers, cattlemen. But I sweat blood until the affidavits were in my pocket, as the "boys" didn't want to mix up in the affair as it was no fight of theirs, they being honorable men.

I then returned home, wondering what the next operation would be.

After a short stay in Denver I was detailed on a case in Colorado Springs, which turned out to be a two weeks' pleasure trip in that noted summer resort. The tourist season was then at its height, it being midsummer; therefore my stay in that clean little prohibition city was a pleasure indeed.

The work was in the nature of an investigation to decide who had stolen a big lot of street car tickets, though only a few of them had been used.

The operation was being conducted by Mr. G. A. Carpp, the president of a principal national bank. I was assisted by Mr. O. J. Lewis, Mr. Wm. Boyd, Dr. Tice and Supt. Latham of the street railway system of that place.

While in Colorado Springs I visited my old friends, Postmaster Dana, Chief of Police Alex. Adams; the cowboy author, Andy Adams, and last but not least, C. W. Kurie, the mining man, and his lovely wife and sons.

Mr. Kurie and his eldest son gave me my first automobile ride in their brand new $4000.00 "Red Devil." I enjoyed it immensely.

As the result of my work a high up employe of the Electric Ry. Co. lost his job. I felt sorry for the poor fellow when I accused him of being the guilty man. The blood rushed out of his face and he became as pale as a ghost. His ears became so transparent after the blood had left them, that I could almost see through them. But the head officials had no disposition to prosecute him.

I had previously confronted other trusted employes on whom a slight suspicion rested, and accused them of the theft as though I had good proof, but they looked me square in the face and showed their innocence by every look and action. Among these were Mr. Carpp's young nephew and on old Union soldier eighty years of age. It was comical to see this old hero of bloody battles climb upon his dignity when accused.

I then bade my friends goodby and returned to the Queen City of the Plains, Denver.

Supt. J. S. Kaiser at once detailed me on an operation in Roswell, New Mexico, just the place I wanted to visit, as I hadn't been there for twenty-three years.

Although my instructions from Asst. Supt. "Hank"

Geary who had charge of the case was to do nothing to retard justice, as the agency couldn't afford to work against his "royal nibs," Uncle Samuel; still, knowing my failing, I felt sure that once in the battle I would fight to win, even though my big Uncle did get his corns stepped on.

Before starting on my trip to Roswell, the manager of our six western offices, Mr. Jas. McCartney, called me into his private office to inform me that I had been promoted to the position of assistant superintendent under Supt. John S. Kaiser of the Denver office; that on my return from New Mexico I was to take the place of Asst. Supt. Carver, who had just resigned to accept a place under Special Agent Ben Williams of the A. T. & S. F. Ry.

I told Mr. McCartney that I didn't want the position of assistant superintendent, but he wouldn't take no for an answer. He told me to take a week to think the matter over carefully, and then to write my decision to Supt. John S. Kaiser, so that my letter could be forwarded to the eastern headquarters.

After reaching Roswell, New Mexico, I wrote a letter refusing the promotion, under the pretense that I didn't think office work would suit my complexion after having led an active outdoor life so long; though in truth I refused it because I didn't consider my education finished. For to accept the assistant superintendency, would be like a pupil in a college taking a position as assistant professor. The facts are, I started out in the Dickenson school to serve fifteen years. Then the time was extended to twenty years, as I found there was much more to learn of the world's ways.

On starting out with the Dickensons, I had just fin-ished "fifteen years on the hurricane deck of a Spanish pony," in the strenuous cowboy school, and I concluded that another fifteen years in the equally strenuous Dickenson College would complete my education; but this school was found to be great and broad, so that a twenty years' course would be short enough.

Boarding a Colorado Southern Ry. train, I started for Amarillo, Tex. There a transfer was made onto a Pecos Valley train of the A. T. & S. F. system.

The journey from Amarillo, Texas, to Portales, New Mexico, an all day ride in a railway coach, was over the level staked plains, and was a rare treat to me. Over this same ground I had ridden horseback, with not a single inhabitant between the L X ranch twenty miles north of Amarillo, southwesterly to Roswell, New Mex-ico, a distance of about 200 miles. This was in 1877 and 1878. Now my train speeds along through a coun-try of fine white ranch and farm houses, with a wind-mill on nearly every section of land. What a wonderful change in about twenty-seven years.

On coming in sight of the Paloduro (head of the Red river) Canyon to our left, I saw the once favorite camp-ing place for Indian and Mexican buffalo hunters. Here after the New Year in 1877, W. C. Moore (the cowboy outlaw seen in Alaska) Jack Ryan, Vanduzan and myself camped, down in the breaks of the Paloduro, where Van-duzan had killed a fat bear. And that day I saw my first Indian buffalo hunt with lances.

Leaving my companions in camp, I had joined a band of fifty Apache Indians and we rode out to a large herd of buffalo which were grazing where my train is now gliding along. The herd numbered about 20,000 to 50,000 head. When within half a mile of the woolly beasts our Indian chief placed us all abreast close together so as to fool the buffaloes who couldn't figure out what kind of an animal we were. They would have stampeded from the sight of horsemen approaching them in a haphazard fashion; but as it was, we were within 100 yards of them before they broke into a run. Then the race of life and death began. We were soon right in the midst of the herd at the tail end. For awhile I did nothing but watch the Indians do their expert lancing. Each buck would run up by the side of a buffalo and reaching over, stick the sharp steel or stone lance, which were fastened to long poles, into the animal's loin. Down the poor brute would go, helpless, but not killed. Then Mr. Buck would select another and another victim for slaughter.

One old grey-haired Indian buck on a large yellow horse, leaned far over in his stirrup and drove the lance home, but his weight on the handle broke it, and off he tumbled and rolled over and over in the short buffalo grass. I happened to be following close behind. It was comical to see this Indian, after he had gained his feet, dodging the buffaloes which were bringing up the rear. They tried to keep out of his way, but in his excitement he would run in front of them. One old bull jumped almost over his head and knocked him down. Then he 'sat still and the rest went around him.

At the windup I emptied my Colts 45 pistol and killed three bulls; my aim being just at the lower edge of the hump. Here the bullet enters the "lights" and does the work.

After the battle was over there were several hundred crippled buffalo scattered along the trail. They were unable to rise to their feet, but otherwise much alive.

I remained to see the several hundred bucks and squaws who had followed behind, kill the wounded animals. Then I rode back to camp in time for the bearmeat supper. Of course I had brought along the humps of the buffalo killed by me.

Soon the train rounded the head of Paloduro Canyon, and here to the right, a few hundred yards, stood the log cabin house built by the Dyer brothers (brothers-in-law of Cattle King Charlie Goodnight) in 1878; this being the first house built between the L X ranch and Roswell. At that time Charlie Goodnight had his ranch at the mouth of Paloduro Canyon about twenty-five miles further east. All around this old Dyer log house now waived fields of ripening grain, and nearby stood up-to-date farm homes.

Finally we crossed Running Water, thence past a large "dry" lake which had looked good to me in the summer of 1881. At that time I was returning with the remnants of my men from a raid after "Billy the Kid" and his gang and the cattle which they had stolen and run into Lincoln County, New Mexico, the winter previous. This raid had resulted in the killing and capture of the whole gang.

We struck this "dry" lake with 2,500 head of famished cattle which had had no water for two days and nights; hence were almost crazy. We and our mounts were about dead for water, too. The bottom of this lake bed contained about two feet of rainwater, which proved a godsend to us. We had been lost, but wouldn't give up the ship by turning the cattle loose.

My cowboys were Frank Clifford ("Big Foot Wallace," afterwards an outlaw), Tom Emory and Lon. Chambers. The last two were in the battle which put "Billy the Kid" out of business, and placed two of his gang, Charlie Bowdre and Tom O'Falliard under the sod. They and Jim East, another of my men, were with Sheriff Pat Garrett when the fight took place.

On flew the train over familiar ground, finally stopping in the lively town of Portales. Here at Las Portales Lake, "Billy the Kid" and his gang had their headquarters in the early days, while stealing cattle. At a fresh water spring coming out of a cliff of rock they had a camp and a stone corral.

From here the train descended from the staked plains down into the Pecos Valley, and in the evening dumped me out in the beautiful little city of Roswell, New Mexico.

Late that evening I walked down the main street of Roswell, and there in front of a real estate office sat my old cowboy friend Tom Emory.

But seeing Emory so often in the weeks following brought back memories of bygone days; for right here in this very spot in the spring of 1881 I had left him to guard the steers which we had recovered from parties to whom they had been sold by "Billy the Kid," while I took Lon Chambers and "Big Foot Wallace" down the Pecos river to attend the roundup on John Chisolm's range, in search of other stolen cattle.

At that time, John Chisolm, whose home ranch was five miles below Roswell, and which is now the beautiful home of millionaire J. J. Hagerman, ranged 60,000 cattle, where now live nearly that many human beings.

And within a stone's throw of where Tom Emory now sits smoking, stands the same adobe residence where Emory took his meals with the family of Capt. J. C. Lea,—one of nature's genuine noblemen, now dead,—during my absence.

In those days Roswell contained two stores, one owned by Capt. J. C. Lea and the others by a Mr. Cosgrove. There were, not to exceed a dozen houses in the town, and Emory used to graze his steers where the busy streets now are, and watch them from the Lea store where he was wont to sit and smoke in the shade, just as he is doing now.

During the forenoon the day after my arrival, I stepped into the Citizens National Bank to make a deposit, and my old friend John W. Poe, the president of the institution stepped to the window to wait on me. I gave him my name as Chas. Tony Lloyd and this threw him off the track. We met several times afterwards and he never recognized me.

Seeing John W. Poe brought back other memories, for I was the direct cause of his first coming to New Mexico, where he has lived ever since and accumulated an independent fortune by having the foresight to see the future of Roswell and the Pecos Valley.

In the winter of 1880 I had followed a herd of cattle supposed to be stolen, to Las Cruces on the Rio Grande river. and there from the notorious desperado "Hurricane

Bill" I found out their destination was Tombstone, Ariz. Then I wrote to my boss, W. C. Moore in Texas, to send a good man by rail and stage to Tombstone, Ariz., to investigate this cattle herd, as I couldn't go that far from my outfit, then in White Oaks.

John W. Poe was a deputy U. S. Marshal in Mobeeta, Texas, with a name for honor and bravery, so Moore employed him for the trip to Arizona; but he reached there too late, the herd having been scattered over that wild country and all trace of them lost. Then Moore ordered Poe to Doña Ana and Lincoln Counties, New Mexico, to prosecute the parties who had "stood in" with "Billy the Kid" in the stealing of L X cattle, as per my reports.

Later when Pat. Garrett's term of office expired, John W. Poe was elected sheriff of Lincoln County, which then embraced a wild territory almost 200 miles square.

After becoming settled in Roswell, I called on Attorney W. W. Gatewood, then my operation was started.

I made many new acquaintances here and was taken out buggy riding often, among the flowing artesian wells and lovely farms and orchards. It was indeed a treat to see the change from an untamed cattle country to fruit and flowers. And a drive through "Lovers Lane," the former ranch home of John W. Poe, on a hot summer's day is next to paradise, especially if the girl is a "good looker."

In Roswell I became well acquainted with Gen. Sherman Bell, who dished out to the Western Federation of Miners in Colorado, some of their own bitter medicine. They made a great howl about being deported from their

21

homes, contrary to the Constitution of the United States; but in these howls they failed to mention the hundreds of non-union men termed "scabs," dragged from the bosom of their families and set adrift without food or shelter in dead of winter by them. I know whereof I speak, for I helped them do it in the Coeur D'Alenes, and the only crime committed by the poor "scabs" was trying to earn an honest living by the sweat of their brows.

This is not meant to condemn all members of the Western Federation of Miners, as that would be unjust. I venture to say that half of the members of that great and powerful organization are kindhearted, law-abiding citizens who are deluded and led astray by rank, bloodthirsty blatherskites.

Gen. Sherman Bell was in Roswell for his health, and to hobnob with cowboy Charlie Ballard and U. S. Dist. Att. Maj. Llewellyn, who had helped him and "Teddy" Roosevelt storm San Juan hill in Cuba.

I remained in Roswell over a month, and before leaving, our side came out with flying colors, while poor old Uncle Samuel took a back seat. But during this legal battle I learned some new lessons in high finance and official trickery, which would have caused President Roosevelt's model teeth and massive jaws to snap together like a steel trap, could he have peeped behind the curtains.

One day previous to my departure, I couldn't resist the temptation of making myself known to my old cowboy chums, Phelps and Tom White, nephews of the old time Texas Cattle Kings, George and Jim Littlefield; the White boys being now wealthy.

Of course we had to "hark back" to old times, and in doing so, Phelps White added a little new history to my cowboy life.

In the late Spring of 1877 at St. Joe, Texas, mounted on my pet racehorse "Whisky Pete," and wearing a satisfied smile decorated with a sprouting mustache, I hired out to the boss of one of the Littlefield trail herds numbering 3,700 head of mixed cattle, en route to Dodge City, Kansas. I was given the job of horse wrangler,—taking care of the "ramutha," about 100 head of saddle horses.

In crossing through the ten mile belt of heavy blackjack timber near Red River, which is the Texas and Indian Territory line, the boss detailed Phelps White, who was then too young to support a mustache, though old enough to "tote" a Winchester rifle and a Colts 45 pistol, to help me through the "blackjacks."

I was trailing the "ramutha" several miles behind the cattle herd, taking my time, when young White and his heavy artillery appeared on the scene. He was informed that his help was not needed as the horses were no trouble. Still, he remained and helped me through the timber.

And now after keeping silent twenty-eight years he comes out with the truth that I was suspected of being a horse thief, and they feared that my Indian Territory pals might be in hiding in this "crosstimber" to help me steal the whole "ramutha." Hence the boss sending him back to help me.

They could hardly be blamed for their suspicions, for I was a tough looking kid and had spent the previous winter among the Chickasaw Indians in the Indian Territory.

While with Tom and Phelps White they introduced me to my old friend Tom Emory, and I found out that he had once recognized me down in Casas Grandes, Old Mexico, but having heard that I was with the Dickensons he thought it best not to speak to me.

I was also made known to my old friends J. S. Lea, now county treasurer of this, Chaves County, and Andy M. Robertson, a prosperous business man of Roswell.

Phelps White pointed out to me old "Uncle Henry" Stephens whom I knew in my boyhood days when he was one of the largest cattle drovers of the old Chisholm Trail, between southern Texas and Kansas. He now represents a Kansas City commission firm, as his great wealth has taken wings and "flewd" away.

In leaving Roswell on my return to Denver, I concluded to try J. W. Stockard's new automobile passenger line over the 107 miles of unsettled country to Torrance, at the junction of the new Rock Island and New Mexico Central railways. I did this so as to visit my pets at Santa Fe.

Bright and early one morning we started with the big Red Devil and the Little Red Imp loaded with gasoline and half a dozen passengers. It was raining hard and the mud flew thick and fast. About night we had reached Charlie Ballard's cattle ranch fifteen miles out of Roswell, and a few of us hired a rancher to take us back to the starting point in his carriage. It was late in the night when we reached Roswell.

This was my second and last ride in an automobile.

The trip was worth something though, as I learned some new cuss words.

I thought of the story about the western farmer who had never heard of automobiles and the green cowboy who had never seen a hay mower, but had heard of automobiles. The angry farmer was on his way to the cross-road town to get an unruly hay mower fixed, at a time when his hay needed cutting. He met the cowboy whose hide was full of "red licker," who stopped him and asked:

"Say mister, is that a au-to-mo-bele?"

The hayseeder replied: "I dunno,—the d—d thing au-to-mo-hay, but it won't."

That was the way with the Stockard Red Devils,—they au-to have landed us in Torrance, but they didn't, thus spoiling my chance of swapping smiles with Eat-Em-Up-Jake.

Next morning I boarded a train for Denver, returning over the same route that I had come.

CHAPTER XXI

A Cowboy Operation in Eastern Oregon—A Trip
to Sombrerete, Old Mexico—A Visit to the
Coeur D'Alenes with James McParland—Laying for Train Holdups in Nebraska—An Operation in Mexico City.

On returning home from Roswell I was sent at once
to Santa Fe, New Mexico, in response to a telegram
from Absolom Stuck, a wealthy retired merchant of that
place who wanted a shrewd detective sent on the first
train.

On arriving in the Ancient City of the Holy Faith,
I found Mr. Stuck greatly worked up over the receipt
of a threatening letter demanding that a large sum of
money be dropped by him at a certain out-of-the-way
place at midnight, on a designated night, or he would be
killed and his fine residence blown up.

Deputy U. S. Marshal Fred Fornoff and U. S. Postal
Inspector A. P. Smithers had started to work on the
case. I joined them and we three worked together for
the next couple of weeks.

We finally decided that the letter had been written as
a bluff, with a chance that Mr. Stuck would get scared
and drop the cash in the roadway, as requested; but we
advised that a guard be kept around the residence at
night, though I didn't think that an attempt would be
made on Mr. Stuck's life, which has proven correct, as

the old gentleman is very much alive up to the present time.

On leaving Denver I had wired to Silver City, New Mexico, for my daughter Viola to meet me in Santa Fe. She had just completed her education in the Territorial Normal College of that place, and therefore was at leisure.

Mounted on offsprings of my race mare Lulu, Viola and I had some exciting races after jackrabbits, led by Eat 'Em Up Jake and Klondike.

Viola enjoyed the races after the jackrabbits, but she hated Eat 'Em Up Jake for his bloodthirsty cruelty in killing the poor bunnies after having them in his power.

After a pleasant two weeks spent with Viola and my Pets, at Mr. Stuck's expense I returned to Denver, thankful to the gentleman who had sent the threatening letter. It is only the ill winds which scatter roses and thorns in the pathway of a Dickenson sleuth. On this occasion the thorns were omitted and placed under Mr. Stuck's feet.

A day in Denver and I was off for Steamboat Springs in the heart of the Rockies, to investigate the burning of a lumber mill for R. H. Manning and his associates in the First National Bank of that place.

A lovely trip over the mountain range on the new Moffat Railway brought me to the terminus at Hot Sulphur Springs. From there I had to make an eighty mile stage ride to Steamboat Springs near the corner of Utah and Wyoming.

While on this operation I made trips into the mountains on deer hunts.

In the town of Yampa I was introduced to Attorney F. E. Brooks, one of Colorado's U. S. Congressmen, but I didn't tell him of how I dodged him and played his client Duke, in Tucson, A. T., "double" during the Clark-Duke mining suit.

After a couple of weeks work in the mountains I placed the crime of setting the Manning mill afire at the door of another mill man, and a bitter enemy. But as he had evidently committed the crime alone, I concluded that it would require several months' time at great expense, to get evidence sufficient to convict. I had gained the friendship of this no doubt guilty party, and he and I hunted deer together.

On meeting the clients in Steamboat Springs I advised against retaining me there unless they felt willing to spend a large sum of money for a conviction, with only a chance of success, as we might fail. They agreed to my advice, and I boarded a stage for Wolcott Station on the D. & R. G. Ry., a distance of over eighty miles over a route which I had traveled on a previous operation.

A week's rest in Denver and I was away for a long operation in the far-off golden west.

On arriving in Portland, Oregon, I called at our office there and consulted with the Supt., Capt. Jas. Bevins and the Asst. Supt. D. G. Doogan, both of whom I was already acquainted with.

An attempt had just been made near Seattle, Washington, to rob a Great Northern Ry. train, and Capt. Bevins took me along with him to investigate this train holdup.

Phil. Berne, an ex-operative friend of mine was the superintendent of the Seattle office, hence I was not a stranger in that city.

Here I put in a couple of weeks and experienced a touch of high life in the lower stratum of society, my work being mostly among the dance-hall "girls" in the six concert halls there.

After running down several clues and getting evidence against suspects, I returned to Portland to take up the operation which had brought me to the far west.

Capt. Bevins, who had the supervision of the Portland, Seattle and Spokane offices, returned to Portland in time to see me off for eastern Oregon on my important operation which had been held for me several months.

I went to Shaniko by rail. There I boarded a stage coach and traveled about seventy-five miles over a rocky road to Prineville, the county seat of Crook County, Oregon, in the eastern part of the state.

In Prineville, a prosperous town of 2,000 people, I secured a nice room and settled down for a long stay. My room was in the house of Judge Bell, and he and his wife made my stay a pleasant one. They were a fine old couple who had lived in Oregon for about fifty years.

Prineville is the center of the finest horse country in the United States, and the rough lava hills are alive with wild horses. There are also many large cattle ranches, but the cattle have to be fed hay in winter, as the snow gets pretty deep at times. The horses require no feed as they can paw the snow from the wild bunch grass in the rocky cliffs.

I adopted the name of Chas. Tony Lloyd and palmed myself off as a horse dealer. I opened a bank account with the First National Bank, and had my first money come through my friend John W. Poe, President of the Citizens National Bank of Roswell, New Mexico, so as to show that I was from that territory.

Owing to it being November, the range horse business was at a standstill, except a few small bunches sold at auction.

At one of these auction sales shortly after my arrival, I made myself solid as a cowboy by roping horses by both front feet. Previous to this there was doubt about my ever having been a cowboy. I had purchased five head of broncos at this sale, and they had to be branded in my own "iron," which had just been recorded.

In order to test my cowboy abilities it was agreed that Charlie Bedell, one of their crack ropers, a young man who stands six feet in his socks and is built from the ground up, and whose face stands "ace high" with the girls, and I were to get in the corral and catch these five horses by the front teeth; the one who caught the greatest number to be the winner.

Luck seemed to be on my side, although I had had very little practice for many years. I never missed a throw and caught four head, while poor Bedell only had one to his credit. He didn't object to "setting 'em up" to the large crowd, so much as being beaten by a "foreigner"; for the Oregon boys think they can beat the world at roping and riding.

For reckless riding over rocky hills the Oregon boys can't be beaten; but if their mounts were not the most sure footed animals on earth, the graveyards there would be more plentiful.

The winter was spent in making friends with the wild and woolly element, scattered over the thinly settled mountainous country for a hundred miles east and south. Trips were made through this country, and a few horses bought or traded for, as a "blind."

Finally I received orders to discontinue the operation and return to Portland. Therefore the dozen head of horses then on hand were sold, and I made preparations to leave under the pretense that I was going to Alaska. My work had been successful. I cannot disclose the nature of the operation as the agency may have other work to do on it.

As a whole I found the people of Crook county, Oregon, good open-hearted citizens, and among them were some pretty girls. One of these, a Miss Dora Crane, woke up little Cupid so that he gave me a dig or two in the ribs with his dart. I had to visit her brother Charlie who owned a horse and cattle ranch up the Ochico River, quite often, and Miss Dora and the cute little dimples in her cheeks did the cooking for us.

On the first day of May, 1906, my friends were bidden goodby and I boarded a four-horse stage coach for Shaniko at the terminus of the Columbia Southern Railway.

In Portland I received instructions from Supt. B. A. Cuppel, who had recently taken the place of Capt. James Bevins, who had resigned to try ranch life on his farm in the state of Washington, to hurry on to Denver, as Mr. Jas. McCartney wanted to use me. I then bought a ticket for Denver, Colo., over the Union Pacific railway, and at Echo we got mixed up in a bad washout, with no prospects of getting through for a week.

I then returned to Portland and went to Spokane, Wash., over the Northern Pacific railroad. But in Spokane I found there were no trains running over the Union Pacific line out of there, owing to washouts. There was nothing to do but lay over all day and take the Northern Pacific by way of Butte City, Mont.

In the Dickenson office here I had a pleasant visit with Supt. J. G. Gascom and his assistant, George Jamesworth, who was an operative with me in the Chicago office twenty years previous. Also met Mr. George D. Bangs, the general manager of the whole Dickenson system, with headquarters in New York City; and Tom F. Kipple, general superintendent of the Portland, Seattle and Spokane offices since the resignation of Capt. Bevins, Mr. Bangs and Mr. Kipple had just arrived from Seattle.

My plans were changed by the receipt of a telegram to meet Mr. James McCartney who would leave Denver next day, in Boise, Idaho.

At 10 P. M. Mr. Bangs and I boarded a N. P. train for Butte, Mont. There we branched off on the Union Pacific for Pocatello, Idaho, where we separated, he going east to Denver and I west to Boise City, the capital of Idaho.

I arrived in Boise a few hours after Mr. McCartney. On meeting him at the Idan-ha Hotel he informed me that contrary to his wishes the Dickenson brothers had insisted that he have me and old Colts 45 accompany him on his trips to Idaho in the future. For it had been learned through secret sources that an attempt would be made on his life by the Western Federation of Dynamiters.

In the early part of the year Ex-Governor Steunenburg of Idaho had been blown up and killed at his home in Caldwell, Idaho. A bomb had been placed at his gate by Harry Orchard, one of the inner-circle of the Western Federation of Miners. Orchard was arrested on suspicion after the murder, and Mr. Jas. McCartney was sent for by Governor Frank R. Gooding of Idaho, and he secured a full confession from Orchard as to how he had been paid by the officials of the Western Federation of Miners to murder enemies of their noble order. He had only helped to blow up twenty-six in all. He had made a big killing when he blew up the Independence railroad depot in the Cripple Creek, Colo., district, killing thirteen so-called "scabs" and maiming many others for life.

Governor Steunenburg in the Coeur D'Alene riots of 1899 had offended this Noble Order of Dynamiters by putting many of them in the "bull-pen," and for doing his sworn duty, as he saw it, he was marked for a horrible death; this being done to intimidate other officials. But in this they underestimated the true, noble qualities implanted in most men whom the people elect to run the Ship of State.

Governor F. R. Gooding, despite the threats of murder through the mail and otherwise, went to work with heart and soul ablaze with right and justice, to run down the murderers of his predecessor in office.

At the Idan-ha Hotel I found our agency conducting a miniature branch office with operative Thiele and stenographer H. in charge and doing the open work. The secret operatives being kept in the dark.

In company with Mr. McCartney I visited the Idaho penitentiary several times, and saw the noted Harry Orchard who had confessed; also Steve Adams who later confessed to Mr. McCartney in order to save his own neck. He too, says he was employed by the Western Federation of Miners to murder enemies. His confession unravels many mysteries wherein detectives and others have been "put out of the way."

The warden of the penitentiary, E. L. Whitney, proved to be an old-time cowboy, he and I having worked for the same Texas cattleman, W. B. Grimes, in 1876; hence we "harked back" to the good old days of pure air, poison liquor, "snap and ball" pistols and long horn steers.

At the penitentiary I found an old acquaintance in the person of Rube Robbins who had been a "bad" man chaser in Idaho for thirty-one years. He had taken part in the Coeur D'Alene Miners' Union trouble of 1892, under Governor Wiley's administration, and it was then we first met.

In the county jail in Boise my friend, George A. Pettibone, the dynamiter who blew up the Frisco Mill at Gem, Idaho, in 1892, was now sleeping behind steel bars. With him were President Moyer and Secretary Haywood of the Western Federation of Dynamiters. They were being held for the murder of Governor Steunenburg.

According to the confessions of Orchard and Adams, Pettibone is the wretch who placed the bomb and pocketbook on a cut-off trail across a vacant lot in Denver, to blow up Judge Gabbert of the Colorado Supreme Court. But a poor stranger coming across the lot in the opposite direction from the Judge, picked up the pocketbook and the buried bomb did the rest, leaving only a hole in the ground and pieces of flesh and bones. Pettibone witnessed the scene from a distance, according to these confessions.

In the course of a week Mr. McCartney and I went to the town of Caldwell where Governor Steunenburg was blown up. We put up at the same hotel where Orchard made his headquarters previous to the murder.

While in Caldwell I saw the widow of Governor Steunenburg and his sons who are bankers there. I also saw the spot where the bomb did its hellish work.

Finally Mr. McCartney and I made a trip to Spokane, Wash. Here many of my old Coeur D'Alene friends were met, among them being "Mace" Campbell and John A. Finch, and their secretary, W. A. Corey; also William Finch, Wm. T. Stoll, the attorney, and the merchant prince, F. R. Culbertson; and last but not least, the fighting sheriff of Shoshone County, Idaho, Mr. Angus Sutherland.

Angus Sutherland had much to tell me of the ups and downs of his county in the Coeur D'Alene mining district after I left in 1892; how he had to fight the dynamiters, and how my friend Dr. Simms, was shot through the head and killed as he was coming out of the theater in Wallace; also the killing of Kneebone and Whitney and many others. In fact his narrative was sprinkled with human gore enough to float a small steamer.

From Spokane Mr. McCartney and I returned to Boise, thence a few days' visit in Salt Lake City, Utah, where I met many former friends. Here "Tex." Rickard presented McCartney with his pet Colts 45 pistol, which he had carried for years.

After over a month of high living at Idaho's expense, we returned to Denver.

My next out-of-the-city operation was a trip to the State of Zacatecas, Old Mexico, for Mr. Pierce Akerman of Colorado Springs, Colo.

Of course, I had to go by way of Santa Fe, New Mexico, to visit Eat 'Em Up Jake and my other pets, including Mr. J. W. Best, my foreman, and old man Atwood who had worked for me on the ranch off and on for many years.

A six hundred mile ride from El Paso, Texas, on the bumpity-bump old Mexican Central Railway, after two long delays on account of wrecks, in which two men were killed, and I arrived in Gutierrez, Mexico. Here at midnight I boarded a six-mule stage coach for a seventy-five mile ride over a rocky road to Sombrerete, a mining camp of 8,000 dark-colored souls. We arrived at our destination the following evening.

An interesting traveler on the stage coach with me was an elderly American gentleman by the name of G. He was going to Sombrerete to round up a 12-year-old boy whom he had found out had a nose just like himself.

Mr. G. had been absent several years from Sombrerete and had become well-fixed financially, near the City of

Guadalajara, Mexico. He said this boy must ue a chip off the old G. block, hence he intended to give him a fine college education in the United States. In Sombrerete, later, Mr. G. showed me this boy after he had been scrubbed up and put into knee-pants, and he showed me the peculiarity of his own nose and of the boy's. There was no doubt in my mind as to where this boy got his nose.

The lad's mother who had other younger children, hated to part with her son, but the promise of a college education for the boy, won the battle for old man G.

Who knows but what this is the starting of another nosy race of people, and who can divine the intentions of old Mother Nature in this case? I tried to peep into the future about 1,000 years, and in imagination I could see a populous race of men with noses just like the elder G. and his son. And in their family trees I read how 'way back in the dim and dusty past, one Mr. G. who was of a roving disposition, left his native land of California and settled in Sombrerete, Mexico, where he married a princess of royal blood and begot sons and daughters.

Thus, in my mind's eye, could I see history repeating itself "all same" when the Spanish soldiers and dons started the foundation of the Mexican race; and the hardy French trappers of the north established the French Canadians; and other Frenchmen in the south laid the foundation stones of the Creoles. Of course they all sprang from royal blood, now that old Father Time has washed away their sins.

Mother Nature seems to have her own peculiar way

in which to improve the human races, and in doing so, she uses the poor white man as catspaws to pull her own chestnuts out of the fire. I could even see at the end of these thousand years where the old lady had completely straightened out the kinks in the negroes' hair.

In Sombrerete and the surrounding country I spent over a month.

In La Noria, a mining camp twenty miles north of Sombrerete, I made the acquaintance of B. Clark W., the energetic ex-son-in-law of the once noted governor of Colorado, "Bloody Bridles" Waite.

I knew Mr. W. in Aspen, Colo., in the early days, but he didn't recognize me as the Chas. Leon he met there in the year 1888. Mr. W. treated me to high wines, and without knowing it, divulged secrets which I had come after. He supposed I was a mining man looking for investments. He himself is operating the La Noria silver mine and has working for him several hundred men.

I also worked on many of Mr. W.'s friends and associates.

On this trip I was using the name of Chas. T. Lloyd.

In Sombrerete I met half a dozen pleasant Americans. Among them was young Arkins, a son-in-law of the wealthy Arkins of New York who founded the "Judge" which is read all over the world; also a jolly Irishman by the name of "Christoval" Mansfield. He and his good wife forced me to be their guest for Sunday dinners. Of course this was a treat, as the hotel food was "on the bum," same as it is all over Montezumaland.

My work being finished, I appointed Mr. Adriano

Agualda, a wealthy Mexican lawyer, to look after our clients' interests, which footed up about $100,000.00. He was instructed to have the trap set and ready to spring at a moment's notice. This freed me, so I boarded the stage at midnight during a howling rain and wind storm, for the railroad station of Gueteras. There the next evening I boarded a railroad train for El Paso, Texas; thence on to Denver, by way of Eat 'Em Up Jake's den.

On arriving in Denver, Supt. "Hank" Geary went with me to Colorado Springs, Colo., to close up the operation with the clients, Mr. Pierce Akerman, Mr. Robert Tolles and Attorney Wm. Breen.

Soon after returning home I had to accompany Mr. Jas. McCartney on another trip to the northwest to see that dynamiters didn't blow him off the face of the earth.

We stopped awhile in Boise, Idaho, and visited Harry Orchard, the self-confessed murderer of Governor Steunenburg, in the state penitentiary.

During our absence the other Western Federation dynamiter, Steve Adams, had been transferred to the county jail as his wife and uncle had been there and persuaded him to go back on his confession in order to help the officials of the Western Federation of Miners.

On this trip in Boise I met many of my former friends in the Coeur D' Alenes; among them being U. S. Judge James H. Beatty, Judge Fremont Wood, ex-U. S. Marshal Joe Pinkham, T. A. Doud, and last but not least, U. S. Senator W. B. Heyburn, all of whom had taken part against the dynamiters after the first riots in 1892.

Much of our time was spent in the office of Jas. H. Hawley & Son, laying plans to outwit the Western Federation attorneys so as to get Steve Adams to Wallace, Idaho, without taking him through an outside state.

In order to reach Wallace in the Coeur D'Alenes by rail, it is necessary to travel several hundred miles either through Oregon and Washington or Montana, and in passing through these states we felt confident that Clarence Darrow, the leading attorney for the Western Federation, would get out habeas corpus papers to delay matters.

Finally sheriff Angus Sutherland arrived from Shoshone County in the Coeur D'Alenes, with a warrant for Steve Adams on a murder charge. After the court had turned Adams over to the sheriff, the Western Federation lawyers and their helpers had guards out all night so that Adams couldn't be taken out of town without their knowing it. But here we played a "dirty Irish trick" and got him headed north in a covered rig. He was taken most of the way overland to avoid entering other states. J. C. Mills, Jr., Deputy Warden, and Geo. C. Huebner, chief clerk of the pen, helped to smuggle Adams out into the cold night air.

Warden Whitney of the penitentiary, and state detective Gene Johnson accompanied the sheriff and his prisoner across the rough mountains, hundreds of miles north into the Panhandle of Idaho.

When Attorney Darrow and his associates found that their bird had flown, they gave vent to a string of sulphuric oaths which would have scorched the lips of some people, so I was told. But they couldn't find out which way their vulture had "flew'd."

WALLA

The X marks the spot where the

DAHO.

r stood when the soldiers arrived.

A few days later Mr. McCartney and I boarded a train for Wallace, Idaho.

The Western Federation attorneys were in Wallace when we arrived, but their client, Steve Adams with his escorts, didn't arrive until a few days later.

Al. C. Watson and Chas H Burkhart, two of sheriff Nesbit's deputies from Denver, Colo., were also in Wallace to take charge of Steve Adams for murders committed in Colorado, in case the court here should liberate him.

Wallace seemed like home to me after my long absence of about fourteen years. More especially after viewing the high timbered mountain south of town where Frank Stark and I made our home until the soldiers arrived.

The town had built up and changed wonderfully. Only a few old landmarks like the Carter Hotel remained.

Also the faces of long ago had changed. Still, there were a few of my old friends and enemies left. Among the friends were: Judge W. W. Woods, Judge Mahew, Mr. E. H. Moffit, a leading merchant, Mr. Al. Dunn, postmaster, Mr. Jack Dunn of the Weekly Press and Robt. Dunn of the U. S. Land office; also Chas. E. Bender and Chas. White, leading merchants; M. J. Flohr, cashier of the First National Bank, Dr. Hugh France, Joseph Turner, lumberman and contractor, merchant J. W. Tabor and my good natured friend, Jerry M. Savage, who formerly owned the Gem Hotel, where I crawled through the window to escape dynamiters; and last but not least, J. G. Boyd, the trusted general agent of the N. P. Railroad in Wallace. It was he who turned the switch and gave the train load of Joe Warren "scabs" a clear track to Burk, while sheriff Cunningham and several hundred union miners, myself included, were eagerly waiting to capture the poor "scabs" and tear them to pieces if they refused to return from whence they had come.

Many of the old Miners' Union gang came from Burk and Mullen to see the dastardly Dickenson detectives, Jas. McCartney and Yours Truly. I recognized many of them and a few looked daggers at me. It was voiced around that they intended making a raid some night on Mr. McCartney and me. From that time on I kept a Winchester rifle and a supply of ammunition in my room, which adjoined Mr. McCartney's.

During the nights, up to bedtime, two learned anarchists who called themselves socialists, from Chicago, made speeches to large crowds on the streets. In these talks they would abuse the officers of the law and detectives in general. They would dare Mr. McCartney to come out and dispute their assertions. Often I would slip into the crowd and on the sly hear their harangue. But with the law-abiding people now in control of Shoshone County and with such brave officers as sheriff Angus Sutherland and his deputies: Thomas McCabe, Harry Williams, C. C. Hicks, William Baily and Phil Chandler, the latter being one of the "scabs" blown up with the Independence depot in Cripple Creek, Colo., at the helm, we felt reasonably safe.

. After a two weeks' stay in Wallace our "bad" man Steve Adams was bound over by the judge, J. H. Boomer, to the District Court, without bail. Then there was much gnashing of teeth by attorney Darrow and his anarchist friends. I came very near writing it social- ist friends, as that dynamiting "bunch" claim to be so- cialists, which ought to give a true, pure-hearted socialist the jim-jams.

According to my views there are many good points in socialism, which, if adopted, would make the world bet- ter; and for the men and women who strive for the betterment of mankind, I have the highest regard.

The charge against Steve Adams was murder. He, Jack Simkins, now a hunted outlaw, and some pals were accused of murdering two men in cold blood at the head of the St. Joe river in the Coeur D'Alenes.

The mother and stepfather of one of these murdered men gave damaging testimony against Adams, and so did Mr. Archie Phillips, whom the same Western Feder- ation gang tried to murder.

Mr. McCartney and I took the Coeur d'Alene lake route by rail and steamer for Spokane, Wash. In that city we laid over a couple of days and visited with our friends.

A couple of days' stop in Boise, Idaho, and Mr. Mc- Cartney and I returned to Denver, Colo.

I hadn't more than reached home when I was de- tailed to help our Kansas City, Mo., office spring a trap on some train holdups. The holdup was due to take place at a small station called Sweetwater on the C. B. & Q. railroad in Nebraska on a certain night. The railroad officials had got a tip that their No. 41 western passen- ger train was to be robbed. Hence they wished to kill or capture the gang while in the act.

Of course I took along my trusty old 30—40 caliber,

smokeless powder, Winchester rifle. I had been told that
the railroad company would furnish us sawed-off shot-
guns for the fight; but a Winchester rifle, and a Colts 45
pistol to "nigger" with, are good enough for Yours
Truly.

Of course I couldn't leave Kansas City without seeing
my old Caldwell, Kansas, friend, Frank Jones, the proprietor of the Jones liquor emporium, even though it
did mean a headache next day.

It was 3:00 o'clock A. M. when I bade Mr. Jones and
his friends goodby, after drinking them the following
toast:

Here's to wine enough to sharpen wit;
Wit enough to give zest to wine;
And wisdom enough to quit at the right time.

Then I "hiked" to the depot and, hic, tumbled into my
Pullman berth.

Early in the day assistant superintendent W. H.
Hart, and Jno. A. Hermanson had supplied me with
ammunition and instructed me to leave in the morning
for Omaha, Nebraska; hence taking my half-grown
"jag" into the Pullman sleeper so as to avoid getting up
to catch the train.

In Omaha, Nebraska, Mr. W. B. Coughman, the superintendent in charge of our office there, introduced me to
the operative who was to be my partner in guarding
train 41 from holdups. He happened to be a young man
after my own heart, whom I felt sure would stick to the
bitter end in case of a show-down.

This Mr. V. L. S. had been an officer under Ben. Williams, special agent of the A. T. & S. F. Ry., also town
marshal of coal camps in northern New Mexico, and

during these periods he had to use his gun more than once.

V. L. S. and I were sent to Lincoln, the capital of Nebraska, there to make our headquarters for the next few weeks.

Four other operatives were also sent to Lincoln to guard other trains running out of that city for the west; this being done as a precaution for fear the holdups might change their plans. But these operatives did their work in the western part of the state, as their trains left Lincoln in the day time.

For the first couple of weeks V. L. S. and I rode in the smoking car and kept our eyes peeled for holdup men. Our train No. 41 left Lincoln at 1:20 A. M. and we would remain aboard 'till after daylight, then get off at Broken Bow, west of the small station of Sweetwater, where the holdup was billed to come off. Then we would catch the eastbound passenger about 9:00 A. M. and return to Lincoln, so as to be ready to take 41 out again the following night. This allowed us from four to six hours sleep in our room at Lincoln, when the return train was on time, which was seldom. Often we would not get to bed at all.

On the night that "41" was to be held up, an empty express car was coupled onto the train next to the engine, and in this, operative V. L. S. and I "sneaked," so no one outside of the conductor knew of our presence. When inside of this car we bolted the two side doors and awaited results. The car was kept dark inside.

That night Supt. Williston of the Kansas City office rode out of Lincoln to Broken Bow in the chair car, so as to be on the ground if the holdup occurred.

About an hour and a half before daylight No. 41 stopped to let off a passenger in Sweetwater station. Operative V. L. S. was guarding the north door, while I watched the south door. We each had our door open about six inches so as to see outside.

Just as our train pulled out, operative V. L. S. called me over to his side to point out three men hiding in some tall weeds about fifty yards from the track. We saw one of them stand up and then sit down again, and as soon as the train had got past them they all struck out towards the south. They were evidently holdup men who had smelled a "mice" on seeing this extra express car attached to the train, which was something unusual.

Operative V. L. S. and I had discussed the putting on of this extra express car and had decided it to be a mistake, as train robbers are not fools.

The railroad agent in Alliance reported selling a ticket to Sweetwater station the day before the robbery was to take place, and two on the day of the proposed holdup. This being something out of the ordinary, it may account for the three men seen in the weeds.

We rode in the express car the next night also, and were then ordered to discontinue the operation. Of course we were glad of it, as we had been losing sleep and rest for more than two weeks, and a cold blizzard had been raging most of the time.

Thus did another of my bloodless battles fade into thin air.

I then returned to Denver after bidding my partner goodby in Lincoln, he returning to Kansas City.

Secret information gained pointed to my friend Bob McGinnis, the train robber lately pardoned from the Santa Fe, N. M., penitentiary, as being connected with this proposed train holdup; also a railroad brakeman who had served a two or three years' sentence in the New Mexico "pen", and who had been a cell-mate of the notorious Bob McGinnis, alias Elza Lay.

On arriving in Denver I was detailed on an operation down in Old Mexico to run down a "bad" man who was supposed to be traveling with Col. W. C. White, the Cananea copper king, in his new private car, the Verde.

I arrived in El Paso, Texas, just in time to catch the Verde as she entered Mexico at that point. She had just come from Cananea, Mexico, through Arizona.

I rode on the same train with the Verde into the City of Mexico. There Col. White and his dozen companions were wined and dined by Mr. Diaz, the president of the Mexican Republic, while poor Yours Truly was wining and dining with Harry King, the negro chef of the Verde.

On the 1,200-mile journey to the Mexican capital from El Paso, Texas, I had made the acquaintance of this yellow New York "nigger" so as to get the names of Col. White's guests, and other secrets.

In taking in the swell hurrah resorts of the city I had to pass Harry King off as a rich Cuban. At one place the landlady got me off in one corner to ask on my word of honor if my chum was not a cottonfield "nigger." I assured the "lady" that the gentleman who tipped the scales at 240 pounds was a blue-blooded Cuban, whose ancestors were of royal descent.

A few days in Mexico City and we were off for Chihuahua, 600 miles north.

Before leaving the city I had the pleasure of examining the inside of the Verde, a palace on wheels. King showed me every nook and corner in the car. I also got to visit all the noted places of the city with the Greene party. They rode in carriages while I followed in a common hack.

In the city I found one old friend, Mr. J. W. Seibert, now superintendent of the Wells Fargo Company there. He was an assistant under Supt. Daniel Turner when I followed the Wells Fargo express robber to Mexico City in 1888. Now poor Turner is a patient in a sanitarium in California, so says Mr. Seibert.

From Chihuahua the Verde went a couple of hundred miles up into the Sierra Madre mountains, where Col. White and his associates are building a new railroad west, to connect with the Greene Cananea railway.

Up in these mountains I found a town named Detrick, after my old friend one-arm Sam Detrick who ran a "bull-train," freighting between Socorro and White Oaks, New Mexico, in 1880, '81 and '82. Now he is said to be quite wealthy. I thought it best not to make myself known to him, as he stands in with the Green outfit, and at that time I was not sure that our "bad" man was not a guest of Colonel White's. One of the men in the Verde answered the description of our "bad" man. I had found out this gentleman's name as he had claimed to be a wealthy capitalist from Waterbury, Conn. I was waiting until Supt. David C. Hornybill of our New York office could investigate the matter in Waterbury. I had wired in cypher, the full particulars to New York.

On arriving in El Paso, Texas, late one night I received a telegram from New York to the effect that the suspect was not our "bad" man. I then bade the Verde goodbye. She returned that morning to Cananea, Mexico.

Our New York client had put us on to this false scent, hence our, failure was not the fault of the agency. Possibly it was a put up job by kind Providence to give me a little winter outing in the tropics after my late tussle with blizzards in Nebraska.

While in El Paso, Texas, I had the pleasure of meeting my old friends, John Y. Hewett and Mr. E. W. Parker of White Oaks, New Mexico. I had not seen Mr. Parker for many years. He is now in the mining business in El Paso with his son Morris Parker. I had first met Mr. E. W. Parker in the spring of 1878, when he and a crowd of Uncle Sam's men were putting through the first mail line ever run over the staked plains of Texas.

The Parker crowd had camped near the L X ranch where there were about thirty cowboys getting ready for the spring round-up. As Parker kept his business to himself, we all suspected them as being Texas rangers in disguise, searching for outlaws; the outcome being that we only had half enough cowboys to start the round-up. About a dozen of our "boys" mounted their pet horses and struck out for "tall timber" in New Mexico and Arizona, where some of them helped to swell "Curly Bill's" outlaw gang.

One of these "boys" who left for Arizona was known to us as a "bad" Texas outlaw. He was supposed to be dead, though. His wealthy uncle had built a fine monument over his supposed grave down in the settlements; this being done to throw the officer off the track. One of his former chums, Cape Willingham, had told the secret to me; hence I was not surprised when George skipped by the light of the stars while Mr. Parker and his crowd of supposed sleuth-hounds were asleep.

We heard of other cattle outfits being short of round-up hands that spring, on account of the presence of this star-route mail-line gang.

I landed in Denver after an absence of about three weeks.

A few days' rest and I was off with Manager Jas. McCartney for Boise, Idaho.

In Boise we visited Harry Orchard in the penitentiary and made other preparations for the coming trial of the Western Federation officials.

The Supreme Court of the United States had just rendered a decision that these dynamiters had not been kidnapped by the Dickenson agency and the Idaho officials out of Colorado where they were arrested; hence there was nothing to prevent the case being brought into court now, to determine if these high union officials really had a hand in the murder of ex-Governor Steunenburg.

Mr. McCartney was anxious to eat Christmas dinner with his wife and little niece in Denver, therefore we hurried back.

On our return we stopped a couple of days in Salt Lake City, Utah. We got back to Denver on Christmas eve. This ended my third trip into the northwest as Mr. McCartney's bodyguard.

ORCHARD AND GUARDS.

Reading from left to right:
1. Pen Guard Ackley.
2. Harry Orchard.
3. R. Barthell.
4. Chas A. Siringo.
5. Bob Meldrum.
6. Warden Whitney.

CHAPTER XXII.

In Idaho with Dynamiters—A Cowboy Operation in the Bad Lands of South Dakota—I Resign from the Dickenson Agency.

During the first half of 1907 I led an easy life, with nothing to do but keep old Colts 45 well oiled for dynamiters and assassins.

I had to accompany that greatest of all detectives, James McCartney, who broke up the Molly McGuire gang—hanging twenty-three and sending thirty-two to the penitentiary—wherever he went. But during these noted trials McCartney would remain at his hotel, or visit with friends, while I helped guard Harry Orchard, the star witness for the prosecution. His life was too valuable to take chances on his assassination.

Orchard made a splendid witness at the different trials in Idaho. Thus did he make partial amends to society for the twenty-six men he helped to murder.

In summing up the Orchard evidence the judge on the bench, Fremont Wood, said he certainly told the truth, as no man could tell the same story at different times and not get mixed up in his statements; more so, under the cross-questioning of such able lawyers as Darrow and Richardson. Furthermore most of Orchard's testimony was corroborated by telegrams, letters and reliable witnesses.

At the wind-up Albert E. Horsley, alias Harry Orchard, was convicted for the murder of ex-Governor Steunenburg and sentenced to death. But shortly after, the death sentence was changed to life imprisonment, which was certainly just. In fact he should be put under parole and given his liberty. I would willingly stake my life that he has had a change of heart since that guiding angel, Geo. A. Pettibone, of the Western Federation of Miners, drilled him in the art of manufacturing bombs and exploding them. For according to the evidence it was this drill-master and his pupil who set the bomb for Judge Gabbert, of Denver, and blew the poor stranger, who picked up the pocketbook, into fragments. The pupil placed the bomb and pocketbook while the instructor looked on from a distance of two city blocks.

The State of Idaho, through her leading attorneys, Senator W. E. Borah and James H. Hawley, secured two "gun-men" to help guard Orchard when taken from behind the penitentiary walls. Their names were Bob Meldrum and R. Barthel; Meldrum being the man-killing town marshal of Dixon, Wyoming, at the time Jim F. of "Wild Bunch" fame, and I took in that burg.

When Mr. McCartney introduced us in Boise under my own name it was comical to see Meldrum's surprise. He remarked that he had met me as Harry Blevins, in Dixon, Wyoming.

Since our meeting in Boise, Meldrum has added to his record as a killer, by shooting a man in Telluride, Colo.

During the summer, in Boise, Idaho, I had a few years added to my life through the meeting of that great actress—Miss Ethel Barrymore.

This beautiful young actress was dying to see Harry

Orchard before returning East. But no one except court officials and his guards were allowed to see him, by strict orders from Governor Gooding.

Miss Barrymore had already pled with the governor, so I was told, but his heart was like a chunk of chilled steel. Then some one suggested that I might help her out. Just one smile and a "good-fellow" hand shake, and she had me kneeling at her feet, figuratively speaking. I informed her that my hands were tied without the consent of Mr. McCartney but that if she would act her part according to my instructions we could get his consent. She agreed.

I had learned that all men, no matter how old, have a weak spring in their make-up which can be snapped asunder by fair women, if they only go at it right. Of course I hated to put up a "job" on Mr. McCartney, but who wouldn't to make a pretty girl happy.

Mr. Gifford Pinchot, Chief of the United States Forest Service, was also anxious to see Orchard, therefore he accompanied Miss Barrymore and me to Mr. McCartney's private reception room. Mr. S. S. McClure, of the McClure Magazine, and the wife of the principal owner of the Idaho Statesman, Mrs. Calvin Cobb, also went along.

On introducing Miss Barrymore I started the ball to rolling by telling Mr. McCartney that I had assured the lady that he would not deny her request.

The play started when the young actress moved her chair close up to the gentleman, so that she could look him in the face.

When the one-act drama was over we all started in a

33

carriage for the penitentiary. Mr. McCartney had given me orders to let the lady see Orchard, but under no condition to let her speak to him That was sufficient, as all I wanted was an entering wedge.

On reaching the penitentiary I had warden Whitney bring Orchard from his steel cell to the warden's private office. Then I turned the natural born actress loose in the room with this star dynamiter, and she talked with him to her heart's content.

And I was repaid for all my trouble by having Miss Barrymore 'phone me after midnight to be at her train and say goodby. This I did, and her happy smile and warm hand-shake lingers with me to this day—nearly two years later.

During the Steve Adams trial in Wallace, Idaho, which terminated in a hung jury—that being no surprise, considering the large slush fund put up by the Western Federation of Miners to save his neck—I had the pleasure of visiting Gem where I made my getaway by sawing through the floor. Mr. McCartney's private secretary, Robt. Shollenbeger, went with me on horseback.

We saw bullet holes through old walls as reminders of those exciting times in 1892. I recognized many old landmarks—but only one live one in the person of Dan Harrington and his flowing grey beard.

On leaving Wallace and the Coeur D'Alene country we stopped for a few days in Spokane, Wash. We were accompanied by that whole-soul honest man, ex-sheriff Harvey K. Brown of Baker City, Oregon. But the poor fellow soon after met the same fate as ex-Governor Steunenburg, and in the same manner, a bomb being

Jas. McCartney and the Author.

placed at his residence gate. Here is Brown's dying statement, as copied from the Denver Post of October 2, 1907:

"BAKER CITY, OREGON, Oct. 2.
Harvey K. Brown, ex-sheriff of Baker county, died yesterday afternoon as the result of the horrible wounds he received from the explosion of a bomb at his front gate as he entered his home Monday night. Shortly before noon he recovered consciousness and his ante-mortem statement was taken by the district attorney. It follows:

" 'I was on my way home from up town when I met a man in front of a residence a block from my house, and spoke. The man made no reply. This man was about five feet ten inches tall, his weight about 165 pounds. He wore a brown suit and a celluloid collar and was clean shaven. I have been conscious of having been followed for the past three weeks, and have no doubt that those who attempted my life are persons connected with the Western Federation of Miners, and that I was marked for death on account of the Steunenburg and Steve Adams cases.' "

This illustrates the danger of being an important witness against that blood-thirsty dynamiting bunch, who some well-meaning people believe are angels.

Another prince of a good fellow blown up with dynamite, but not killed, soon after giving his testimony against this "noble order" was Mr. Bulkley Wells, manager and part owner of a rich mine in Telluride, Colo., the former manager of this mine, Mr. Arthur Collins, being shot and killed through a window by that villain, Steve Adams, according to his own, and Orchard's, sworn confession.

We have been expecting to hear of the assassination of Governor Frank Goodin, as his life has been threatened more than any one else, unless it is ex-Governor Jas. H. Peabody of Colorado, who has escaped two attempts at assassination.

All law-loving citizens should adore the names of

these two governors who did their duty in the face of hourly danger. This dynamiting brigade had, no doubt, figured that the blowing up of ex-Governor Steunenburg would put the fear of death in the hearts of other officials who believed in law and order. But they didn't reckon on that noble trait implanted in the breasts of some men which defies death, and even torture, when it comes to sacrificing principle and justice.

When the trial of Haywood, secretary and treasurer of the Western Federation was ended, and Mr. McCartland and I were back in Denver, Colorado, I resigned from the Dickenson Agency to try the "Simple Life" on my Sunny Slope ranch at Santa Fe, New Mexico.

I had not been out of the agency long when I was requested, by Mr. James McCartney, to undertake a cowboy operation up in the Bad Lands of South Dakota. Members of the South Dakota Stock Growers' Association, Mr. James Craig being president, and Mr. Frank Stewart secretary, were short thousands of steers and could not figure out what had become of them. Hence I was sent up there to unravel the mystery.

I spent the fall and winter in South Dakota working on cattlemen, cowboys and Indians. Much of my work being on the Pine Ridge and Rosebud Indian Reservations.

My reports showed where thousands of steers had been stolen and butchered, the year previous to my arrival, to furnish beef for the grading crews of the two new railroads, the Milwaukee and St. Paul, and the Northwestern, building west through that country.

Some of my cowboy chums, on whom I worked, had

become well fixed financially by butchering these cattle. Most of the stealing was done through half-breed Indians who lived on the reservations.

Much of my time was spent in Rapid City, Interior Kadoka, Wasta and the White Owl country. My name was Chas. Tony Lloyd. I experienced some hardships from the terrible blizzards which rage in that country during the winters. On closing the operation in the White Owl Country I had to ride in a cold blizzard for over one hundred miles, with snow belly-deep to a horse, in places, to the railroad town of Wasta.

I was indeed glad to get back and bask in the warm sunshine of New Mexico, and to be with my pets, Eat 'Em Up Jake and Rowdy, my favorite saddle stallion, the off-spring of Lulu; also Miss Pussy-cat, who has a history in connection with the "Wild Bunch;" she having been given to me when a wee kitten up in Ft. Steel, Wyoming, by cowboy Charlie Ivey, who little dreamed that this supposed Harry Blevins had once been a cowboy companion of his, in the early-day cattle business of Texas.

Mr. Geo. S. Tweedy, who was in charge of my ranch, had cared for my pets during my absence.

Now, dear reader, in closing my twenty-two years of experience in studying human nature, let me say that I have come to the conclusion that there is more good than bad in mankind. I believe most of the viciousness in man could be smothered by doing away with liquor and greed for the almighty dollar. For through these great evils I have seen bitter tears enough wrung from the eyes of men, women and children to float a washtub.

Saloon men should not be condemned for the liquor evil, for there are good, pure-hearted men among them. They are conducting a lawful business so long as they pay a license to the government. The people as a whole are to blame for not putting a stop to it by law; and at the same time establish poor men's club rooms to take the place of saloons, which are a blessing to a cold and hungry stranger when he lands in a town broke. Good men sometimes run short of cash and cannot pay for lodging in a warm hotel. Then is when the saloon is a godsend.

Every greedy old "Money-bag" in the land should be sat down on hard. I would be in favor of screwing his hands to a long-handle shovel, or a heavy wheel-barrow, for months at a time, to let him know how it feels to work ten hours a day to keep body and soul together, while such as he do nothing but gloat over gold, and wring the life-blood from humanity.

It is a great pity that old Father Time and Mother Nature cannot get married and start a new breed of cattle, with cows giving a large flow of the milk of human kindness. For then we would have something to feed to greedy capitalists and blood-thirsty labor union agitators.

Had I the power our glorious American flag would be constantly waving over every school house in this fair land. On one side would be printed in large letters of gold:

Down with liquor, cruelty and greed; up with manhood, kindness and virtue.

And on the other side:

Preservation of noble thoughts and deeds, for the upbuilding of ideal man.

In bidding you adieu I ask if the world has been benefited by my having lived in it? I answer, yes. For have I not planted trees and grass on a sun-kissed desert at the end of the old Santa Fe Trail—at the very spot where once grazed the tired oxen and mules after their journey across the plains?

The bible says he who makes two blades of grass to grow where only one grew before has benefited mankind. And that hits Yours Truly.

THE END.

CPSIA information can be obtained
at www.ICGtesting.com
Printed in the USA
BVHW050340301121
622797BV00001B/9